IMPROVISED CITY

IMPROVISED CITY

*Architecture and Governance
in Shanghai, 1843–1937*

COLE ROSKAM

A Samuel and Althea Stroum Book

UNIVERSITY OF WASHINGTON PRESS | *Seattle*

Improvised City was supported by a grant from the Samuel and Althea Stroum Endowed Book Fund.

Copyright © 2019 by the University of Washington Press
Printed and bound in the United States of America
Composed in Minion, typeface designed by Robert Slimbach

23   22   21   20   19   5   4   3   2   1

UNIVERSITY OF WASHINGTON PRESS
www.washington.edu/uwpress

LIBRARY OF CONGRESS CATALOGING-IN-PUBLICATION DATA
Names: Roskam, Cole, author.
Title: Improvised city : architecture and governance in Shanghai, 1843-1937 / Cole Roskam.
Description: Seattle : University of Washington Press, 2019. | Includes bibliographical references
    and index. |
Identifiers: LCCN 2018046903 (print) | LCCN 2018049735 (ebook) | ISBN 9780295744803 (ebook) |
    ISBN 9780295744780 (hardcover : alk. paper) | ISBN 9780295744797 (pbk. : alk. paper)
Subjects: LCSH: Architecture and society—China—Shanghai—History—19th century. |
    Architecture and society—China—Shanghai—History—20th century. | Sociology, Urban—
    China—Shanghai—History—19th century. | Sociology, Urban—China—Shanghai—History—
    20th century. | Shanghai (China)—Politics and government—19th century. | Shanghai
    (China)—Politics and government—20th century.
Classification: LCC NA2543.S6 (ebook) | LCC NA2543.S6 R65 2019 (print) | DDC 720.1/03—dc23
LC record available at https://lccn.loc.gov/2018046903

COVER ILLUSTRATION: Detail of map of Shanghai designed by Carl Crow, drawn by V. V. Kovalsky,
published by Shanghai Municipal Council, 1935. 94 × 72 cm. Held by the Norman B. Leventhal Map
Center Collection, Boston Public Library.

The paper used in this publication is acid free and meets the minimum requirements of American
National Standard for Information Sciences—Permanence of Paper for Printed Library Materials,
ANSI Z39.48–1984.∞

CONTENTS

ACKNOWLEDGMENTS

Over the course of this book's development, I have depended upon the support of many, many friends, colleagues, and institutions around the world. I would like to acknowledge the financial and administrative support provided by numerous sources, including Harvard University, the Fulbright Scholar Program, the Shanghai Academy of Social Sciences (SASS), the Mellon Foundation, the American Council for Learned Societies (ACLS), and the Department of Architecture at the University of Hong Kong.

One of the many challenges in completing this book was the time and travel required to visit archives in which Shanghai-related material is located. I cannot thank enough the staffs at the following institutions: the Harvard College Library system; the National Archives and Records Administration (NARA) at College Park, Maryland; the Library of Congress, Washington, DC; the National Archives, Kew; the Library and Museum of Freemasonry, London; Guildhall Archives, London; the Syndics of Cambridge University Library; the National Library of France, Paris; Les Archives diplomatiques du Ministère des Affaires étrangères, Nantes; L'École des Ponts ParisTech, Marne-la-Vallée; Le Ministère des Affaires étrangères, Missions étrangères, Paris; Special Collections, the University of Hong Kong Libraries, Hong Kong Government Records Service; Special Collections, Shanghai Library; the Shanghai Municipal Archives; and the Shanghai Urban Construction Archives.

The conceptual roots of this project originated in my undergraduate studies at Connecticut College. Danny Abramson inspired me to become an architectural historian and encouraged me to pursue the study of Chinese architecture. The Toor Cummings Center for International Studies and the Liberal Arts (CISLA) provided me with an opportunity to seek answers to my questions abroad. I remain indebted to Neil Levine and Eugene Wang at Harvard University for all of their invaluable guidance in shaping my interest in architecture and China into a substantive intellectual project. Their scholarship continues to motivate me. Time spent in Beijing at the Inter-University Program for Chinese Language Studies and in Shanghai at the Shanghai Academy of Social Sciences and Tongji University enabled me to engage with places and people that influenced my research significantly, including Lu Yongyi, Ruan Yisan, Xiong Yuezhi, and Xue Liyong. More generally, I have benefited tremendously from advice, questions, and insight offered by Marie-Claire Bergère, Barry Bergdoll, Jeff Cody, Chanchal Dadlani, Françoise Ged, Denise Y. Ho, Christian Henriot, Bill Kirby, Lai Delin, Yuko Lippit, and Liz Perry, among many others.

Niccole Coggins, Lorri D. Hagman, Regan Huff, and Julie Van Pelt at the University of Washington Press have been instrumental in shepherding this project through to completion. Dan Clem, Kristin Holt Browning, and Susan Murray provided keen editorial insight at crucial moments. I am grateful to the two anonymous readers of the manuscript for their constructive comments. John Carroll and Alex Bremner, both wonderful historians and friends, generously combed through the manuscript and offered suggestions for improving it. Jiang Naixin did an amazing job of helping me collect and organize the images for this book. Any of the book's shortcomings remain entirely my own.

Portions of chapters 1, 2, 7, and 8 were originally published as "The Architecture of Risk: Urban Space and Uncertainty in Shanghai, 1843–74," in *Harbin to Hanoi: The Colonial Built Environment in Asia, 1840 to 1940*, ed. Laura Victoir and Victor Zatsepine (Hong Kong: Hong Kong University Press, 2013); "Recentering the City: Municipal Architecture in Shanghai, 1927–1937," in *Constructing the Colonized Land: Entwined Perspectives of East Asia around WWII*, ed. Izumi Kuroishi (Farnham, Surrey, UK: Ashgate, 2014); and "Situating Chinese Architecture within 'A Century of Progress': The Chinese Pavilion, the Bendix Golden Temple, and the 1933 Chicago World's Fair," *Journal of the Society of Architectural Historians* 73, no. 3 (September 2014): 347–71.

Every day I wake up feeling so fortunate to have Diana and Clay in my life. They have been incredibly supportive and patient with me as I brought this project to completion, providing laughter and love that buoyed me whenever work weighed too heavily. This book is dedicated to my parents, Craig and Nancy, and my sister, Amanda, who have been there since the beginning.

IMPROVISED CITY

Introduction

AFTER arriving in the recently established international treaty port of Shanghai in early November 1843, the British missionary and translator Walter H. Medhurst (1796–1857) summarily dismissed the Qing government's existing administrative buildings there as "particularly insignificant. The reason of this is, that when government offices have to be erected, an order is issued to the people generally to build accommodations for such purposes; and as the officials are seldom or ever favorites, the people do as little for them as they possibly can. Hence they procure the smallest sized timber, and the most fragile materials, so as to run up sheds of a given size in the cheapest manner."[1] To Medhurst, a well-traveled Congregationalist with nearly twenty years of experience in Malacca, Penang, and Batavia, the material and structural deficiencies evident in Shanghai's public buildings suggested more than shoddy construction. Medhurst considered the condition of Shanghai's civic architecture analogous to the decay of the Qing Empire itself. Walls "never above half a brick thick," tiles "spread over as thinly as possible," and flooring "made of the thinnest planks and smallest supporters that can be found" all evinced an imperial authority on the wane. "Generally speaking," he concluded, "the government offices are little better than stables, and present nothing but a grand gateway, with a couple of stone lions, to keep people in awe, while within they are full of rottenness and uncleanness."[2] Imperial Chinese architecture (figure I.1), and by extension, the Qing government, required a new set of standards.

Medhurst's critique reflects widely held European notions at the time concerning the ability of buildings, particularly those of a distinctly public significance, to evoke political and cultural ideals emblematic of the political entity responsible for their construction—ideals that could, in turn, move people in intellectual and emotional ways.[3] By conflating architectural and national character, Medhurst illuminated the ways in which architecture's presumed and public purposiveness was employed to rationalize Great Britain's nearly

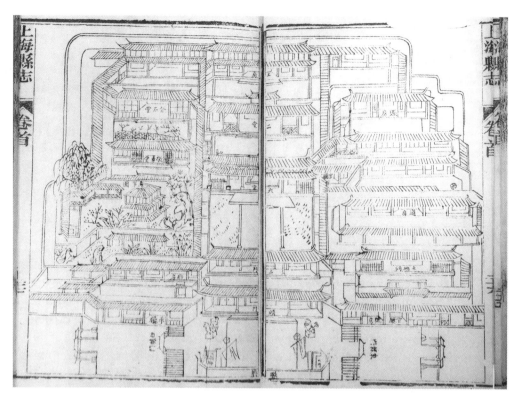

FIGURE I.1. *Daotai* compound, Shanghai. Reprinted from Yu Yue, *Chongxiu Shanghai xianzhi: Yi juan* (Shanghai, 1871), Special Collections, University of Hong Kong Libraries.

three-year military operation against Qing China, known as the Opium War (1839–42), as a civilizing mission devoted to China's modernization. The conflict resulted in the opening of the Qing Empire's most commercially active coastal cities, including Shanghai, Ningbo, Fuzhou, Xiamen, and Canton (as Guangzhou was then Anglicized), to the purportedly enlightening influence of British trade and was inspired by the liberative potential of incubating European economic and social formations within imperial China.[4] Yet such an unanticipated, violent act—and architecture's central role in its justification, its immediate aftermath, as well as its subsequent reverberations over time—present several fundamental questions. What was the spatial and political nature of these new interventions? What physical forms would they take, and how would they be governed? What were the broader geopolitical and cultural ramifications of such formations?

This book examines architecture's role in the development of so-called modern political power in Shanghai over the course of its nearly one-hundred-year history as a treaty port, from 1843 to 1937 (maps I.1 and I.2). It attends specifically to the ways in which an architecture of governance—buildings, sites, and infrastructure designed to organize and control interchange between different segments of a diverse populace—participated in the management of a

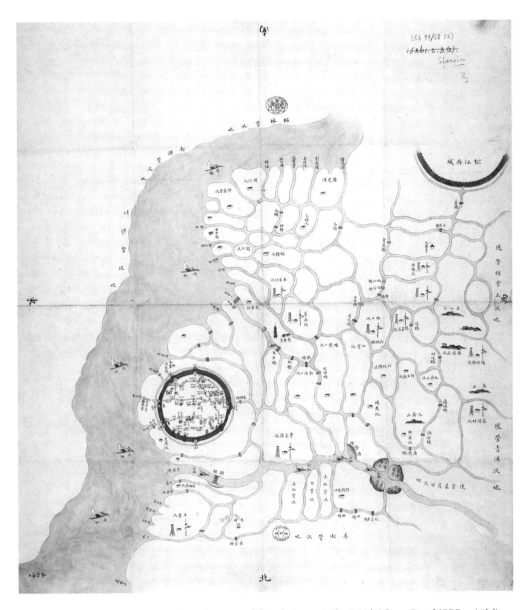

MAP I.1. *Hydrographic and Battalion Map of Shanghai*, 1870. © The British Library Board (ORB 99/58[2]).

cosmopolitan community designed for unfettered economic exchange. Shanghai was already a bustling regional hub prior to British arrival, but its urban composition was significantly altered by the construction of a British settlement north of the city's walls beginning in November 1843.[5] This development was followed, in June 1844 and January 1848, by the establishment of an American settlement as well as a French concession, respectively.[6] The British and American settlements were neither transferred nor leased in the name of their respective governments, and technically they remained Chinese territory—a series of

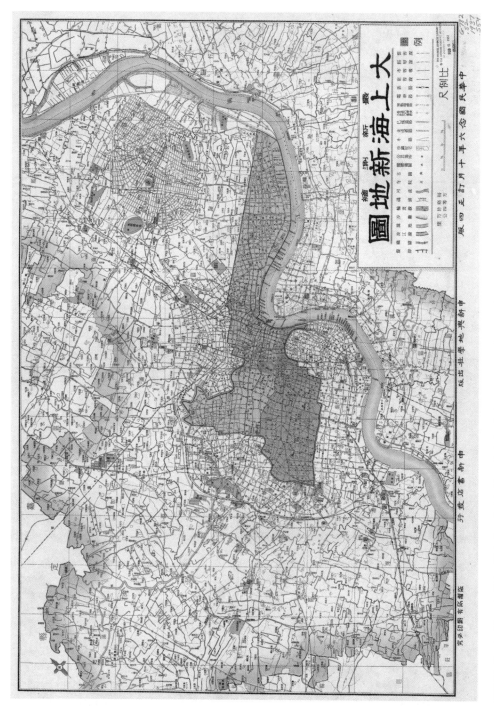

MAP 1.2. *Greater Shanghai Map* (Zui xin cehui da Shanghai xin ditu), 1937. Harvard Map Collection, Harvard University.

individual plots rented by individual merchants from individual Chinese land-owners. The French Concession, by contrast, initially comprised a parcel of land rented in whole by the French government itself, though it eventually adopted the same title deed system as the International Settlement. In both cases, governing these quasi-independent municipal entities proved challenging. Qing officials initially made Britain's first consul to Shanghai responsible for the city's fledgling foreign community. Over time, however, more localized, representational forms of municipal governance took shape in the forms of the Shanghai Municipal Council, an administrative body founded in 1863 and run by elected foreign councilors in the International Settlement, an amalgam of the city's British and American areas, and the French Municipal Council, established in 1863 by the French Concession and managed by the French consul. The Chinese city remained under the nominal control of the Qing government until 1912, when it fell into a state of administrative flux before a formal civic authority was reestablished by the Nationalist government in 1927. These three municipal entities operated independently, and roughly within a mile and a half of each other, until the Japanese occupation of the city in 1937.

The legal apparatus of extraterritoriality was the key catalyst enabling the production of these ambiguous landscapes. Beginning in 1842, treaties signed between Qing emperors and virtually every foreign power interested in commercial exchange with China ensured that all foreign nationals, left to their own capitalistic devices, would be given extraterritorial rights and allowed to remain subject to the legal codes of their own respective governments.[7] The British government predicated the need for such exception upon "the inglorious uncertainty" of Chinese law, particularly with respect to homicide.[8] Qing officials, deeming their British counterparts to be equally inscrutable, obliged Britain's demands, which they rationalized as being roughly equivalent to preexisting freedoms granted to Chinese *huiguan*, or mercantile organizations, throughout the kingdom.[9] In granting British merchants the freedom to abide by their own laws and customs, Qing officials believed such activity could be accommodated within the Qing dynasty's own bifurcated system of governance—an interlocking system of informal economic networks extending into northern, central, and southeastern Asia and maintained through political affiliations, religious patronage, and ritual practice.[10] This loose legalistic and spatial framework, composed of overlapping jurisdictional and diplomatic interests, allowed foreign citizens to operate independently within Qing China's imperial sphere while reassuring Qing officials that their territory remained stable and whole.

Architecture needs to be understood as an important if undertheorized force within these tangled modes of governance. Consulates, town halls, memorials, exhibition halls, and large-scale public works initiatives—each constituted new technologies and types in China designed to delineate some particular contour of Shanghai's uncertain geopolitical, legal, and cultural terrain. Collectively, these architectural objects helped to produce an extraterritorial spatial imagination—a vision of urban organization intended to enable foreign officials to disrupt but not devastate established logics of governance, and the conceptual basis for a physical environment that was believed to be somehow distinct from preexisting colonial enterprises in other parts of the world.[11] The political mechanisms that developed in connection to extraterritoriality, and the architecture designed to both represent and facilitate them, were not simple administrative extensions of sovereign authorities back in Europe or North America. Foreign communities in China often welcomed and requested the projection of metropolitan authority until such oversight was perceived as encroaching upon their own, more localized spheres of influence, at which point undue supervision was challenged and eventually usurped.[12] In this respect, and over time, a nation's diplomatic interests often diverged from the particular municipal concerns of its own expatriated citizens in China, resulting in complex, occasionally contradictory palimpsests of municipal, regional, and international power that tested architecture's ability to manage and control.

Shanghai was by no means an effective municipal system, nor did its various administrative assemblages operate as originally imagined. Shanghai's anticipated tenure as an international treaty port was never clear, nor were its ever-changing boundaries ever permanently demarcated. Yet its governing structures mediated between a dizzying array of political, social, and economic forces over time, and at a variety of local, regional, and global registers. The treaty port consisted of a multitude of multiethnic, international communities, each with distinct claims of identity. By the late nineteenth century, at least 75 percent of Shanghai's population had migrated from other places, including 89 percent in 1895, more than 82 percent in 1910, and more than 90 percent in 1930.[13] By 1932, Shanghai had become the world's fifth-most-populous city and the most commercially profitable treaty port enterprise in China.[14] Migrants hailed from each of China's provinces as well as at least fifty countries. Many arrived to find these identities rendered newly malleable by Shanghai's own political transitions and the cultural, physical, political, and social vagaries that resulted.[15] Communal, regional, national, and ethnic allegiances mutated in particularly rapid and unpredictable ways, with regard to both Qing China's own established cultural and political frameworks as well as a shifting world order. Problems of legitimacy as well as legibility resulted not only from ever-changing shifts in who and what composed the Shanghai public but in what Shanghai itself was made of—from individualized segments of the city's population, to an urban archipelago of diasporic constituents, to the city as an imagined whole.

The interplay between Shanghai's legal and physical architecture has been generally understood as constituting a kind of "semi-colonial" or "transnational colonial" landscape—a term that gestures toward the variegated and oppressive nature of foreign administration operating within China between 1840 and 1943 yet ultimately fails to illuminate the distinctive dynamics of treaty port politics, economics, culture, and space.[16] Notions of semi-colonial governance obscure the established Qing imperial system that operated both before and after foreign arrival while suggesting that those foreign imperial powers with an interest and presence in China had a shared and determined mode of rule in mind. Terms like *semi-* or *transnational colonialism* thus fail to capture the multiple, often-competing skeins of power that took shape within Qing borders over time—a complex array of anomalous strategies and sites that by one count totaled more than 250 distinct "foreign places" within China.[17] Treaty port–era Shanghai was an exercise in violence and oppression, but it was not designed according to plan—a much-theorized requisite for modern colonial systems and power.[18] The extraterritorial spatial imagination that took root in China, too, represented something less tangible than the assertion of one's perceived authority through the physical occupation of territory, though it certainly relied on physical objects and spaces to cruel and devastating effect. Chinese landowners were often coerced but not required to rent property to foreign residents, and distinct "mixed" courts facilitated the uneasy coexistence of Chinese and foreign laws. Municipal systems were designed to maintain the guise of Qing sovereignty while protecting the economic and territorial interests of those rival foreign states with a commercial interest in China. Great Britain, Qing China, France, the United States of America, Japan, Germany, and Russia, among others—each invested in the diplomatic and commercial potential of the treaty port system, though these investments took different forms, and each investment was imagined with a unique set of geopolitical concerns in mind. In this respect, Shanghai's accumulation of local, regional, national, religious, as well as ethnic forms of sovereignty produced an urban environment that needs be understood as distinctive from those of other colonial domains around the world at the time.

Refocusing scholarly attention on the physical dimensions of extraterritoriality through architecture offers new insight into the procedural and spatial variability at work within China both prior to and following the establishment of the treaty port system. Such work reinforces the notion that extraterritoriality was less a system of rigid and orderly rules than a practice dependent upon a changeable and legally pluralistic environment.[19] It also opens up the possibility for comparative study in relation to other kinds of extraterritorial zones for "experimental rule-making" that emerged around the world during the nineteenth and early twentieth centuries, including the Suez Canal Region and Tangier.[20] Shanghai may have shared specific attributes with other colonial and imperial contexts around the world, many of which were also unstable and uncertain in nature.[21] Ultimately, however, the extraterritorial environment requires a different method of spatial analysis—one in which architecture figures as an active force in the multiple conceptualizations of citizenship, sovereignty, and territory that emerged within the city, and illuminates the ways civic spaces demarcated and defined them.

Despite a rich body of Shanghai-related scholarship, previous studies have not comprehensively analyzed the treaty port's architectural development in specific relationship to questions of political control and municipal administration.[22] Few of the city's constituencies had any opportunity to engage with the aesthetic, programmatic, or spatial details of Shanghai's civic or diplomatic architecture. Nevertheless, as members of Shanghai's population, they interacted with civic objects and spaces in ways that both reinforced and challenged standard systems of rule. In Shanghai, buildings of a distinct and ostensibly public significance helped to establish and gradually render normative competing notions of authority and citizenship to a fluid and heterogeneous population. Collectively, Shanghai's civic and diplomatic architecture formed constellations of intersecting, often-competing municipal and imperial dominions operating in immediate, physical relationship to each other and within the broader national and regional networks of people and objects coursing through the city.

The relationship between so-called modern governance in China and forms of modern architecture remains a relatively undertheorized subject within the field of Chinese architectural history despite several valuable historical studies on the topic.[23] Most histories of modern Chinese architecture begin with the new commercial and residential structures foisted upon Qing China by the British government beginning in 1842 and subsequent Chinese efforts to both absorb and domesticate these influences through material and aesthetic amalgamations with imperial-era Chinese building methods and forms.[24] The new objects, practices, and modes of experience produced at least in part by the city's fragmented management have been traced to a range of distinctly nongovernmental physical spaces, including teahouses, brothels, parks, department stores, as well as gardens, among others, rather than to the administrative mechanisms that were in place.[25] The analytical binary of traditionalism and modernism is often used as the main theoretical lens through which the history of these forms and spaces are understood. Yet crucial questions remain. For example, numerous preexisting accounts of Shanghai's architectural history ignore the fact that key characteristics of modernity, including intensified feelings of dislocation from the past and shifting perceptions of place in the face of commercial and technological exchange, can be identified in forms of Chinese artistic production that existed outside Shanghai, and long prior to the British arrival in 1843.[26] Moreover, if particular moments or spaces in treaty port–era Shanghai's history can be understood in relation to some distinct formulation of architectural or political modernity, they were paradoxically enabled by the distinctly premodern diplomatic and legal framework of extraterritoriality.

I do not delve extensively here into the more widely researched subjects of Shanghai's architectural history, including residential typologies like the *lilong* alleyway houses or the city's iconic Bund skyline, though these examples certainly participated in the city's governance. Instead, my focus on the relationship between municipal governance, diplomatic representation, and architecture aims to provide a new theoretical framework for understanding the city as an extraterritorial environment. This objective stems from an interest in the power of institutions as organizational and physical entities, and the extent to which the exceptional architectural and political formation of a treaty port may itself be understood as a cultural act.[27] Shanghai's complex cultural milieu is generally understood to have materialized "within the fissures among different agents of control" in the city rather than springing directly from the mechanisms of control themselves, namely, the imposition of variegated notions of a so-called international law upon Qing China.[28] Evidence of effective administration within Shanghai has been attributed to a range of factors extrinsic to the history of its political institutions themselves—interpersonal and familial networks developing through the city over time, for example, or the pioneering labor of visionary individuals committed to the city's survival.[29]

By examining the linkages between architecture, governance, and the law in late Qing China, I also seek to both expand and challenge the ways in which notions of the modern are generally defined and understood in relation to Shanghai's built environment. Architecture's relationship to law has been recently highlighted as a consequential component of the modernist project and is explored here as an important catalyst in extraterritorial Shanghai's development.[30] My work acknowledges pre–treaty port–era forms of modernity in China while recognizing that the treaty port system was something new, with powerful political, economic, and cultural implications that continue to resonate today. Situating Shanghai's architectural history within these overlapping spheres of influence focuses our attention on the tensions existing between governance and capitalism within China before and subsequent to the Opium War. Long prior to the treaty port system, in fact, Qing China relied upon law and space to mediate other forms of conflict between various ethnic, professional, and social factions.[31] The Qing legal code was subdivided to accommodate numerous ethnic and religious constituencies and allow for certain exceptions based upon class standing. These distinctions took physical form through various districting policies imposed by the Qing regime beginning in the 1640s in direct response to Han Chinese resistance to Manchu leadership.[32] The treaty port system was itself built upon a foundation of commercial networks and institutions established by an active Chinese mercantile class whose members were not part of the Manchu banner elite, and whose activities helped to loosen the bonds between spatial and political control so essential to Qing imperial administration.[33] Geographical, topographical, and scalar variation was thus evident among Chinese cities prior to the Opium War.

A closer look at architectural design, production, and representation suggests each actively participated in inscribing new sets of political, economic, and social relations upon an urban milieu over time. The administrative "mechanisms of security" and mobilization identified by theorists such as Michel Foucault, Giorgio Agamben, and others as being so essential to the modern political state generated ruptures between Confucian ritual, or *li*, and alternative systems of governance that architecture illuminates in ways other forms of cultural production do not.[34] Architecture also contributed to the production and amelioration of feelings of alienation, powerlessness, and disjuncture these changes generated both before but particularly after 1842. The projects I explore in this work—the completion of Shanghai's British consulate, the ceremonial inauguration of a French memorial to soldiers lost in China, and efforts to tear down the Chinese city wall, among many others—were physical projects and processes that evinced the competing forms of citizenship and sovereignty on display within the treaty port.[35] The attrition of Qing political sovereignty in Shanghai represented an erosion of values, meanings, and ideals in which entire new "reference-worlds" took shape within others.[36] It was a process bound up in materialities, policies, and boundaries specific to the built environment. Shanghai's public architecture did more than testify to the city's changeable political and economic conditions over time. It also actively produced them.

Ultimately, understanding architecture's engagement with the legal abstractions of extraterritoriality expands our understanding of architecture's representational capacity to convey and command meaning within a uniquely global urban context. That a number of these projects were not completed, or went unrealized altogether, does not diminish their individual or collective significance as historical artifacts. Rather, it highlights the numerous, often-overlooked efforts to mediate the tensions existing between Shanghai's administrative composition and the economic forces at work within the city through architecture. Projects were routinely proposed but not realized for financial reasons. Several were interrupted by the threat of war, only to be completed later. Others depended upon a degree of public consensus that proved impossible to achieve. In many respects, these proposals embody the ephemerality of treaty port Shanghai itself. Once imagined, they remain preserved within the archives of Shanghai's various governments as drawings, photographs, and written descriptions. With this work, I aim to bring them to light.

A MODERN ARCHITECTURAL AND POLITICAL ORDER

Before considering the relationship between architecture and extraterritoriality in treaty port–era Shanghai, it is important to first clarify architecture's role within the broader dynamics of Qing international relations over the course of the eighteenth and early nineteenth centuries. Architecture and urbanism were essential components of imperial Chinese governance. Chinese buildings comprised four-sided, orthogonal volumes realized through timber frame construction organized into standard sets of spatial and tectonic modules. Elaborate polychromatic combinations of pillars and *dougong*, or bracket sets, supported broad, overhanging roofing systems initially designed to wick away water from the building's foundation; over time, they took on greater representational significance. Clear hierarchical rankings of buildings determined the particular proportions used, which in turn informed column height, beam span, and the number of bracket sets. Formal and spatial characteristics such as symmetry, flexibility, and modularity also predominated.[37] Individual structures were parts of larger north-south-oriented clusters typically organized around a courtyard. Such directionality, reinforced by standard, square- and circular-shaped urban forms protected by city walls, was believed to ensure that any fickle, intangible cosmological forces would not disrupt the city or the empire.[38] As physical extensions of Beijing's authority, these works comprised a matrix of physical form and imperial ritual that helped to bind the Qing dynasty's political, diplomatic, and social administration together.

Over the course of the seventeenth and eighteenth centuries, European encounters with imperial Chinese architecture played an active and essential role in shaping European conceptions of the Qing Empire as a geopolitical entity. China's built environment adhered to a procedural, compositional, and structural logic many European visitors struggled to comprehend (figure I.2). To Johannes Nieuhof, a member of an unsuccessful 1655 Dutch East India Company mission to seek an audience with the Ming Shunzhi Emperor, Chinese architecture lacked a certain material durability or financial efficiency as compared with European edifices. Nevertheless, the uniform nature of its buildings in relation to each other, and their careful integration within an overall urban composition, projected an impressive degree of political coordination and control.[39] "In each Chief City," marveled Nieuhof, "are at least fifteen or twenty great Houses belonging to the Governors; which in regard of the Magnificence of their Building, may compare with Kings' Palaces. In other [lesser cities] are eight or nine great Houses, and in every small City four, which are all alike in fashion, only they differ in largeness, according to the Quality of the Governor."[40] More than any particular material or tectonic feature, China's imperial buildings possessed a singular, standardized compositional quality that projected an undeniable political and architectural authority. Louis Le Comte (1655–1728), a member of a 1687 French Jesuit mission to China, was overwhelmed by the power implicit in Beijing's scale. At its widest, Paris measured 2,500 paces, which was "but a quarter as large as all Pekin. . . . Indeed to outward appearance our most populous cities are wildernesses in respect of this. . . .

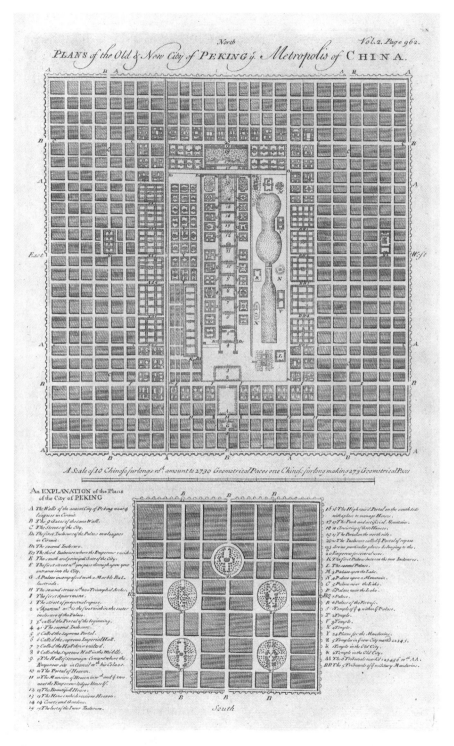

FIGURE I.2. Emanuel Bowen, engraver, *Peking—Plans of the Old and New City of Peking ye Metropolis of China.* Reprinted from J. Harris, *Navigantium atque Itinerantium Bibliotheca, or Complete Collection of Voyages and Travels* (London, 1744), Houghton Library, Harvard University.

When a man approaches Pekin, he must own that these immense buildings, and, if I may speak it, the rudeness of these august buildings have a beauty preferable to all our ornaments."[41] Many European observers interpreted such constancy as essential to the enviable stability of China's dynastic rule, which stood in contrast to the turbulent economic, political, and social forces beginning to roil Europe's cities during the late seventeenth and eighteenth centuries.[42] The French Jesuit historian Jean Baptiste (J. B.) Du Halde (1674–1743) did not himself travel to China but relied upon such information in crediting the empire's political and social stability to the physical and ideological structure on display in Chinese architectural and urban design. "Tis owing to this good Order which is observed at Peking, and that sets an Example to other Places," he theorized in 1736, "that the Empire enjoys such a long Peace and happy Tranquility."[43]

European perceptions of China's architectural, and by extension political, exceptionalism began to change over the course of the mid-eighteenth and early nineteenth centuries. Qing efforts to limit Jesuit activity within their kingdom resulted in fewer missionary accounts of the empire while giving way to the more critical writings of British merchants and political emissaries. Increasingly pejorative European analyses of Qing architecture's Otherness began to feed a curious European imaginary. These observations were informed not only by direct European engagement with China but also by the proliferation of Chinoiserie-inspired artifacts and objects throughout Europe, which had begun to influence perceptions of what it meant to be both European and modern.[44] The British writer Daniel Defoe (1660–1731) never visited China but nevertheless felt compelled to include a fictional account of the kingdom in his novel *The Farther Adventures of Robinson Crusoe*, published in 1719. In that section, his protagonist acknowledges the beauty of China's cities but challenges the quality of life they sustain. Nanjing was "regularly built, and the streets are all straight. . . . But when I come to compare the miserable people of these countries with ours, their fabrics, their manner of living, their government. . . . What [is] their trade to the universal commerce of England, Holland, France, and Spain? What are their cities to ours, for wealth, strength, gaiety of apparel, rich furniture, and infinite variety? What are their ports, supplied with a few junks and barks, to our navigation, our merchant fleets, our large and powerful navies? Our city of London has more trade than half their mighty empire."[45]

The growth of European trade around the world, and with it emerging perceptions of commerce's effects on social stability and political health, prompted consequential shifts in European impressions of China's civilizational sophistication. Views on Chinese art and architecture changed as well. Critics such as the architect Robert Morris (1701–1754) dismissed Chinese-inspired pavilions, temples, and gardens in Great Britain as art forms unattached to the visible hardships of Chinese society or any semblance of Europe's reality, and "unmeaning" in style.[46] William Chambers (1723–1796), an admirer of Chinese architectural expression who lived in Guangzhou as an employee of the Swedish East India Company from 1743 to 1745 and again in 1748, was influential in polarizing perceived differences between foreign and Chinese architecture, which he described as possessing an "oddity, prettiness, and neatness of workmanship" that revealed no "certain rule" at work. To Chambers, such preciousness was at odds with the sturdy and "practical" designs of the "modern" architects working in Europe at the time.[47] In 1757, the Qianlong Emperor (1711–1799) restricted European merchants to the southeastern Chinese city of Guangzhou for the limited duration of a defined trading season.[48] The decision only confirmed prevailing sentiment in Great Britain concerning the Qing government's perceived irrationality with respect to emerging European political-economic theories of liberalism and its purported value in promoting social and political stability. For example, the economic theorist Adam Smith (1723–1790) lamented in his famous 1776 text *An Inquiry into the Nature and Causes of the Wealth of Nations* that while Europe's own progressive commercialism moved forward, "China seems to have been long stationary."[49]

Architecture seemed to offer a useful index of the Qing Empire's cultural and economic obduracy. A stubborn reliance upon wood construction, for example, left China's architectural expression crippled by a "lightness and tawdriness" indicative of a creeping cultural as well as political stagnation.[50] Such recalcitrance, both to the gospel of international economic expansion and Europe's own architectural advancement, exposed deficiencies in China's cultural and political character in need of immediate reform. Many pointed to signs of structural decay in China's archaic political system, where, wrote Edward Augustus Freeman (1823–1892), "fixed laws have forever bound down every effort at genius, so that no improvement or development can be looked for."[51] China's architectural fixity was dismissed on similar grounds. By 1793, Beijing's formal composition lacked "taste, grandeur, beauty, solidity, or convenience" and possessed all the spatial charms "of a large encampment."[52] Such depictions reduced Chinese architecture, and by extension, the Chinese government, to "a proud, extravagant and finally unsound structure supported on a flimsy framework of ceremony and artifice."[53] In the eyes of many British merchants dependent upon the China trade, the Qing Empire's institutional rot demanded urgent action. Eventually, it led to war.

CHAPTER 1

The Architecture of Extraterritoriality

O N September 4, 1839, British frigates and Qing war junks exchanged fire off the coast of Kowloon (Jiulong), a peninsula southeast of the Pearl River Delta. News of the episode reached London in December. By March, parliamentary debate was held regarding the launching of an official British expedition to China. A British blockade of Guangzhou began in June 1840, followed by a series of joint assaults by British commercial and military naval forces along the Chinese coast (map 1.1). On July 4, British frigates arrived at Zhoushan, an island located just off the coast of central China at the mouth of the Yangzi River, and proceeded to pummel the Qing defense into submission. In October, Britain claimed the port city of Ningbo. A tentative agreement to end the war and cede Hong Kong to Great Britain was negotiated, but both the British and Chinese governments ultimately found the terms unacceptable. An attack on Shanghai occurred the following June. On August 29, 1842, imperially appointed Qing commissioners led by Qi Ying hurried to Nanjing to sign an armistice treaty, known as the Nanjing Treaty. The treaty concluded the Opium War while formally opening Shanghai, Ningbo, Fuzhou, Xiamen, and Guangzhou to foreign trade, confirming Hong Kong's redefinition as a Crown colony, and rewarding Britain's military efforts with a substantial cash settlement, among other concessions.[1]

Given the Opium War's obvious and dramatic economic, geopolitical, and social implications, it is easy to overlook the fundamental, spatial dimensions of Britain's efforts to expand its commercial access to Qing China. British merchants had long chafed at the restrictive physical confines of Guangzhou's

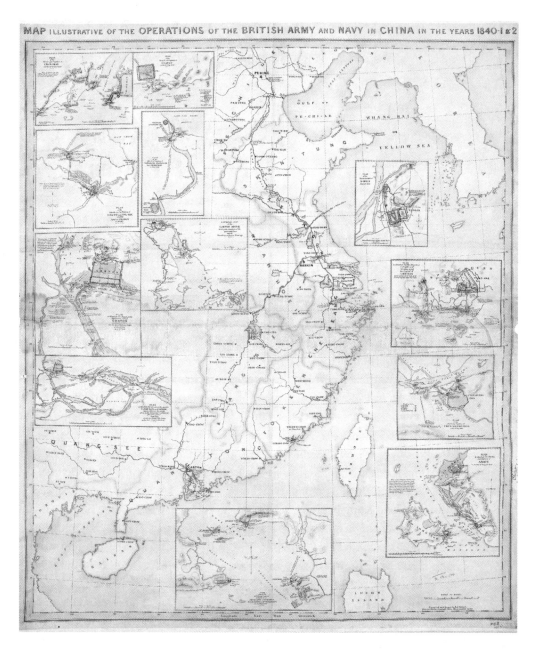

MAP 1.1. *Map Illustrative of the Operations of the British Army and Navy in China in the Years 1840–1 and 2.* National Archives, Kew, London (WO 78/990/3/33).

thirteen "Factories," or trading houses—a row of narrow, cramped rectangular compounds through which all foreign trade in and out of China (with the exception of Macau) was required to operate beginning in 1757 (figure 1.1). "It may, perhaps, seem incredible that the whole frontage of the buildings, in which foreigners of all nations are shut up together, for the prosecution of their trading business at Canton, does not exceed between seven and eight hundred feet," remarked John Francis Davis (1795–1890), formerly superintendent of British trade in China, in 1836, just several years prior to the outbreak of war. "The confined state of these, and their utter inadequacy to accommodate an increased number of traders, at the same time that the Government refuses any increase of space, is a subject which must very soon be debated with the local [Qing merchants]."[2] In the eyes of many Guangzhou-based British merchants, new sites were desperately needed within which British and Chinese commerce could freely intermingle, unimpeded by the perceived regulatory archaism of the Qing government.

Of these potential sites, Shanghai figured prominently. The city's position in the Jiangnan River Delta, some fourteen miles from the mouth of the Yangzi River and the Pacific Ocean at the confluence of the Huangpu and Wusong Rivers, had made it a valuable regional transfer point for agricultural and commercial products dating back to the twelfth century. By the early nineteenth century, Shanghai had become one China's most active ports; one foreign observer estimated some 1,600 ships typically passed through the port on an annual basis, including vessels from Singapore, Java, Malacca, Sumatra, India, and Polynesia.[3] British merchants were eager to capitalize on the city's bustling international traffic, though how to do so posed challenges. The Qing government prohibited European traders from accessing the port, and Great Britain was wary of forcefully expanding its global imperial administration into China.

As mercantile dreams clashed with the messy reality of diplomacy, architecture represented an important focus in the debate over how to impose a more flexible and universal legal and physical system upon China. A new spatial paradigm was needed, distinct from the restrictive Factory system forced upon foreign merchants by Qing officials in Guangzhou, within which Britain and other advanced nations could more freely engage in trade with China without incurring the particular liabilities of imperial responsibility. William Chambers, a veteran of the Factory system, observed in 1759 that architecture had an uncanny ability of "prepar[ing] the way for Commerce by conquering every obstacle that nature opposes to her progress."[4] Great Britain hoped for similar results—an integration of environment and economy based upon sets of Western legal principles that would help to reconfigure British-Qing commercial relations without destabilizing the Qing government. Yet establishing a new physical and legal framework within the preexisting confines of the Qing Empire was fundamentally disruptive, and it raised ethical and logistical questions

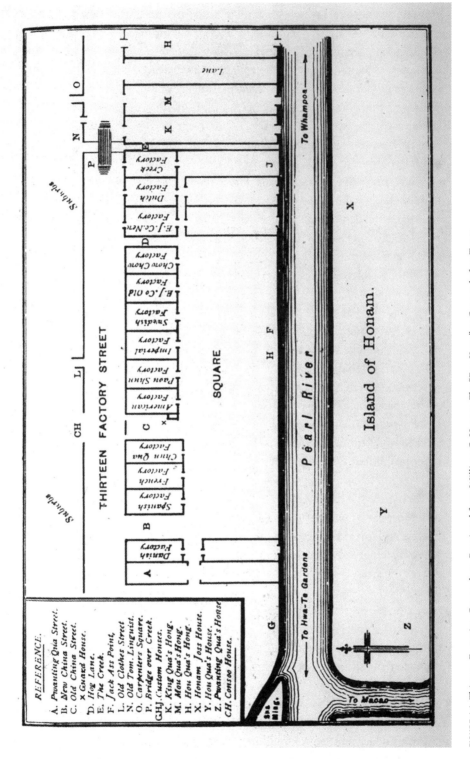

FIGURE 1.1. Thirteen Factories, Guangzhou. Reprinted from William C. Hunter, *The "Fan Kwae" at Canton before Treaty Days, 1825–1844* (London: K. Paul, Trench and Co., 1882), Special Collections, University of Hong Kong Libraries.

concerning the morality of such an aggressive intervention, how such enterprises would be both designed and governed, and for how long they might last.

OPIUM

Understanding the motives behind the Opium War and the expectations attached to its outcome requires some discussion of the commodity in whose name it was fought and the spaces through which the commodity flowed. Opium was the most financially profitable good exchanged between the British Empire and Qing China prior to the war. Politically and socially, it also proved the most corrosive. Most, if not all, of this trade moved through the British East India Company and its massive network of growers, brokers, and distributors. By the late eighteenth century, the Company's monopolistic straddle between China, India, and Great Britain made it the largest corporation in the world.[5] By separating its own production system from decentralized distribution networks, the Company was able to both profit handsomely from the drug's sale while maintaining its reputation as the exclusive and dependable British representative for all legal commercial dealings with the Qing Empire. Opium poppies were first harvested, processed, and dried within Company-controlled territory around Patna in northeastern India. Chests of the drug, known as catties, were packed and sent to Calcutta, where they were auctioned off to independent Company-affiliated merchants, or country traders. Traders then transported the commodity to southeastern China via ship, where networks of Chinese merchants, boatmen, and corrupt Qing officials ensured its safe delivery into China through Macau, Guangzhou, and miles of unprotected coastline.

The drug had been initially banned in China in 1729 due to fears over its negative impact on Qing society, but that decree, as well as a formal Qing prohibition of the trade in 1797, went unheeded by many China-based British representatives and their Chinese accomplices. Following the advent of Britain's formal economic expansion in India in 1757, British merchants continued to sell the drug to China in an attempt to offset the growing trade imbalance between the British and Qing Empires attributed to Britain's thirst for Chinese tea. One popular destination was Macau, a small concession located south of Guangzhou on the Pearl River Delta and leased by the Portuguese government beginning in 1557 for the purposes of trade. Portuguese and Chinese officials independently managed the city's foreign and Chinese populations, respectively. Guangzhou, another port located farther north along the Pearl River, was another landing point. Following a Qing decree opening additional Chinese cities to international trade in 1684, in fact, Guangzhou quickly superseded Macau to become the official epicenter of all foreign trade in southeastern China.

Two years later, in 1686, the Factory system was created to accommodate national joint-stock companies like the British East India Company. The arrangement was controlled by the city's Cohong, or Gonghang (公行) in standard Chinese (Mandarin). The Cohong guild consisted of a handful of Chinese mercantile houses, or hong, that operated all of the commercial compounds along the Guangzhou River, southeast of Guangzhou's city walls. Architecturally, the Factories consisted of offices and warehouses for foreign traders, with origins that dated back to Company quarters in seventeenth-century India, where merchants had been similarly restricted to specific spaces within British-controlled garrisons.[6] In Guangzhou, the site consisted of a dense architectural aggregate comprising all of the dwelling and work space for every legal foreign business in China.[7] Designed to resemble Cantonese mercantile compounds and oriented west to east along the river, these spaces housed all of the city's foreign representatives and included the Danish, Spanish, French, Chunqua's (later Minqua's), American, Paoushun, Imperial, Swedish, Old English, Chow-chow, English or New English, Dutch, and Creek Factories. The entire complex measured approximately 245 meters long by 140 meters wide. Several major streets, including New China Street, Old China Street, and Hog Lane, cut through the complex lengthwise from north to south. Each was occupied by a variety of businesses tailored to the wants and needs of their foreign neighbors. A fenced public terrace and square known as the Respondentia separated the Factories from the riverfront and the Chinese city and provided merchants with their only space for recreation. Each factory was rented by foreign representatives and remained the property of individual local hong merchants ostensibly responsible for the goods bought and sold within each lot. Flags hoisted in front of each façade suggested strict national and corporate designations, though the interplay between commercial agents and particular state or company sponsors was, in fact, fluid and ill-defined. Over time, each plot became subdivided into individual buildings for independent companies and agents extending one behind the other, separated by a web of narrow alleys and courtyards. Ground floors contained counting and storage rooms, with dining and sitting rooms located on the second floors. Third floors comprised the sleeping quarters.

For most foreign representatives, the Factories embodied an exhausting, lonely engagement with the Qing Empire. Foreign women were prohibited from living in Guangzhou, meaning any family members had to stay in Macau during the business season, which extended from September to March. Mercantile representatives worked an average of twelve to fifteen hours each day during this time, interrupted only by meals, a "hurried trot" around the square, and an occasional boat ride, leaving most foreign agents "as pale as their jackets" thanks to limited time for exercise and "the deep shaded hongs that they pass their days under, unexposed to the sun."[8] Foreign merchants were not allowed into the walled city, though many ignored this decree to partake in the urbanity of the dense, vibrant metropolis.[9] In general, however, foreign activity was legally restricted to designated areas of the city, where the pressures of confinement were aggravated by the demands of business. Originally designed to control and contain a select number of foreign mercantile operations in China, the Factory system struggled to accommodate expanding foreign—particularly British and American—trade with China over the course of the late eighteenth and early nineteenth centuries.

In 1813, British officials decided to terminate the Company's monopoly over the India trade, which further opened the market to smaller opium producers and country traders and increased demand for commercial space. Increased competition between opium businesses in British-controlled Bengal and India's Princely States led to a drop in prices and a spike in Chinese demand, but country traders struggled to expand their operations given the legal and spatial restrictions imposed by the Qing government. While Guangzhou remained the key physical conduit through which all legal commercial exchange with China operated, the emergence of Kumsingmoon, Lark's Bay, and Lintin Island, a largely uninhabited tract of land in the Pearl River Delta, as off-loading sites for the drug complicated both the geographical and jurisdictional policing efforts. Publicly, Cohong merchants like Houqua (1769–1843) registered their disapproval of the drug, but their close personal and business ties with foreign firms often made them complicit in the commodity's sale.[10]

By 1823, opium had become "scarcely matched in any one article of consumption in any part of the world."[11] As the number of opium catties entering China jumped from four thousand in 1820 to eighteen thousand in 1828, pressure to modernize the Factory system was met by strong Qing resistance. Growing tension between foreign merchants and their Qing supervisors manifested itself in a series of violent interactions around the organization and use of the Factories, precipitating the demands for more commercially oriented domains that would be placed upon Qing China after the Opium War. In 1822, a massive fire swept through Guangzhou, destroying twelve thousand Chinese homes and all but one of the Factories and contributing to general foreign unease.[12] A wall separating the Respondentia from its urban surroundings was destroyed, enabling Chinese residents to walk through the public square with ease. Efforts were made to reassert some mercantile domain over the property, but in 1831, new regulations for foreign residence in Guangzhou were announced that further restricted foreign activity in and around the city. Two years later, in 1833, and again in 1834, intense flooding inundated the Factories in several feet of water, leading to disease outbreaks among foreign residents. "There is no remedy for these evils excepting permission to erect additional factories in a more healthy situation," warned Davis, who would eventually become the second governor of Hong Kong.[13]

Some foreign observers defended the system, finding its security a reassuring bulwark from the unknown Chinese environment. For example, the American trader William C. Hunter could think of "no part of the world" in which "the authorities have exercised a more vigilant care over the personal safety of strangers who of their own free will came to live in the midst of a population whose customs and prejudices were so opposed to everything foreign."[14] Many other residents found the situation unbearable, however. Foreign merchants were restricted from entering a street for fear of being mobbed and discouraged from looking out a window by the prospects of attracting the gaze of Chinese observers. Many paced the Factory grounds in perpetual, anxious unease. "The strong desire to leave China is an idea that has been quite familiar to me since the first moment I entered the Celestial Empire. . . . The root of the evil lies in the confinement we are subject to, and that confinement has more seriously undermined my constitution than those abodes of black vomit and yellow plague, Vera Cruz and the West Indies," lamented Robert Thom, an employee of the British trading firm Jardine Matheson who would later become the first British consul to Ningbo.[15] By 1835, it was estimated the Factories contained eighty sets of apartments for foreign merchants, coolies, and servants, with an estimated 1,060 people living and working within the complex.[16] Mounting tensions contributed to an attack on the Factories by Chinese residents in December 1838, followed several months later, in May 1839, by an imperial edict demanding that all back doors to the Factories be bricked up, all streets and passages through and near the Factories be blocked, and walls "be built higher and thicker for greater security."[17] All shops with foreign characters were closed, and Chinese shop owners operating within proximity to the Factories were moved to other parts of the city.

Frustrated foreign commercial agents interpreted Qing recalcitrance in the face of such distress as evidence, not merely of the Factory system's obsolescence but of the Qing Empire's imperial envy. "The jealousy of the Chinese, and their fear of a permanent footing being obtained by foreigners in the Celestial Empire, will militate very strongly against any extensive additions or conveniences, as they in every instance discountenance an arrangement by which the residents may be made more comfortable," complained William Wightman Wood (1804–?), an American journalist who also briefly served as editor of the *Canton Register*, a publication founded by Jardine Matheson and thus inclined to criticism of the arrangements.[18] Qing authorities interpreted the situation differently and saw little need to alleviate the suffering of uninvited guests unwilling to acquiesce to the laws of the territory within which they lived. In May 1839, Lin Zexu (1785–1850), Qing governor-general in Hubei and Hunan, threatened the Cohong with violence unless they convinced their foreign partners in trade to give up any and all opium-filled cargoes on either island. Their draconian efforts caused the drug's price to fall dramatically while steeling foreign opinion against the Qing government and its antiquated Factory system once and for all. Open naval conflict began four months later, in September 1839.

As news of the events in Guangzhou arrived back in England, there arose significant resistance to both the commodity and the war launched in its name. "The opium trade is now so very unpopular in England that we cannot be too cautious in keeping it as quiet and as much out of the public eye as possible," warned James Matheson (1796–1878) to the commander of his South China-based opium fleet in April 1843.[19] Vocal opponents of the war included China-related manufacturing interests in Britain who felt the drug inhibited Chinese demand for their products as well as British missionaries who had seen the debilitating effects of addiction firsthand.[20] In response, pro-trade advocates scrambled to construct a sturdy moral imperative for the war's necessity. Popular and long-circulated impressions of China's architectural and urban obsolescence helped to fortify Great Britain's own evolving justification for the war's necessity—not in defense of the drug but of Britain's pride and commitment to unfettered commercial trade. In fierce debate on the floor of Parliament, proponents of the war employed architecture to frame the situation as a necessary defense of the free market in the face of an obstinate imperial rival. British lawmakers were eventually swayed by tales of their innocent countrymen trapped in the blockaded Factories with only the British flag serving as a reminder that "they belonged to a country unaccustomed to defeat, to submission, or to shame."[21] Able-bodied, willing Chinese trading partners could be easily found elsewhere in China, if only Qing authorities would enable such open exchange. "Without the walls of Canton," wrote one British observer, the Chinese were "as good shopkeepers as are to be found in any part of the world."[22] Architectural metaphors resonated with readers charmed by Chinese goods and convinced by the argument as to why China's latent entrepreneurial spirit needed to be released from the antiquated confines of Qing society.

Such imagery also speaks to the ways in which European perceptions of China's architectural culture informed broader British consciousness concerning the Qing government's capability to build and govern effectively. Following the conflict, Lieutenant John Ouchterlony, a Madras engineer sent to China in 1840 to help coordinate Britain's offensive in the Opium War, prefaced his memoirs with an aforementioned quote from Daniel Defoe, whose writing had begun to reshape British perceptions of China's architectural and political cultures more than one hundred years previously.[23] These efforts reconceptualized China's physical landscape as a decayed impediment to progress in need of dramatic reform. As British officials and merchants set about asserting themselves within the Qing landscape, these perceptions continued to affect what was built, where, and why. For example, China-based British officers determined to leave all of their wartime masonry infrastructure along China's coast "standing and in good order" to "give the Government of China a proof of our wish to make amends for this destruction and will likewise establish a character for civilization."[24] New extraterritorial visions predicated on the organization of new spaces through which international commerce would flow unimpeded began to circulate both along the Chinese coast and in Great Britain. The London *Times*, reporting soon after the war's conclusion, compared the Qing dynasty's (1644–1911) violent opening to the 1666 London blaze that led to the city's dramatic reconstruction under Sir Christopher Wren: "Was not the fire of London in 1666 a good? Did it not lead to immense improvement in the appearance, in the accommodation, and the health of the British metropolis? The question must be answered in the affirmative."[25] Like wooden London's glorious rebirth in stone, Qing society's violent dislocation from its past would enable the creation of new environments within which an empire's political and economic redefinition could commence.[26]

REDEFINING SHANGHAI

British troops first fired upon and invaded Shanghai in June 1842, two months prior to the Opium War's eventual conclusion. Four British battalions were quartered in the city's City God Temple (Chenghuang Miao) for several days—a decision designed to produce, according to John Ouchterlony, "as may be conceived, an imposing effect."[27] British occupation of the City God Temple represented a particular and humiliating violation of the Qing Empire's political legitimacy. Imperial-era Chinese cities comprised spatial and administrative mechanisms designed to maintain imperial order over a particular county, prefecture, or provincial region and, ultimately, the kingdom at large.[28] Chinese cities did not operate as independent, physical entities distinct from either the countryside or each other; rather, they embodied nodes in a spatio-political network organized around the maintenance of Qing governance itself. Any physical desecration of that system signified a defilement of the Qing bureaucracy itself. As Shanghai's largest and most sacred public space, the temple's occupation prompted what Chinese witnesses described as mayhem and panic throughout the city, though published British accounts reported no violence and highlighted only the "orderly and forbearing conduct" of British troops and the "confidence" of Chinese shopkeepers willing to feed them poultry and vegetables.[29] Such acts were designed to unsettle but not dismantle Shanghai's preexisting administrative framework, thereby enabling British officials to position themselves, both physically and administratively, within the city and at last "place Trade on a tangible and controllable footing" in China.[30]

Shanghai was a county capital with regional economic clout, and it maintained an active role in this imperial sphere. The city's physical core consisted of a series of major religious, educational, and political edifices built primarily over the course of the Ming and Qing dynasties—a Confucian-ordered constellation of temples, academies, and government offices that ultimately reinforced

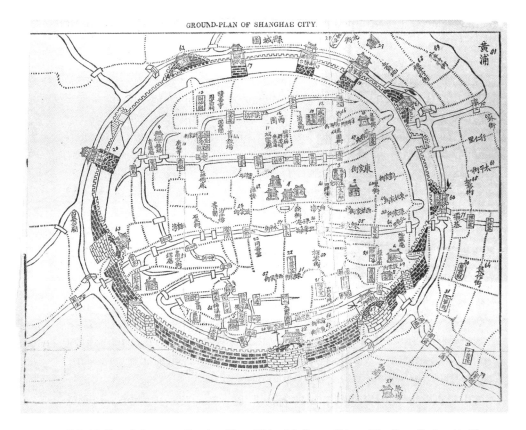

MAP 1.2. Shanghai, ca. 1845. Reprinted from Walter Medhurst, *Chinese Miscellany: Designed to Illustrate the Government, Philosophy, Religion, Arts, Manufactures, Trade, Manners, Customs, History and Statistics of China*, No. 4 (Shanghae: Printed at the Mission Press, 1845), Special Collections, University of Hong Kong Libraries.

the emperor's right to rule through a spatial and ceremonial calibration of ritual, architecture, and urban space (map 1.2). The Qing state may have exerted less formal control over the physical spaces of a second-tier commercial port like Shanghai, but imperially sanctioned rituals (*li*) were nevertheless carried out within and around the city in keeping with its status as an administrative center.[31] The city was protected by a stone and brick wall, constructed in 1554, to guard against the risk of plunder by seafaring marauders of Chinese and foreign origin. It served as a striking physical testament not only to Shanghai's significance as a seat of government or commercial entrepôt, but to the broader social stability and security of both the region and the empire at large.[32]

At the time of British arrival, the city's bureaucracy was headed by a *daotai*, or circuit intendant of the Susongtai region; a district subprefect; a *haifang tongzhi*, or subprefect in charge of coastal defenses; and the county magistrate, or *xianzhang*. Architecturally, however, this administrative hierarchy was not reflected in terms of spatial proximity to the city's center. For example, the county magistrate was only the fourth-highest-ranking Qing official in the city, but as his was the oldest administrative position within the city, his yamen, or residential compound, was located within the city's physical center. The magistrate represented the emperor in the city's daily bureaucratic operations, including tax collection and local adjudication. Although his compound was physically separated from the rest of the city by a carefully prescribed series of walled courtyards and gates, the magistrate himself was expected to maintain regular and direct contact with locals.[33] The compound itself consisted of a main hall (*dating*) flanked by a series of ancillary structures intended for the magistrate's clerks. The magistrate's private quarters were located in a second set of courtyards just beyond the public affairs courtyard to the north but still within the main compound. Two secondary axes were composed of courtyards and buildings for the magistrate's assistant, county records, archives and library, as well as his eunuchs.

The City God Temple was positioned north of the magistrate's compound (figure 1.2). The structure was originally constructed in the city between 1403 and 1425 and underwent reconstructions and renovations in 1602, 1683, 1753, 1747, 1798, and 1836. It served as the home of Shanghai's magisterial deity, a spiritual equivalent to the county magistrate whose jurisdiction included the city's dead. The temple's main hall, open daily to the public, was consistently packed with Shanghai residents beseeching the god's favor in anticipation of the afterlife.[34] A second, smaller hall, located just north of the main building and open only on the first and fifteenth days of the month as well as festivals, featured a sculpture of the spiritual magistrate himself. The living magistrate was expected to make bimonthly visits to the temple on the first and fifteenth of every month to exhort city residents as to how they should behave.[35]

The county magistrate's yamen and the City God Temple formed a locus of imperial power that bound the city's real spaces to its spiritual dominion. A variety of institutional, educational, and religious edifices such as Confucian, Daoist, and Buddhist temples, as well as ancestral halls, radiated from these two main constructions to form the administrative and cosmological matrix of Qing governance. Each structure adhered to the same spatial principles as the city's other major constructions: orientation along cardinal directionality, a strict division of public from private spaces, and adherence to basic courtyard spatial composition.[36] A thick urban fabric of local vernacular constructions known as *sanheyuan*, or residential compounds assembled from southern-facing one-story brick and timber constructions and open courtyards protected by enclosure walls, surrounded the city's major religious and civic monuments.

Communal belief in geomancy, also known as fengshui or *kanyu*, stitched these spaces together. Fengshui provided a kind of psychological linkage between an individual's well-being and his or her urban environment. Shanghai

FIGURE 1.2. City God Temple, Shanghai, ca. 1871. Reprinted from Yu Yue, *Chongxiu Shanghai xianzhi: Yi juan* (Shanghai, 1871), Special Collections, University of Hong Kong Libraries.

lacked any substantial hills to deflect the malevolent energy known as *qi* believed to emanate from the north and was thus considered to be more susceptible to the whims of geomancy than other parts of China. Any minor disturbance caused by the erection of new houses, high towers with pinnacles, the planting of poles for scaffolding, the cutting down of trees, or the building of houses carried with them significant risk to the local community. The lack of major north-south avenues within the city, for example, was attributable to this vulnerability. Instead, most of Shanghai's major streets extended east to west, lest negative *qi* spill directly into the city. In addition, all of the city wall's six main gates and guard towers were bestowed with names conjuring strong fengshui connotations in the hope of ensuring a continued healthful flow of positive *qi* and the simultaneous rejection of negative energy through its spaces.[37]

Beginning in the early seventeenth century, increased regional commercial development as well as the arrival of French missionaries into the area began to challenge Shanghai's insular, concentric civic composition. In 1608, a Jesuit church was built three miles west of the city center by the local scholar and Matteo Ricci protégé Xu Guangqi (1562–1633) on his own family's land. This was followed, in 1640, by the construction of a Catholic church within the city wall's northeast quadrant. The Chinese-built compound was later converted into the city's God of War temple in 1724 amid disagreement between the Jesuit mission and Rome over the recognition of Confucian rites in relationship to the Church's own teachings.[38]

In 1684, a rise in regional commerce triggered more dramatic physical change. Nonlocal *huiguan*, or guild alliances, began to cluster around northeastern Shanghai, prompting the establishment of a regional customs house, or *jianghaiguan*, in 1735.[39] The Suzhou prefect's circuit intendant was also transferred to Shanghai in response to growing coastal trade in and out of the city, with a circuit intendant compound built adjacent to the *huiguan* construction occurring both within and beyond the city's eastern walled boundary, not far from the city's customs house. His responsibilities included customs collection and general government oversight of the diversifying economic activity catalyzed by increased *huiguan* activity. As professional organizations established by sojourning merchants from Ningbo, Guangzhou, Quanzhang, Chaozhou, Zhejiang, and Fujian, *huiguan* offered spaces where other residents from the same parts of China could meet, network, and establish relationships in response to expanding regional and international commodity flows along the coast (figure 1.3). A second major guild organization known as *gongsuo*, run by local craftsmen and based around specific trades, became another civic and architectural influence within the city at the time. Administratively and architecturally, both *huiguan* and *gongsuo* signaled important precursors to foreign mercantile activity in Shanghai.[40] The guilds offered commercial and social counterpoints to the sprawling Qing government compounds located in the heart of the city, with elaborately decorated, multicourtyard arrangements, and numerous halls and offices available for business meetings, banquets, and theatrical performances collectively signifying their status within the city.

Although both the *huiguan* and Cohong systems figured prominently as administrative and spatial models upon which the Qing government would structure its relationship to the foreign commercial community in Shanghai, *huiguan* had a destabilizing impact upon Shanghai's economic and urban growth. By the early 1830s, Shanghai was a bustling commercial port of at least five hundred thousand people.[41] The City God Temple remained at the city's physical core, underscoring its prominent political and spiritual role within Shanghai's civic system. Yet commerce had begun to shift administrative activity within the city eastward toward the river. There, clusters of nonlocal Chinese-operated mercantile businesses and wharves began to loosen the civic bonds existing between Shanghai's local mercantile community, its government, and the ceremonial spaces designed to enforce such linkages. Following the Opium War, the *huiguan* and preexisting native place networks remained in place, and they facilitated an additional influx of nonlocal merchants into Shanghai from Zhejiang, Jiangsu, Xiamen, Guangzhou, and other growing

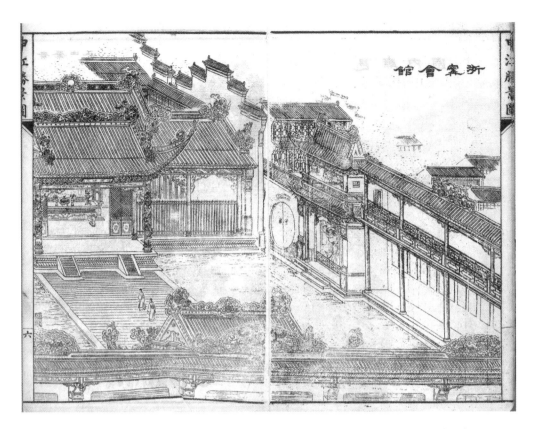

FIGURE 1.3. *Huiguan*, Shanghai, ca. 1905. Reprinted from *Li chuang wo du sheng huitu Shanghai zaji: Ba juan* (Shanghai, 1905), Harvard-Yenching Library, Harvard University.

interior markets. These networks provided the groundwork for more expansive, direct foreign-Chinese commercial collaboration.

DESIGNING EXTRATERRITORIALITY

British officials arrived in Shanghai to find a dense, urban landscape composed of a tartan-like overlap of crisscrossing alleys, bridges, and canals relied upon for the passage of goods and people spread throughout the city. Three major arteries extended across the city east to west, along with just one significant north-south street, which brought visitors to the magistrate's yamen. Charitable institutions, pagodas, temples, pawnshops, teahouses, storefronts, and markets punctuated an urban fabric otherwise "densely studded" with one-story residential compounds.[42] The City God Temple's ornate aesthetics and central location suggested its primary importance within the city's architectural and political hierarchy—a central factor in Britain's decision to initially occupy the structure on the premise that a shocking disruption of Shanghai's political topography would facilitate future commercial transformation. Yet British observers such as Walter Medhurst also noted the contrast between the city's government buildings and the bustling commercial and building activity taking place east of the city's walls along the water.[43] While British officials initially intended to disturb the city's center for diplomatic purposes, it was ultimately along Shanghai's peripheral zones that Great Britain's commercial aspirations would be planted.

Extraterritoriality engendered the legal, physical, and psychological conditions necessary for such an endeavor. Extraterritoriality is a state of judicial exception premised on the belief that members of one particular political, religious, or ethnic group may require exemption from the laws of another people or territory.[44] Its roots extend back throughout the history of global commercial and diplomatic exchange; in imperial China, for example, one can find evidence of commercial and diplomatic exchange with non-Chinese people that was treated as an exceptional activity requiring distinctive laws, practices, and spaces.[45] In Europe, the Treaty of Westphalia (1648) may have established territorial sovereignty as the fundamental bedrock of diplomatic relations within Europe, but European powers actively wielded extraterritoriality to assert diplomatic and commercial privileges in the Middle East as well as Asia well into the eighteenth and nineteenth centuries.[46]

In Shanghai, extraterritoriality ensured British merchants would not be subject to what they considered to be the capricious barbarism of Qing law, which foreign observers perceived to be etched into the Qing commercial landscape itself. "They have no more free or open characters among them than they have free or open ports," opined a contributor to the *Canton Miscellany* in 1831. "Their theories and standards of politics, morality, and philosophy are of native production and formation; they share them with no other people. They will ever consider themselves the most superior nation in the world, until convinced by some other argument than mere reason that this perhaps is not the case."[47] Such insolence demanded a legal and physical architecture of equivalent exception—what the political scientist Timothy Mitchell has described, in his analysis of the agricultural estate in late nineteenth-century colonial Egypt, as "a new structure of difference."[48] This framework, designed to counter the perceived asymmetries of Chinese knowledge and control on display in Guangzhou, was defended on the basis of the Qing Empire's perceived unwillingness to abide by the rules of the modern nation-state. If Qing officials insisted upon existence beyond "the pale of 'civilization,'" British officials would demarcate their own legal and spatial domain for some new form of development.[49]

Britain's extraterritorial rights in China were first formalized by the "General Regulations of Trade" signed by representatives of the British and Qing governments in July 1843 outside Guangzhou and subsequently included in the Supplementary Treaty of the Bogue, signed on October 8, 1843. The Treaty of Wangxia, signed between the United States and the Qing Empire on July 3, 1844, included a more explicit description of the jurisdictional rights at stake. The Qing-French Treaty of Huangpu, concluded on October 24, 1844, detailed the specific acts deemed to be criminal by both parties.[50] All of the nations and kingdoms who signed their own treaties with China over the course of the late nineteenth century insisted upon similar exceptions for their own citizens, though how these rights were defined and interpreted by different nations varied.[51]

Extraterritoriality became the main jurisdictional mechanism through which all foreign officials and merchants inserted themselves into the Qing imperial sphere with minimal diplomatic effort in the name of commercial exchange. The extraterritorial logic imposed by Great Britain and followed by other foreign powers was rooted in the perceived righteousness of a more universal rule of law and the reasoned principles of the free market—polices for which some Qing precedent existed.[52] Importantly, however, extraterritoriality put forth a vision for jurisdictional sovereignty untethered from the formal control of physical territory. Extraterritoriality produced a spectrum of exceptionalities, each framed as somehow more universal than Qing law, yet each paradoxically dependent upon its own particular principles of legal order. Importantly, because extraterritoriality was without a physical reality, one had to be produced—localized administrations and spaces capable of facilitating commercial exchange regardless of the spatial basis of Qing social order.

For British officials and merchants committed to China's economic liberalization, the design of an extraterritorial system on the scale of the treaty port presented an unprecedented administrative and engineering opportunity. Pre-existing British strategies for colonial economic expansion generally involved an aggressive reordering of an urban landscape in the name of greater efficiency, safety, and an overarching sense of British control. Known as the "grand model," the standard British colonial plan was characterized by a symmetrical grid, a series of green belts used for recreation, and racial segregated zones for work and residence.[53] In some cases, the process involved the destruction of a sovereign power's preexisting physical fabric, or otherwise subverting it, as in British colonial authorities' redistricting of Ceylon over the course of the 1830s, and in the demolition of Lahore's city wall and the alteration and desecration of Mughal-era structures there beginning in 1848.[54] By contrast, Shanghai's urban landscape would not be destroyed. British representatives feared that doing so would "inevitably lead to the total dissolution and subversion of the existing Government, and would be tantamount to a dismemberment of the Empire," thereby producing a condition of colonial dependency on Great Britain and threatening the future of British commerce in the process.[55] Instead, British officials hoped the treaty port might enable a more complete integration of local and foreign commercial interests and more genuine, flexible, and substantial trade relations. The goal was "not to create separate interests between the merchants of both countries which would result from granting privileges, but also to unite as much as possible as many points in common, so as to induce the self-interests of all English and Chinese to aid in the establishing that peace and confidence so essential for mercantile affairs."[56]

If interregional commerce implicitly tested the jurisdictional parameters of the Qing Empire, the treaty port system similarly challenged the territorial sovereignty upon which these boundaries were based. In this respect, the treaty port presented an exercise in both jurisdictional and spatial design. Asserting free market principles into China required some physical method of introducing and maintaining them. Islands figured as one popular spatial trope for the kind of administrative and physical flexibility envisioned by British merchants. In 1836, George Thomas Staunton (1781–1859), a young member of Lord Macartney's 1793 embassy to Beijing who had grown to become a seasoned veteran of British-Qing affairs, noted the "infinite number of intermediate islands, possessing every facility and convenience both for navigation and commerce," which could be claimed by Great Britain without violating Qing law.[57] Zhoushan Island, located due east of Ningbo at the mouth of Hangzhou Bay and known to the British as Chusan, was targeted as one early potential site for British commercial expansion. There, merchants "looked fondly to an English home, with charming villas and gardens amidst picturesque valleys and crystalline cascades, with orchards and pasturage on the exuberant plains."[58] Moreover, such a site would not represent the "territorial aggrandizement" of Britain's colonial empire insofar as the physical limits of an island presented a prescribed, measured space for trade.

Macau represented another potential model. British officials may have bristled at the administrative oversight the Chinese imperial government had long maintained over the Portuguese enclave—Ming and Qing court appointees had worked with Portuguese officials to manage the city's Chinese population, levy duties, and distribute the licenses necessary for Portuguese residents to build any new structure since 1557—but they envied the relative degree of self-governance on display there.[59] New Orleans, which was managed by three independent municipalities beginning in 1837, offered another possible precedent, though it was not officially acknowledged as a paradigm at the time.[60] Both cities functioned as open ports, amenable not only to commercial exchange with other parts of the world but to flows of enlightened, European-influenced dialogue and exchange, producing an urbane cosmopolitanism that some believed would combat "the prejudices and arrogant pretensions, which surround this wonderful [Qing] government and unfit it for intercourse with all other Nations" on striking display in Guangzhou.[61]

In the absence of any formal military or colonial bureaucracy, Britain relied upon its own nascent consular corps to provide a basic administrative structure. Shanghai's first foreign consul-general, General Sir George Balfour (1809–1894), was uniquely qualified for such a mission. Balfour had entered into the Madras

Artillery in British India in 1825 after an education at the Military Academy in Addiscombe, England. He served in both Malacca and India before being transferred with Madras forces to China in 1840, where he had helped coordinate Great Britain's occupation of Zhusan, Guangzhou, as well as Xiamen during the Opium War. In 1841, he was elected one of the British army's public agents for captured property, a position he filled until all outstanding disputes were resolved in 1844.[62] Balfour, who had begun to study Chinese in connection with his role as public agent, was formally appointed British consul to Shanghai in February 1843. His appointment was followed in May by the transfer of Gong Mujiu (1788–1848), a Qing administrator from Suzhou, to Shanghai to manage foreign trade as *daotai*. Balfour moved to Shanghai six months later, on November 8.

Shanghai was not a colonial territory whose boundaries could be aggressively redrawn by military engineers, leaving British officials to determine other means of asserting themselves into the city's spatial and administrative core and subverting Qing precedent and legitimacy in the process. British officials and residents were still beholden to certain dictates of Qing law, including rules governing the owning and maintenance of property. Faced with these limitations, Balfour insisted upon maintaining a physical consular presence within Shanghai's walls in the hope of avoiding the kind of marginalized existence suffered by British merchants in Guangzhou. Balfour's instincts are substantiated by the recollections of Daniel Brooke (D. B.) Robertson (1810–1881), former British consul to Guangzhou, who claimed that the British consulate's move within Guangzhou's walls following the Opium War produced an effect that "did more to break down the barrier which existed between the Chinese and foreigners, than any other plan that could have been devised."[63] Although Balfour later acknowledged his personal preference for the convenience and comfort of a "foreign-styled" house located outside the city, establishing an official British presence within Shanghai's walls was seen as offering numerous valuable commercial as well as diplomatic advantages, including a presumed measure of respect from Chinese residents and better communication with Chinese authorities.[64]

Qing officials quickly rejected Balfour's request, however, arguing that there existed no unoccupied space within the city's walls for a British consulate. An enterprising Cantonese merchant by the name of Yao quickly stepped forward to offer his own property for rent after Balfour purportedly threatened to either pitch a tent in the courtyard of the City God Temple or reside in the harbor on his boat, the *Medusa*, until suitable consular premises could be found.[65] The British contingent eventually learned that the merchant had actually been preselected by the *daotai* to serve as a sponsor to arriving British merchants.[66] British officials accepted his offer but drove him from the premises, which was described as a "Chinese mansion" composed of four two-story buildings and a total of fifty-two rooms.[67] Even from afar, however, the Chinese landlord continued to keep a close watch on the foreign consul and his retinue, who were subjected to constant interference from locals wandering into the complex at all hours of the day.[68]

Upon securing a consular base for British operations, Balfour worked to purchase land from the Qing government for a foreign settlement. Qing officials rebuffed the effort, however, and British merchants were required to negotiate their own deals with individual Chinese landowners. Ironically, it was Daotai Gong who insisted upon the market-based principles British officials argued were universally applicable and true. They offered a laissez-faire strategy for stretching but not breaking Qing law. Balfour subsequently initiated negotiations over land rent, and in consultation with Gong, they devised a system by which British merchants could obtain property from Chinese landowners. Foreign merchants would lease plots "in perpetuity" from Chinese owners—a phrase identified in the English contract but which is lacking from the Chinese version.[69] Down payments would be made to the Chinese landlord, and an annual land tax, or rent, was owed to the Qing government. Merchants, defined as land renters, could decide when they wanted to stop renting land, and land-owners could not increase their rent. Gong and Balfour also agreed on a fixed price per *mu* to deter speculation.[70] Chinese landholders who were unwilling to "admit of innovations and in some degree to the obstructions raised by various interested Parties" were summoned to meet with officials, and following extensive negotiations, were coerced into rental agreements.[71] Deeds were initially registered through the consular office, who would then submit an application to the *daotai*. From there, deeds were forwarded to the city magistrate, who would pass them onto the Chinese Land Office, the political body responsible for measuring and registering the land.[72]

Shanghai's opening to foreign trade signaled a new era in British-Qing relations, though Britain's early presence in the city eventually seemed to conform to the spatial generalities of Qing urban precedent on display in Guangzhou. For example, most foreign rental activity took place beyond the city's walls, where Balfour had identified ample space for mercantile anchorage and storage north of the preexisting city. No formal designation of space was agreed upon, though Balfour apparently laid out a rough and nonextant plan for streets extending from the banks of the Huangpu River to the east; Wusong River, also known as Suzhou Creek, to the north; and the southern boundary of Yangjing-bang, a small canal just several hundred yards from the Chinese city's walls. A western boundary was not initially defined but was later delimited as a small stream known as Defense Creek. It was along this designated foreshore that the first British and American merchants arrived in Shanghai for the legal opening of the city to foreign trade on November 18, 1843 (map 1.3).

Although many preestablished norms of the Qing governing strategy with respect to foreign residents remained in place, including the relegation of

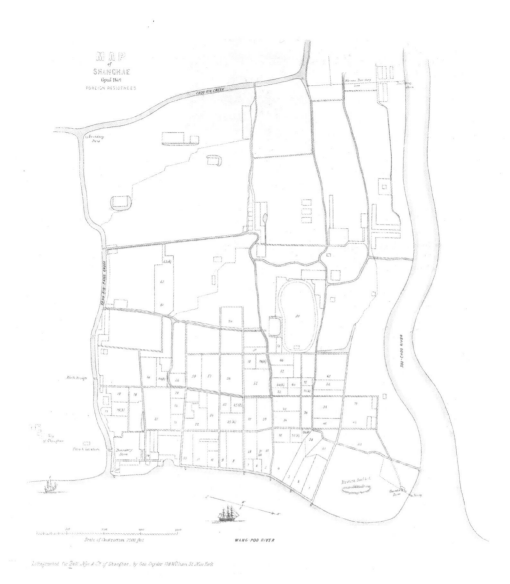

MAP 1.3. Geo. Snyder, lithographer, *Map of Shanghae, April 1849: Foreign Residences.* Bull, Nye & Co. Map Collection, Pusey Library, Harvard University.

nonlocal merchant guilds outside the city's walls, important distinctions remained. By transgressing the boundaries of the Qing administrative domain embodied by the walled city, Britain disrupted the architectural and urban framework considered so crucial to Qing legitimacy. Moreover, British merchants were no longer beholden to commercial exchange with one set of Chinese merchants. Nor were they legally restricted to the physical or social confines of Qing society. Foreign women were free to live within the British Settlement, and merchants could settle in the Chinese city if they were so inclined. Importantly, a legal architecture believed so crucial to free commerce, and eventually found so lacking in Guangzhou, had also been put in place—one that was more conducive to the production of frameworks of taxation, maritime, and insurance law required by international agencies. Such legal support was accompanied by a physical architecture capable of ensuring security and reinforcing difference. Buildings designed for the demands of commerce would directly challenge preexisting Chinese building customs and Qing imperial mandate in a number of substantial ways, though few, if any, predicted it at the time. Few could foresee the scale of international commercial exchange that would soon engulf the vacant land just north of the city, or the extent to which capitalism's fluid, transactional nature would become so fully imbricated within Qing society.

BUILDING EXTRATERRITORIALITY

More than any other decision made with respect to the treaty port's eventual development, the designation of British merchants to the banks of the Huangpu River rendered, in distinctly spatial terms, the new asynchronies now present within and around the city. Groups of British and American merchants, working with recently arrived Cantonese and Fujianese counterparts, quickly exploited the spatial and legalistic vagaries of the treaty port enterprise in ways the city's nascent governing system did not anticipate. All of the city's first foreign mercantile houses were Guangzhou- and Macao-based operations already engaged in the opium trade, and each rented Chinese structures along the Chinese city's riverfront from enterprising Chinese merchants in search of contact. They included the Scottish firm Jardine Matheson, their rivals Dent & Company, Gibb and Livingston, as well as the American firm Russell & Company. Most of these firms' representatives were young bachelors eager to secure the immediate safety of their own property and aided by Chinese middlemen known as compradors who helped to establish these firms and their first partnerships with Chinese traders.[73]

To foreign merchants seasoned by the various restrictions imposed upon them in Guangzhou, Shanghai offered an unimaginable degree of procedural and spatial flexibility. The cramped confines of the Factory system had necessitated an uncomfortable conflation of personal and professional space that alienated foreign merchants while aggravating the potential risks posed to goods and people by fire and disease. With these changes, there was also a sense that some degree of cultural propriety had been restored. Foreign merchants "are as uncomfortable in Canton as a Chinese woman would be in New York," remarked Osmand Tiffany (1823–1895), an American visitor to Guangzhou between 1844 and 1849.[74] In Shanghai, merchants found spacious plots relatively unencumbered by the autocratic demands of the Qing government or the discomforts of undue exposure to a foreign place. C. A. Montalto de Jesus, author of the first comprehensive history of treaty port Shanghai, surmised that the "unconventional simplicity" of the city's land regulations were designed to allow merchants absolute freedom to "build houses and godowns, churches and hospitals, charitable institutions, and schools" while "cultivating flowers, plant trees, and have places of amusement."[75] Writing home in 1855, the young American mercantile representative Albert Heard (1833–1890) reassured his parents that "the difference between Canton and [Shanghai] is most striking and in many respects agreeable, with plenty of room and a widely extended settlement instead of a narrow garden."[76] Ample space existed to construct individual warehouses, known as godowns, within which the company's goods could be more effectively organized and secured, along with individual mercantile houses and compounds. The subsequent self-mythologizing of Shanghai's foreign community as a "Model Settlement"—a town born of little but foreign determination and ingenuity—may, in fact, have stemmed in part from the site's early idealization by British merchants in contrast to the cramped nature of mercantile life in Guangzhou.[77]

Shanghai's spatial amenities served both psychological as well as commercial purposes. Positioning the British Settlement outside the city's walls was done not merely in the name of segregation but due to the lack of "storage . . . insurable under any reasonable risk" within the Chinese city.[78] The godown represented the normative spatial cell through which additional uncertainties would be mitigated and neutralized. Derived from the Malay word *gudang*, or "warehouse," godowns were simple, relatively standardized structures designed to keep surplus commodities safe and dry (figure 1.4). As a form of social and economic organization, the godown represented a valuable space within which "almost every article either Eastern or European could be procured, and most of them, at not very unreasonable prices."[79] The building type originated in seventeenth-century India as one individual module of a foreign mercantile compound, which comprised an enclosed and fortified demarcation of territory for business.[80] Within more cramped commercial quarters, such as those found in Guangzhou, a ground-floor room would typically be converted into storage and referred to as a godown. In general, however, godowns were autonomous structures. Found in all corners of the British Empire, godowns were not all exactly alike, though they tended to follow a basic spatial and structural model of four walls and a roof ideally impervious to external weather conditions. In Shanghai, they were the first structures built for the temporary storage of each company's goods, though new prefabricated models constructed of iron were eventually imported into the city as well.[81]

The godown was quickly followed by the materialization of the city's first foreign mercantile compounds. Like the godown, the compound can also be traced back to early European mercantile architecture in India. Typically designed as one large, two-story structure on a measured plot of land, the compound served as the major residential and commercial epicenter of each

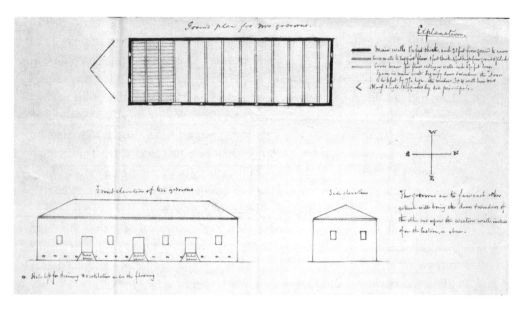

FIGURE 1.4. Ground plan and elevation for two godowns (warehouses), undated. "Heard Family Business Records, 1754–1898," Baker Business Historical Collections (*Mss:766 1754–1898), Harvard University.

individual mercantile company. The political, social, and commercial vicissitudes of the Shanghai enterprise demanded compounds capable of functioning as supralocal nodes within a global network along which commodities could flow safely, and with minimum hassle. Undated plans for an efficient post-and-beam structure constructed by the American mercantile firm Augustine Heard and Company, founded in 1840 in Guangzhou by Heard, a former Russell & Company partner originally from Ipswich, Massachusetts, reveals an orthogonally arranged series of internal and external spaces designed to accommodate both professional and personal activities (figure 1.5). The building's ground floor included a tea room, dining room, drawing room, and main office, while a second floor featured five bedrooms clustered around a central hallway and two toilets. Another unattached block of rooms included servant spaces, a kitchen, and storeroom. Reliable oversight and space were crucial to an effective business, and the integration of personal and professional spaces suggested both a degree of economy and a manager's careful supervision of the company's business. A matrix of regularly distributed posts emblematic of Chinese construction standards at the time held both structures together. This system allowed for the addition and rearrangement of ancillary spaces over time depending upon market-driven, professional, or personal needs. Writing to his Boston-based brother in 1856, for example, Albert Heard hoped to redesign the firm's compound as a "hollow square," creating a courtyard around which

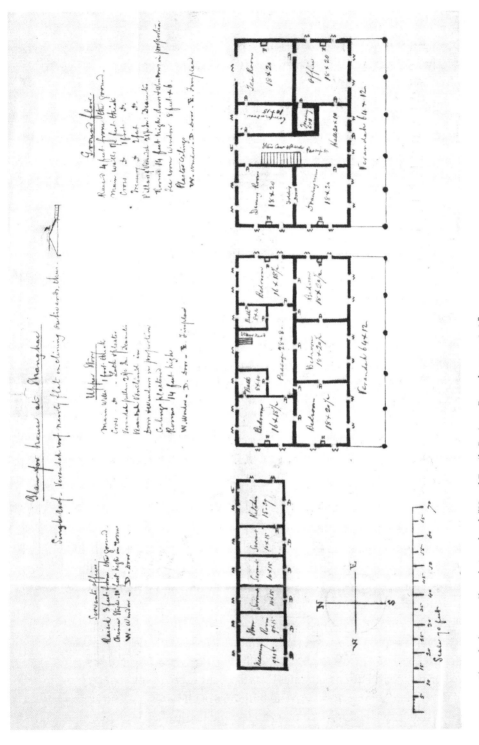

FIGURE 1.5. Plans for house at Shanghai, undated. "Heard Family Business Records, 1754–1898," Baker Business Historical Collections (*Mss:766 1754–1898), Harvard University.

offices, a tea room, and lodging for the comprador could be provided.[82] Given the inherent unknowns of the place, architectural and spatial adaptability was of critical importance.

The verandah was a third important architectural element in the treaty port's early existence.[83] If the godown mediated between a merchant's goods and the outside market, and the compound organized a merchant's private and public spaces and practices, the verandah moderated a merchant's exposure to climate and the natural environment. Typically built on at least one side of a structure, the verandah was an open-air porch or gallery produced by extending a compound's roof over its exterior walls. It offered a main structure protection from the elements while allowing residents to enjoy sheltered access to external breezes out of the sun.[84] It also likely derived from Indian precedent, though similar spaces existed in other parts of the British Empire, such as the "piazza" in eighteenth-century Jamaica.[85] The verandah also satisfied several social needs, both in Shanghai and in other parts of the imperial British sphere. Within the particular colonial context of Mumbai, for example, verandahs operated both as the main living spaces of families during particularly hot and humid times of the year while also mediating quasi-public interactions between foreigners and natives.[86]

Most importantly, the verandah fulfilled several structural functions. In Shanghai, as in other colonial contexts, early foreign-built structures were often deemed clumsy and insufficient European responses to the specific climatic contingencies of the locales in which they were constructed.[87] Shanghai's first compounds, for example, were hastily built structures completed in wood, stone, and local brick, an unreliable and unfamiliar building material. The city's monsoon-like rains proved devastating to these constructions, while the relatively small, fragile composition of Shanghai's bricks made them even more susceptible to deterioration.[88] The main walls of a mercantile compound thus required a substantial buttressing, along with adequate protection from "the driving rains which prevail during the southwest monsoon and the action of the frost in winter."[89] Here, in fact, the verandah also proved its worth. Although it was often dismissed as an ineffective building adaptation imported without any particular forethought into the city's climate, which was both cooler and drier than the tropical environs of colonial Hong Kong or Singapore, the Shanghai verandah helped to reinforce foreign compounds against buckling and dilapidation while protecting a building's foundation from the risk of rot.[90] An 1852 British government dispatch describing the condition of the first constructed British consulate corroborates this role: "The exceedingly changeableness of the climate is most destructive to buildings of all kinds. . . . The greater protection than can be afforded to them are verandahs, as they keep the main walls dry and therefore prevent most of the deterioration that results from exposure to the weather."[91] The city's position on the soft alluvial deposit of the

Yangzi River basin, too, made construction projects susceptible to constant shifting, cracking, and sinking, requiring additional support as necessary.[92]

As construction types, the godown, compound, and verandah each may be traced back to earlier British colonial settlements in tropical climates, including those in the West Indies and British-controlled India. Their arrival in Shanghai illuminated the circulatory flow of goods, people, and ideas through Great Britain's imperial domain into the treaty port, where they served as vital architectural components of the larger commercial mechanisms stitching Great Britain, Asia, the Caribbean, and Australia together. In this respect, they also played crucial representational roles in assuaging the initial anxieties of life in an unfamiliar environment for which no certain legal basis existed. One early foreign resident explained Shanghai's compounds existed to "protect life and property from causes of national disturbance in the country where they were located," and residents would later reminisce about the dependable, fortress-like durability of these structures in the face of the settlement's uncertain future.[93] Ironically, such constructions depended heavily on Chinese builders from Shanghai, Hong Kong, and Guangzhou. One such Cantonese contractor, Chop Dollar, has been credited with the construction of no fewer than three of Shanghai's first mercantile buildings. These include the Jardine property, which featured a unique southern Chinese roof based on designs sent from Guangzhou; the Dent and Beale compound, which allegedly featured wide-enclosing verandahs and the first foreign-introduced trees in Shanghai; and the Russell House, purportedly constructed of solid granite in 1847 with assistance from Russell's representative Edward Cunningham (figure 1.6). His name refers to the term "chopped dollars," or the gold Spanish coins used as the standard currency in each of China's treaty ports—an acknowledgment perhaps both of his worth to the foreign community and the circulation of figures like him up and down the Chinese coast.[94]

Embarking upon a global enterprise was a daunting logistical proposition fraught with danger, necessitating reliable staff and architecture capable of maintaining regimented schedules and ensuring the safe and efficient storage of goods.[95] Images and plans of the first foreign compounds convey simple, measured spaces of both a professional and domestic variety. Projecting a visible order through images reassured family members, creditors, and company executives that the business was composed of clean, well-organized spaces through which their investments would circulate.[96] While the planting of landscape around these structures projected an aura of domesticity insulated from the busy commercial environment just beyond its walls, the infrastructure that financed the merchant's home lay immediately adjacent to it and consisted of a series of standardized godowns, built of fire-resistant stone and accessible to the Bund to allow for the rapid transport of goods. Fire and marine insurance helped to provide additional security against the risks of investment, presuming

FIGURE 1.6. Chow Kwa, *Shanghai: The Bund, with the Premises of Russell and Company*, ca. 1855. Oil on canvas, 60.96 × 93.98 × 5.08 cm. Peabody Essex Museum, Museum purchase with funds donated by the Friends of Evelyn Bartlett, in memory of Evelyn Bartlett and in honor of Dr. H. A. Crosby Forbes, 2000, AE85781. © Peabody Essex Museum, Salem, MA. Photograph by Walter Silver.

merchants could attest to the dependability of their compounds through written confirmations as well as visual evidence. Images of the settlement's waterfront offered a different yet equally valuable form of visual currency and a broader civic perspective of the enterprise's physical and financial potential.[97] These representations were based upon earlier pictorial precedents set in Guangzhou and colonial Macau; many, in fact, were painted by the same Chinese artists. Most depicted only the British Settlement as a distant row of individual mercantile compounds from some imagined perspective across the Huangpu River. In one of the oldest paintings of the treaty port dated to the early 1850s, the Bund appears detached from any urban context, with only the presence of the Qing Customs House suggesting the community's location in China (figure 1.7).

These paintings, like their architectural subjects, were based on British colonial artistic precedent, though they diverged from earlier examples in several notable ways. Colonial enterprises such as British-controlled India or Australia relied upon an extensive range of artistic forms and methods to help document and catalogue unfamiliar places, people, and practices for offices of technocratic colonial administrators and curious collectors back home.[98] Images of Shanghai, by contrast, lacked the taxonomic ambition, breadth, and detail of their colonial counterparts. In the absence of any administrative or jurisdictional precedent

FIGURE 1.7. Artist unknown, *View of a Portion of the Shanghai Bund*, nineteenth century. Oil on canvas, 55.88 × 68.58 × 6.35 cm. Peabody Essex Museum, Gift of Charles H. Taylor, 1932, M3795. Courtesy of the Peabody Essex Museum, Salem, MA. Photograph by the Tokyo Institute of Oriental Culture.

for the city's extraterritorial nature, there was no real governing desire for insight into the colonial subject, and thus no systematic effort to document or catalogue the Chinese environment or people surrounding the settlement. Instead, pictorial attention attended to the settlement itself. Officials and residents alike were more interested in both rationalizing and promoting the loose interactivity between capitalism and governance taking place within the confines of their own environment. Here, architecture and its pictorial representation helped to project the image of a stable commercial enterprise possessing all of the presumed securities and comforts of a standard colonial outpost. "A little town has sprung up in less than four years at the Northern Extremity of Shanghai on the banks of the Huangpu," trumpeted Balfour's consular successor, Rutherford Alcock (1809–1897), to his Hong Kong–based superiors in 1847, "which presents the appearance of a British colony rather than the settlement of Foreigners on Chinese Territory."[99] The desired illusion of colonialism achieved through the visual depiction of recognizable architectural motifs in an otherwise foreign context suggested a community on the margins of Britain's imperial domain but safely isolated from the Qing imperial context within which it was physically and administratively attached.

In 1844, one year after Shanghai was declared open, the foreign population consisted of twenty-three merchants, two Protestant missionaries, and Balfour.[100] One year later, the foreign settlement's population had more than tripled, to ninety residents. In 1847, it stood at 108, of whom eighty-seven were English, four Parsee, and seventeen American. Over the course of 1844 and 1845, Balfour and Gong struggled to provide the regulatory framework capable of containing the settlement's expanding and diversifying population. Ensuring that all merchants adhered to preexisting laws, or, more generally, that the British consular authority would even be able to control the foreign community, proved difficult.[101] American merchants, for example, took advantage of their rival's efforts despite official American condemnation of Great Britain's overaggressive imperialist actions in the Opium War, only to find themselves subject to Balfour's representation in any and all official negotiations—a situation neither British, American, nor Qing officials were prepared or willing to handle.

In 1845, Balfour and Gong agreed upon a formalized set of land regulations composed of twenty-three articles. The British Settlement's boundaries were delineated from those of the American Settlement established north of Suzhou Creek. No flammable building or dangerous materials were allowed within either settlement, the purpose being "to render houses and property insurable, and to afford lasting peace and comfort to the mercantile community."[102] Any Chinese residents not employed as servants by foreign residents were prohibited from living within the foreign areas. Foreign nationals were allowed to rent land and build houses, storage facilities, churches, cemeteries, hospitals, charitable institutions, schools, and shops on any acquired land within the British Settlement's prescribed limits.[103] The regulations also strengthened the administrative authority of the British consul himself. Balfour was given the jurisdiction to preside over legal cases involving every nationality except those of Chinese origin. Hong Kong–based British authorities disagreed with the provision, but it accorded with Qing precedent and was eventually accepted.

The privileging of British diplomacy proved politically and socially unpalatable to both of Britain's major rivals, the United States and France, however. Each mounted challenges to Britain's diplomatic and commercial predominance within the city through physical form, employing space as a medium for dissent while testing the Qing dynasty's pluralistic sense of legal order in the process.[104] In May 1845, Henry Wolcott, an American merchant working in the city on behalf of the American firm Russell & Company, established the United States' first Shanghai-based consulate by hoisting an American flag over Russell & Company's temporary compound within the British Settlement. Balfour subsequently demanded, with no apparent trace of irony, the removal of Wolcott and his flag as a violation of Britain's diplomatic sovereignty within the city and on the basis that the Qing government had presumed any Shanghai-based foreign merchants would operate exclusively through the British consulate on any and all land-related deals. With the United States engaged in war with Mexico and unable to provide any financial support, Wolcott was left alone to tackle negotiations with local Chinese officials while scrambling for equal footing with a more organized and official British diplomatic corps based not only in Shanghai but also Beijing.

Wolcott's efforts were paralleled by the work of Louis Charles de Montigny (1805–1868), France's first Shanghai consul, who sought to acquire French consular property somewhere within the city following the signing of the Treaty of Whampoa by the French statesman Théodore de Lagrené (1800–1862) and the Qing representative Qiying (1787–1858) on October 24, 1844. Upon his eventual arrival in the treaty port in 1848, Montigny secured a three-hectare, 100-meter-long slice of land sandwiched between the Chinese city and Yangjingbang to be administered exclusively by French authorities (map 1.4). Though technically part of the Chinese city, the parcel was occupied only by a handful of Chinese houses and graves, while its western section was incorporated land controlled by the nearby French Jesuit mission in Xujiahui. The original treaty signed by the French and Chinese at Whampoa articulated boundaries within which French residents could establish commercial operations but did not stipulate any method of municipal organization. French insistence on its own spatial autonomy within the city and independence from its British rival fit within the country's broader, global aims at imperial dominance.[105]

The assertion of American and French consular representation in Shanghai was both substantiated and institutionalized, albeit unimpressively, through architecture. A new US consulate was established in 1847 within rented property north of Suzhou Creek beyond the subsequent limits of British jurisdiction in the designated American Settlement, though American consular jurisdiction in China would not be officially formalized until August 11, 1848. Only in 1853 did the US government appoint Robert Murphy (1827–1888) as the city's first professional American consul. France's consulate was founded in 1848 in rented premises described by Marie-René Roussel de Courcy (1827–1908), the secretary of the French legation, as a "Chinese house of the most humble appearance, inconvenient and unseemly, located between cemeteries and the most disreputable quarter of the suburbs."[106] Beyond serving as the home and office of Montigny, his wife, three daughters, mother-in-law, and sister-in-law for five years, the structure, which was also referred to as a "shed," a "barracks," and a "frog's nest" in correspondence from the time, was also used to host ministers from France, Great Britain, and the United States as well as Chinese authorities.[107]

The materialization of an independent commercial class consisting of international merchants sparked anxiety on the part of British officials over the expanded atmosphere of exceptionality originally designed to take form. Of

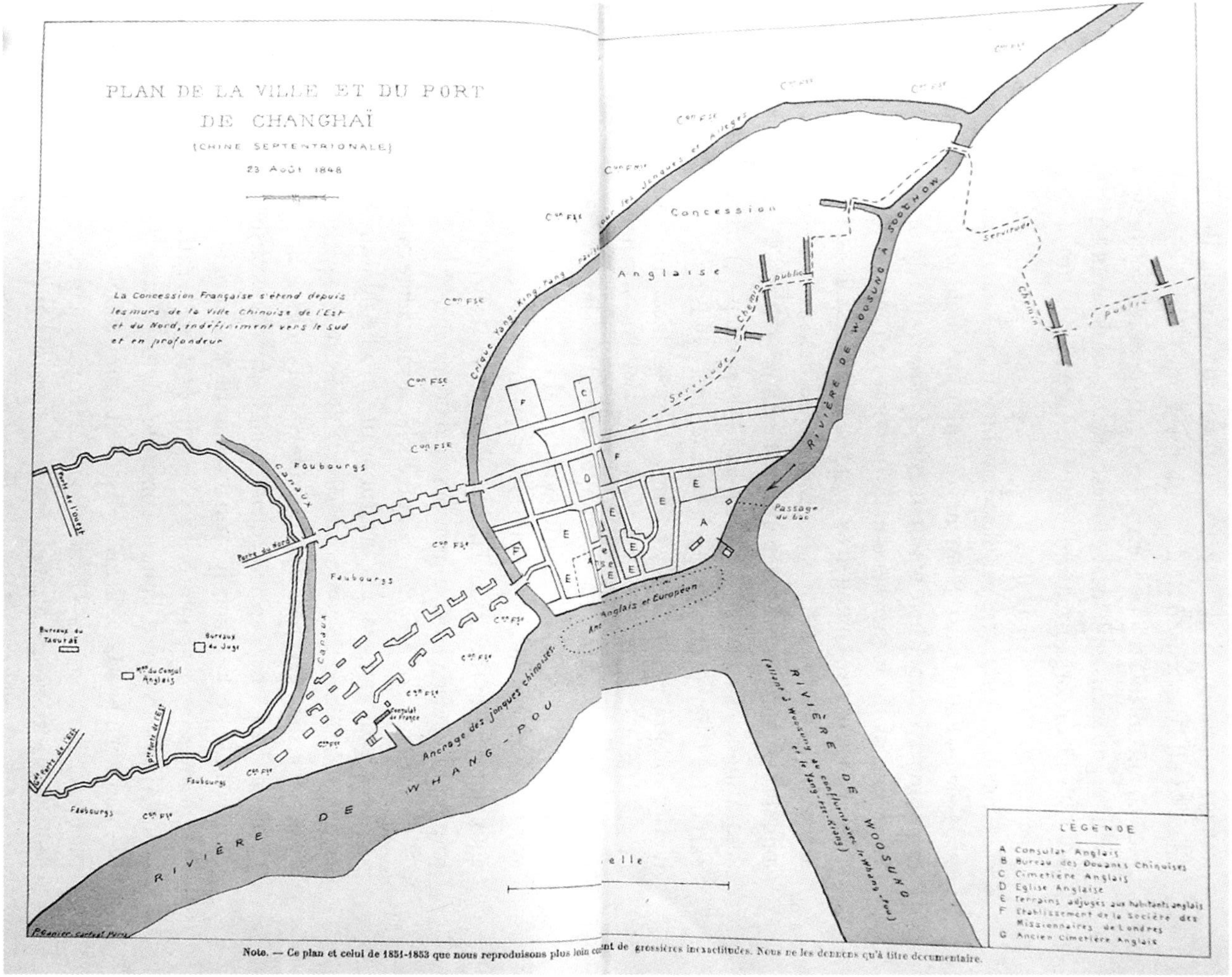

MAP 1.4. French Concession, Shanghai, 1848. Reprinted from Charles Maybon and Jean Fredet, *Histoire de la Concession Française de Changhai* (Paris: Librairie Plon, 1929), Special Collections, University of Hong Kong Libraries.

particular concern was the fact that extraterritoriality was being claimed by other foreign powers to achieve equal rights independent of Britain's consular oversight, thereby neutralizing Britain's perceived legal and commercial advantages. These fears were further fanned by British merchants themselves, who began to assume consular duties for nations otherwise not represented in Shanghai. The British firm Dent and Beale, for example, became diplomatic representatives for both the kingdoms of Netherlands and Portugal. The American merchant Edward Cunningham of Russell & Company also served as consul for both Sweden and Norway, while the Heard & Company compound housed a small Russian consulate. Official consular designation assured these firms greater access to Qing officials and the lucrative commercial benefit of such engagement. It also suggested a certain political acquiescence to the liberalized commercial impulses of the city.[108]

A MODEL SETTLEMENT

By 1846, it was clear a new spatial logic was taking shape around the city's walls. Twenty-four foreign mercantile firms operated within the British Settlement, including twenty-one British firms and three American operations. A second customs house was purportedly opened northeast of the city along the British Settlement's Bund for the exclusive and convenient administration of foreign tariffs.[109] A Landrenters' Association was founded in 1845 and a Committee of Roads and Jetties in 1846; both ensured that every foreign land renter would build a road to the river's edge, both for each individual's obvious commercial benefit as well as the overall advantage of the community. In 1850, the city's foreign population numbered 119, including five doctors and seventeen Protestant missionaries. The vast majority were British, followed by the French and a handful of Americans. Chinese residents were technically forbidden from dwelling within the foreign settlements, though Cantonese servants were allowed to live there within the compounds of their respective foreign mercantile employers. The Chinese city's population, estimated at 250,000, was composed of its own diverse, occasionally combustible mixture of sojourning merchants from Guangdong, Zhejiang, and Fujian, among other far-flung locales.

Shanghai's second British consul, Rutherford Alcock, hailed the new treaty port's emergence as the future of Qing-British relations. The city's first Masonic lodge, the Northern Lodge—an influential organization in the British construction of an early civic consciousness—was established in 1849.[110] There existed committees for parks and races, while the community's first newspaper, the *North-China Herald*, began publication on August 3, 1850. A theater company, library, and church were all in operation, and a drainage and sewage system were each proposed and implemented beginning in 1852. That year, a proposal was also made for a "central Institution" capable of organizing the settlement's various interests into one physical form, including space for public meetings, a newspaper reading room, billiard hall, Masonic lodge, and the headquarters for a chamber of commerce.[111] Importantly, Shanghai had almost overtaken Guangzhou as the primary port of origin for all Chinese goods shipped to Great Britain—40 percent to 51.7 percent respectively.[112] If the cramped physical quarters of the Factories encapsulated the history of Britain's commercial relations with China, Shanghai's ample acreage embodied the promise of an unbridled mercantilism. Each city embodied "two different epochs and systems. Our relations in the north are full of promise—partaking largely of the character of free International intercourse, while our position at Canton appears . . . with the heavy arrears of past injustice, and bad policy on both sides. The Retrograde and the Progressive elements (the governing principles of the past and the Future, of the Eastern and Western Civilization) meet in the daily intercourse and the actual relations of Chinese and Foreigners, and are not unfrequently brought into hostile collision."[113]

Alcock's acknowledgment of the tensions between Chinese and foreign residents belied friction between Shanghai's foreign commercial forces and consular efforts to control them. Two years earlier, in 1847, Alcock had moved the British consulate to the British Settlement on land secured years prior by his predecessor, Balfour. Alcock, a lifelong envoy and Britain's first diplomatic representative to live in Japan, found the Chinese city unsuitable for family life, and he negotiated the construction of Britain's first new consular premises in China. In so doing, Alcock also hoped to regain some measure of authority over the site. In fact, Balfour had originally imagined the eventual maintenance of two British diplomatic compounds within the Chinese city as well as the British Settlement—a vision that had not come to fruition. Alcock's decision to operate one British consulate outside the city walls represented a tacit acknowledgment that the political advantages brought about by close contact with Qing officials had been eclipsed by the commercial prospects of the city's unpredictable foreign community.

The new consulate, designed and eventually completed in 1852 under the guidance of George Strachan, was located at the confluence of Suzhou Creek and the Huangpu River on arguably the most visibly prominent plot in the British Settlement. It was a basic, purpose-built facility with few amenities.[114] In claiming such a valuable site for diplomatic and administrative purposes, however, Alcock risked upsetting the liberal free market principles Alcock himself extolled as so crucial to the future of Qing-British relations. A number of merchants greeted the new building with aversion, revealing the emerging divide between commercial and consular visions for the city and its future. An 1852 *North-China Herald* editorial noted that the site itself had been earmarked for British consular construction in 1843, at a time in which the future of the treaty port was "altogether unknown."[115] Since then, however, the materialization of a foreign community signaled a degree of localized, self-sustained communal organization that, to many merchants, invalidated the need for more substantive consular representation of any kind. Relative calm between Qing China and Great Britain further served as a testament to the civilizing influence of capitalism—a calm engendered by "the freedom of circulation" afforded to foreign merchants in Shanghai, which had "created a feeling of great friendliness, with both the officials and the people of the district."[116]

Nearly ten years after Great Britain relied upon its own brute naval strength to pry Shanghai open to British trade, Shanghai's merchants confidentially believed future prosperity would depend upon little more than the theoretical reassurances of economic exchange articulated through physical architecture. The consulate's new site, once targeted for its military potential, now possessed more value as leasable property. The *North-China Herald* suggested the site, no longer needed for war, be turned over to the abstractions of the real estate market, which now represented the community's "best security."[117] Such laissez-faire optimism, underscored by the belief that Shanghai's foreign areas had "just growed" spontaneously through initiative and the free market, lay at the conceptual core of the treaty port system, and would remain one of its lasting legacies.[118] In practice, however, full-throated belief in the market had already begun to fray the bonds between the consulate and commerce, evincing deeper instabilities at the institutional heart of the treaty port system itself.

Although the British consulate had played an active role in most, if not all, of the settlement's early civic engineering projects, the sense of entrepreneurial self-sufficiency engendered in part by these works produced a general apathy for administrative oversight and some of its more visible forms. In 1857, for example, Shanghai's third British consul-general, Daniel Brooke (D. B.) Robertson, complained to his England-based superiors that while Shanghai's British merchants were frequently painting and repairing their own property to combat the effects of Shanghai's climate, the consulate had received but one coat of paint in the previous ten years, with little local interest in such efforts.[119] British gunboats continued to ply the Huangpu River in case of emergency, but the settlement lacked a formal police force; instead, the foreign areas were protected by watchmen subject to approval by Qing and British officials. The intangible, transactional reassurances of the market, embodied by the settlement's emerging urban grid, the self-protective, adaptable nature of the foreign compounds themselves, and the "delicious sense of safety" these structures provided, left merchants confident in their own abilities to weather any financial, political, or natural disaster looming on Shanghai's horizon.[120]

These founding tensions remained critical influences in the city's subsequent development as a treaty port. With physical access to China now legalized and spatialized in the form of treaty port, hundreds of merchants, missionaries, sailors, soldiers, and adventure seekers arrived in the city in the early 1850s in search of opportunity. The influx of foreign money had doubled, even tripled local profits compared to what Shanghai-based Chinese merchants were making prior to the Opium War. Privately, officials feared the consequences of such unbridled cosmopolitanism. In 1847, Consul Alcock warned his Hong Kong–based superiors that "with a large number of vessels anchoring throughout the year at Shanghai, with Crews among whom are very indifferent characters— British, Lascars and Manila Men—mutiny on board, drunkenness and violence on shore are by no means uncommon, requiring the strong arm of authority to be used upon men not in a state to render ready obedience to the law."[121] Shanghai had begun to transform into "a second San Francisco," a "New Orleans of the Empire," and "a second Singapore"—an incalculable and impermanent assemblage of ethnicities, classes, and nationalities hailing not only from each of China's provinces but also from Edinburgh, Bombay, New Orleans, Liverpool, Manila, Marseilles, and Boston, among other places.[122] Within the Chinese city, "natives of the place live mixed up together with strangers in the streets," reported Walter Medhurst.[123] Fire represented another serious concern, particularly within the Chinese city, with "ruinous losses . . . frequently experienced, leading to robbery and plunder."[124] The presence of foreign as well as nonlocal Chinese charitable missions, guilds, and fraternities only contributed to the palpable cultural and social fluidities within the city.

Shanghai's development prompted new questions concerning the diplomatic dynamics through which cross-cultural commercial intercourse would continue to take place. In many ways, the perceived structural weaknesses Walter Medhurst identified within Shanghai's civic architecture in 1843 did portend deeper instabilities in mid-nineteenth-century Qing society aggravated by the ferocity of the free market. The spacious, neat row of solid, mercantile compounds lining the Huangpu River belied their own set of unresolved political and commercial vulnerabilities. A series of domestic disturbances would soon encircle the treaty port and capitalize upon these weaknesses in traumatic ways.

CHAPTER 2

Commemoration and the Construction of a Public Sphere

O N the morning of September 7, 1853, residents of Shanghai's Chinese City awoke to find it occupied by groups of outlaws from southern China collectively identified as the Small Swords Society.[1] The group surrounded the city's yamen and killed Magistrate Yuan Zude (1811–1853), though Daotai Wu Jianzhang (1791–1866), a former Cohong-affiliated merchant in Canton, was able to escape and hide in the Russell & Company compound. Reverend Matthew T. Yates (1819–1898), an American missionary living within the city walls, fled to the British Settlement to report the incident to the United States minister to China, Humphrey Marshall (1812–1872). Marshall could not believe his account and asked Yates to accompany him back to the city as an interpreter. There, they "found the city in quiet possession of six hundred men."[2] This number quickly grew to three thousand rebels, resulting in an eighteen-month occupation that triggered the influx of thousands of Chinese refugees into the foreign settlements in search of safety before French soldiers eventually aided the Qing forces in inducing the rebels' surrender in January 1855.

The Small Swords occupation coincided with an attack on Nanjing that same year by another southern Chinese regional faction known as the Taiping Heavenly Kingdom.[3] This strife, which grew into a civil war popularly known as the Taiping Rebellion, transformed China in multiple ways, casting an uneasy pall of disorder over the entire empire. Although exact figures vary, a recent study put the number of total Chinese deaths between 1851 and 1864 at seventy to one hundred million people.[4] John Scarth, a British businessman traveling around the country at the time, reported sights in Guangzhou "at which humanity shudders. I shall not detail them. Suffice it to say, that in the city of Canton alone, during six months, 70,000 men were executed."[5] Lamented an anonymous Chinese solider, "Ah, me! The sights I saw! Corpses, corpses, everywhere. I know them every one, kindly souls, my friends, my neighbors—there they lay, left where they had been shot, or speared, or slashed with swords."[6] The scope and severity of the carnage seemed to obliterate any sense of Chinese solidarity under an already diminished Qing regime.

In Shanghai, the unpredictability of violence reverberated through the city's population and its spaces in consequential ways. If extraterritoriality produced one measure of exception within the city, war enabled another—a state of siege that defied the city's preexisting administrative and commercial systems as well as the fragile physical and psychological demarcations that had taken form since 1843. Taiping rebels would not occupy Shanghai, but they threatened the city in 1860 and again in 1861. More generally, the threat of battle produced new commercial, social, and political alliances that inalterably changed the city's demographics, its collective psyche, and its physical composition. An estimated five hundred thousand Chinese residents flooded into the British, French, and American settlements during both the Small Swords Uprising and the Taiping Rebellion. Both crises exponentially expanded the city's overall population while integrating the foreign communities, then believed to number approximately 1,657 British residents, several hundred French and Americans, and an uncounted number of merchants and mercenaries from other countries, kingdoms, and territories.[7]

Like war, profit figured as another powerful force capable of eroding any ideological bonds of nationality, race, and class existing within the city. Many foreign merchants capitalized upon the disruption by building houses to be rented to hundreds of thousands of Chinese refugees in search of shelter within the foreign settlements. In doing so, they dismissed official efforts to maintain the segregationist spatial policy upon which the foreign settlements' existence had been predicated. As one British resident famously argued to Consul Alcock in the wake of the Small Swords Uprising:

> No doubt your anticipations of future evil have a certain foundation, and, indeed, may be correct enough—though something may be urged on the other side as to the advantages of having the Chinese mingled with us, and departing from the old Canton system of isolation—but upon the whole, I agree with you. But in what way am I and my brother landholders and speculators concerned in this? You are Her Majesty's Consul, are bound to look to national and permanent interests—this is your business.... Our business is to make money, as much and as fast as we can; and for this end, all modes and means are good which the law permits.[8]

Wartime frictions triggered questions over Shanghai's potential as a permanent civic entity. These deliberations also took physical form as a series of urban and architectural initiatives, each of which illuminated new, previously unforeseen degrees of international competition and cooperation. Of particular concern was the construction of war memorials to soldiers lost during the violence, both Chinese and foreign. In the absence of any shared public memory within the city, these sites were the first physical manifestations of some shared conceptual public sphere in Shanghai. As permanent, public objects designed with specific sets of residents in mind, they also challenged the capitalist reflexivity at the heart of the treaty port enterprise.

THE SMALL SWORDS UPRISING

The Small Swords Society (Xiaodao Hui), a collection of southern Chinese rebels, guild members, and mercenaries from Fujian and Guangdong, successfully subjugated the city in 1853 in coordination with several non-Shanghainese guilds located there.[9] Between September 1853 and February 1855, several thousand men occupied the entire walled city. Accounts differ as to whether the faction used the gardens of the City God Temple or the former British consulate as their main control post.[10] Doubt over the occupation's root cause as well as its potential outcome prompted each of Shanghai's foreign consuls to officially declare the settlements' collective neutrality from the conflict, though many foreign residents were partial toward the rebel faction and their efforts to undermine the Qing regime.[11] More generally, however, foreigners had long feared the impact of the Chinese city's perceived administrative neglect, spatial inscrutability, and hygienic malfeasance upon the foreign settlements' body politic.[12] The society's uprising brought these anxieties to life.

Initial Qing military efforts to retake the city proved ineffective, prompting the launching of a series of Qing counterattacks on land due west of the British Settlement near its new racecourse (map 2.1). These maneuvers also involved the movement of Chinese soldiers around and through the French Concession's territory immediately north of the city, a violation of its extraterritorial rights that transformed the concession into a staging area for battle. These intrusions, coupled with French fears over the occupation of a Roman Catholic church located within the city, eventually led to French military involvement in the conflict. On the morning of January 6, 1855, French and Qing troops initiated a joint artillery bombardment of the city, blowing a hole through the city wall itself near its north gate (map 2.2).[13] French officials also committed two ships, *la Jeanne-d'Arc* and *le Colbert*, and some 250 French sailors and soldiers to aid in the purging of the estimated six to eight thousand rebels. The Qing-French collaborative assault eventually ended the conflict, but it threw the wartime foreign consular alliance of neutrality into doubt.

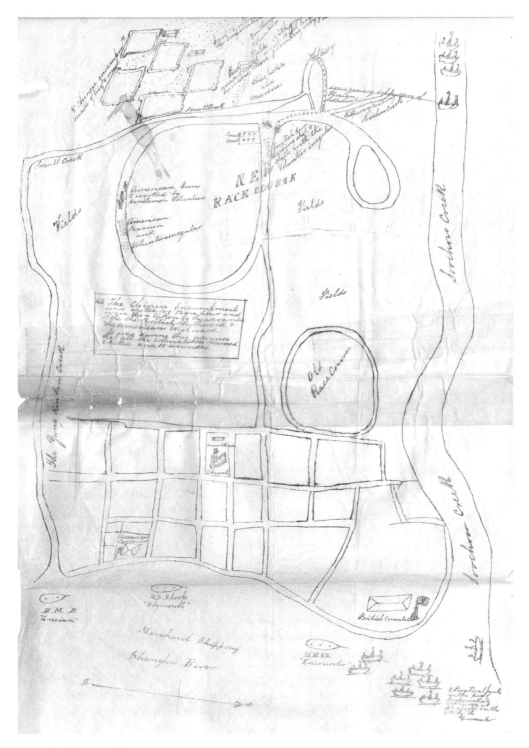

MAP 2.1. The British Settlement, Shanghai, April 1854. RG 59, Records of the Department of State, Consular Correspondence (Despatches), 1785–1906, vols. 2982 and 2999 (M112), National Archives and Records Administration, College Park, MD.

MAP 2.2. Chinese City with positions of Qing and French barricades, 1854–55. © Compagnie de Jésus—Archives Jésuites (FCh250).

The Chinese city's occupation by the Small Swords Society, and the spatial and psychological effects of the bloodshed, quickly began to generate "chronic" feelings of civic disorder throughout Shanghai.[14] The death of multiple Qing and French soldiers in the conflict's protracted climax and the simultaneous discovery of numerous British and American deserters within the rebels' ranks further aggravated diplomatic animosity between French, British, and American consular authorities. Qing officials rightfully accused American and British merchants of supplying the rebels with food, which had unnecessarily prolonged the conflict. In fact, many British and American merchants opposed attempts by any foreign government to prop up what they saw as a failed Qing political regime. At one point, a self-organized group of British and American merchants even took their aggression to the battlefield, battling Qing troops directly in the infamous Battle of Muddy Flat and infuriating Qing officials and embarrassing foreign consuls in the process.

The bloodshed proved disquieting for many Chinese residents, who had never before witnessed such a large-scale domestic affront to Qing rule. Cao Sheng, a low-level municipal official living within the city at the time, described the occupation as a horrific series of dreamlike illusions punctuated by a range of unimaginable evils, including starvation, fire, and plague.[15] Great swathes of the Chinese city's residential and commercial districts lay in ruins. Foreign inspections of the city were organized informally as well as officially with local Qing representatives. They revealed at least half of its urban fabric and suburban areas to have been destroyed either by rebels or Qing troops, and its most notable gardens and edifices reduced to ash.[16] Like British occupation during the Opium War, the Small Swords Uprising's violation of the Chinese city undermined Qing governing legitimacy as well. Many of the city's major monuments required a complete rebuilding, including the Confucian Temple, the western portion of the City God Temple, the county magistrate's yamen, and the city wall itself. Bodies continued to lie in the Chinese city's streets days after the rebels' retreat, "disgusting the sight and shaming public decency for days together." Suspended from the city walls were many "bloody heads dangling, to the horror of every sensitive beholder."[17] That additional foreign military support was required to end the conflict added insult to Qing imperial authority while prompting Chinese residents to reconsider the historical role played by foreign residents within the city. In his own firsthand account of the occupation, for example, Cao reminded readers that, for all of the collective trauma generated by Shanghai's initial foreign occupation in 1842, the event had included only three days of chaos. Moreover, any major physical damage inflicted upon the city at that time had occurred outside its walls at the hands of thirty-five Chinese miscreants who were subsequently captured and killed by foreign soldiers.[18]

Cao's recollections underscore the reevaluations taking place with respect to Qing-foreign municipal relations in light of the Small Swords violence. The bloodshed produced a new web of conflicted, contingent alliances that subverted the neat ethnic- and national-based distinctions relied upon by all segments of the city's population in the crafting of the treaty port's founding narrative and subsequent physical delineation of its spaces. The self-sustaining talismanic power of the market had not, in fact, defended Shanghai from danger. The rebels' protracted seizure of the Chinese city had crippled the port's economy and inspired calls for greater municipal oversight within all sectors of the city. This shift, away from the perceived virtues of a largely unregulated commercial urbanism, and toward more civic-minded determinism, directly affected the physical and social fabric of the city.

WAR AS CIVIC CATALYST

The uprising upended any pretense of racial segregation's effectiveness as social policy. Amid sporadic violence, general anxiety over the uprising's intentions, and broader social unrest in the surrounding area, approximately twenty thousand Chinese refugees flowed into the foreign settlements in search of safety between 1853 and 1855. Foreign and Chinese merchants quickly responded with the construction of hundreds of wooden and brick tenement homes southeast of the British Settlement's old racecourse along North Gate Road, Barrier Road, and the north side of the Yangjing Canal to rent to families fleeing the Chinese city's violence. The settlement's population, estimated at three hundred residents housed in 150 homes on 1,500 *mu*, or approximately one square kilometer, was suddenly dwarfed by thousands of Chinese residents crammed into approximately eight hundred tenement houses on little more than 200 *mu*. Structurally, the tenements were roughly hewn log structures that provided basic shelter and borrowed from preexisting Chinese vernacular dwellings accompanied by an assortment of godowns, opium shops, brothels, and gambling houses. Chinese and foreign officials considered the solution temporary and agreed to find a more permanent solution to the "strange" situation taking shape once the conflict concluded.[19] Eventually, the structures triggered the first direct interventions in Shanghai's market economy by the city's consular powers. "The evil is already too great, and too largely increasing at a rapid rate, to be overlooked," lamented Alcock to superiors in 1854.[20] Gone was the "uniform cleanliness and cheerful appearance" of the British Settlement. In its place stood a "New Shanghai" comprised of an "ill-assorted" array of buildings along with the greater risks of "fire, robbery, and disease" caused by overcrowding.[21]

In calling attention to the uncertainties of uncontrolled construction on the British Settlement, Alcock illuminated the broader existential crisis underlying these structures, namely, the extent to which unfettered market forces would be allowed to reshape Shanghai's foreign-administered areas more generally. As physical testaments to the tension between capitalistic impulse and its governance, the tenements exposed differences of opinion among Qing, French, British, and American authorities as well as residents over the foreign areas' desirable racial composition, physical maintenance, and, by extension, commercial future. All members of the city's foreign community were ostensibly committed to the pursuit of profit—a citizenship of capitalists interested in the collective exploitation of the free market. Yet the extremes to which foreign residents were willing to resort to realize such objectives varied. Some merchants embraced any opportunity to make money, while others considered integration to be a breach of founding treaty port principles, producing "inconveniences which did not exist even in the miserable factory days of Canton."[22] Differences of opinion also cleaved along national lines. For example, British consul Alcock worked hard to protect the original principles of the Nanjing Treaty, which included the prohibition of Chinese residents from all British settlements. American representatives, by contrast, found the city's segregation unnecessary and counterproductive to their own long-term interests in China, evoking the American community's own experience of commercial subjugation under British control just years prior as justification for integration. American minister to China Humphrey Marshall (1812–1872) argued that only through cross-cultural inclusivity would Shanghai become "the greatest city of Eastern Asia."[23]

Public fears over an uncontrolled Chinese population within the foreign areas eventually prompted recognition that organized municipal governance within the foreign settlements was necessary. At stake, however, was what "form" such a body might take, both with respect to its administrative organization and its ideological essence.[24] In July 1854, French, American, and British consular officials formally authorized the creation of an elected municipal council. With the establishment of such an organization, Shanghai's foreign population sought to ensure "the better order and good government" of the foreign areas through the shared implementation of infrastructural improvements such as public drainage, road construction, and "fifty other circumstances" within the settlements.[25] The council's membership represented an imbrication of consular and mercantile interests that included figures like William Kay, council chairman and director of the British firm Blenkin, Rawson and Company, and Edward Cunningham, American representative for the firm Russell & Company and consular representative for Sweden and Norway, among others. Officially appointed consular representatives included Alcock of Great Britain, American Robert Murphy, and French citizen Benoît Edan (1803–1871).[26] Collectively, the body was designed to operate with only a basic modicum of municipal oversight—a minimal standard deemed necessary only after egregious displays of Qing negligence, as foreign land renters pointed out.[27]

Faced with a diverse and divided body politic, council officials set about realizing public construction projects that would give the British, American, and French settlements more definitive, physical shape. Within the British Settlement, for example, these initiatives included the construction of granite footways along the settlement's streets, the provision of public lighting provided at each Chinese house's entrance, and bilingual street signs in Chinese and English. These gestures aimed to illuminate the benefits of a more active regulatory regime, particularly in relationship to what foreign residents perceived to be the uncontrollable ills of disease and disorder existing within the Chinese population. Paying for such services, however, remained a problem. The British

Settlement, for example, was neither a transfer nor a lease of land in the name of the British Crown; rather, it remained Chinese territory and subject to Qing land taxes. Any perceived violation of this policy represented a rejection of Qing sovereignty, with potentially dire diplomatic results. Diplomatic and Qing representatives eventually agreed that additional taxes could be collected from land renters in the British Settlement for the payment of municipal services, a plan which paved the way for greater municipal coordination.

On February 24, 1855, immediately following the conclusion of the Small Swords Uprising, the French Admiral Adolphe Laguerre (1792–1862), the French consul Edan, and three hundred troops made an unprecedented visit to the Shanghai yamen to wish the magistrate a happy Chinese New Year.[28] The public display of new political allegiances was followed by plans to physically extend the British Settlement's Barrier Road southward toward the French Concession. Shortly thereafter, a second stone bridge linking the French-controlled area to the Chinese city over its moat was also initiated. Affectionately known to French residents as the "Bridge of the Breach," it aligned with the Chinese city's newly repositioned secondary north gate, the reconstruction of which was being undertaken by the Qing government following its destruction by French cannons. In December 1855, the construction of a new, permanent bridge over Suzhou Creek was launched that would allow residents to walk between the British and American Settlements for the first time (map 2.3). Privately financed by Charles Wills of Jardine Matheson, Thomas Beale (1805–1857), and William Hogg, the Wills' Bridge was completed in October 1856, and was acknowledged by the city's Qing authorities with a public memorial reminding Chinese residents to pay the required toll upon crossing.[29] By 1857, streetlamps were erected at all of the British Settlement's jetties and at the corner of most of its streets, along with large water tanks positioned along several prominent streets in case of fire.[30] The French Concession followed with the construction of 169 streetlamps in 1867. Within the Chinese city, too, a degree of civic reorganization began to emerge. Many of the Chinese city's public buildings were restored to their original condition, while others were rebuilt in different parts of town; the city's literary institute, for example, originally located in the east, was moved to the city's west section, foretelling what would become the city's main academic sector. Repairs undertaken on the magistrate's yamen included the reconstruction of its first ceremonial gate. Evidence that the Small Swords occupation had been orchestrated with conspiring nonlocal Chinese residents prompted an immediate ban on Cantonese and Fujianese sojourners living within the Chinese city's walls, the gates of which were now closed at sunset every evening, along with a curtailing of nighttime street activities.[31]

Foremost among Shanghai's early collaborative architectural projects was the Inspectorate of Foreign Customs. British officials had long lamented the process by which Qing customs were collected from foreign ships. Shanghai's

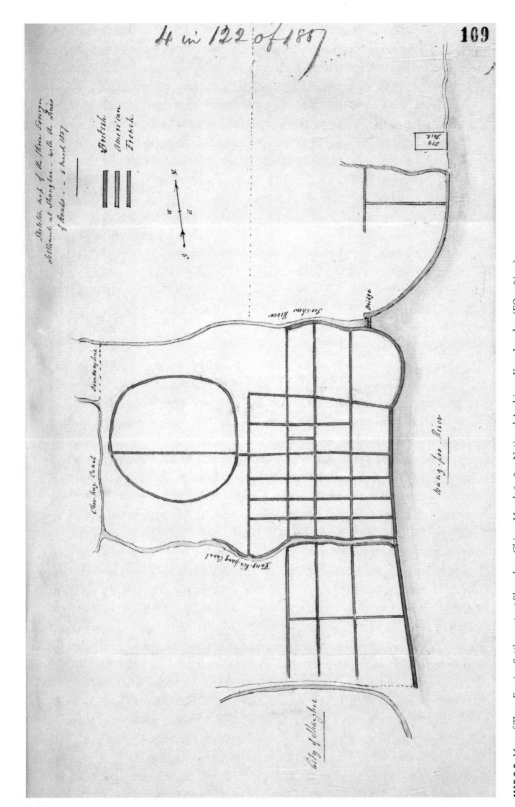

MAP 2.3. *Map of Three Foreign Settlements at Shanghae, China, March 6, 1857.* National Archives, Kew, London (FO 228/241).
The French Concession is far left, British center, and American far right.

main customs house had been seized and destroyed by the Small Swords rebels soon after their initial occupation of the Chinese city, leaving Qing officials without a physical site within which tariffs could be collected and preventing ocean-bound traffic from legally entering or exiting the port. However, Alcock refused to retake the customs house on the grounds that such action would unnecessarily aid the Qing government while defying Britain's claims of neutrality in the conflict. By the late winter of 1854, illegal cargo began to flow in and out of the city without the payment of any requisite tariffs, effectively transforming Shanghai into the kind of open port British merchants envisioned when the city was first opened to British trade.[32] In June, and following meetings between Xu Naizhao (1799–1878), the Qing governor of Jiangsu; John Bowring (1792–1872), Britain's plenipotentiary to China; Robert McLane (1815–1898), America's minister to China; and the French minister and Shanghai consul Alphonse de Bourboulon (1809–1877), a system was agreed upon whereby tariffs would again be collected from foreign vessels by a foreign inspectorate staffed by three foreigners, each working on behalf of the Qing government.[33]

Beginning in the fall of 1855, the inspectorate was temporarily headquartered on the corner of Park Lane and Church Street on the site of the city's preexisting customs house (figure 2.1).[34] As a physical nexus of foreign procedure and Qing bureaucracy, the reconfigured Imperial Maritime Customs House rechanneled the localized diplomatic coordination taking place in Shanghai around the treaty port's founding mission, namely, the collective pursuit of commerce. Each foreign board member was allowed to work within the Qing Customs House itself and given unprecedented access to all documents issued by the imperial customs authority.[35] The yamen-style courtyard compound design, which represented the only Chinese-controlled structure along the Bund, included a series of administrative halls extending behind the red-lacquered main gate and building. It adhered to the basic imperial model for official architecture, including a main hall flanked by structures on either side, organized around a central courtyard used for particular rituals. The influence of Chinese shop architecture on the complex included the additional construction of a long, narrow building along the main entrance, where it may have served as an intermediary chamber for waiting merchants.[36]

The aesthetic and structural incorporation of ostensibly Western and Chinese architectural features captured the odd administrative alliances crystallizing within the compound. Such syncretism was most evident in the two massive two-story wings flanking the main structure, which were added in 1857. The first floors of both wings were constructed in brick with rusticated stonework that highlighted their exterior corners; each floor also included shuttered, paneled window treatments. Chinese-tiled entablature-like banding distinguished each building's first and second floors, which were clad in floor-to-ceiling wooden wall paneling punctuated by shuttered openings and topped by hipped

FIGURE 2.1. Imperial Maritime Customs House, Shanghai, 1857. Courtesy of the Virtual Shanghai Project.

and gabled roofs. Intersecting flying eaves and masonry chimneys on each building's east and west façades capped the architectonic and cultural juxtapositions on display.

The embellished, somewhat inharmonious décor of the customs house evinced the awkward, unprecedented administrative realignments taking place. Recast in aesthetic and programmatic terms, the employment of foreign inspectors by the Qing Empire for its own bureaucratic operations suggested a willing international coordination that masked the self-serving interests at work. Neither Qing nor foreign officials were entirely satisfied with the arrangement, but British insistence that successful trade depended upon "the existence of order"—an order demonstrated most importantly by a stable and capable Qing government—required that concrete steps be taken to improve the treaty port's administration.[37] The physical and bureaucratic centralization of customs collection stabilized the coordinated management of Shanghai's finances while projecting a prosperous commercial future for all engaged parties.

Amid such organizational progress diplomatic challenges remained, however. For example, British and American representatives remained perturbed by France's decision to attack the Chinese city, which they saw as an undermining of claims of foreign neutrality. Less-connected foreign mercantile interests within the foreign settlements also resisted the imposition of a more normative civic order by their wealthier British, French, and American cohabitants; at least one design scheme emerged suggesting that the settlement be isolated and transformed into an island by dredging a canal around the British Settlement from the Yangjing Canal to the Wusong River.[38] The scheme reinforced lingering, utopian imaginings of the treaty port as an open marketplace within which both Chinese and foreign merchants could interact yet nevertheless maintain their own, segregated environments. Such impressions seemed unlikely given the messy physical realities of war and the market speculation it fanned. In reality, negotiating the various fissures within Shanghai's population required some new mode of extraterritorial governance—one that acknowledged the need for a degree of Chinese and foreign coordination while affirming the ideological differences between the various powers present within the city.

THE TAIPING REBELLION

Qing officials had only recently completed their reconstruction of the city's walls when the Taiping Rebellion (1850–64) threatened another, potentially more devastating occupation. The faction's leader, Hong Xiuquan (1814–1864), was a failed imperial examination candidate and Han Chinese subject who subsequently declared himself the brother of Jesus Christ. The Taiping revolt originated in the southern province of Guangxi before moving northward toward the major urban centers of Qing administrative authority. Its escalation exposed the resentment existing among many Han Chinese for their Manchu rulers. Such anger stemmed not only from the legal and political privileges afforded to Qing leaders but from the Qing government's inability to defend the empire from foreign aggression; in particular, the extension of extraterritorial rights to foreigners after 1842.

In 1853, the Taiping movement successfully claimed the former Ming capital of Nanjing for its own. As the civil war crept northward, foreign fears concerning Shanghai's potential invasion grew. Consular officials and foreign residents, to say nothing of audiences in Europe and the United States, were divided over whether the foreign community should support the purportedly Protestant, pro-Western rebels or the beleaguered Qing establishment, however. French officials pledged their military backing to the Qing government in the hope it might strengthen their own political influence within the city, and they used their support to justify a series of unprovoked attacks on purported rebels living around the Shanghai city walls that resulted in the illegal expansion of the French Concession's area.[39] American representatives publicly maintained neutrality, though privately, there were numerous conflicted opinions concerning the rebel movement, particularly given America's own, concurrent civil war. Great Britain also struggled to maintain its stated neutral position. Between 1856 and 1860, Great Britain and France waged the Second Opium War against the Qing Empire after Qing officials detained the crew of a Chinese ship known as the *Arrow*, which was registered under the British government in Hong Kong. The episode prompted a British occupation of Guangzhou and coordinated British-French military maneuvers on Beijing, resulting in the infamous looting of the Summer Palace, the opening of all of China's ports to the opium trade, the establishment of a foreign legation in Beijing, and the expansion of Christian missionary activity throughout the empire. At one point during these events, and much to the amusement and consternation of observers in England, the United States, as well as Hong Kong, British troops were simultaneously engaged in attacks against both the Qing government in Beijing as well as Taiping rebels outside Shanghai.[40]

There also existed a shifting spectrum of views over the course of the conflict among foreign residents. Martha Crawford (1830–1909), a Shanghai-based American missionary, estimated that most foreign residents not aligned with the Protestant Church firmly sided with the Qing government.[41] Protestant missionary representatives were understandably intrigued by the purportedly Christian teachings at the heart of the Taiping movement, though subsequent reports of the rebels' violent excesses eventually prompted a number to disavow their cause. A number of foreign firms selling military equipment to both sides, including Jardine Matheson, feared any opposition to the rebels would threaten business. The lack of consensus among Shanghai's foreign interests notwithstanding, the city's foreign population was in agreement over the need to protect themselves from the risk of invasion. Moreover, the array of local gentry and foreign-supported defense initiatives mobilized for this effort—conscripted British and French troops, American and Filipino mercenaries, foreign and Chinese volunteers and policemen, Punjabi infantry, as well as the multiethnic Ever Victorious Army—underscored the diversity of constituent interests at work.

Although no rebel attack materialized, the war affected Shanghai in other direct and physical ways. Another deluge of Chinese refugees into the foreign settlements between 1860 and 1863 triggered a second wave of unregulated construction. In June 1861, British consul Walter Medhurst (1822–1885), son of the missionary, reported that "whole streets of houses fitted for native use" had been built within the British Settlement by foreign merchants—informal development that pushed the British Settlement's porous western boundary westward, from 100 to 470 acres (map 2.4).[42] Approximately 8,740 such structures were eventually built and rented to Chinese residents, particularly wealthy elites from Hangzhou and the Suzhou, the provincial capital. Wang Tao (1828–1897), the well-known translator and writer, recalled a spontaneous, "bustling gaiety" in the city during the rebellion that "far surpassed that of former days. Men of prominence fled their native places and came here to take up refuge. And through gambling and drinking, conversation and poetry, they almost forgot the ravages of war."[43] Uncounted numbers of Chinese and dozens of other diplomatically unrepresented residents moved in and out of the city at will,

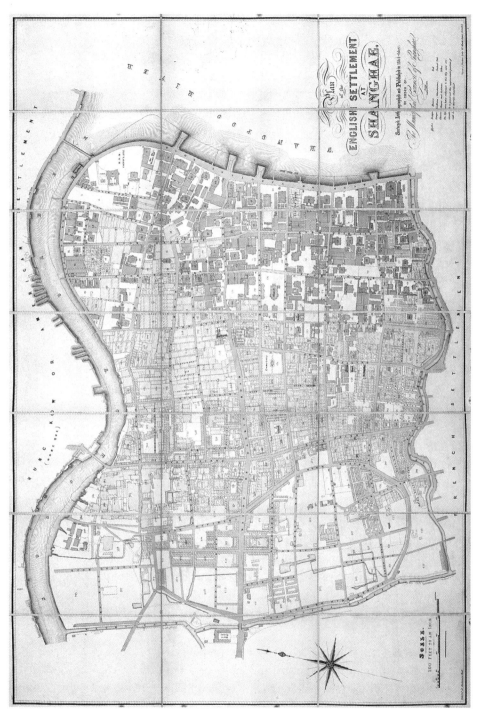

MAP 2.4. *Plan of the Hong Kew (Hong que) or American [sic] Settlement at Shanghae,* 1866. China Ward Collection, Phillips Library, Peabody Essex Museum (912.512.S528). Courtesy of the Phillips Library, Peabody Essex Museum, Salem, MA. Photograph by Mark Sexton. The area predominantly inhabited by Chinese residents occupies the left two-thirds of the map.

including Greeks, "vagabond Malays, Manilamen, and Cantonese [who] infest the settlement."[44]

These makeshift residences, arranged in rows and exhibiting a certain degree of aesthetic and material standardization, revealed the grip of capital over the city, and they catalyzed efforts to establish a more comprehensive foreign municipal administrative system.[45] Following the war, these structures were replaced by similar but sturdier brick-and-timber construction known alternatively as *lilong* or *linong*, or alleyway housing units. Urbanistically, the *lilong* composition structured the lives of Chinese refugees more visibly than had their Small Swords–era predecessors. They allowed for the implementation of systems of tax collection and racially categorized building codes. Economically, too, the transfer of elite Chinese wealth into the foreign settlements had significant long-term implications on the settlements' growth. The speculators behind these constructions included small and established American and British firms as well as Chinese entrepreneurs, many of whom became the city's first real estate developers.[46] Anonymous, independent former smugglers and more prominent commercial operations like D. Sassoon & Company, Jardine Matheson, and Gibb, Livingston & Company all capitalized upon an unparalleled opportunity to transfer wealth from one mature resource, opium, to another, less proven but potentially more lucrative one. In this respect, the *lilong* system helped to strengthen the political foundation and diversify the economic basis upon which the foreign community depended.

Foreign officials did not initially consider such speculation advantageous to the settlements' long-term governance. Had the foreign settlements simply developed on their own accord while preserving "the foreign character which it was from the first intended it should maintain," British consul Medhurst reasoned, the municipal system devised in 1854 would have survived "for a long time to come."[47] The power of capital produced a problem of administration. "I am inclined to think that the whole system at Shanghai is a mistake," Frederick Bruce (1814–1867), British envoy extraordinary and foreign plenipotentiary to China, subsequently warned Shanghai-based British consular authorities. "Our management is both extravagant and oppressive. . . . It is a great source of danger and insecurity to our interests: and by ignoring the jurisdiction of the Chinese Government over the inhabitants, we release it from any claim under the Treaty in case of incendiary fires, etc. That is a point not sufficiently borne in mind by the community."[48]

The reconvergence of China's civil strife, entrepreneurial opportunism, and consular mismanagement laid the groundwork for a new era in the city's municipal history. In May 1862, as foreign and Qing officials in both Shanghai and Beijing continued to struggle to reformulate the foreign settlements in physical and administrative terms, French officials extricated themselves from the binds of the International Municipal Council. Pronouncing itself weary of perceived slights at the hand of British and American consuls, France intended to establish its own municipal body without official Qing approval despite the fact that only 50 percent of the French Concession's total land was actually occupied or owned by French citizens.[49] Regardless, French officials maintained their concession's autonomy from any preexisting British-Qing regulatory framework and formed a French municipal council under the administrative authority of the French consul general—a unique bureaucratic structure in which the concession's main diplomatic representative would also be responsible for daily municipal administration. Concession officials subsequently began to tax their growing Chinese population at rates far exceeding those previously agreed upon by British and Qing officials in order to generate the revenue needed to sustain the concession's administration.

In 1863, the British and American Settlements joined to create the International Settlement. British and American officials remained infuriated that France's decision had ignored "the moderation, painstaking, and wisdom of the people of other nationalities" represented in the city, which had, in turn, left "the safety of all endangered, and the foreign name degraded throughout the Empire."[50] The fragile efforts to localize and strengthen municipal collectivity during the war had been seemingly shattered by the changeable realities of extraterritoriality. "[Shanghai] has become a seaport of great magnitude, no less than 270 vessels, having been last year numbered at one time within its waters," the International Settlement's Landrenters' Committee warned Bruce in June 1863. "It is the resort of people of all nations, including a large admixture of rough and lawless characters and of a Chinese population collected from various quarters, and representing nearly all the provinces. This Chinese element combines with the European mercantile and missionary community to the formation of an improvised City. . . . For this City the present residents must perform hastily and at enhanced cost the various municipal works, usually distributed in most places over many years and successive generations."[51]

Entrepreneurial experimentation begat new, more reflexive systems of governance, which in turn necessitated new architectural and urban interventions. In 1862, the British Settlement's east-west roads were renamed after Chinese cities and its north-south arteries after Chinese provinces in an effort to accommodate the now dominant Chinese population.[52] A numbering system was also established whereby foreign houses were identified by Roman numerical addresses printed on oval markers, and Chinese houses were marked with rectangular markers featuring easily recognizable characters derived from the *Thousand Character Essay* (Qianziwen), imperial China's earliest and most widespread standardized literary text.[53] These efforts were followed, in 1863, by an American-led initiative to open a new gate along the eastern section of Shanghai's existing city wall, thereby improving circulation and air flow in and through the Chinese city while complementing a French gate already constructed along the wall's west side that helped to channel access to French-controlled territory from the Chinese city. Edward Cunningham (1823–1889), American consul and director of Russell & Company's Shanghai offices, hailed the proposed twenty-four-foot-wide street as "an avenue for air and health" that would provide Chinese authorities with "direct and dignified access" to the foreign settlements.[54] Chinese authorities rejected the overture, but it registered the arrival of a new spatial paradigm within the city—an idealized urban condition shaped by new, modern conceptions of public health and circulation designed to better manage human behavior. It was soon followed by official efforts to reconfigure the city's cultural landscape.

CONSTRUCTING A COLLECTIVE MEMORY

The public monument was an important site through which Shanghai's various international and local interests attempted to begin to build consensus among a diverse and traumatized populace. These projects embodied the first efforts at representing the city as a shared urban environment. In nineteenth-century Europe and the United States, decisions made with respect to public monuments, including site, form, and style, typically involved a governing authority working with particular segments of a community speaking on behalf of some greater, imagined collective. These processes were interpreted as evidence of broad public consensus and engagement, though they were also often commandeered by a specific ethnic or socioeconomic group seeking to claim or maintain a degree of social and political power over another, resulting in physical symbols of one particular constituency's values.[55]

In Qing China, memorialization was a sacred, imperially sanctioned process involving ritualized practice and architecture. Memorial gateways, or *pailou*, commemorating particular scholars or virtuous women could be found in and around Shanghai, and throughout China. Such monuments inscribed state-supported values such as loyalty and chastity directly onto the built environment.[56] Following the violation of the Chinese city during the Small Swords Uprising and the Taiping Rebellion, new forms of physical memorialization emerged. These objects, initially supported by the city's foreign communities, represented physical testimonials not only to the foreign lives lost in the name of defending the city but to foreign efforts to build for themselves environments worthy of recognition within the broader imperial spheres that intersected in Shanghai.[57] The emphasis on shared experience and material permanence at the heart of these commemorative acts and spaces made them consequential interventions, particularly given the treaty port's contested origins and uncertain future. Vanquishing the Small Swords faction had required cooperation among an international body of troops that few residents, Chinese or foreign, could have predicted or necessarily desired. In addition to untold numbers of Chinese residents, Qing troops, as well as rebels, thirteen French men had been killed in the fighting, including a first lieutenant, two second lieutenants, a second mate, three quarter mates, five sailors, and a soldier. Following the battle, Qing governor Ji'erhang'a (d. 1856) paid his respects to French Consul Edan. Two days later, Edan acknowledged in a public circular that "French blood was spilled for a just and worthy cause on the walls of Shanghai" and that such sacrifice would be acknowledged in the form of a monument to be erected within the French Concession and funded by donations from French troops still stationed there.[58] At least one Chinese observer also noted the conflict's significance as representing a unique moment of shared loss.[59] Most of the city's British and American residents remained physically unharmed but psychologically shaken by the violence.[60] The battle to retake the Chinese city represented a rare moment of shared sacrifice within the city, and it triggered an important collective psychological shift regarding Shanghai's status as a civic mass.

The construction of a memorial to the French troops killed during the uprising signified a new expression of physical and mnemonic conjunction for the city (figure 2.2). The twenty-five-square-foot tomb, within which the thirteen fallen combatants were interred, was completed by mid-March 1855. A squat, pyramidal obelisk and supporting base made of black and green granite was positioned atop the tomb, while four subterranean entrances located on each of its four sides provided access from above. Each of the memorial's four faces also featured a white marble plaque inscribed with commemorative text. The first, written in French, paid homage to the soldiers lost in the battle, and its three other sides featured Chinese inscriptions from Magistrate Lan Weiwen (d. 1857), Governor Ji'erhang'a, as well as the Xianfeng Emperor (1831–1861) thanking France for its contribution to the battle.

The monument's recognition of an unparalleled diplomatic and military alliance was matched by the transnational theatrics on display in the internment ceremony itself—the first such event in the treaty port's history. On March 15, 1855, a bilingual service for the soldiers was held at Francis Xavier Cathedral in Dongjiadu, which was built by French missionaries just south of the Chinese city between 1840 and 1850. The memorial service was followed by a procession of French and Qing officials as well as pallbearers for the soldiers in their Chinese-built coffins along the Huangpu River to the French consulate, where their sacrifice was solemnly acknowledged by a gun salute fired in the air "against the city wall." Even the *North-China Herald*, which had harshly criticized both France and the Qing army during the siege, acknowledged the event's commemorative significance: "We trust this will be the last sad remembrance of the disastrous struggle in this unfortunate war, and that brighter and happier times will now dawn upon this improving Port. . . . War, at any time, ill assorts with the quiet pursuits of peace. We trust our settlement will never again be tried by such melancholy scenes as the past thirteen months have witnessed."[61]

FIGURE 2.2. Memorial to French soldiers killed in the Small Swords Uprising, Shanghai, 1855. Reprinted from Charles Maybon and Jean Fredet, *Histoire de la Concession Française de Changhai* (Paris: Librairie Plon, 1929), Special Collections, University of Hong Kong Libraries.

More than an index of the competing and conflicted loyalties at work in postuprising Shanghai, the monument and its inaugural ceremony formed the basis of a new, imperially charged form of shared public memory within the city. French and Qing officials certainly shared a mutual distrust of the British community, and the memorial concretized an important and productive moment of collaboration between the two. Ultimately, however, the monument's position on the grounds of as yet unbuilt French municipal offices underscored its singularity as an emblem of French imperial beneficence. As physical form, the obelisk had long represented an Orientalized European appropriation used to demarcate and delineate boundaries. By the mid-nineteenth century, the monument took on particular significance in France as a distinctive marker of imperial territory.[62] Erected in Shanghai, the pyramidal mass indicated the scope of France's interests in Asia. News of the monument's construction circulated around the French imperial network; in 1856, one year following its completion, the Parisian newspaper *L'Illustration* published an article and accompanying image of the monument, along with a reminder of France's long-running missionary presence in China in an effort to differentiate France's commitment to China from that of Great Britain, the United States, and Russia.[63]

The monument's ceremonial opening represented an unprecedented transnational event in the treaty port's history, but it was a coerced spectacle that aggressively nationalized the city's spaces more than ever before. The object itself specifically honored slain French troops, with written gratitude expressed by Qing officials as a perpetual reminder of the Qing Empire's dependence on a foreign power in a dark time of need. Private correspondence revealed official Qing discomfort with the proceedings and Qing efforts to omit the episode from the Qing government's official public newspaper, *Jingbao*, prompted French complaint.[64] The notion of municipal coordination, let alone its commemoration, remained an open-ended question.

The Taiping conflict, which like the Small Swords Uprising had involved a number of foreign combatants killed in the defense of the Qing dynasty, presented similar challenges. The rigid hierarchies within the Manchu army made it difficult to situate and honor these figures within its ranks. Acknowledging their sacrifice involved the reconciliation of Qing ritual processes with commensurate foreign memorial practices and, by extension, commemorative architecture. Of these cosmopolitan combatants, Frederick Townsend Ward (1831–1862) and Charles George Gordon (1833–1885) remain the most notable. Ward, an American seaman from Salem, Massachusetts, with experience in the Crimean War, arrived in Shanghai in the autumn of 1859 intending to organize a mercenary force to attack Taiping forces in defense of the Qing Empire. Gordon, a British army veteran who also saw action in Crimea, arrived in Tianjin in late 1859 and participated in the British destruction of the Summer Palace, though he, too, would eventually defend the Qing from their southern Taiping rivals. The decisions made by Ward and Gordon to pledge allegiance to the Qing cause made them extraordinarily controversial characters with local, national, and international audiences during the conflict. British officials, for example, saw the active involvement of foreign mercenaries as risking foreign complicity in the continued support of a decrepit regime.[65] Shanghai's foreign community greeted Ward's death in battle on September 21, 1862, with ambivalence, believing that his involvement in the conflict had put the entire city at risk of possible retaliatory invasion from the Taiping. Li Hongzhang (1823–1901), commanding general of the Anhui army and governor of Jiangsu, successfully petitioned the emperor to acknowledge Ward's sacrifice, which was eventually captured textually, architecturally, and ceremoniously through a series of Qing representational conventions.

Ward was the first American to hold an official rank in the Qing military hierarchy, and he was memorialized in appropriate fashion. Following the issuing of an imperial decree, his body was buried in full Qing uniform outside Shanghai as part of a Qing funeral procession that included surviving officers of the Ever Victorious Army, Qing officials and military leaders, and British naval and army officers.[66] Two memorials were built in his honor, including one

FIGURE 2.3. Frederick Townsend Ward's memorial hall, Songjiang, 1867–77. China Ward Collection, Phillips Library, Peabody Essex Museum.

near his grave at Songjiang as well as Ningbo (figure 2.3).[67] Both structures were completed in 1877 and consisted of imperial halls within which were positioned altars with inscriptions and offerings devoted to the soldier. Both the cosmopolitan nature of the Qing burial ceremony and the memorial tablet positioned above his altar reading "Joined in opposition to the same adversary" (*tongchou dikai*) acknowledged the transcultural peculiarity of the situation (figure 2.4).

Following Ward's memorialization, the Qing government facilitated the construction of a second monument in honor of the Ever Victorious Army in Shanghai (figure 2.5). In April 1864, and with the Taiping faction in gradual retreat, Li requested permission from the emperor to honor the achievements of Ward's successor, Charles Gordon, and the Ever Victorious Army. Gordon had been summoned to return to England for military service and had already begun to disband the militia in preparation for his return home. Nevertheless, Li petitioned the Qing government to issue a gold medal "in keeping with foreign precedent" that would symbolize Gordon's services to the Qing government.[68] This was followed, in January 1865, by a similar request on behalf of the entire Ever Victorious army.[69] Some portion of this financial support was subsequently reapportioned by Gordon, transferred to the British consulate, and used to construct a memorial honoring the Ever Victorious Army. A sculpture

FIGURE 2.4. Altar, Frederick Townsend Ward's memorial hall, Songjiang, 1867–77. China Ward Collection, Phillips Library, Peabody Essex Museum.

was commissioned in Hong Kong from a contractor named "Chang-yee" before being shipped to Shanghai, where it was erected adjacent to the foreign garden along the Bund, and without municipal council approval, on April 25, 1866.[70]

Like its massive Small Swords–inspired predecessor, the more modestly scaled Shanghai memorial, which became popularly known as the Gordon Monument, took physical form as an obelisk. However, the Gordon sculpture lacked the semiotic complexity of the earlier monument, which operated as both a physical site of entombment and a catalyst for remembrance. The Gordon memorial was placed atop a small stepped granite base surrounded protected by a chain fence and marked only by an affixed plaque proclaiming its significance "in memory of the officers of the 'Ever Victorious Army' who were killed in action while serving against the Taiping Rebels in the province of Kiangsu, A.D. 1862–1864."[71] The sculpture's position along an intersection in the settlement, rather than set back within the public garden itself, gave the monument a prominence, but it also prevented passersby from stopping and reflecting on its significance. In many respects, the Ever Victorious Army memorial represented an object to be viewed but not fully contemplated. A Qing-funded physical act of memorialization within the parameters of the International Settlement troubled residents for whom the city remained a contested political entity. The *North-China Herald* described the obelisk as a "relic of barbarism. . . . The good taste of the community has for some months been outraged by the erection, on one of the most prominent parts of the bund, of—a monument we suppose it must be called, which, whether regarded as a work of art, or as an intended memorial of honor to a number of brave men, is utterly unworthy."[72] The monument's construction was not accompanied by any public fanfare; over time, it even became the object of occasional vandalism.[73] Rather than providing a kind of formal and mnemonic certitude to Shanghai's foreign population, the monument seemed to suggest foreign acquiescence to the greater stability of the Qing domain itself. In fact, responsibility for determining the memorial's location had been transferred to the British consular treasurer along with the Qing

FIGURE 2.5. Memorial to the Ever Victorious Army, Shanghai, 1866. Photograph by John Thomson (British, 1837–1921). Glass photonegative, wet collodion. Reprinted from *Shanghai, Kiangsu Province, China* (1871), Wellcome Collection.

funds for the monument, suggesting a hasty decision emblematic of shared foreign and Chinese doubt over the war's immediate as well as long-term implications for Shanghai and, more generally, China.

Although there is some evidence the Chinese community was generally aware of these physical acts of commemoration within the foreign settlements, it is not known whether Li or other local leaders were cognizant of the controversy generated by the monument within the foreign community.[74] Nevertheless, foreign resentment of the Qing memorial signaled the extent to which public memorials wielded a certain instrumentality within specific segments of the city at particular moments of time. If France's participation in the Small Swords Uprising had first sparked foreign debate over the complex confluence of local and global interest in China's domestic affairs, the Ever Victorious Army obelisk, which monumentalized deeply dubious moral and political behavior on the part of American and British residents, further stoked such passions. The Small Swords Uprising may have threatened the city's livelihood, but the Taiping Rebellion directly imperiled the survival of the Qing Empire, a goal with which a number of Shanghai's residents were privately, if not publicly, sympathetic. The rebels' defeat and the perseverance of the Qing regime illuminated the conflicted multiplicity of cultural and political relationships at work within the treaty port—relationships that, in turn, tested architecture's ability to articulate them.

POSTWAR SHANGHAI

Acts of architectural memorialization did not fully address the causes of either the Small Swords Uprising or the Taiping Rebellion, nor did they compensate for the feelings of despair and loss that followed. In their curation of the past, these projects were designed with Shanghai's future in mind. Public memorials sought to establish some command over the city's fluid population through the construction of collective memory, even as the privileging of particular narratives—French decency in the face of crisis, or the gracious efforts of an international army devoted to the Qing cause—legitimized particular narratives at the expense of others, and in ways that often generated disagreement. As such, they marked a profound and consequential shift in Shanghai's public consciousness. Gone were the days in which the Qing government could presume control over its own populace within the safe confines of Shanghai's wall, or when foreign merchants could rely on the perceived securities of their own self-contained, segregated community.

As the Taiping Rebellion raged and eventually came to an end, officials and merchants gradually came to terms with a radically transformed urban landscape and its political, social, and cultural implications. The Chinese city had been cleaved by regional factions, while the foreign settlements now formed a "Chinese City" of their own, stitched together with a dense urban fabric of Chinese tenements.[75] All of the perceived security and comforts of autonomy achieved following the Opium War had been sacrificed to the same capitalistic caprice used to justify the war effort in the first place. For all of the upheaval resulting from China's own domestic upheaval, the foreign settlements' character had been "entirely altered" by the acts of foreigners themselves.[76] Despite these initial efforts at projecting a kind of civic consciousness throughout the city, doubts over the treaty port's viability remained. The settlements' inflated real estate market collapsed following the war's end, dragging the city's economy down with it. A decline in global commodity prices, generated in large part by America's own civil war, helped to further plunge the city into recession. "Probably no year ever opened on the trade of this port with gloomier prospects than 1865," lamented Charles Winchester, Shanghai's newly appointed British consul general.[77] London-based papers, it was reported, could no longer reasonably feed British youth with "glowing pictures . . . of long-tailed celestials rushing frantically to beg freight for their goods in foreign vessels" or dreams "of profits of all these things."[78] The cold logic of the free market did not protect the city from the risks of war as once imagined by foreign merchants in 1849. Instead, capitalism preyed upon war's viciousness. In so doing, it generated new spaces and apprehensions even the talismanic powers of extraterritorial opportunity could not help to dispel.

The particular systems of governance required to sustain this new order—its cost, its constituents, and its duration—all remained open-ended questions. For some, rendering Shanghai's diversity "amenable to authority" still represented an important objective despite the treaty port's founding principles of laissez-faire commercialism.[79] If commercial prosperity was to return to the city, a "feasible plan for keeping order in the settlements" was urgently needed.[80] Such anxiety permeated a series of political and social structures designed and built in the wake of China's civil war, each of which gave physical form to the emergent municipal alliances and practices taking shape.

CHAPTER 3

Building a Shanghai Public

THE first foreign maps appeared depicting Shanghai as a single urban entity—
a cohesive whole stitched together by the urban fabric of the *lilong* built during the war—beginning in the 1860s. The first Chinese map of Shanghai to include the foreign settlements followed in 1875 (map 3.1). The production of these images signaled the physical and social integration taking place within the city during and subsequent to the Taiping Rebellion.[1] Both maps rendered the city complete and legible for local and global audiences. In doing so, each tacitly acknowledged Shanghai's emergence as a commercial hub and its broader participation within the internationalized geography of capitalism during the mid-nineteenth century. As physical records of change and contiguity, they also registered shifts in the visual representation of Shanghai as a city for all segments of its population.

Qing and foreign officials understood physical proximity to be a powerful if unpredictable force, not only in commercial and social intercourse but in municipal governance. As the Qing government pursued a strategy of technological development vis-à-vis its foreign adversaries, Shanghai's foreign residents prepared for the physical and psychological effects of greater, more direct exposure to the ebb and flow of China's domestic affairs. In 1863, two new administrative organs were established within Shanghai, including municipal councils within both the French Concession and what would become known as the International Settlement, comprised of the former British and American districts. These two bodies emerged in direct response to a growing need to manage civic activity within the settlements and amid growing foreign and

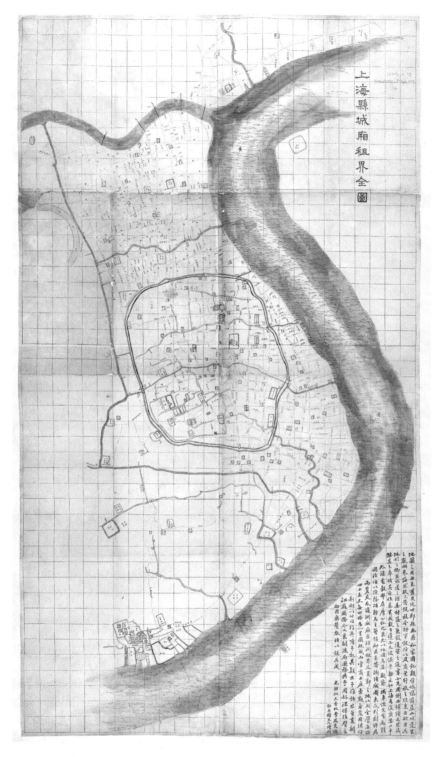

MAP 3.1. *Downtown Map of Shanghai County and Concession Areas* (Shanghai Xian Chengxiang Zujie Quan Tu), 1875. © The British Library Board (Or 15406.a.58).

Chinese fears over the Qing Empire's ability to govern, as both Shanghai's local Chinese gentry and the foreign settlements' more vested mercantile interests sought to stabilize their positions within the city following years of civil strife.

In colonies around the world, architects recognized that public buildings needed to first make visible the ruler's "imperial position"—a strategy that often involved the aggressive seizure of local lands, large-scale urban interventions within preexisting cities, and the construction of monumental edifices, many of which incorporated indigenous motifs as evidence of conquest and control.[2] In Shanghai, the dynamics of extraterritorial power operated differently. There, local, regional, and national allegiances had begun to blur, producing new conditions, processes, as well as sites within which emergent, occasionally conflicting definitions of municipal citizenship began to be tested and articulated in all sectors of the city. Architecturally, these amalgamations resulted in a heterogeneous mixture of programs and scales. Several Qing initiatives, including the cofounding of the Mixed Court with the International Settlement and the construction of the Jiangnan Arsenal, endeavored to accommodate the new technologies and procedures demanded of the nineteenth-century world order. Within the foreign zones, a series of new municipal structures, including French Municipal Council offices and a civic center for the International Settlement, aimed to demarcate the hardening and expanded physical and cultural boundaries of their respective municipal domains. Projects such as the Trinity Church and the Masonic Hall expressed new religious and social contours within the city's cosmopolitan population. These buildings, and the local architectural discourse they inspired, were designed to accommodate the shifting municipal, regional, and international loyalties at work. As such, they tested the hypothetical constitution of a collective Shanghai public and how that public might be both engaged and represented in formal and aesthetic terms.

"SELF-STRENGTHENING" THE CHINESE CITY

The Qing government faced a reconfigured physical and political landscape following the ravages of the Taiping Rebellion. The conflict shredded the calibrations of ritual, urban form, and architecture required for imperial Chinese legitimacy in ways that eclipsed the damages inflicted during the Opium War. Of particular concern was the Taiping Rebellion's origins in domestic discontent on the part of the empire's predominantly Han Chinese population over perceptions of Manchu privilege and broader social inertia. Rather than addressing these systemic ills, however, Qing officials instead attempted to buttress themselves from future domestic or foreign attack. In 1861, the empire initiated a program to modernize Qing military technology known as the Self-Strengthening Movement (Ziqiang Yundong). These activities represented part of a broader imperial pivot toward "Western affairs," or *yangwu*, a new category of Qing government activity created through the establishment of a new bureau, the Zongli Yamen, in Beijing in 1861.[3]

Few Qing observers framed the empire's relationship to the West in specific architectural terms, but the production and representation of these new shared spaces presented another complex dimension to the process of Qing modernization itself.[4] The term "Western affairs" broadly encompassed both the intangibilities of diplomatic contact and the physical infrastructure through which such contact occurred, including treaty ports, arsenals, and shipyards. The initiative took shape through the advocacy of several provincial-level officials, including Zeng Guofan (1811–1872), commander in chief of the Hunan army, and Li Hongzhang, commanding general of the Anhui army and governor of Jiangsu. Zeng and Li each harbored resentment toward foreign forces, but they also had firsthand experience with British, French, and American soldiers, officials, and engineers on the battlefield and understood the advantages of learning from foreigners "without always having to use their men."[5] Importing and mastering foreign technology was one step; understanding the symbolic power these machines derived from their own foreignness—most Chinese people had never seen such equipment before—was another important lesson.[6]

Significantly, the Qing dynasty's first experimental spaces for self-strengthening began to materialize within several of the empire's treaty ports. In 1862, Zeng established a small arsenal and ammunition plant staffed by Qing engineers in Anqing, a city near his army's major base for operations in and around Anhui. This was followed, in 1863, by Li's launching of a munitions production enterprise in Shanghai, where he had lived since 1861. Li also served as the governor of Jiangsu, the province within which Shanghai was located, and thus was acutely aware of Shanghai's own administrative awkwardness and the new architectural modes of municipal influence and authority being wielded within and through its urban spaces. In 1864, for example, he and the city's *daotai*, Ding Richang (1823–1882), financed the manufacture of a small cannon there. Li also helped establish the city's first Chinese school for foreign languages.[7]

In 1865, Li and Ding founded the Jiangnan Arsenal, which began as a weaponry shop located in the American Settlement north of Suzhou Creek and operated by the American manufacturer Thomas Hunt & Company. Li and Ding initially rented the factory before eventually purchasing it from Hunt, along with all of its equipment, eight foreign technicians, and six hundred workers.[8] In 1867, they used this investment to establish a new arsenal just south of the Chinese city's walls along the Huangpu River. The arsenal's plan, produced and published in an 1871 Qing gazette, highlights each of the complex's major edifices (figure 3.1). The image's aerial perspective captures the entire facility's thirty-two buildings and seventy-three acres, suggesting the macrocosmic, procedural flow to the space itself. In addition to shipbuilding

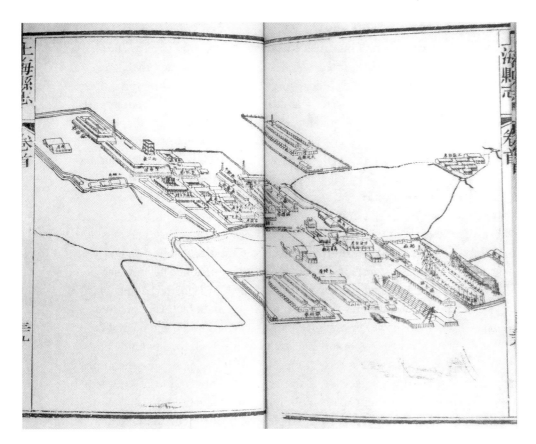

FIGURE 3.1. Jiangnan Arsenal, Shanghai, ca. 1871. Reprinted from Yu Yue, *Chongxiu Shanghai xianzhi: Yi Juan* (Shanghai, 1871), Special Collections, University of Hong Kong Libraries.

operations, the site included an educational workshop, lodging for foreign and Chinese workers, as well as a temple. Shipbuilding warehouses were positioned along the water. The complex's administrative offices and drafting department occupied the arsenal's center, and the site's noisier, more combustible operations were located farther to the west. There, living quarters for the arsenal's foreign technicians, or *yang jiang*, could also be found; the first of these experts, an American employee of Hunt's named T. J. Falls, arrived in 1865. A preexisting Buddhist temple known as Gaochang Si lay between the workshop and foreign quarters. A steam hammer factory was erected beyond the workshop, with a gun manufacturing facility and translation, engineering, and surveying departments located in the site's southwest quadrant.[9] Chinese builders were housed in a separate location outside the main grounds.

The arsenal's architecture both acknowledged and attempted to transcend the technical disparity existing between the Qing Empire and other parts of the world. As a result, its space was embedded with far-reaching political implications. Here was a platform for exchange and engagement unlike any other existing in Shanghai at the time—a sublimation of Qing humiliation into an architectural expression of imagined collaboration and productivity. The plan's orthogonal matrix of planes, façades, and constructed solids, captured in precise detail, projected the new technical processes at work within the empire. Although foreign engineers were separated from their Chinese counterparts, their coexistence within the facility implicitly acknowledged the value of cross-cultural interchange, even as many Qing officials believed segregation was both necessary and desirable to the survival of the empire. Li famously summarized the initiative as being little more than "seeking the machines which make machines"—a functionalist vision that dictated the site's interlocking composition, with all of its major facilities organized around main administrative offices in a display of procedural rationality.[10] Nevertheless, the juxtapositions of people and skills on display, like the differences between the arsenal's iron and wooden shipbuilding processes, revealed a new, imperially sanctioned heterogeneity.[11]

In practice, the arrangement initially succeeded. By 1870, the Jiangnan facility had arguably become one of the most proficient manufacturing sites in East Asia.[12] Over time, however, the forced arrangement limited the possibility of deeper, more spontaneous knowledge exchange between foreign and Chinese workers. The arsenal's architectural representation projects a visual and programmatic formality suggestive of the compartmentalization of knowledge taking place on-site. Examples of Sino-foreign exchange and friendship existed; the British scientist John Fryer, for example, described his colleague Xu Jianyin (1845–1901) as "a brother. . . . We work very much together and he often comes to my house and dines."[13] Technical work ultimately remained in the hands of foreign experts, however, and as new technologies emerged, neither the arsenal's facilities nor its employees could adapt. Similar tensions were at work in other Qing initiatives such as the Fuzhou Shipyard, built between 1867 and 1871 under the supervision of two French naval officers, Prosper Giquel (1835–1886) and Paul d'Aiguebelle (1831–1879).[14] The complex consisted of more than forty-five buildings on 118 acres, including a mixture of foreign and Chinese-styled structures designed to produce new hybrid technologies. Yet Chinese workmen, "whose language European staff did not understand," were "altogether ignorant of what they were about to be taught," lamented Giquel, while a number of European instructors refused "to act in harmony with a race considered by them to be their inferiors."[15] In both projects, heavy Qing investment in the state-sanctioned form and space of knowledge exchange could not overcome interpersonal obstacles of language and racism.

Despite these setbacks, integration remained a goal that began to infuse architectural thought in Shanghai over the course of the 1870s. The Shanghai Polytechnic Institution and Reading Rooms (Gezhi Shuyuan), founded by British consul Walter Medhurst and Fryer in 1874, was designed "to extend the knowledge of the Chinese in regard to Foreign countries and topics generally,

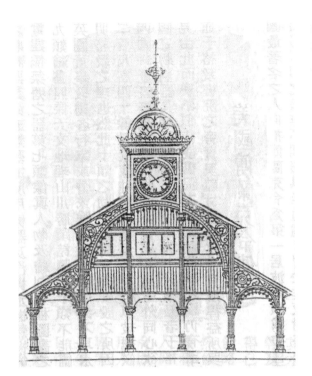

FIGURE 3.2. "Crystal Palace" design for Shanghai Polytechnic Institution (proposed), 1874. Reprinted from *Gezhi huibian* (1877), Fung Ping Shan Library, University of Hong Kong Libraries.

and thereby to promote good feeling between foreigners and Chinese."[16] Contributions were raised from foreign and Chinese donors, including Li and Shen Baozhen (1820–1879), directors of the Fuzhou Arsenal. The building's program included lecture and reading rooms, a library, and an exhibition hall featuring examples of foreign and Chinese machinery and tools. What such a facility might look like was of primary concern. Several supporters argued that the unprecedented and progressive collaboration warranted an aesthetic based on London's Crystal Palace, a magnificent cast-iron and plate-glass hall constructed to host the 1851 London Exhibition, the first world's fair. Not only would such materials signal the Polytechnic's progressive purpose, proponents reasoned, but the material and spatial experience would produce an unprecedented "object lesson" in consumption for the city's Chinese residents (figure 3.2). "Our mission in this country is to create wants," reasoned a *North-China Herald* editorial.[17] Organizers dismissed this preliminary scheme as too impractical and expensive, however, and a "plain" two-story Chinese building designed by Xu Shou, an engineer employed by the arsenal, was eventually completed in the interest of suiting "Chinese tastes" along the International Settlement's Guangxi Road in 1876.[18] Following its opening, however, the project was met with public indifference. Few Chinese residents visited the building, which featured a library collection of only several hundred volumes, while a number of foreign businessmen, convinced the project had been advocated by ambitious Qing officials in an effort to copy foreign manufactured objects, refused to donate any goods.[19] Like the Jiangnan Arsenal, the Shanghai Polytechnic imagined an architecture charged with collaborative agency that proved disconcerting and ultimately unfeasible.

The new Mixed Court building, established in 1864, adhered to the aesthetic and programmatic precedent of previous foreign-Qing interactions, in which Chinese administrative systems were identified through a recognizable Chinese architecture, even though the site itself was located within the International

Settlement. Daotai Ding Richang stationed a Chinese official within the settlement to administer Chinese court cases at the behest of foreign ministers eager to limit the foreign settlements' jurisdictive powers over Chinese residents and address the growing institutional crisis prompted by integration and the unsteadiness of the municipal council enterprise.[20] Initial sessions took place on the British consular grounds before British consul Sir Harry Smith Parkes (1828–1885) provided a Chinese-built structure, composed of overhanging eaves and traditional building materials, to permanently house the court. The visible presence of a Chinese jurisdictional authority was intended to assure locals and outside observers alike that any Chinese interests in the foreign settlements were being appropriately considered. Indeed, it was observed that the court seemed more inclined toward Qing influence when it was located within "the specific Chinese surroundings" of the Nanjing Road area than when it had been "under the roof of a European institution."[21] However, many foreign residents perceived the new building and the procedures taking place within it as evidence that their extraterritorial privileges were under threat, and council members insisted that a foreign consular representative sit on the court to ensure that non-Chinese interests were secure and that court procedures, in keeping with "Western ideals," be acknowledged and followed where appropriate.[22] The court building itself thus represented a form of social and cultural interpenetration that proved controversial for foreign and Chinese residents alike. "A scheme so entirely new to China has, as a matter of course, to be worked under many and great disadvantages," wrote Fryer of the Polytechnic in 1875. "Every step being on new and untried ground, has necessitated the expenditure of much time and trouble in feeling the way."[23] Discomfort with these spaces and the institutions they supported underscored the new conditions they proposed—an anticipated reality residents were as yet unwilling to accept.

A NEW CONCESSION

Designing for extraterritoriality was in itself a political project, and the city's municipal governments used architecture to assert what they interpreted to be their rightful positions within the city's administrative framework. Following their resignation from the International Municipal Council, for example, French representatives quickly embarked upon an extensive public works program to reinforce France's colonial aims within the city. French residents were aware of their "opulent neighbor" to the north, and they sought an architecture capable of unequivocally proclaiming France's political and economic esteem.[24] Importantly, post-1864 efforts to improve communication and circulation between each of Shanghai's three municipalities repositioned the French Concession as a pivot point through which people, goods, and traffic could flow between the

International Settlement and the Chinese city. The concession's emergent centrality imbued plans for new civic construction with additional import.

In 1864, the French Concession Municipal Council Hall was completed just beyond the Chinese city's north gate, and within proximity to Henan Road, the north-south artery linking each of Shanghai's administrative zones together. As the intended headquarters for the French Concession's newly established Public Works Department, the building was expected to support a road building committee and police force as well as the French Municipal Council, led by the French consul general. A second edifice, positioned along the French Concession's Bund, comprised a new French consular residence and offices to replace the more modest structure occupied by the French consul since 1848. Both buildings sought a more visible presence for France in Shanghai's urban composition and, more generally, France's larger imperial framework in Asia.

With the construction of the French Municipal Council Hall, French officials cemented their physical and administrative independence from their British and American neighbors (figure 3.3). Yet French officials were hobbled by their own limited organizational expertise within the city—a shortcoming that proved particularly glaring with respect to building knowledge and experience. Given the obvious national interests involved in both projects, one can presume desire on the part of French representatives to employ a French architect for the construction of these two important civic monuments. Yet all of the two or three self-proclaimed "trained" architects and engineers in Shanghai were British Freemasons.[25] French officials ultimately relied upon Frederick H. Knevitt, a British-born engineer and architect, for the municipal offices' design.[26] One aesthetic linkage may have been a factor in the selection; Knevitt practiced in the United States for several years under the architect Frederick Clarke Withers (1828–1901), who nurtured an interest in European neoclassicism, including Victorian Gothic and French Second Empire styles, the latter of which had become internationally admired following the expansion of the Louvre beginning in 1852.[27] The building incorporated several key architectural embellishments that distinguished it as a peripheral participant in Second Empire architecture, including an arched colonnade along the building's first-floor porch and an abstracted triumphal arch used to accentuate the building's grand entrance. An elaborate pedimented portico and second-floor balcony drew additional attention to the façade. All of its furniture purportedly originated in France.[28] Four municipal clock faces and a French flag crowned the building's central dome.

Construction began along rue du Consulat with the Chinese contractor Wei Yongchang in 1863. Upon its opening on August 10, 1864, the building offered an unprecedented visual, figural, and aural projection of French municipal independence over the city. The hall's conjoined municipal and consular

FIGURE 3.3. French Municipal Council Hall, Frederick Knevitt, Shanghai, 1863–65. Reprinted from Arnold Wright and H. A. Cartwright, *Twentieth Century Impressions of Hongkong, Shanghai, and Other Treaty Ports of China: Their History, People, Commerce, Industries, and Resources* (London: Lloyd's Greater Britain Publishing, 1908), Special Collections, University of Hong Kong Libraries.

programs reinforced the concession's unique administrative structure, in which the French consul also maintained administrative control over the French Municipal Council. Equally importantly, its clock tower asserted French authority through unprecedented aural and physical means—one of the first public displays of time in the city. Time-keeping was not in itself a new method of structuring routines and behaviors within Shanghai; although the Chinese city lacked bell and drum towers, residents had long relied on the twelve two-hour branch system to structure their schedules, with night watchmen beating the time at two-hour intervals.[29] However, time was a particular Victorian-era obsession, and the notion that its careful measurement revealed some universal sense of civilizational worth made it a political instrument in both the British and French imperial spheres.[30] The International Settlement and French Concession each emphasized numerous public forms of time keeping, from noon-time cannon blasts, to the use of wind-flags and time-balls along the Bund, to the punctual ringing of church bell chimes throughout the city.[31] However, the concession's clock projected a new municipal standard for temporal synchronization that extended French authority beyond the physical boundaries of the concession itself. Each of the tower's four clock faces supposedly featured chimes collectively timed to sound "near and far" at fifteen-minute intervals.[32] Ge Yuanxu's 1875 travel guide to the city, *Miscellaneous Notes on Visiting*

Shanghai (Huyou Zaji), noted that the visible and aural projection of time prompted passersby to unconsciously intone, "slowly, slowly walk by."[33] In this respect, the French Municipal Hall's modern time-keeping mechanism structured not only routines but notions of civic behavior.

The hall itself contributed to this effort. In 1870, the French consul cleared a "large, open space" around the municipal offices that freed the site from its "former, half-strangled condition," defying the predominant tendency within the city to crowd houses together in the name of profit.[34] Privately, French officials considered the edifice a final step in the "ordering, cleaning up, and Gallicizing" of the concession initially begun during the Small Swords Uprising.[35] The demolitions also enabled the establishment of public marching grounds in front of the building and a ceremonial, cascading staircase used for public events—spectacles that borrowed from French colonial precedent in an effort to link the concession to the broader French imperial constellation in Asia. A statue of Vice Admiral August Léopold Protet (1808–1862), commander of the French navy in the South China Sea killed in the Taiping Rebellion in 1861, was added to the grounds in 1870. If the Municipal Council building's clock imposed a temporal structure upon the city, the Protet statue asserted a new, Euro-American–inspired form of commemorative representation—the figural sculpture. Protet was the first French officer killed in the Taiping uprising while leading French, British, Punjabi, and Chinese soldiers into battle outside Shanghai. His death triggered immediate retaliation in the form of a massacre of three thousand people, including women and children, in the neighboring village of Zhelin.[36] His statue was completed by the Paris-based French sculptor Jean-Auguste Barre (1811–1896) in 1869 before being shipped to Shanghai, where its distinctive Gallic origins lent the project a cosmopolitan credibility (figure 3.4).

Positioning the statue on the Municipal Council grounds necessitated the displacement of the consulate's Small Swords Uprising memorial, which was relocated to the newly founded French cemetery at Baxianqiao, located approximately two hundred meters west of the Chinese city wall. Like the Small Swords obelisk, the Protet statue was created to remind residents of French sacrifice on Qing China's behalf. Unlike the earlier memorial, however, Barre's sculpture harbored no formal allusions to its Asian context or to the role played by the Qing government in the conflict. At its inaugural ceremony, held on December 10, 1870, the statue was hailed by French Municipal Council president Millot as "one of the principal ornaments, not only of the French Concession, but also of that which we might call the Model Settlement," the nickname of the International Settlement.[37] Millot referred to the "united efforts" of the city's defenders during China's civil strife, indicating that for all of the administrative factionalism within the city, the war's violence remained a potent symbol of municipal coordination in the name of one shared space, and the "common property of all."[38] The Chinese *Dianshizhai Pictorial* (Dianshizhai

Huabao) reminded readers of the statue's commemorative significance with an image depicting the solemn international ceremony, which included foreign volunteer corps, representative foreign consuls, Qing officials and soldiers, and officers of the French, American, and English men-of-war who had participated in the battle.[39]

Both the Municipal Council Hall and its accompanying, commemorative grounds seemed to elevate France's political standing within the city above the local into an imagined, imperial sphere of global influence. Just prior to the construction of the municipal offices, in fact, the French government completed an eight-kilometer road that connected the concession to the French mission at Xujiahui, located southwest of the city.[40] This artery offered catalytic potential for future urban growth predicated on an emergent, westward spread of Chinese homes,

FIGURE 3.4. Statue of Admiral Auguste Léopold Protet, French Municipal Council Hall, Shanghai, 1870. Courtesy of the Virtual Shanghai Project.

French businesses, and now a municipal hub. For all of its performative décor, however, the French Municipal Council Hall was considered to be a structural failure. In 1875, the French consul was purportedly forced to reduce the height of the dome to mitigate the building's subsidence into the city's soft, alluvial soil.[41] Each of the building's original four clocks were removed and replaced with one clock, which was embedded in the pediment above the building's main entrance. In 1877, less than one year following that renovation, French municipal engineer Dupré reported on lingering ill effects of building settling seen in window ledges and façades.[42] Significant faulty paneling was also apparent, and two walls had lost plumb, necessitating multiple renovations over time. These various structural and material deficiencies exposed the compromises and deceptions at work in the concession's governance—an uncertain municipal representative body claiming for itself a position of imperial authority its administrative and technical infrastructure could not necessarily support.

The newly constructed consular residence betrayed similar deficiencies (figure 3.5). The residential quarters, along with the soon to be completed

FIGURE 3.5. French consulate following renovations, Shanghai, 1870. Archives du Ministère de l'Europe et des Affaires étrangères—La Courneuve, France (A050984).

Messageries Maritime building, were both expected to offer undeniable aesthetic and material evidence of France's growing commercial clout within the city and, more generally, in Asia. As in the French Municipal Council Hall, however, the limited availability of design expertise in Shanghai necessitated the involvement of British architects. French officials were determined to hire the city's most accomplished architect for their consul's residence, and in July 1863, Consul Victor Mauboussin commissioned the British architectural firm Whitfield and Kingsmill for the project. Following Mauboussin's untimely death later that same year, France's consul designate, Paul-Dominique Chevrey-Rameau (1836–1914), took over the project and dropped Whitfield and Kingsmill in favor of a deal with the French mercantile firm Rémi Schmidt and its architect, Monsieur A. Dupré.[43]

The commission consisted of two structures, including a consul's residence and a secondary structure for office and residential space to accommodate consulate employees. Ground-floor plans no longer exist, but both buildings featured a mixture of personal and private spaces for the consul general, his family, staff, as well as the French Mixed Court. A degree of programmatic flexibility was critical, with an array of professional and personal accommodations provided, including private bathrooms. Second- and third-floor plans alternatively labeled as "bureau," "logement," and "hôtel consulaire" suggest a fluid conflation of imagined consular roles, tasks, and spaces and a need for regular consular oversight. As an exercise in diplomatic representation, officials anticipated a building whose very material diversity would capture the cosmopolitan nature of the French Concession. In a lease signed in July 1864, Chevrey-Rameau insisted that the building "be equal in every respect (solidity, quality, and finish) to the best house constructed and existent in Shanghai."[44] Imported French manufactured fastenings and hinges, Singaporean wood for the structure's transverse beams, New Zealand timber for its floor planks, and main supporting beams hewn from Californian redwood trees lent the building a distinctive architectural internationalism.

Soon after the consular residence's completion in March 1867, however, a series of embarrassing complications began to arise. Despite the provision of plans as well as a wooden scale model of the building to the Chinese carpenter, a misinterpretation of the symbol for an English foot transformed an intended twelve-foot span of space between the new structure and its neighboring property to two and a half feet, effectively preventing the opening of doors and windows on that side of the building.[45] A subsequent inspection conducted by architects Thomas Kingsmill (1837–1910), Dupré, and William Kidner (1841–1900) revealed more problems, including severe cracking throughout the building's interior and rapidly deteriorating foundations.[46] The building's untreated wooden cornice had been unnecessarily exposed to the elements, zinc had been used rather than tile for the building's roof, Chinese fir had replaced American timber, and the requested French hinges, bolts, and hooks had been substituted with Chinese-manufactured fixtures.[47] The consulate required significant repairs in 1872 and 1873, though the absence of existing plans make the extent of interior and exterior renovations difficult to assess.

The embarrassing setbacks in the construction and maintenance of both buildings encapsulated the difficult physical and representational space within which Shanghai's foreign powers operated. French officials desired a building that would resonate with the city's cosmopolitan community and an imagined audience beyond China. In the absence of any singular power, systematized regulatory framework, or reservoir of expertise, however, it was difficult to realize an architecture of authority. Collisions with the realities of local construction methods were inevitable, but the concession seemed to lack the overarching professional ideals on display in the International Settlement. The material cosmopolitanism in evidence at the consular residence may have suggested France's commercial stature within the city, and the building's elaborate use of imported resources from around the globe reinforced distinctly French claims of taste and connoisseurship. Yet both buildings ultimately took shape as elaborate rehearsals of colonial prestige that lacked the underpinning knowledge and procedural mechanisms for such rule.

AN INTERNATIONAL SETTLEMENT

On September 21, 1863, the British and American Settlements joined to form the International Settlement. The zone was controlled by a joint British-American municipal administration, or municipal council, composed of elected foreign land renters who would continue to report to the settlement's consular body, and it bore influences from the administrative structure of the English municipal council, the less formal, public-meeting format of a New England town hall, and a corporate board of directors.[48] Theoretically, the council was free of direct diplomatic engagements with the Qing government, but its establishment required Qing approval, which was granted on the condition that the interests of the settlement's Chinese residents would be represented, a request that went unfulfilled until 1927.[49] Over the course of its existence, the council included American, German, Russian, and, later, Chinese and Japanese representatives, but the majority of members were British, and they doggedly defended British commercial interests when necessary.[50]

The council's independence in relation to its overarching consular authorities made the architecture of governing the International Settlement a unique challenge. Council members were aware of civic improvement efforts undertaken in a range of colonial contexts as well as in Europe and North America and looked to London's own Metropolis Management Act of 1855 in search of some successful municipal paradigm upon which to base their own nascent body. Yet many remained hesitant to impose taxes or administrative oversight over an environment founded in the name of economic liberalism, making lessons from London or even colonial Hong Kong difficult to apply.[51] Perceived cultural and social differences posed another consideration. "Is it fair," asked land renter Thomas Hanbury, "to compare natives of Shanghai with Englishmen or even with Cantonese? The Shanghai people are perhaps the most sheep-like, stupid, and easily managed people in the world, while Hongkong, it is well known, has often obtained an unenviable notoriety as a resort for the worst portion of the Canton population—perhaps the most turbulent and daring in China."[52]

Debate over the need for a town hall within the settlement, its funding, and its civic goals emerged shortly after the International Settlement was founded, and spoke to deeper uncertainties over the design of authority—how it would be financed, who was responsible for its maintenance, what it looked like, and for how long it might last. Many believed the council's civic responsibilities should be limited to the construction of basic physical infrastructure capable of supporting private initiative; this included basic road and drainage maintenance, gas lighting (1862), an electricity system (1882), a centralized waterworks and plumbing (1881), and tramline construction, which was begun in 1902.[53] Other residents considered the notion that the settlement could lower its taxes, build a town hall, and sustain other infrastructural improvements to be a

"Utopia."[54] Advocates of a more visible, civic-minded architecture pointed to the French Concession's proposed municipal offices as evidence that the settlement could retain its tax base and embrace the spirit of entrepreneurial impulse at its core while providing residents with civic objects they could see and admire.[55]

The proposed construction of a new town hall also aggravated sensitivities between the International Settlement's emerging private and public interests, particularly within the building profession. In 1870, a census revealed five civil engineers living within the British community. When plans for the project were announced in 1866, several of Shanghai's few but notable professional designers entered the building competition, including Kidner, Kingsmill, and Knevitt.[56] In the end, Elihu H. Oliver, a young engineering novice and settlement employee, received the job. Both Kidner and Kingsmill complained about the decision, arguing that the hall's status as a prominent public façade justified the need to reopen the competition to the public. Opponents, however, feared the financial costs involved in such a contest. Consensus proved elusive, and the proposal was shelved until further notice. Plans for permanent municipal offices resurfaced in 1873, though the project again stalled over a lack of consensus over the expenditure of public funds and the possibility of a public competition.[57]

In the face of doubts over the settlement's long-term potential, individualized segments of the foreign community began to express themselves more aggressively through architectural form, revealing the vital nongovernmental linkages connecting residents back to Guangzhou, London, Berlin, San Francisco, and New York. Of these networks, foreign missionary organizations were particularly active, and ecclesiastical architecture proved instrumental in forging and indexing international exchange within China.[58] In 1863, the settlement's British Episcopal Church Society wrote to Britain's most preeminent Gothic Revival architect, George Gilbert Scott (1811–1878), concerning the construction of a new Holy Trinity Church in Shanghai. The settlement's preexisting Trinity Church was constructed in 1848 in large part through the organizational efforts of the American missionary and bishop William Jones Boone (1811–1864) and the British government's financial support. The edifice had required constant repair, and following the Taiping Rebellion, the settlement's Christian community lobbied for a new church capable of hosting a congregation of eight hundred people, at a construction cost of no more than twenty thousand pounds. Scott replied favorably to the request, eventually producing drawings for an "early-thirteenth-century Gothic style" design in November 1864.[59] Unfortunately, however, his plans proposed a church without a spire, which residents desired as archetypal of ecclesiastical architecture back home, as well as seating for only 460 members. Kidner, a Scottish designer employed by Scott who relocated to Shanghai in 1864 to assist with the project's construction, was subsequently asked to make revisions to the scheme while an additional twenty thousand taels were raised.[60]

Scott ultimately embraced Kidner's proposed revisions, purportedly expressing relief that Kidner, who "so thoroughly understood his views and who appeared to be so capable of carrying them out satisfactorily," would see the project to completion (figures 3.6, 3.7, and 3.8).[61]

The completed structure measured 152 feet long and 54 feet high, featured a ribbed vault ceiling and a detailed mosaic floor, and became a cathedral in 1875. Kidner's redesign accommodated three hundred more people and featured brick construction rather than Scott's proposed stonework; it also included a wooden ceiling, rather than brick, to alleviate the building's weight and accommodate the skills of the city's Chinese workforce, connoting both the design partnership behind the project's realization as well as the church's geographic position within a British community in Asia. Externally, a buffering cloister wrapped around the nave, in addition to a narthex; both represented adaptations to the particularities of Shanghai's climate. Internally, the material and aesthetic interactions between the church's brickwork and its carved stone moldings lent the space a simple but refined flourish of craftsmanship that spoke of the settlement's humble beginnings and lofty aspirations. The church's organ was manufactured by Walkers of London, while its stained-glass windows were gradually accumulated and installed through local donations.[62] Only

FIGURE 3.6. Holy Trinity Church, George Gilbert Scott with William Kidner, Shanghai, 1866–69. Reprinted from Arnold Wright and H. A. Cartwright, *Twentieth Century Impressions of Hongkong, Shanghai, and Other Treaty Ports of China: Their History, People, Commerce, Industries, and Resources* (London: Lloyd's Greater Britain Publishing, 1908), Special Collections, University of Hong Kong Libraries.

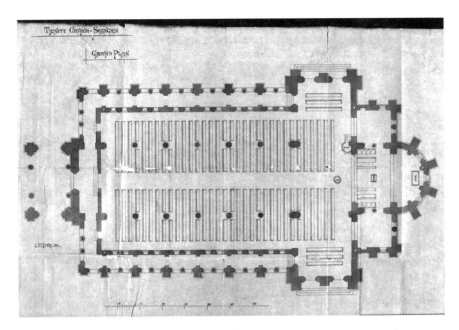

FIGURE 3.7. Plan, Holy Trinity Church, George Gilbert Scott with William Kidner, Shanghai, 1866–69. National Archives, Kew, London (FO 17/454).

FIGURE 3.8. Interior, Holy Trinity Church, George Gilbert Scott with William Kidner, Shanghai, 1866–69. Courtesy of the Virtual Shanghai Project.

the church's spire remained an unresolved issue; Scott had initially expressed interest in designing it, but a lack of funding ultimately prevented its realization until 1893.

Holy Trinity Church represented Shanghai's first commissioned and designed building attached to an architect of any international renown, and it provided Shanghai's British population with the kind of physical benchmark they had long sought to affirm their legitimacy within the broader, global British imperial realm. Scott's participation in the project also offered its supporters a welcome, clarifying sense of status at a time in which Britain's involvement in Shanghai seemed impossibly mired in the murky jurisdictional ambiguities of extraterritoriality. Like the 1857 mutiny in India, both the Small Swords Uprising and Taiping Rebellion triggered retrospection with respect to the nature of British governance abroad.[63] Navigating the indeterminate loyalties at stake in Shanghai required a fresh dose of Victorian resolve, which the city's own muddled municipal organization seemed incapable of mustering. No architect was arguably more closely associated with architectural representations of Britain's evolving imperial ideology at the time than Scott; he "stood at the head of his profession as a Church architect," with projects in Great Britain, Newfoundland, India, South Africa, and Australia, and a reputation "entitled to a place amongst those of Wren, Jones, and [Vanbrugh]."[64] Through his involvement, the settlement's British community connected itself, albeit tangentially, to active and ongoing public debate back in England over London's Government Offices, the search for an appropriately British architectural style, and, not unrelatedly, the future of British imperialism.[65] Not everyone was convinced of the bond's solidity in the extraterritorial environment, however. In 1887, an anonymous visitor noted that while foreign residents appeared proud of their cathedral, so few of them attended services there that one could not help but conclude that "after all Shanghai is in China, and the Chinese have a marvelous power of making those who live amongst them, whether Mongols or Europeans, grow like themselves in habits."[66]

Over the course of the 1860s, the influence of British-dominated social norms and trends continued to manifest itself in a number of new edifices designed not by or for its International Municipal Council, but by a plethora of social clubs and organizations. It was to these social organizations that British residents increasingly turned in search of a reprieve from the city's social and commercial uncertainties, as was simultaneously occurring in London.[67] Sailing and racing clubs were established in 1848 and 1853, respectively, followed by the formation of the British Club in 1865 and the German Club in 1866. All, however, paled in political and social influence to the city's Freemasons. The organization had held critical sway within the city since its redefinition as a treaty port.[68] In many respects, it was Freemasons who most first and most fully embodied and promoted ideals of the civic then emerging in Shanghai. "There is probably no community in the world which pays so much attention to the cultivation of Masonry as Shanghai," opined the *North-China Herald* in 1870.[69]

The settlement's first Masonic Hall was initially proposed by the Northern Lodge of China in 1852, though it was subsequently delayed by the Small Swords Uprising. Designed by George Strachan, the structure was eventually completed on Park Lane in March 1855. The one-story building featured a main lodge room, several "preparation rooms," as well as a banqueting hall.[70] A second Northern Lodge hall was completed 1861 on Canton Road. Land for a third and larger Masonic Hall, to be jointly financed and used by the city's Northern, Royal Sussex, and Tuscan Lodges, was subsequently purchased along the Bund in 1865. A third headquarters, completed in 1867 along the Bund, was initially designed by the Mason John Clark before being completed under Kidner's guidance, with costs shared among the three sponsoring lodges (figure 3.9). This building would serve as a "permanent" home for Masons in Shanghai—a long-cherished goal of the organization there, not only insofar as it cemented Freemasonry's status within the foreign community but in the hope that it would earn the respect of the city's Chinese population and international observers alike.[71]

The Masonic Hall, like each of Shanghai's new clubs and social headquarters, sought to mediate the inherent contradictions between the treaty port's commercial origins, the recognition that greater civic integration had particular economic and political, benefits, and fears of what such integration what would mean in social and cultural terms. "There can be no doubt that Freemasonry exercises an important influence over many members of the community," reported the *North-China Herald* in 1870. "We may also note the observation of Lessing: 'Wherever Freemasonry has appeared, it always has been the sign of a healthy, vigorous government, as it is even now the token of a weak and timid one, where it is not sanctioned.'"[72] In Shanghai, and similar to the continued influence of Chinese *huiguan* and native place associations operating concurrently within the city at the time, Freemasonry functioned as a kind of quasi-municipal body that provided communal services and spaces at a time in which organized governance still remained controversial or, in the case of the Chinese city, ineffective. These organizations and their architectural settings helped to stabilize if not entirely fix foreign as well as Chinese perceptions of the treaty port as a complete urban whole.

The ceremony for the building's foundation stone, held on July 3, 1865, conveyed Freemasonry's local and international reach. That November, for example, the *Illustrated London News* highlighted the dramatic pageantry of the procession, which involved more than fifteen various ranks of Masons from several of the city's Masonic bodies.[73] Local reviews of the completed structure were mixed, however.[74] The building's three-floor frontal façade diminished to a two-story back section, suggesting two different types of architecture melded into one—a physical embodiment of Freemasonry's indeterminate status as both an exclusive

FIGURE 3.9. Masonic Hall, John Clark and William Kidner, Shanghai, 1867. Reprinted from *Masonic Annual for Northern China* (1893). Courtesy of The Library and Museum of Freemasonry, London.

social club and one of the first public spaces in which a majority of the city's foreign ratepayers could gather. The building's interior, too, adhered to its own, disorganized spatial logic and included a central lobby, kitchen, servants' quarters and storage, a large public hall, two reading rooms, a library, banquet hall, as well as an organ room used to mark and orchestrate official Masonic events. These programs spoke to an array of civic services the building was expected to provide, including the hosting of annual ratepayers' meetings. By 1870, the building's spatial responsibilities had grown to accommodate each of the city's eleven Masonic lodges, including those of Scottish, English, and American provenance.

The unprecedented scale of both the Trinity Church and the Masonic Hall, both in terms of the completed, physical structures and the broad, geographic reach on display in their respective design, realization, and subsequent promotion, conveys eagerness on the part of British residents to establish an identity for the settlement commensurate with other parts of the British Empire. In 1867, British consul Charles Winchester reported that "notwithstanding the prevailing impecuniousness several buildings of a public nature were commenced during the year; a Church designed by an eminent ecclesiastical architect, an imposing Masonic temple, a neat little Theatre, and a Handsome Racquet court."[75] The British-dominated Shanghai Club was opened in 1864. The German-speaking Concordia Club was established in 1865. "There is no doubt that more attention is now being paid to matters of purely local interest," opined the *North-China Herald* in 1867.[76]

Amid the rapid materialization of British-oriented institutions, other segments of the city's expatriate population struggled to compete. For example, American expatriates were outnumbered ten to one in the city by British residents, and their commercial prospects had been severely affected by the social and financial impact of America's own civil war. Following that conflict's conclusion, Shanghai-based Americans urged officials in Washington to consider the construction of a permanent consulate in the belief that it might help to buttress what was perceived to be the country's inferior position in China. The United States consulate consisted of a rented premises housing a post office, courtroom, offices for the consul general, vice consul, judge, and interpreter, bedroom for the vice consul, as well as several verandahs. The structure, located north of Suzhou Creek on Huangpu Road, was considered "an embarrassment of the gentlemen who fill the office of the United States Consul to maintain the respectability of the Government in the eyes of the Chinese."[77] In 1874, a proposal emerged for a permanent consulate to be designed by William Kidner (figure 3.10). Plans included a series of buildings with a variety of private and public programs for consular staff. However, the project was eventually derailed by the involvement of both Consul Seward and Vice Consul Oliver Bradford in the illegal construction of the Wusong Railway, an ambitious effort to link Shanghai to the mouth of the Yangtze River, which prompted Chinese protests against what was considered the illicit seizure of land for the project's completion.[78]

Great Britain's dominance over the physical development of Shanghai's foreign-administered areas did not go unnoticed by visitors from other parts of the world. Upon his travels through the city in 1870, for example, the Austrian Count Joseph Alexander von Hübner (1811–1892) understood the International Settlement as an urban expression of "the initiative of individuals, aided by moral strength and, exceptionally and temporarily, by the military and naval force of the government," composed of a physical fabric demonstrative of some "supervising if not controlling" authority.[79] Hübner was not particularly impressed by the architecture, but he admired the evident industriousness behind it—an "elastic, energetic, indefatigable genius" he attributed to the Anglo-Saxon race, and occuring independently of the formal skeins of power on display in a formal British colony. By contrast, the French Concession represented "the work of the government, accomplished with or without the help of individual citizens," that betrayed an inclination "to control and often to reign."[80] Hübner surmised that when French officials were eventually withdrawn from the concession, and "the French flag pulled down. . . . I would bet 10:1 that in several years, the [concession], too, would disappear, while the International Settlement, following the departure of British officials and the Queen's soldiers, would continue to provide for themselves and maintain order, and if required, a defense against an external enemy. . . . It is important to remember this in understanding Shanghai."[81] To Hübner, the settlement evinced a visually satisfying urbanity that seemed to transcend the physical limitations of its architectural objects in ways that both reinforced impressions of Britain's civilizational superiority but, equally importantly, also challenged

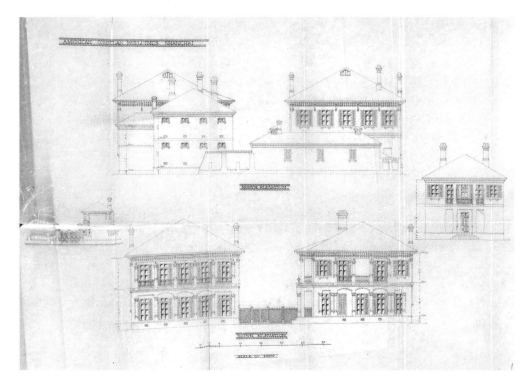

FIGURE 3.10. Plans and elevations, American consulate (proposed), William Kidner, Shanghai, 1874. RG 59, Records of the Department of State, Consular Correspondence (Despatches), 1785–1906, National Archives and Records Administration, College Park, MD.

the necessities of colonialism. It offered a potent urban trope for a form of entrepreneurial capitalism theoretically unbridled by the constraints of governance itself.

CONTESTED PUBLIC SPHERES

Living in extraterritorial Shanghai directly informed foreign perceptions of what could be accomplished in China through commercial intercourse. It also had an influential bearing on Chinese residents, many of whom saw a need to aggressively compete with the city's foreign interests. Chinese frustration toward foreign intervention within China's physical and cultural landscape stemmed in part from the new urban aesthetics taking shape in cities like Shanghai, the sense of permanence they evoked, and the segregationist impulses underlying them. "Foreign Governments say they lease our lands," wrote Li Hongzhang in an undated diary entry. "We know [the lands] are gone forever."[82] By 1871, the total foreign population living within Shanghai's International Settlement stood at 2,773, while Chinese residents living within the International Settlement numbered 51,421.[83] Chinese-language tourist publications suggest Chinese residents and visitors were aware of the new public services and edifices within the foreign settlements, including the French Municipal Council Hall, while Qing acquiescence to foreign methods of architectural and spatial representation indicated the government's recognition that more dialogic forms of civic architectural expression were inevitable. Nevertheless, all of Shanghai's social organizations barred Chinese residents from entering their premises, even as certain groups, such as the Freemasons, took seriously the selection of an appropriate Chinese name for their new hall so that it might ensure "the respectability of the institution in the eyes of the Chinese."[84]

Chinese resentment occasionally turned violent. On June 21, 1870, six months prior to the Protet statue's inauguration in Shanghai, a Chinese mob of seven thousand attacked and killed the French consul and nineteen other French residents in the northeastern treaty port of Tianjin. News of the violence prompted a joint parade of the Shanghai Volunteer Corps and their French comrades through the streets of Shanghai that September.[85] In response to the attack's brutality, Shanghai's General Chamber of Commerce issued a warning: "Ever since the opening of the various ports of Nanking, the security of foreign life and property has been practically, though tacitly, guaranteed by the presence or near proximity of one or more of Her Majesty's vessels-of-war. The mass of the people, both at the open ports and in the interior, have always been well-disposed towards foreigners. . . . For various reasons, which it is unnecessary here to recount, this conviction has been rapidly dying out, and within the last two years many outrages have been committed on Europeans."[86] Four years later, a violent Chinese riot aimed at foreign residents erupted in Shanghai over the French government's attempts to build a road through the Ningbo guild's burial grounds following the expansion of the concession's grounds during and after the Small Swords Uprising.[87] Approximately 1,500 Chinese residents took to the streets and attacked both the French Municipal Council Hall as well as the home of M. Percebois, the French inspector of roads. French police retaliated by opening fire on the crowd, killing four Chinese. Both sides eventually compromised, though the French government's acquiescence to the Chinese requests earned a great deal of derision within the foreign community, particularly for its perceived pandering to a Chinese social organization.[88]

A Chinese-produced map of the event illuminates the contested spatio-temporal landscape taking shape within and around the city (map 3.2). A constellation of four Chinese bodies overlays the concise gridded lines of the expanding French Concession and its major municipal edifices. Godowns line most of the concession's streets, though several landmarks stand out. To the north, a colophon identifies a large facility with a smoke-belching chimney as a French *huofang*, or kitchen, though the structure likely served as some kind of large incinerator. The image's southern boundary is marked by the Ningbo guild compound as well as the serpentine form of the Chinese city wall. One

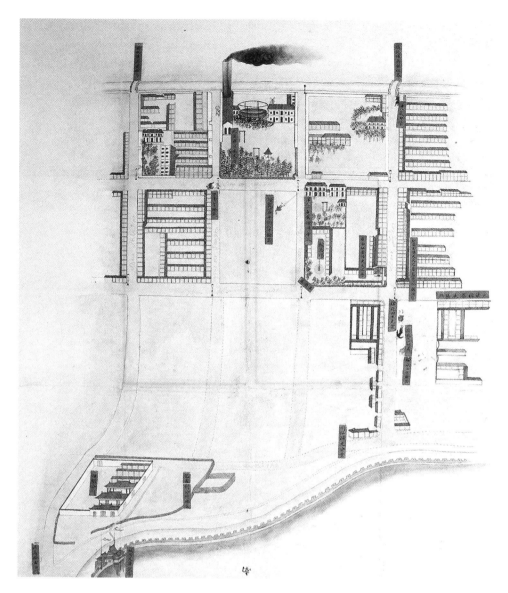

MAP 3.2. French Concession following the Ningpo guild's protests, Shanghai, 1874. Archives du Ministère des Affaires étrangères, Centre des Archives diplomatiques de Nantes, France (635PO/Extrait/B/27).

diagonal in particular violently mars the scene's overarching orthogonality—a bullet line stretching from the verandah of Percebois, who purportedly opened fire from his compound in self-defense.

Multiple episodes of foreign-Chinese violence throughout the empire were sobering reminders that China's foreign settlements were not temporary insertions into the broader Qing political system that would be subsumed over time as mercurially as they had arrived. The treaty port system continued to operate as an unresolved interstitial organ within the broadly organized Confucian-ordered Qing body politic. Despite lingering questions of legitimacy and long-term survival, however, an institutionalization of extraterritoriality's economic and legal abstractions had begun to materialize. Regulating architecture through code and aesthetics offered an important next step—a means of moderating the speed and abstraction of international capitalism and its corrosive effect on national and ethnic difference while maintaining a comforting degree of control. Regulation required a specific kind of authority not necessarily present within the city's existing structures of governance, however. To that end, the professional architect, engineer, and builder emerged as public figures within the city, and experts capable of mediating the city's physical, political, and cultural sensitivities through architectural form. The codevelopment of these forces—agents of architectural expertise and the regulatory regimes within which they were expected to operate—projected new discipline upon the city's spaces, producing a new urban condition in the process.

CHAPTER 4

Regulation, Professionalization, and Race

BUILDING regulations were instruments in the enforcement of colonial rule.[1] In designating the alien customs and spaces of a foreign colonial elite as normative, architectural codes and guidelines produced taxonomies used to mark and monitor physical, racial, and social boundaries. British colonies, for example, often depended upon regulatory regimes that provided a sense of procedural and aesthetic order as well as some quantifiable measure to observe and control indigenous behavior and practice.[2] France, too, imposed architectural and urban regulations throughout much of its empire, thereby linking colony to metropole through standardization while also transforming colonial cities into "laboratories" within which so-called foreign and indigenous cultures could be more easily studied and policed under these new conditions.[3]

Shanghai's precarious position along the "edges" of multiple empires necessitated different methods of regulation.[4] Building codes were not originally a prescribed means of asserting authority within the treaty port upon its founding. Indeed, it initially appeared little more was needed to project a degree of foreign exceptionalism throughout the city than the market itself in coordination with the construction of individual objects such as mercantile compounds that would "magnify . . . and maintain an invincible prestige," thereby ensuring that their foreign progenitors were considered in "the eyes of that alien world . . . heroes."[5] War and the spontaneous integration of the foreign settlements transformed the city's spatial dynamics, however. The first quantifiable defining and measuring of urban space in Shanghai began to take place in 1854, following the violence of the Small Swords Uprising. Then, British Settlement officials worked to establish a method by which foreign homes could be distinguished from Chinese constructions for tax purposes. The settlement was a self-funded entity, and building codes facilitated the collection of municipal revenue from residents while also helping to control Chinese construction practices. The integration of the foreign settlements by Chinese residents produced a lucrative real estate market, but such proximity fanned fears of pestilence and other unregulated ills originating from Chinese builders and homes that could render International Settlement property "valueless."[6] This paradox illuminated the central contradiction at the heart of extraterritoriality itself—the desire for nearness to China's economic markets without incurring the attendant risks of adjacency.

Over time, building regulations came to serve important mediating functions in the treaty port's governance and economy. The International Settlement's regulatory fabric soon necessitated professionals capable of producing and enforcing its rules. Subsequent efforts to register professional architects and engineers represented a complementary measure designed to inscribe a sense of control through expertise. Shanghai's diversity possessed a tangible if unruly physicality that made it "not only the most cosmopolitan city in the world, but . . . the most representatively cosmopolitan—the most dangerously cosmopolitan."[7] Building categorization and professionalization were mutually supportive mechanisms intended to stabilize such hazards. In theory, architects provided a degree of authoritative professionalism in a fluid, pluralistic environment; regulations, in turn, offered a tool by which the professional architect's role within the city could be established, defined, and clarified. In reality, however, it was difficult to regulate building activity without a coordinated citywide effort undertaken with the cooperation of both French and Chinese municipal authorities.[8] Nevertheless, codes and professionalization aimed to produce a reassuring, quantifiable rubric at a time in which Shanghai's extraterritorial qualities had become difficult to quantify.

Not everyone embraced such measures. Indeed, some considered them to be in violation of the treaty port's founding principles of economic independence and entrepreneurship. By the mid-1860s, however, it was clear that integration had transformed the Shanghai enterprise into a very different urban environment than what its founders had intended. Even the city's most visibly Chinese- or foreign-controlled sections were perceived as fostering an intricate and, to many, often illegible mixture of local, regional, ethnic, national, socioeconomic, and professional configurations. Building codes and professional regulation signified a degree of legibility, and with it, cultural identity at a time in which increased postwar cross-cultural interactivity had begun to produce acute anxiety, particularly among, but not restricted to, well-positioned foreign residents.[9] Building rules figured as influential instruments designed to manage, if not completely subdue these shared spaces and activities—an exercise in reshaping the city around some new economic and social ideal.

Between 1854 and 1862, Shanghai's foreign consuls, council officials, and Beijing-based diplomats collectively tangled with the Qing government over the design of some basic administrative mechanism by which tax revenue could be collected within the foreign-administered areas, and people thus more effectively counted. To foreign officials, such a system signified Shanghai's progress as a metropolis of internationally recognized standards. "With such a Code," trumpeted British consul Rutherford Alcock, "Municipal Government of a comprehensive and effective character [has] become for the first time a possibility."[10] Instituting such a system required population data, which led to the first official municipal survey map of the British Settlement, begun in 1864. The survey identified 6,256 inhabited Chinese homes, along with 2,461 deserted structures, within the settlement, along with an estimated 125,000 Chinese residents.[11] By 1866, the Chinese population numbered approximately 110,000 people, making the British Settlement, which covered just 0.57 percent of the city's area, home to 12.5 percent of Shanghai's population.[12] Disagreement arose between foreign consular authorities and Qing officials over whether Chinese residents within the settlement could be taxed by the foreign council or remained subject to the Chinese government, however. Since the Qing government continued to tax land in the foreign settlements, representatives on both foreign councils ultimately determined they could begin to tax the buildings built upon it. Foreign officials also argued that Qing taxation of individual Chinese residents within the foreign-controlled boundaries was an unwieldy and illegal expansion of Qing legal authority into extraterritorial space.[13]

Faced with an institutional crisis, Settlement officials took advantage of perceived structural distinctions between "Chinese" and "European" constructions to both implement and rationalize a native and foreign house tax beginning in 1863.[14] Combatting the financial and health risks posed by the hundreds of wooden tenements built by foreign and Chinese entrepreneurs for Chinese refugees on foreign-leased land during the Small Swords Uprising and the Taiping Rebellion necessitated more municipal revenue. Identifying "native" or "Chinese" homes by their wooden columnar support systems, and "foreign" architecture by the presence of load-bearing stone or masonry walls, offered a method of categorizing those structures and their inhabitants that may have been based upon entrenched foreign perceptions of Chinese architecture as an archaic, stagnant art, but such classification was also considered defensible in the name of public safety, and it formed the basis for a new source of municipal revenue.[15] Following the Taiping Rebellion, the inhabitants of Chinese structures were charged 7 and 8 percent rates "for the price of protection" afforded them by the settlement's government, while occupants of foreign architecture were taxed at 5 and 6 percent of a structure's assessed value; only in 1898 were both Chinese and foreign residents charged equally.[16] Much of the income collected was spent on fire protection, policing, and physical defense—expenses representatives justified by the need to protect foreign life and property in China.[17] "We are not of the number of those who would expel the Chinese residents from the Settlement," observed the *North-China Herald*. "The benefits to the trade of the port arising from [the Chinese] presence within municipal limits, where they have been comparatively free from the interference and exactions of their own government officials, have been neither few nor unimportant; but, while thus supporting the cause of the Chinese residents, it is only right to remember that the foreigner is entitled to at least equal consideration."[18]

In 1870, the newly formed Committee on Land Registration and Building Regulations for Native Houses called for the banning of flimsy wooden plank–constructed structures from the International Settlement. This was followed, in 1874, by a public proposal forbidding the construction of so-called "Chinese" structures east of Henan Road.[19] Such measures responded to foreign anxiety over alterity without affecting the commerce these spaces produced. By 1878, the Shanghai Municipal Council tallied 15,605 Chinese homes as existing within the settlement as opposed to just 568 "foreign dwellings."[20] Nevertheless, the extraterritorial model of urban life was foreign derived, and it demanded a more visible indication of regulation without inhibiting profit. Additional measured followed. In 1878, the municipal surveyor proposed that all future construction projects within the settlement include fire walls built no farther than ninety feet apart from each other. Single-storied houses were required to include at least twelve inches of solid brickwork from the basement to the ground level, while two-storied houses needed to include fifteen inches, and three-storied houses, twenty.[21] In 1890, officials implemented building permits in a further effort to prevent the construction of unapproved structures while regulating the number of those approved by the Public Works Department. In 1900, Shanghai's consular powers rephrased Land Regulation XXX to give the municipal council the authority "to make Rules with respect to structure of new buildings, whether foreign, semi-foreign, or Chinese."[22] Both foreign and Chinese-designated codes now required three provisions upon application for a building permit: designated wall thicknesses and heights in the interests of rat-proofing and structural soundness; blueprints showing the foundation's existing and future pipelines and plumbing; and plans showing the distances between the building and the surrounding street or road.[23] Chinese homes built after 1904 needed to include four-inch-thick concrete floors designed to prevent rat infestations within them. A more careful articulation of "foreign" building rules was also suggested at the time, though they would remain "as workable as possible" to avoid the possibility of future friction between the city's foreign architects and its municipal engineers.[24]

Efforts to distinguish "foreign" and "Chinese" building categories belied a rich history of architectural interchange and appropriation within Shanghai, all undertaken in the name of Shanghai's freewheeling commercial expediency. The provision of a "semi-foreign" building category within the council's regulations spoke directly to such interplay while also illuminating the difficult and, at times, contradictory negotiations between municipal governance and capitalism. Chinese builders working under the alleged supervision of foreign merchants, none of whom had received significant formal training as professional designers, produced architectural forms and practices mythologized in the city's early treaty port history. One notable example was the "compradoric" architecture on display in the British Settlement's first mercantile structures, which foreign observers lauded for their combination of Western and Chinese forms and acquiescence to the Chinese building practices and cross-cultural context at hand.[25] Early experimentation was not limited to the city's built environment, however. Following the Opium War, Chinese shipbuilding practices relied upon the borrowing of foreign-originated sails, hulls, and flags as a kind of cultural camouflage that helped to elude international port laws, thereby ensuring a ship's safety from taxation or undue regulation—a "hermaphrodite rigging" that passed as foreign at sea but looked Chinese in port.[26]

Many of Shanghai's Chinese residents, elite and poorer classes alike, reveled in the exotic, transgressive environments produced through cross-cultural contact. Throughout the Qing Empire, the late nineteenth-century city composed shifting commercial, political, and social terrain.[27] Architectural practices adjusted accordingly. Physically, these changes registered through the arrival of new building types and technologies such as the railway station and museum, though the basic urban pattern of a city like Shanghai largely endured—a city wall within which was found a dense urban fabric comprised of temples, administrative compounds, and residences. Beyond these walls, however, an atmosphere of spectacle offered a release for Chinese audiences eager to forget the horrors of the Taiping Rebellion.[28] Two- and three-story teahouses along Fuzhou Road, for example, featured Western building elements such as balconies, decorative staircases, plate-glass windows, and kerosene lamps that blurred distinctions between foreign and Chinese architecture in an effort to create atmospheres of fantasy and escape for Chinese sojourners (figure 4.1). One popular establishment known as the Chinese Food and Tea House (Zhongguo Fan Cha Guan) offered Western food and alcohol for those with Western-inclined palettes, while the "Western room" of a well-known courtesan's brothel featured silver wallpaper, rugs, and a ceiling fan.[29] Such items were considered generally "Western" because they seemed new and different, with

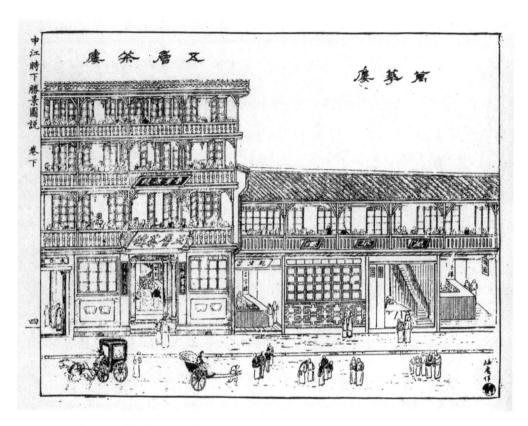

FIGURE 4.1. "Five Story" Teahouse, Fuzhou Road, Shanghai. Reprinted from Meihua'anzhu, *Shenjiang shengjing tushuo* (1884; repr., Taipei: Dongfang Wenhua Shuju, 1970), Hong Kong University of Science and Technology.

little actual regard for their true national origins.[30] Most of these structures also existed within the foreign-controlled settlements. Descriptions of "magnificent" foreign structures "soaring to the sky" or "reaching to the clouds" were quite common in Chinese newspapers and guides as promotional efforts to sell these new architectural and spatial experiences to recent Chinese immigrants as well as tourists from other parts of the empire.[31]

Economically, architectural mimicry proved lucrative. By the end of the nineteenth century, some Chinese shop owners employed foreign architectural vernacular within the city in an effort to attract customers. Chinese commercial newspapers and magazines began to promote a stylistic blurring of the *jiushi*, or "old style," which connoted China's traditional architecture, along with the *yangshi*, or foreign style, with all of its connotations of exoticism and luxury, as a savvy means of modernizing a storefront display in order to attract more business.[32] For those shopkeepers unable to afford renting new space in prominently located and Western-operated buildings, the improvement of their existing shop fronts through foreign-imported aesthetics represented a means of overcoming an otherwise underwhelming two-story structure with commonly employed features including metal *pailou*, concave and convex mirrors, fountains, and Western figural sculptures.[33] Over time, the appropriation of Western ornament soon became not merely a superficial but a necessary cost of conducting business. Plate-glass windows and doors were less expensive to maintain than traditional Chinese storefronts featuring paper-screen windows and elaborately carved wood thresholds, for example.[34] By the 1920s, the use of elaborate corner towers, such as those crowning "many Wren churches and commercial buildings of all descriptions," had become ubiquitous indices of large-scale palaces for consumption along Nanjing Road, including the Wing On and Sincere department stores.[35]

Cross-cultural appropriation was an exercise in which foreign residents also actively participated. The mixture of architectural styles and eras on display in Shanghai amazed and befuddled Chinese and foreign residents and visitors alike. *L'Echo de Chine* noted that "the convergence of old and new building styles within the city over such a short period of time has created spectacular juxtapositions of immense homes and factories, the proportions of which are astonishing, not so much in their grandeur as much by the new, curious spectacle they offer in comparison to their neighbors of another age."[36] Foreign touristic propaganda described a city of "two souls," with a physical and cultural divide established between the modern and the undeveloped, the East and the West, and the familiar and the exotic.[37] Only upon arriving in Shanghai did many foreign visitors realize that some three blocks beyond the Western edifices along the Bund lay the rest of the city, consisting "mainly of Chinese buildings, with here and there a European edifice."[38] Nevertheless, numerous foreign buildings borrowed from Chinese ornamental and structural details, thereby channeling foreign fantasies of cultural subversion while reinforcing foreign preconceptions of Chinese architecture as trifles of playful entertainment.

Missionaries and educational initiatives appropriated Chinese architectural aesthetics for different programmatic intentions, though with similar aesthetic results. Sino-Christian architectural hybrids were initially products of circumstance and available Chinese labor, though they quickly became valuable promotional tools signifying ecclesiastical adaptation and acculturation.[39] The buildings of Shanghai's St. John's University, founded by missionaries in 1879 for the education of young Chinese men, originally featured traditional Chinese materials and architectural motifs out of expediency, having employed a number of Chinese laborers for its construction. Later construction such as Schereschewsky Hall, completed in 1894, or Anniversary Hall, erected in 1915 to house the Low Library, deliberately incorporated foreign masonry construction and Chinese-style roof treatments to ensure they did "not look like a foreign importation" while also acknowledging the university's diverse mix of Chinese students, American faculty, and Chinese and foreign donors (figure 4.2).[40]

FIGURE 4.2. Anniversary Hall, St. John's University, Shanghai, 1915. Reprinted from V. L. Wong, *The Low Library: A History* (Shanghai: St. John's University, 1924), Special Collections, University of Hong Kong Libraries.

For architects, toying with culturally specific building categorization at the expense of the settlement's regulatory infrastructure had political, economic, and social implications. In 1907, for example, the Shanghai-based British designer and RIBA associate Sidney Halse applied to build nine Chinese houses and a stable in the International Settlement. According to Halse's application for a building permit, the buildings' roofs were supported by brick walls, and their interiors included "foreign" staircases and fireplaces, features not typically found in Chinese structures. Halse contended that the fireplaces and the inclusion of brick walls would strengthen the buildings and give them greater protection against fire, resulting in Chinese homes that were "a little better than customary."[41] The case of Halse's "Chinese" structures presented representatives with a dilemma that highlighted the categorical subjectivities at the heart of its architectural regulatory regime. Halse insisted that the buildings were to be "owned by Chinese . . . and solely for Chinese occupation," but council engineers suspected foreigners willing to sacrifice their living standards for cheaper rents would inhabit them, and they could not condone the exploitation of such codes through an architectural hybridization designed by, and ostensibly for, such residents. Halse was promptly instructed to make the buildings conform to either Chinese or foreign standards.[42] Although the architect's entrepreneurial initiative gestured toward the treaty port's founding principles, his subversion of the revenue system upon which the settlement's municipal enterprise had come to depend revealed the racist logic at its heart.

Nineteenth-century Shanghai's fascination with and repulsion from architectural eclecticism was by no means unique to the treaty port but should be seen as an extension of broader race consciousness taking shape in Europe and the United States at the time, particularly in relation to the colonial enterprise and the risks of cultural subversion associated with hybrid objects.[43] Architects, historians, and theorists shared disquietude over how the era's architectural heterogeneity would be defined, categorized, and remembered. As the French architect Eugène-Emmanuel Viollet-le-Duc (1814–1879) lamented in his celebrated "Tenth Discourse," "Is this epoch, so fertile in discoveries, so abounding in vital force, to transmit to posterity nothing better in art than imitations, hybrid works without character and impossible to class?"[44] These threats had specific architectural dimensions, particularly within the colonial environment. There, architects often incorporated local architectural motifs into their buildings to demonstrate their mastery of them, thereby rendering them subservient to the overarching design of the colonial enterprise. By the early twentieth century, however, these strategies had lost favor as an unfortunate kind of "architectural miscegenation" to be avoided.[45] Interpenetrations of racial, sexual, and architectural categorization within the colonial milieu challenged its systematic efforts at social stratification, producing worries that could only be assuaged by additional, more obvious expressions of subjugation. For example, Sir Edwin Lutyens's (1869–1944) designs for the new imperial capital at Delhi aimed at an emphatically British project unencumbered by the kinds of Indian architectural details evident in "half-caste" Eurasian buildings constructed in Bombay and other cities decades earlier. The project's eventual incorporation of Indian architectural elements was the result of the designer's subtlety and taste in successfully avoiding the creation of a "bastard form of architecture."[46]

Shanghai's municipal representatives took their cues from these colonial discourses, but it was difficult to realize these strategies given the treaty port's political and economic particularities. By the 1870s and 1880s, the transcendence of building categories that had once seemed so emblematic of the port's value now signaled a harbinger of some broader erosion of cultural and, by extension, political sovereignty. One important trigger of extraterritorial anxiety was the International Settlement's shift from opium to real estate as a key generator of wealth. The economics of real estate heightened the perceived threats posed to the city's financial as well as physical well-being by so-called Chinese, semi-Chinese, and semi-foreign building types. In 1911, the International Municipal Council created a committee on Chinese houses to better articulate the physical and structural distinctions between foreign and Chinese homes and ascertain who was living where and what they were paying. Following renewed public calls for zoning standards prohibiting the construction of Chinese-inhabited homes within certain sections of the city, a set of new, more specific building rules was proposed in 1915, including the prohibition of Chinese homes more than two stories in height.[47] The council passed these rules in 1916.

The French Municipal Council struggled to impose its own set of regulations within the French Concession's boundaries. There, foreign residents favored prescribing certain architectural styles to specific sections of the concession as a means of limiting the construction of structures of an outwardly Chinese appearance to designated areas. The practice had precedent in Paris, where laws limited development around famous sites such as the Arc de Triomphe, the Champs-Élysées, and Place Vendôme, and advocates were hopeful such a policy could work in Shanghai.[48] Zoning proposals included the restriction of new Chinese buildings of wood or earthen wall-construction to the east of the concession's Hengshan Road. Others proposed that Western architectural façades be built on any land bordering roads, a Potemkin-like solution that would allow interior blocks to remain Chinese while projecting a more refined, European veneer to the general public.[49] Ironically, some observers pointed to European construction standards, and not unregulated Chinese building, as the main culprit in the lack of quality architecture within the city. One French resident urged his fellow residents to assume personal responsibility for the aesthetic choices made within the city's Chinese teahouses, which he attributed to a certain stylistic slovenliness modeled by the foreign community itself: "We arrive here with the idea of being educators, giving to the Celestials lessons in what constitutes the taste of "civilized" as far as construction goes, but we find that the average building is erected without art, without grace, only bricks or stones. . . . Where is the construction erected by Europeans that denotes a certain degree of art?"[50]

The fragmented nature of municipal oversight contributed to the difficulties in imposing and enforcing regulation. In both the French Concession and the International Settlement, officials and residents argued over whether Shanghai's continued survival as an international port depended upon the containment of its viral cosmopolitanism, even as such cosmopolitanism continued to produce profit for merchants across the city. Alfred Charles Clear, president of the Engineering Society of Shanghai, warned in his 1915 annual address that throughout the International Settlement, "behind the garish fronts of semi-foreign buildings great quantities of flimsy houses are being thrown up for human habitation with scant regard to health or safety from fire or epidemic. . . . [It] is not a subject altogether for congratulation as the style and quality of the buildings is far from ideal."[51] Official fears over the risks of aesthetic and structural mixing notwithstanding, the illogical sets of building rules proposed in support of the settlement's burgeoning real estate industry continued to produce, rather than prevent, hybridity. Cement flooring, for example, was an acceptable modernization of Chinese architectural form because it prevented rat infestation, thereby improving public safety. Modern fireplaces, however, were deemed as improvements only in specific residents' lives and, consequently, of little communal worth. If Shanghai was to offer some urban model for China's modernization, it would take a preemptive and discerning eye independent of any prescribed municipal guideline—a vision molded by the practical and discursive expertise of the architectural discipline itself.

PROFESSIONALIZATION AND THE ARCHITECT

In the treaty port, a great deal of tension surrounding municipal governance was triggered by "order versus opportunity"—the value of commercially speculative ventures that fueled economic growth weighed against the foreign consular and municipal responsibilities to control such activity through greater regulation, which in theory could stabilize such growth over time.[52] These frictions informed architectural production, in particular, when and how to build. It also shaped discussions as to who should build. By the end of the nineteenth century, the presence of designers and builders from the United States, France, England, Germany, and Spain, among other countries, along with carpenters arriving from places like Hong Kong, Guangdong, Zhejiang, Ningbo, Shaoxing, Jiangsu, and Suzhou, gave rise to numerous national and ethnic fissures within the city's construction community. Calls for professional registration grew out of such heterogeneity. On one hand, architectural expertise possessed an agency that was of significant value to the city's governance, insofar as it offered reassurance that Shanghai's physical environment was being built in a proficient and skilled manner. At the same time, expertise could be instrumentalized in ways that privileged certain segments of the city's architects and engineers over others.[53]

Many of Shanghai's first professionally trained designers were Masonic-affiliated British engineers sent by foreign mercantile companies to China to facilitate the construction of commercial infrastructure along the Chinese coast.[54] Beginning in the 1880s, these figures were joined by other, nonaligned architectural entrepreneurs in search of opportunity. The end of the 1895 Sino-Japanese War, for example, came with more Chinese extraterritorial concessions that offered foreign companies the right to establish commercial and industrial operations throughout the country. In Shanghai, construction opportunities blossomed, as did competition among designers. Between 1897 and 1910, the number of foreign firms in Shanghai rose from six to fourteen. Over the same period, many Chinese contractors also began to diversify their own services, erecting and renting so-called "foreign" buildings to foreign clients unable to afford the services of an architect.[55] Registration advocates sought to eradicate such behavior and the competitive tensions it fueled. In sublimating their own interests within broader public discussions taking place at the time regarding urban order and the risky implementation of building plans "not in accordance with the local regulations," advocates of registration attempted to frame professionalization as a public good that would help to ensure a higher overall building quality and better service.[56] Designers considered their knowledge as valuable not only to the settlement's long-term safety and security but to its continued economic growth.

The emergence of professional design bodies in Shanghai, and more generally around the world, intensified these debates.[57] In 1901, the Society of Shanghai Engineers and Architects was founded by Charles Mayne, a British citizen and the chief engineer of the International Settlement; Joseph Julien (J. J.) Chollot (1861–1938), chief engineer of the French Concession; J. Reginald Harding, British engineer in chief to the Imperial Maritime Customs; and Cecil Simpson, the acting surveyor to Her British Majesty's Office of Works.[58] Society founders considered the proliferation of unapproved construction within the settlement to be a serious concern, in particular the potential cost of municipal oversight and loss of business such illicit activity signified.[59] Importantly, each founding member was also part of the foreign settlements' administrative infrastructure, revealing the extent to which the organization's goals dovetailed with those of the city's foreign municipal organizations from its inception. The society's establishment was followed, in December 1907, by the creation of the Institute of Architects in China, which was formed by several of the city's prominent foreign architects in the name of securing professional registration for architects, and prompting the Shanghai Society of Engineers and Architects to change its name to the Engineering Society of Shanghai.[60] In 1910, the Japanese Architectural Society was formed in an effort to produce a standardized schedule of fees and regulations for Japanese architects practicing in Shanghai.

In 1903, the settlement's Public Works Office began to require that building plans be submitted in accompaniment of any building permit application. The decision represented a shift not only in how projects would be represented but in how construction could be evaluated and monitored. The requirement also institutionalized a degree of architectural skill; no longer could untrained draftsmen apply to build structures on the basis of an available plot or financing alone. "The practice of erecting foreign houses without technical assistance or the services of an architect has grown with the demand for cheaper European dwellings," argued Mayne in 1907. "The trend of the value of land has been upward for many years, and speculation in real estate has thus consistently proved profitable. There comes a point, however, when 'changing hands' ceases, a return is looked for, and development must follow."[61] As a valuable conceptual intermediary between the settlement's speculative physical environment and municipal oversight, architectural knowledge offered potential to stabilize and ensure Shanghai's prosperous future. A formal movement by the Municipal Public Works Department to require the registration of architects and engineers practicing in Shanghai followed in 1907, which necessitated an amendment of the Land Regulations articulating that any approved construction or renovation project would require an architect's registration beforehand. The concurrent publication of an annual registry of names of all qualified architects and engineers to be altered and approved by the committee as new professionals moved into or left the city was framed as ancillary to these efforts.[62]

Calls for professional registration exposed the various national and ethnic rifts at the core of Shanghai's cosmopolitanism. Consular representatives saw major components of the regulatory scheme, including the proposed establishment of an advisory subcommittee organized by the Shanghai Municipal Council consisting of four architects and three civil engineers, all of British nationality, as driven by British self-interest.[63] Members of the public understood the registration effort as a gambit on the part of the city's architects to claim for themselves some distinction within the foreign community's established socioeconomic hierarchy. Although residents occasionally wrote to the council with complaints of shoddy construction, the issue of professional registration generally seemed to garner little public support.[64] At least one resident expressed shock over the general public's "apathy" about the issue, warning that in "any ordinary building, Chinese traders, self-styled architects rule the day for a mere pittance."[65] Others expressed gratitude to the city's consuls for their efforts to protect residents, not from unlicensed Chinese builders but from the potential monopolistic control of Shanghai's building industry by a self-selected cabal of professional architects:

> There are a few people interested in this question besides the architects and they are very much gratified by the action of the Consular Body. There are men of moderate means, wage-earners, shipping people and others who have looked ahead, bought a small plot of ground when it was still cheap, saved up some more money and now propose to build a four-roomed house or two, or even a smaller sort of house. An ordinarily intelligent person . . . is well able with the help of a Chinese contractor to build his own house without the help of an architect.[66]

In April 1913, the secretary of the Shanghai Municipal Council informed all interested parties that the council would not take any further action concerning the registration of architects or engineers.[67] The obstacles inherent to professional organization and other related issues of regulation and standardization in Shanghai stemmed in some part from a romanticized glimpse back at the treaty port's laissez-faire origins, and the notion that self-made entrepreneurs could establish themselves without unnecessary regulation. Yet they also spoke to anticipation over the prospects of China's future development. Many believed efforts to standardize practices and measurements in Shanghai would likely influence China's eventual adoption of a particular standard or approach—a model that would then be accepted by all of China's international manufacturers and professionals. In the words of one British engineer, the introduction of more standardized systems of measurement offered pragmatic and economic potential "to lessen the cost and to expedite the construction of works designed by engineers as well as to enable British manufacturers to meet the keen competition which was to be found everywhere."[68] With American and British designers accustomed to binary, duodecimal measurements, and those originating from Continental Europe more familiar with the decimal and metric system, standardization of any form was a matter of geopolitical as well as economic significance.[69] At stake in the struggle over issues of registration and standardization, then, was not simply the perceived health and well-being of the treaty port but a broader, much more lucrative claim to the industrial future of China.

IDENTIFYING THE BUILDER

By registering Shanghai's architects, settlement officials hoped to bring an end to what they understood to be a major source of unregulated construction and urban disorder—the Chinese builder. The professional practice of architecture did not exist in China prior to the arrival of foreign architects and engineers; the Chinese term for the profession of architecture, *jianzhu*, and the architect, or *jianzhushi*, both represented neologisms that first entered the Chinese lexicon via Japan sometime in the late nineteenth century. Such terms seemed to conflate definitions of "architecture" and "building" into one general practice, and in Shanghai, they led to confusion as to the roles and responsibilities of an architect in relation to those of an engineer or a builder. "Chinese so-called 'Architects' do not hesitate to promise that if they are entrusted with work they can get plans approved which others could not," warned Charles Godfrey, municipal engineer and surveyor, in 1913.[70] By the early twentieth century, distinguishing them in the name of good governance was a priority.

Generalized depictions of the Chinese builder as a cunning and at times duplicitous character essentialized a diverse community of imperial builders, contractors, and laborers. Large-scale Chinese migration into the city over the course of the late nineteenth and early twentieth centuries disrupted standard building procedure in the Chinese city and generated significant friction with the local building community. Different dialects, building methods, and levels of expertise further complicated processes of design and construction. For example, local Shanghai carpenters adhered to the *gong*, the standard Chinese unit of measurement used in land surveying, and equal to 1.673 meters. At least two other standards could also be found in the countryside surrounding Shanghai, while cities like Ningbo or Suzhou used their own variations, resulting in a spectrum of measures, standards, and customs.[71] Temples devoted to Lu Ban, a contemporary of Confucius and the patron saint of carpentry, served as loci for China's building industry. Shanghai's Lu Ban temple was dominated by the city's own builders' guild, or *benbang*, a native clique that included carpenters from the walled city and nearby towns such as Chuansha, an important village located east of the city in Pudong. Following the opening of the port to foreign trade, the Shanghai guild proactively limited its building activity to the construction of local Chinese homes, leaving the erection of foreign structures to non-Shanghai guilds from Guangzhou and southern China, collectively known as *hongbang*, and named for a particular anti-Qing faction in southeastern China.[72] *Benbang* and *hongbang* factions competed for business opportunities, with evidence of nonlocal expansion into local Chinese business interests met with swift and violent retribution.[73] At the same time, the ebb and flow of sojourners into the city rendered these boundaries negotiable and fluid over time, with guild partnerships dissolving and reforming over time in response to specific commercial opportunities.[74]

The Chinese contractor, or *jiangtou*, rose as a dominant player in late nineteenth-century Chinese building culture. With many laborers unable to read English, and the majority of foreign merchants unable to communicate in Chinese, language skills were an important part of any successful business model in Shanghai. Consequently, an ability to communicate in English, decipher foreign building plans, and comprehend Western building contracts helped distinguish the city's most successful contractors from competitors. One of the city's earliest and best-known contractors, Yang Sisheng (1855–1908), was born in Chuansha to a family of carpenters. Yang opened the first private Chinese construction firm in Shanghai, and he became one of the first native Shanghai builders to use Western-style blueprints and formal work contracts, earning the trust of several prominent foreign clients in the process. Yang's reputation throughout both the city's Chinese and foreign sections was purportedly established through his involvement in the 1893 construction of a new Shanghai customs house. The building's successful completion and his subsequent increase in notoriety brought him into contact with Huang Yanpei (1878–1965), the young educational reformer and, like Yang, a Chuansha native. Yang was propelled to national attention through the funding and construction of several Chinese elementary schools in Shanghai and Pudong under Huang's mentorship, with features in newspapers and magazines around the country extolling his selflessness and commitment to educational reform, particularly following his death in 1908.[75] His memorial service followed standard Qing imperial ritual, including the burial of peacock feathers in his coffin, the placement of salt in his mouth, as well as the use of a horizontal inscribed headstone at his burial site.[76]

Yang was an early and broadly popular personification of China's own modernizing building industry, and his iconic status predated the canonization of other influential architects like Liang Sicheng (1901–1972), Yang Tingbao

(1901–1982), and Liu Dunzhen (1897–1968) in modern Chinese building culture and history.[77] Long ignored within Qing society as manual laborers, he and other contractors emerged as important conduits for Chinese-foreign cultural and professional interchange. Such collaboration made these builders wealthy local celebrities.[78] As early as the 1880s, for example, contractors could be seen parading around Shanghai in elaborate rickshaws, their families having become influential and well known within the Chinese community.[79] Such financial largesse left contractors uniquely positioned between the professional realms of manual labor and the new white-collar workforce emerging not only within Shanghai but throughout China.[80] By the turn of the century, Shanghai had become home to nearly one hundred Chinese building companies. Growing discrepancies in the use of measurement standards, salary expectations, common currency usage, and a basic lack of general means of communication exacerbated intercompany competition.[81] In 1898, and amid the pressures of growth and professionalization, Shanghai's Chinese building leaders called for a need to organize and standardize architectural and engineering qualifications within the city, eventually leading to a merger of the Shanghai and Shaoxing contingents in 1907. The reconciliation revealed contractors were aware of the negative consequences professional infighting could produce, even as the reputation of certain contractors rose relative to others. With language obstacles constituting a major issue in cross-cultural collaboration, foreign architects and Chinese builders both preferred to work with dependable partners and reliable, nonlinguistic methods of communication to realize their projects.[82]

Despite these alliances, Shanghai's Chinese construction industry, like its international architectural community, still struggled to accommodate new standards for architectural design and practice circulating around the world. Given the language obstacles involved in construction projects, building collaborations often took initial form as physical models rather than drawings. Models became the primary means of conveying construction details between foreign foremen and Chinese laborers because they communicated issues of scale, ornament, and massing without text. With Western and Chinese drafting talent at a premium, drawings were also difficult and expensive to produce.[83] Lingering confusion as to the nature of the disciplines of architecture and engineering within the context of Chinese society remained an impediment to sustained, quality construction. In 1904, the International Settlement founded a Public School Committee and funded the construction of a school building in an effort to improve training among local Chinese boys, particularly in relation to professional engineering and technical expertise.[84] The program was established by chief engineer Charles Mayne, who imagined potential graduates would apprentice within the Public Works Department. The endeavor ran into difficulties, however, when Mayne discovered that those young Chinese recruits deemed by foreign evaluators to be of the requisite intellect and class for training in the field of engineering considered the profession to be "manual work" and beneath them.[85] The challenges of ensuring quality within the industry thus stemmed not only from interpersonal and regional rivalries among builders, or linguistic or procedural obstacles arising in part through Shanghai's extraterritorial environment, but from questions of class, and the ambiguous status of architecture as a discipline in late Qing China. Establishing the value of both the contractor and the architect relative to professions like engineering in Chinese society remained important issues in each profession's gradual development and legitimization over time.

INSTITUTING ARCHITECTURE

The pressures of design and building practice were compounded by the fluid, extraterritorial uncertainties of Shanghai itself—difficulties that reverberated not only through the professional community but through the architecture it produced. Two major projects proposed for construction within the city between 1908 and 1911 embodied the labored negotiations within Shanghai's building community over its own fluctuating aesthetic, structural, and professional standards. The six-story Palace Hotel, commissioned by Central Stores Limited, designed by Walter Scott of Scott, Harding & Company, Architects, and built by Wang Maomao and the Wangfa Construction Company with assistance from Yang Sisheng, was instantly hailed as the tallest, most elegant modern building in Shanghai upon its completion in January 1908 (figure 4.3).[86] The hotel was built along the Bund at the intersection with Nanjing Road, one of the International Settlement's most prominent corners, and was designed to replace the former Central Hotel. Constructed with a combination of timber, brick, and reinforced concrete, the six-story building's exterior façade featured an assortment of arched and peaked window moldings, elaborate cornices, rusticated stonework, and decorative railing. Half columns extending the height of the building's fifth and sixth floors provided the illusion of their projection slightly beyond the rest of the structure's footprint. Two decorative cupolas and a small garden crowned the rooftop. Inside, amenities included two hundred rooms, a 250-seat dining room, modern plumbing facilities imported from the United States, and one of the city's first elevators.[87]

The Palace Hotel revolutionized Shanghai's burgeoning tourist industry by offering a luxurious and modern setting as well as large-scale meeting and conference facilities where none had previously existed.[88] Yet the building's unprecedented height also sparked significant public safety fears within the foreign community as to its stability. Following its completion, the structure faced criticism both publicly by Shanghai residents as well as privately by council officials and inspectors. One Shanghai resident found the hotel's six-story height and placement upon a busy intersection to be a "danger," adding that "this building is *very* lofty and has none of the usual so to say, protection in Shanghai of architectural ornamentation. The Palace Hotel is a distinct menace to the Public and should not be tolerated in its present state."[89] The Chinese press, too, noted its "towering" six-story façade.[90]

The Public Works Department subsequently commissioned a confidential building inspection from the architects Robert Moorhead and Sidney Halse in an effort to calm public anxiety concerning the structure and confirm its physical integrity. Moorhead was an engineer with expertise in railroad construction; Halse, a former employee of Scott's, had previously run afoul of municipal building regulations himself. Their report found numerous construction and design flaws in the building. Its foundation had been built without any attempt to

FIGURE 4.3. Palace Hotel, International Settlement, Walter Scott, Shanghai, 1908. Reprinted from *The Palace Hotel Guide to Shanghai* (1909), Widener Library, Harvard University.

support the load it was expected to sustain, resulting in unequal settling and significant cracking throughout the building's supporting structure. The distribution of loads over the building's main girders was imbalanced, and its rear wall consisted of a system of column stanchions and girders Moorhead and Halse determined should never have been used in view of the only "slight" advantage gained. The building contract had omitted "many of the important points of construction," making it "difficult, if not impossible, to convey to the Contractor in any other binding manner." The report also found a "paucity of drawings and instructions given by the Architects at the time the [building] estimates were obtained and the Contract settled," a gamble that likely made the contractor's job "impossible." Discrepancies also existed between the plans provided to the Shanghai Municipal Council and those provided to the contractor.[91] Aesthetically, too, the building was found wanting. "Unsightly" pierced pediments affixed to building's north side served no constructional purpose, and Venetian windows installed on the building's south side were badly framed, with many of their components not properly secured and loose. Numerous other deficiencies were identified throughout the majority of the building's guestrooms. The report concluded that "the design of the building is neither well considered nor good from a constructional point of view."[92]

Importantly, and in stark contrast to public debate at the time concerning the unreliability of the Chinese builder, Moorhead and Halse's confidential report placed all responsibility for the building's workmanship with Scott, the architect in charge of construction and then vice president of the Institute of Architects in China. This is not to say a measure of culpability did not also rest with the Chinese contractors; in the early stages of the building's construction, for example, and prior to his death, Yang purportedly advised Wang and Wang on how to ensure the successful construction of the building without attracting the undesirable attention of the council's building inspectors.[93] However, the fiasco was an embarrassment for a foreign design community advocating professional registration as a means of ensuring a certain architectural quality. Halse and Moorhead's report was never publicly disclosed, and following the hotel's official opening, promotional literature celebrated the building as "the most comfortable hostelry in the Orient," with an emphasis not on structural integrity but on its latest technological and accommodation marvels. These included the city's first wireless telegraph service, the settlement's largest dining room, electric lighting, and several fast-running Otis elevators.[94] By 1916, just five years following the building's opening, the Shanghai Municipal Council had to limit the number of people allowed into the building for parties and other large-scale social functions.[95]

Less than one year following the hotel's completion, plans were announced for the construction of the tallest building in Asia—a 343-foot-tall reinforced concrete pagoda to be built within the International Settlement on the western end of Canton Road (figure 4.4).[96] Reinforced concrete was a relatively new technology in Shanghai and had been previously used only on a handful of projects, including the Shanghai Mutual Telephone Company Ltd. building (1908), a new wharf built by the Butterfield & Swire trading firm, and the foundations of the Garden Bridge.[97] The project was initiated by Cheng Tingyi, manager of the Hubei Cement Works and manufacturer of Pagoda brand cement, and Einar Jonsberg Müller, a Norwegian resident and former municipal engineer in the settlement who had worked on the Telephone building. The sixteen-story tower would be primarily for the use of Chinese residents and tourists and was divided into a gymnasium, library, museum, cinema, theater, public baths, billiard rooms, tea rooms, refreshment rooms, restaurants, a rooftop viewing platform, and a fire lookout to be offered for use by the Shanghai Municipal Council.[98] The completed structure would top out at more than twice the height of any preexisting tallest structure within the city, including the newly completed Palace Hotel and the Holy Trinity Cathedral. It was a daring proposal that represented an early prototype for a vertical shopping mall, and

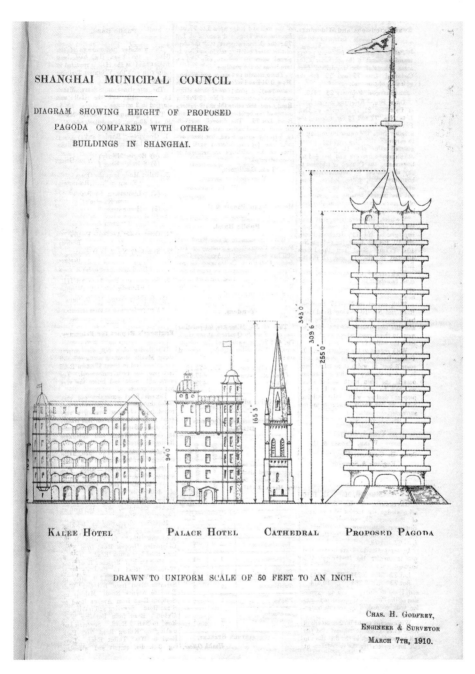

SHANGHAI MUNICIPAL COUNCIL

DIAGRAM SHOWING HEIGHT OF PROPOSED
PAGODA COMPARED WITH OTHER
BUILDINGS IN SHANGHAI.

KALEE HOTEL   PALACE HOTEL   CATHEDRAL   PROPOSED PAGODA

DRAWN TO UNIFORM SCALE OF 50 FEET TO AN INCH.

CHAS. H. GODFREY,
ENGINEER & SURVEYOR
MARCH 7TH, 1910.

FIGURE 4.4. Reinforced concrete pagoda (proposed), Cheng Tingyi and Einar Jonsburg Müller, Shanghai, 1910. Reprinted from *Shanghai Municipal Gazette* 3, no. 120 (March 17, 1910), Special Collections, University of Hong Kong Libraries.

the city's first international skyscraper. As a Chinese-inspired concrete structure on par with what was being constructed in New York or Chicago at the time, it posed a test, not only to the perceived carrying capacity of Shanghai's soft, alluvial soil but to the nascent regulatory fabric undergirding the entire extraterritorial enterprise.

By the late nineteenth century, the risks of building settling were becoming increasingly obvious around Shanghai, with reports of architectural cracking, sinking, as well as collapse.[99] The pagoda's embrace of reinforced concrete construction pushed the limits of what the city's architects and engineers knew about the soil and reinforced concrete technology. In a letter to the Shanghai Municipal Council written January 17, 1910, Müller and Cheng explained the innovative concrete engineering principles behind the project's construction, its cross-cultural potential as a destination for both Chinese residents and tourists.[100] Upon examining the project's request for a building permit, then chief settlement engineer and surveyor Charles H. Godfrey declared that "the whole question of the erection of tall buildings in Shanghai rests upon the present application."[101] Godfrey was unequivocal in his support of the pagoda, particularly as it pertained to Shanghai's future growth. The visionary proposal presented a new urban planning model for the city, one that later echoed in iconic modernist plans such as Le Corbusier's 1925 Plan Voisin—the erection of several high-rise structures surrounded by parks and undeveloped land, rather than the proliferation of short buildings separated by narrow alleys and roads.[102] The pagoda also prefigured later experimental translations of Chinese architectural form through concrete by designers like the American architect Henry Murphy (1877–1954).

Other responses to the project were more tepid. For one, there was some confusion over how to categorize the structure—whether it might be best categorized as a building, which would require a reconfiguration of the settlement's existing height restrictions, or as a pagoda, which technically made it a religious structure and thus conceivably exempt from official building regulations.[103] Though settlement officials eventually defined it as a building, doubts remained concerning its exceptional form and innovative materiality, and council representatives surveyed those owners and tenants of the properties adjoining the land on which the pagoda was to be built. Eight landlords, including seven foreign and one Chinese businessmen, of which one was purportedly an architect, spoke out against the project based on a range of concerns. These included fears of the tower's potential negative impact on the neighborhood's real estate prices, the pagoda's structural stability, and concern on the part of their Chinese tenants over the pagoda's effect on the area's fengshui.[104]

That foreign landlords raised the issue of geomancy as an obstacle to the pagoda's construction after years in which it had never emerged as a potential deterrent to other large-scale engineering projects within the city struck both

Müller and Cheng as absurd. In letters to the council, Cheng advised that "this talk of fengshui is really without basis," while Müller noted that "everything a foreigner has ever done in China has been bad joss at the outset. Railways, tramways, were very bad joss. But pagodas are specially considered to be 'very good joss' all over China, but to suit the opposition the good old Chinese rule is reversed."[105] Local Chinese business leaders were subsequently questioned; of the eleven guilds queried, five responded in favor, two objected to the project, and four were unresponsive, suggesting the potential for any fengshui disturbance was not a significant concern. The affected landlords continued to object to the project, however, prompting the council to schedule a proxy vote at the next ratepayers' meeting on March 21. In the interim, Müller presented the project in a meeting of the Shanghai Society of Engineers and Architects, where response to the scheme was encouraging. Members were particularly excited by the pagoda's daring challenge of the prescribed limits of tensile strength and height limits imposed by the council's building regulations.[106] Its potential success would herald a new era of technological advancement for the city. Only Thomas Kingsmill, the celebrated, longtime British resident, Freemason, and author of the settlement's first survey in 1864, offered a dissenting opinion, believing that not enough attention had been paid to the particular "architectural aspects" of the project and that anything the pagoda's façade might feature not completely in accordance with "the Chinese style of architecture would be an eyesore."[107]

Kingsmill's comments exploited a gap in public opinion over the proposal's technical merits versus its perceived aesthetic value—a question of taste that had been wielded in the past in an effort to control unwanted Chinese construction. Concurrent debate over professional registration, for example, hinged on the belief that professional architects would be better able to discern architectural quality as opposed to substandard building production. Yet the Palace Hotel and the pagoda proposal challenged these presumptions in consequential ways. In an effort to discredit the project, opponents subsequently fixated upon the building's so-called Chinese elements, including its form, and the potential desecration of a traditionally religious Chinese building type for the purposes of entertainment. That the pagoda had been proposed by a Chinese businessman with presumed knowledge of the cultural significance of its form, and that its potential construction had not offended selected members of the Chinese community, went unnoted. The pious defense of Chinese architecture by foreign residents, following decades of foreign criticism of imperial Chinese building practices and forms as weak and decayed, demonstrated how effectively architecture could be used to either demarcate or subvert the various boundaries—cultural, social, and otherwise—imagined by various segments of the city's population. One concerned citizen conjectured, with no apparent irony, "How would, say, Englishmen like it if Chinese were to erect a replica of one of their noble cathedrals, say in the suburbs of Brighton, and devote the building to such objects as theatres, swimming baths, penny gaffs, and lavatories? Then, its commanding height and appearance, surmounted by a Chinese flag, will give good ground to the Celestials to say that our Settlement has been taken back by the Chinese government. And the poor Cathedral spire what an insignificant finger pointing to heaven it will appear, when overshadowed by the great monstrosity."[108] In the only surviving image of the pagoda, drawn by municipal engineer Godfrey, printed in the *Municipal Gazette* on March 17 and reprinted in the city's largest Chinese newspaper, *Shenbao*, on March 20, the pagoda is juxtaposed next to the city's preexisting tallest structures. The image gestures toward an unsettling reterritorialization of the settlement—an overscaled, ostensibly Chinese monument of uneasily categorized architectural licentiousness borne of Shanghai's ineffective municipal regulation.

At the ratepayers' meeting, however, the proposal was defended on grounds of its technical innovation and symbolic value. Charles Edward Pearce, head of the Shanghai Municipal Council's Electricity Committee, argued that the tower represented an homage to the history of China's most famous pagodas and that its cutting-edge engineering bravado would help position Shanghai as one of the world's great cities.[109] A vote was held, and the pagoda was approved, 138 to 112, though construction was made contingent upon a counterproposal made by the affected foreign landlords to move the building to Nanjing Road, where the pagoda's collection of Chinese and Western shops and entertainment facilities would augment the street's profitability as a shopping hub.[110] The project was eventually thwarted not by the settlement's regulatory framework but by the market itself. Property adjoining Nanjing Road proved too expensive to rent or purchase, and following two appeals to the council seeking approval for construction upon its originally proposed site, Müller and Cheng abandoned the scheme in June 1910.

CONTROLLING COSMPOLITIANISM

Regulation and registration were designed to both control and profit from a physical landscape originally envisioned as an unfettered international marketplace. This shift, and the contradictions it institutionalized, was justified largely on the basis that some speculative enterprises—the illegal construction of homes, for example, or the fabrication of architectural credentials—were prohibitively disruptive to others, namely, a carefully controlled real estate market. Yet both the Palace Hotel and the concrete pagoda underscored the extent to which treaty port Shanghai could not produce a singular vision of progress or a unified body of practices. The competing modes of architectural production and representation taking place subverted the modern urban vision of Shanghai envisioned by settlement officials as a well-governed landscape borne of hygienic streets, measured spaces, and segregated aesthetics. Rather, a very different yet no less compelling iteration of the modern was taking shape in the form of physical objects designed to accommodate the complex mediations taking place between China and the rest of the world.

In their formal, material, and programmatic innovations, both projects represent harbingers of a new Chinese nation-state. The pagoda proposal offered a striking and identifiably Chinese formal response to an emerging, international architectural expression shaped by unprecedented scales and structural systems. By responding to the innovations taking place in Europe and the United States and incorporating them into the centuries-old traditions of Chinese architecture, the project imagined a new China forged through internationalism. The Palace Hotel, with its ill-formed foundations and inferior structure, nevertheless contained programmatic and technological qualities designed to serve the global circulation of travelers through China from around the world. More than an index of change, the hotel also served as its catalyst: the anti-Qing political dissident Dr. Sun Yat-sen (1866–1925) stayed in the hotel following his swift return home from an extended diplomatic trip to the United States and Europe upon hearing the news of the Wuchang uprising against the Qing in October 1911. He spent several days there in negotiations with Wu Tingfang (1842–1922) and other Qing representatives before traveling to Nanjing to become inaugurated as the first president of the Republic of China on January 1, 1912. On January 5, a banquet attended by one hundred leaders of the revolutionary movement was held on his behalf in the Palace Hotel's main dining room.[111]

Architectural hybridity remained controversial in Shanghai, but the possibility of adapting and learning from architectural difference empowered segments of China's intellectual community to advocate cultural borrowing as a necessary step in China's modernization. For example, late Qing reformists like Liang Qichao (1873–1929) and Kang Youwei (1858–1927) both employed buildings to illustrate the country's broader cultural, political, and social ills in juxtaposition to the wealth and grandeur of Western architecture.[112] Chinese fascination with foreign building techniques, methods, and styles offered a prophetic sign of an ascendant modern Chinese nation-state committed to interrogating the strengths and weaknesses of its own cultural traditions. The newly founded Republic of China embodied just such a vision—a new political edifice grounded in certain historical conventions but committed to the cause of change.

The new Chinese nation-state's establishment signaled a shift in how the Chinese government would define and argue for its own embattled territorial and jurisdictional domain. The design of the extraterritorial system had been predicated on the perceived gulf between Qing China and western European systems of governance, and the need for some transitional form of statecraft until China adapted to the modern world order. Changes in the nature of Chinese governance, from the affective nature of Manchu "ethnic sovereignty" to the more ascriptive nature of the modern territorial border, indicated such adaptation was taking place, and with it, a transformation of the geopolitical dynamics of Chinese administration. [113] No longer could diplomatic relations with China be understood or rationalized through some imperial Chinese standard, imagined or otherwise. A new Chinese republic represented a form of modern liberal governance with new, internationally accepted legal and architectural standards that would make the argument for extraterritoriality and its spaces increasingly difficult.

CHAPTER 5

Engineering "Face" in an Emergent Chinese Nation-State

FOLLOWING the rejection of the Qing dynasty and the founding of a new Chinese republic, it appeared China had taken a step toward legal and political synchronization with the West. Over the course of the 1910s and 1920s, China's new leadership asserted itself on the global stage in ways their Qing predecessors did not. Enforcing the geopolitical legitimacy of both China's territorial boundaries as well as the popular sovereignty of the Chinese people was a paramount concern. Initially, however, these efforts gained little traction. Extraterritoriality, once rationalized as a necessary condition given the perceived uncivilized nature of the Qing dynasty, was repositioned as a defense against an inexperienced and untested Chinese nation's development. "Not until China reforms her laws and law courts so as to be in harmony with the West, can she rid herself of extraterritorial jurisdiction and be treated as an equal," argued Dr. Gilbert Reid (1857–1927), a well-known American Presbyterian missionary, in a speech to the International Institute of China in Shanghai in February 1914.[1] Nevertheless, the shift in China's sovereign status prompted foreign representatives to begin to think about how to reconfigure and preserve their extraterritorial regimes. A post-extraterritorial China suddenly loomed as a distinct possibility.

By the Revolution of 1911, Shanghai had cemented its reputation as the country's industrial and banking capital. Between 1900 and 1910, the number of ships visiting the port jumped from 7,322 to 45,870.[2] Over roughly the same period, Shanghai became home to forty-three new foreign factories, each with an initial capital investment more than ¥100,000, compared to 104 total factories for the entire country.[3] Chinese manufacturing and investment was more limited but still significant in its impact; by 1911, Shanghai supported seven Chinese-owned cotton mills and five Chinese-owned flour mills.[4] To some observers, such industriousness possessed a long-term trajectory that rendered the extraterritorial model obsolete. "The business of foreign traders in China has outgrown extraterritoriality and extraterritoriality is now meaningless. Today they are in closer personal contact with the Chinese people than ever before, and through the gradual doing away of the compradore system, with the market itself," reasoned Dr. Philip Tyau, Great Britain's acting councillor of the Ministry of Foreign Affairs in Beijing.[5] Yet many expatriates living in China's treaty ports had grown accustomed to the tangible and intangible benefits of the extraterritorial life. Its potential disappearance drove a wedge between national governments in Washington, Paris, and London and their China-based citizens. Home governments considered émigré-led efforts to insulate Shanghai from China's new political realities to be an ill-conceived attempt to maintain foreign privilege at all costs, and antithetical to the political and commercial intentions of the countries to which members of Shanghai's foreign community were bound. In 1906, for example, the "Act Creating a United States Court for China" established an extraterritorial court in Shanghai with jurisdiction over all Americans in China, dramatically curtailing the judicial powers of individual US consuls within the country. The act, intended to subordinate treaty port Americans to their home country, expanded America's imperial interests in Asia while increasing the global ramifications of municipal-level politics in treaty ports like Shanghai.[6]

With Shanghai's extraterritorial status now linked to the transformative process of China's revolution, residents felt its spaces imbued with new agency, at both the local and international scales. "The average Shanghai-lander, whether Chinese or foreign, has had no particular inducement or encouragement to think of Shanghai as a whole or of its future," noted the chief engineer of the Huangpu Conservancy Board to members of the Engineering Society of China in Shanghai in 1919.[7] Political revolution, which had prompted a modest bump in the city's property values, offered the potential to at last draw Shanghai together and "finally merge . . . into one unified community at least in certain respects."[8] Fears concerning the Chinese Other remained, but foreign officials and residents alike increasingly understood that their political and commercial future depended upon international capital's ability to improve the lives of Shanghai's dominant Chinese population. Shanghai's Chinese elite also recognized that their own prosperity was linked with the commercial prospects of their foreign neighbors.

In reality, however, the prospects of institutional integration remained slim. In 1899, a new, foreign-styled Mixed Court building was completed by the firm Atkinson & Dallas. Procedurally as well as physically, the former Mixed Court complex had not been effectively maintained by the city's Chinese *daotai*, and the court's major buildings, which lacked proper cooking and sanitary facilities, had fallen into visible physical disrepair after decades of Qing neglect.[9] The court's new premises possessed a "dignity" and order that anticipated larger procedural shifts, and in late 1911, both the International Municipal Council and French Concession assumed control over the Mixed Court system and its building, quickly appointing Chinese magistrates on their own without Qing governmental approval to ensure court cases would continue to be heard.[10] The decision meant the court was no longer a Chinese-administered office but would instead be operated by the city's consular body without diplomatic authority or legal justification. It also suggested that despite the reestablishment of a Chinese civic entity capable of reassuming certain administrative responsibilities, foreign interests in both settlements would continue to resist substantive municipal integration.[11] Some members of the foreign community still held out hope the International Settlement might one day become independent; to "[cease] to be a concession or place set aside for the residence of foreigners in China under treaty, and [take] its rank as an important metropolitan city, self-governing in regard to its municipal affairs, as are Calcutta, Bombay, Rangoon and Singapore."[12]

Amid questions concerning Shanghai's future, each of the city's various political interests undertook a set of architectural and infrastructural initiatives to create the spaces, surfaces, and experiences capable of negotiating the national and racial fissures at work within and around the extraterritorial environment. On one hand, examples of urban and architectural fragmentation were abundant throughout the city. The Bund's appearance changed noticeably as one moved from the International Settlement to the French Concession, while the Chinese city, prior to 1912, remained physically divorced from the foreign settlements by its imposing wall. Different pockets of Shanghai tended to resemble the provincial origins of their residents.[13] One observer likened the city's atmosphere to an international dogfight in which "so many dogs . . . crowded together in a small back lot, keep one eye on the coveted bone, and the other on the remaining members of the pack who covet it."[14] Nevertheless, many considered architecture an essential force in improving the city and, more generally, facilitating China's transition into the modern world order. "The modern Chinese building will not be like traditional Chinese architecture nor will it be like ours," wrote the Shanghai-based French columnist Pol Korigan in 1909. "It will be a new building that elaborates, bit by bit, upon everything that is eclectic. It will preserve national, indestructible customs while also following progress and the needs created by inevitable reform."[15] Such visions emerged at a time of political transformation around the world and amid growing interest in architectural internationalization.[16] They also inform an intensification in municipal construction projects within the city in the years prior to the fall of the Qing Empire through the end of World War I.

"FACE" AND ARCHITECTURE IN A GLOBALIZED LOCALITY

One popular perceived commonality suggestive of the city's shifting geopolitical dynamics was foreign appropriation of the Chinese notion of "face"—the English translation of several Chinese terms, including *mianzi, yan,* or *lian,* and roughly characterized to be an index of one's social position in a community based upon reputation, influence, as well as the respect of others.[17] Over the course of the late nineteenth and early twentieth centuries, face figured as a object of fascination within foreign communities throughout China.[18] The term's popularization in English was in large part due to the American missionary and Sinologist Arthur Smith (1845–1932), whose book *Chinese Characteristics* (1894) framed face in pseudosociological terms as a kind of social projection akin to Euroamerican notions of prestige, esteem, or character. More recent scholarly assessments of the term suggest face is a more complex construction that may operate more as a kind of site—a conceptual two-dimensional surface composed of one's relationships from which potential interactions begin and a degree of social status materializes.[19]

By the late nineteenth century, Chinese and foreign observers began to apply traditional notions of "face" to the Chinese body politic, particularly in relation to international affairs.[20] For foreign residents, face seemed to offer insight into the Chinese psyche, particularly in relation to politics and international relations. The Shanghai-based American correspondent Elsie McCormick (1894–1962) believed that face connoted a form of social negotiation that "blossoms at its fullest in national politics."[21] Chinese intellectuals made similar observations. The writers Hu Shih (1891–1962) and Lin Yutang (1895–1976) considered the Republican Chinese government's obsession with its own face, and foreign efforts to preserve the "face" of their own privilege in treaty ports like Shanghai, to be key impediments to Chinese democracy.[22] In 1934, the author Lu Xun (1881–1936) remarked that foreigners found face "extremely hard to understand, but believe that 'face' is the key to the Chinese spirit and that grasping it will be like grabbing a queue twenty-four years ago—everything else will follow."[23]

In each case, face was interpreted as a mediatory device between two opposing forces—a metaphorical "skin" or membrane upon which a degree of social standing could be externalized and rendered visible to others. In this respect, face had equivalences to an architectural surface. Physiognomic readings of architecture date back to the eighteenth century, and like face, a building's façade has long been theorized as a legible layer upon which a degree of social standing and meaning, or "the aspirations and anxieties of the architectural

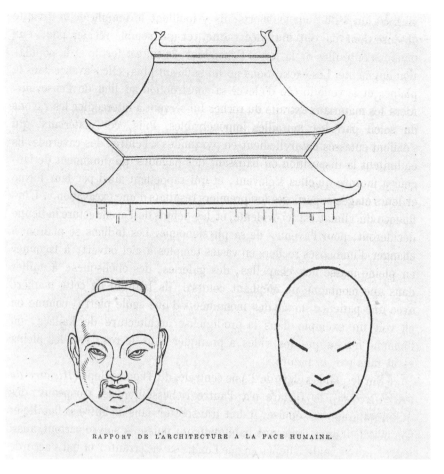

RAPPORT DE L'ARCHITECTURE A LA FACE HUMAINE.

FIGURE 5.1. Study of correlation between architecture and the human face, reinforcing Orientalist tropes. Reprinted from Charles Blanc, *Grammaire des arts du dessin—Architecture, sculpture, peinture* (Paris: Librairie Renouard, 1876), Fine Arts Library, Harvard University.

culture of its time," could be read (figure 5.1).[24] A building's so-called character—its ability to influence both individuals and society at large through optical and psychological effects while also revealing aspects of an architect's or even a culture's internal qualities—was understood to be most clearly expressed through the lineaments or contours of its façade. Over the course of the mid- to late nineteenth century, theorists like Gottfried Semper (1803–1879) and John Ruskin (1819–1900) argued persuasively for the significance of a building's surface and its ornamental detail to social meaning. For Semper, surface represented the point at which labor was transformed into a aesthetic emblematic of communal activity—notably, a quality Semper specifically identified in imperial Chinese architecture.[25] Ruskin also privileged a façade's ornamental detail for its unique ability to index the work involved in a particular project, which could, in turn, generate feelings of empathy within the observer.[26] In both cases, a building's surface figured as a means of communication between two distinct bodies or environments.

Physiognomic readings of art and architecture became popular in post–World War I Europe amid internationalization and distrust in the ability of languages to express meaning.[27] These methods emerged even earlier in an extraterritorial port like Shanghai, where miscommunication and cultural difference played an active, daily role in one's social and physical negotiation through the city's spaces. By 1915, the International Settlement's population totaled 620,401 Chinese residents and 18,519 foreigners, including 4,822 British, 7,169 Japanese, 1,323 Portuguese, 1,307 Americans, and 1,009 Indians. The French Concession totaled 146,595 Chinese residents and 2,405 foreign residents. The city's overall population stood at approximately 1.5 million people. Face was presented as a valuable social and architectural metaphor by which officials and architects could negotiate ethnic, national, and socioeconomic difference amid the geopolitical shifts taking place. In Shanghai, popular media likened a store's architectural façade to a person's face, with attractiveness and novelty seen as critical to financial success.[28] More generally, face also presented a visually extrinsic method through which the foreign presence could be situated within Chinese society and culture while reinforcing racist Orientalist tropes of Asian people as somehow more emotive or responsive to their senses than their more rational, intellectual Western counterparts. As one local American publication explained: "American trade in the Orient suffers heavily from a loss of prestige due to the deplorable housing conditions of its government representatives. . . . In the Orient . . . the surface appearance counts much more, and 'face' is one of the important elements in conducting business. The Chinese trader in the interior imagines that a merchant from a nation whose consular property is in constant danger of collapsing is not as worthwhile dealing with as a merchant from a nation which can build ample and imposing consular buildings to house its agent."[29]

In Shanghai, foreign interpretation of face and its architectural implications inform a series of building and infrastructural projects undertaken there between 1894 and 1922. A new waterworks for the French Concession, new Shanghai Municipal Council offices within the International Settlement, and long-anticipated plans for a new American consulate may each be seen as participating in the intensifying international commercial competition within China amid the deterioration of the Qing dynasty and the founding of the new Chinese nation-state. As British, French, and American officials continued to negotiate China's extraterritorial legal landscape, Chinese leaders, too, recognized that the city's physical, political, and commercial fate lay beyond its imperial-era walled confines. To that end, steps were taken to demolish the city wall itself in an effort to open the Chinese city to greater economic opportunity while countering foreign claims to additional land beyond established settlement and concessionary boundaries. The demolition proved an index of Shanghai's own transformed appearance.

AMERICA'S ARCHITECTURAL INDECISION

China-based American diplomats, missionaries, and journalists framed the establishment of the new republic as a positive development in the United States' diplomatic and economic future in Asia. Although European powers were tainted with the residue of imperialist baggage, pro-China American supporters reasoned, the United States could promote itself as a key mentor and important political model for the young Chinese nation-state, even as the American government continued to seek investment opportunities in the country, and despite America's recent colonization of the Philippines and Guam.[30] Many young Chinese interpreted America's remission of its share of the Boxer indemnity funds, which had been sent by China to those foreign powers affected by the Boxer Rebellion (1900–1901), to support the establishment of Chinese universities, as evidence of America's altruistic commitment to China's political and intellectual freedom. A young Mao Zedong (1893–1976) imagined "the two Republics East and West will draw close in friendship and cheerfully act as reciprocal economic and trade partners," producing an alliance that could stand as "the great endeavor of a thousand years."[31] Shanghai represented a valuable site in these efforts, as it offered American firms access to the Chinese market while also serving as an established showcase that allowed Chinese residents from other parts of the country to learn more about the country's industrial and political achievements. "Already we are seeing the truth of this in Shanghai in a small way," intoned a 1903 British government pamphlet titled *The Threatened Decline and Fall of Great Britain in China*. "This city, destined to be one of the greatest in the world, is slowly spreading what it has already learnt over the rest of China."[32] America's ability to imprint itself and its values upon the Shanghai landscape would, in turn, affect how Chinese citizens would see the United States.

Active consular construction in the city beginning in the 1890s suggested the seriousness with which foreign powers took Chinese perceptions of their commercial reputations. In 1894, France built a new consulate to replace its rickety consular premises along the Huangpu River, commissioning a private Chinese contractor, Cao Qingzhang, for the project under the direction of then chief municipal engineer J. J. Chollot.[33] The project came less than ten years after the Sino-French War, in which France wrested control over Tongking (northern Vietnam) from the Qing government and fully exposed its imperial objectives in southeastern and eastern Asia. The new French consulate, clad in a more ornate, Second Empire style emblematic of its expanded imperial aspirations, along with a cornice ringed with a decorative balustrade and capped

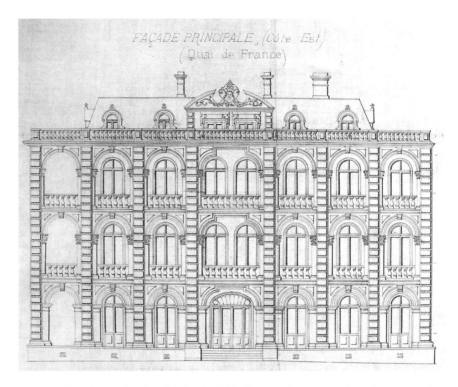

FIGURE 5.2. French consulate, Joseph Julien (J. J.) Chollot, Shanghai, 1894. Archives du Ministère des Affaires étrangères, Centre des Archives diplomatiques de Nantes, France (635PO/Extrait/B/28).

with a square-domed roof, reflected these ambitions (figure 5.2). Second and third floors provided the spaces necessary to secure France's imperial interests in East Asia, including the consul's office, several salons, a dining room, a billiard room, three bedrooms, and two additional offices.

Japan's monumental new consulate, completed in 1909 and designed by the Japanese architect Yajo Hirano, included a Court of Justice, housing for the consul general, as well as Japanese police officers' quarters and a prison (figure 5.3). The building incorporated what Hirano termed a "Renaissance" style, with strong echoes of the recently completed French structure, including a showy neoclassical façade, stately square dome, and prominent riverfront orientation. Its exterior featured a rusticated first story upon which sat two additional stories of arched verandahs, their bays distinguished by embedded Ionic pilasters. The ambitious structure was completed in 1911, and it was subsequently used by the local press to highlight just how quickly "Japan is climbing the ladder of nations and that it has the pride to legitimize and hold its rank" in Shanghai.[34] A new Russian consulate, designed by Hans E. Lieb and completed in 1916, was similarly positioned along the Huangpu to maximize its exposure to arriving vessels (figure 5.4). A cambrel roof sheltered three floors of office and residential space, with both attic and basement floors provided. Rusticated stonework

FIGURE 5.3. Japanese consulate, Yajo Hirano, Shanghai, 1911. Reprinted from *Architecture and Building* (September 1911), Special Collections, Loeb Design Library, Harvard University.

wrapped around the building's basement and first and second stories, while balconies distinguished the third story, which may have served as consular residences. The consulate's prominent tower further accentuated the structure's size, indicating Russia's outward confidence in itself as well as Shanghai's economic future. Preexisting British and German consulates each expressed the operational sophistication and stability of modern diplomatic regimes. The British consulate, prominently sited at the confluence of Suzhou Creek and the Huangpu River, comprised twenty-four rooms, including thirteen offices devoted to consular work and consular and judicial staffs of eleven and eight, respectively. The German consulate consisted of two three-story buildings and a staff of seventeen.

Such development came as home governments began to identify problems with their citizens in extraterritorial zones, in particular, a general tendency on the part of expatriate communities to ignore the "national interests" of their native countries in such places.[35] Despite the cost and rhetoric paid to these projects by the foreign community, there was little empirical evidence suggesting they actually affected a community's allegiance to a particular domain, a country's commercial prospects in China, or Chinese perceptions of a country's commitment to China. For example, Ge Yuanxu's popular Shanghai guidebook *Miscellaneous Notes on Visiting Shanghai* (Huyou Zaji) described the city's consulates as "majestic government agencies anchored along the river's edge" with

FIGURE 5.4. Russian consulate, Hans Lieb, Shanghai, 1915. Reprinted from *Far Eastern Review* (October 1916), Cornell University Library and Cornell Digital Consulting and Production Services.

little to distinguish them architecturally from the city's mercantile compounds apart from the presence of their flagpoles, which "pierced the clouds."[36] Ge found them less impressive than equivalent Chinese governmental compounds, however, suggesting that universal determinants of quality architectural design remained elusive within the city. Any shared degree of architectural legibility proved difficult, given the various constituencies at work.

Shanghai-based Americans were eager to inscribe their own influence upon the treaty port, and they sought the attention of popular America media outlets to draw Washington's attention to their plight. "American business men ought to be up and doing about a great, permanent, effective exposition in China, with branches in several of the larger cities, and with additional ramifications such as traveling shows" urged the *New York Times*. "Ours is a path not of war and intrigue, but of open, honest, commercial dealing."[37] For all of America's perceived advantages in China, however, Shanghai's other consulates conveyed a degree of coordination and investment that stood in striking contrast to the American consulate, a five-room office rental located on a back street, along with those of Denmark, Holland, Belgium, Austria-Hungary, and Sweden, and thus a "humiliation" to patriotic Americans who considered their nation to be on par with those of "first-rate" powers like France and England as well as Germany and Japan.[38]

In 1899, US consul to Shanghai John Goodnow (1858–1907) promised American expatriates a permanent consulate and American exposition hall that would feature displays of American goods and products in an effort to promote American industry and its national "character."[39] Character, like face, was considered a particular, localized barometer of social status bound by distinctive, national parameters, with architectural implications generally understood to be conveyed through the stateliness of a particular façade.[40] Yet American officials could not agree as to the quintessential elements of American character or how to best represent character in architectural terms. Differences of opinion between officials in Washington and those based in China, as well as between American political and commercial representatives, complicated the United States' official diplomatic position, with many American politicians vocally supporting the "modern trinity" of "democracy, the rule of law, and Christianity" in China, but America's commercial interests clearly benefiting from extraterritorial access to the country's markets.[41]

The United States' inability to secure a site for a permanent American consulate underscored these unresolved ideological contradictions. In October 1907, Secretary of War William Howard Taft (1857–1930) arrived in Shanghai as part of a broader regional tour that included the country's recently acquired territory, the Philippines. A boisterous welcoming reception was organized in Shanghai, including representatives from thirty-two Chinese guilds, in a display of how America's commitment to China might aid both countries' economic development. Taft seemed to recognize the value of a sizable consular appropriation, noting that "in the Orient, more than anywhere else in the world, the effect upon the eye is important."[42] A 1908 US Department of State report in support of the construction of a new American consulate also argued that "when the representative of our country is found in modest simplicity, in a tumble-down building, in a second-class street, the Oriental mind is slow to believe that the government he represents can be of much importance, and this unfavorable impression is of considerable importance to our commercial development."[43] This was followed, in 1911, by a congressional report advocating for the purchase of land and buildings for consulates in China, Japan, and Korea using money provided as part of the Boxer Indemnity Fund.

In anticipation of future construction, American consul general Amos Wilder (1862–1936), father of the American writer Thornton Wilder (1897–1975), negotiated a temporary lease for property located along the Huangpu River between the German and Japanese consulates (figure 5.5).[44] In 1914, following the Chinese Revolution, Wilder began to lobby the secretary of state for US$360,000 for property and a new building to be constructed entirely of American materials in the name of "American trade and prestige."[45] Unbeknownst to Washington, however, a localized struggle for the purchase of land in Shanghai had begun to produce an additional geopolitical strain on the project. The consulate's current plot was being sublet to the American government by the Japanese business firm Mitsui Bussan Kaisha, which rented it from

FIGURE 5.5. American consulate, Shanghai, 1911. National Postal Museum, Smithsonian Institution, Washington, DC.

a Chinese family. As the deadline for the lease approached, Wilder's successor, Thomas Sammons (1863–1935), began to worry that the Japanese government coveted the land and was trying to force its Chinese owners to sell it to them instead.[46] Back in Washington, a US$375,000 appropriation for the purchase of land and a building for the US consulate at Shanghai was inserted into H.R. bill 15762 on June 17. By July 22, however, the bill still had not passed, leaving Shanghai-based officials scrambling to renegotiate a two-year extension on their existing lease until 1916.[47]

Sammons subsequently engaged Edward Ezra, a local British property magnate and known opium merchant, into helping US interests buy the property for US$291,656, trumping their Japanese competitors in the process.[48] He also commissioned the local architectural firm Atkinson and Dallas to prepare a report on the various geographical positions of foreign consulates throughout the city in an effort to prove America's interests in China were ill-served by its continued inability to secure permanent property.[49] On July 1, 1916, the Diplomatic and Consular Act was approved with a US$355,000 appropriation for the purchase, alteration, and repair of consular premises or the erection of new consular buildings at Shanghai—the most expensive American embassy or consulate project in the world at the time.[50]

Ironically, the nine-year effort undertaken to secure the property for American interests in the name of American prestige and dignity within the community generated backlash in Shanghai against the US consulate itself.[51] The underhanded purchase of such a valuable property in Shanghai, and the construction of costly, permanent quarters for both the American consulate and the U.S. Court of China, seemed to contradict America's goals of promoting China's own "rule of law"—a system that would no longer require any foreign jurisdictional presence within the country.[52] Originally trumpeted as a potential symbol of America's unwavering loyalty to China, the still unconfirmed American consular project had instead exposed embarrassing incongruities of opinion concerning the future of extraterritoriality in China between Washington, American consular and jurisdictional proxies in Shanghai, and the city's American expatriate community.

In the absence of consensus between Washington and Shanghai over what shape America's interest might take, Shanghai's American commercial representatives set about expressing their own economic objectives to the young republic. In 1914, the National Association of Manufacturers of the United States proposed a district headquarters, consular compound, and museum for the display of American products to be constructed in Shanghai in honor of Frederick Townsend Ward as well as Anson Burlingame (1820–1870), America's second minister to China.[53] The only extant image of the project reveals an interplay of overtly foreign and Chinese architectural forms, including arched entrances and mullioned window treatments topped by two Chinese-styled towers (figure 5.6). An accompanying quote attributed to Francis Bacon—"Before anything is effected, we think it impossible, but when it is done, we stare—and wonder—why it has not been done before"—alludes to the Chinese Revolution and America's involvement in the young country's progress. Architecturally, the incorporation of Chinese ornament within an American institutional program seems designed to project an optical effect of cooperation.

FIGURE 5.6. Burlingame-Ward memorial (proposed), Pond & Pond, Architects, Shanghai, 1914. China Ward Collection, Phillips Library, Peabody Essex Museum.

FIGURE 5.7. American Club, R. A. Curry, Shanghai, 1923. Photograph by Paul Lee with funding provided by the National Endowment for the Humanities.

The failed Burlingame-Ward project was followed, in 1924, by the design and construction of the American Club by R. A. Curry (figure 5.7). The club provided a long-awaited hub for American expatriate activity within the city. Funded by the American Chamber of Commerce, it represented the third chamber of commerce formed by Americans outside of the United States. The building itself was composed of a six-story brick façade highlighted by Italian marble detailing. A denticulated marble belt course distinguished the structure's first floor from its upper stories, while the top floor, comprised of marble pilasters and arcaded windows, accentuated the building's height. Internally, a series of clubrooms, dining halls, and bar offered an array of amenities to the city's American population. Wherever possible, American detailing and fixtures were used. Following the building's completion, the *China Press*, Shanghai's largest American-financed newspaper, assured readers that the American Club represented "a standing guarantee that Americans are in China to stay, and that they are fully determined to bring about, by every legitimate means within their power, an enlargement of their commercial relations with China and an intensification of the present good will that exists between the two nations."[54]

GREAT BRITAIN'S MUNICIPAL INFLUENCE

Great Britain's architectural and administrative prominence in Shanghai seemed to give credence to foreign perceptions that architectural appearances could somehow sway commercial and political fortunes in China. Its consulate, arguably the treaty port's most notable political façade, had once been celebrated for its "magic influence" over Chinese authorities and its charmed effect on Britain's early commercial prosperity in Shanghai.[55] At the local, civic level, the Shanghai Municipal Council had long served as an essential mechanism in maintaining Britain's commercial and diplomatic supremacy over its foreign rivals; between 1871 and 1914, there were, on average, seven British, one German, and one American on the council.[56] Paradoxically, however, British influence over council proceedings, coupled with general public antipathy for long-term civic investment, had long problematized efforts to realize a permanent municipal headquarters.

Calls for a town hall first surfaced in the early 1860s following the city's stabilization after the Taiping Rebellion and continued into the 1870s amid growing demands for space to support the International Settlement's police force, fire brigade, tax and land offices, post office, council chamber, and drill space for the Shanghai Volunteer Corps and its artillery.[57] New, nonextant building plans were commissioned but eventually shelved by the council due to budgetary concerns, before being revived in 1884 and delayed again.[58] In a ratepayers' meeting on February 18, 1890, a resolution was passed authorizing building plans along with an estimated budget.[59] Three years later, however, on the anniversary of the settlement's Silver Jubilee, neither a plan nor a budget had been agreed upon. The postponement prompted one resident to publicly declare that any visitor, initially and presumably dazzled by the "manifest destiny" embodied in Shanghai's commercial expansion, would be astounded to learn that the city had actually existed as "a community of civilized beings" for fifty years without possessing a permanent civic office.[60] The cudgel of civilization, having long been wielded against China, had been turned upon the settlement. What was required was visible evidence not only of administrative organization but of long-term municipal stability—a physical monument to extraterritorial governance.

In 1896, the British architect and Shanghai resident Henry Lester (1840–1926) completed designs for a town hall to host ratepayers' meetings and other municipal council business. The stone and wood building was constructed along Henan Road and was decorated with a modest series of arched doorways and windows. Its unique use of tiles and ironwork inspired Chinese residents to nickname the building "the Iron House," or *tie fangzi* (figure 5.8). A large public hall for gatherings occupied the building's first floor, while a second floor featured smaller meeting rooms and offices. Settlement affairs quickly outgrew the town hall's modest premises, however, necessitating additional public debate over a new municipal façade. In 1910, it was determined that any new office building should be centrally situated and, if possible, located within the council's existing compound, which had been built piecemeal around the town hall as specific programmatic needs arose. British government representatives in Hong Kong supported the decision, revealing the interlocking relationship between Britain's imperial and quasi-imperial domains in East Asia.[61] A special committee was convened to look into the issue, and Robert Charles Turner, the council's chief architectural assistant and a sitting member of the special committee, was selected as project architect.[62]

In 1912, British residents called for the construction of new municipal council offices to address the International Settlement's expanding administrative needs. Public interest in the municipal office project was largely driven by

FIGURE 5.8. Town Hall, Henry Lester, Shanghai, 1896. Reprinted from Arnold Wright and H. A. Cartwright, *Twentieth Century Impressions of Hongkong, Shanghai, and Other Treaty Ports of China: Their History, People, Commerce, Industries, and Resource* (London: Lloyd's Greater Britain Publishing, 1908), Special Collections, University of Hong Kong Libraries.

Shanghai's middle-class British residents, known as "Shanghailanders."[63] Shanghailanders considered Shanghai to be their rightful and permanent home and were psychologically and socially tied to the treaty port in ways that other, wealthier foreign residents were not.[64] In the United Kingdom, town halls represented active vessels for the communication of particular civic values and norms to a community while also mediating the relationship between local and national authority.[65] Supporters of the new edifice saw the project as having similar agency, particularly with respect to legitimizing their presence in China and cementing extraterritoriality's legacy. "Shanghai is no longer a mere place of temporary sojourn, but the abode of numbers yearly increasing," noted the *North-China Herald* in 1913, "and in every city in the world there is the same demand today for beauty and space in town-planning."[66] The complex was proposed for construction in the center of the International Settlement at the intersection of Fuzhou and Henan Roads, where it would stand as a monument not only to Britain's administrative know-how, but to the perseverance of its expatriates. Yet project supporters also feared the building might not have the financial or political support to transcend Shanghai's ill-defined status along the periphery of Britain's imperial domain.[67] The complex thus had to operate at two registers, local and international—the charged municipal context of Shanghai and the broader, global sphere of the British Empire.

Conveying a distinctive kind of bureaucratic responsiveness to the emerging, modern municipal needs of a rapidly growing population was crucial to the project. Council members assiduously studied city-planning trends back in England, where empirically based planning models as well as the Garden City movement had begun to attract attention.[68] Numerous preexisting examples in the United Kingdom as well as a number of other British colonial offices and territories were discussed, including projects in Singapore and Hong Kong, municipal offices in Cardiff, Birmingham's Council House extension, and the Lambeth municipal buildings in Brixton Hill, designed by Septimus Warwick (1881–1953) and Herbert Austen Hall (1881–1968) and built between 1906 and 1908.[69] In response to an inquiry regarding Singapore's civic edifices, Singapore Municipal Council president R. Peirce reminded Shanghai chief engineer C. H. Godfrey that "it is very desirable that Public Offices should be set back from the roads wherever practicable to reduce the noise and dust, and give dignity to an important public building. At home the practice varies."[70] At one point, it was proposed that the final building plans be submitted to an eminent architect "at home," that is, Britain, though at least one committee member felt that local conditions rendered the views of a European architect of little value.[71] In the end, the municipal architect Turner completed the building's designs.

Indications of new architectural priorities at work in Shanghai are evident in the project's programmatic schemes, including an emphasis on bureaucratic efficiency over the spectacle of visibility and physical monumentality. Five final iterations were eventually presented to the council, each of which offered a different composition of building volumes and scales. Final approved plans comprised a three-story organization of offices distributed in five individual blocks of buildings wrapped around an open central core to be used for artillery drills, marching, and stables. A series of public and recreational amenities spoke to the municipal council's relationship to the British constituency that supported it, while accommodations made to the Shanghai Volunteers Corps conveyed the sense of guarded defensiveness around the foreign community itself. The complex's main basement housed a drill hall and lobby, and its ground floor included an armory and repair shop, a gymnasium, and cloakrooms. A tailor's shop, reading room and library, lecture room, billiard room, and clothing store comprised the building's first floor. On the second floor were various offices and staff quarters. The third floor featured quarters for the Shanghai Volunteer Corps' commandant, with three sitting rooms, four bedrooms, and a kitchen. Lavatories on each floor were distinguished by gender and race.

The concentration of programs within the complex, and their proximity to each other, attended to the intimate and overlapping relationships driving the personal and professional lives of the settlement's dominant minority. In this respect, the building provided more than simply a well-designed mechanism for municipal management. It also figured as a means by which the city's British community could retain its social and political standing. Emphasis on pro-grammatic efficiency notwithstanding, however, officials still saw value in the project's potential monumentality—a value primarily derived by perceptions as to how Chinese residents might view the political stability of the International Settlement.[72] Paradoxically, officials who doubted "the peculiar and not neces-sarily permanent system of administration" in Shanghai tended to favor a sys-tem of high buildings. It was presumed a tall, more slender structure would use its space more efficiently while producing lower land rental costs, a strategy recently employed in the construction of the Shanghai Mutual Telephone Com-pany. By contrast, those residents who regarded "the continuous prosperity of the Settlement as assured" advocated for a cluster of lower buildings occupying a larger parcel of land. In these debates, the building's face or social surface registered not necessarily as an aesthetic condition but rather as an index of ground surface and the perceived social value of its overall mass. An initial published scheme of the municipal office design featured both a large square area as well as a tower, though the tower was later abandoned for budgetary reasons and uncertainties about the city's soil (figure 5.9).

The municipal council offices eventually consisted of a series of buildings "of no greater height than is usual in European provincial towns, and surrounded by streets of a greater breadth than is strictly demanded by traffic, buildings which may be said to be likely to gratify the civic pride of the Landrenters and Ratepayers of the future."[73] Final building plans were submitted to the Royal Institute of British Architects (RIBA) for evaluation, where they were shep-herded through by Charles Mayne, who had served as Shanghai municipal engineer from 1889 and 1909 before returning to London. Following RIBA suggestions to clad the structure in granite, the building contract was entrusted

FIGURE 5.9. Shanghai Municipal Council Offices, preliminary scheme, Robert Charles Turner, Shanghai, 1912–14. Reprinted from *Shanghai Municipal Council Report for 1914 and Budget for 1915*, Special Collections, University of Hong Kong Libraries.

to the Chinese construction company Fuchangtai. Construction began in the late autumn of 1914, though the project was immediately slowed by the concurrent outbreak of World War I and the subsequent loss of many building supply shipments from England through submarine warfare. Prolonged delays in interior work, coupled with several changes to the building's program, including the addition of a Municipal Electricity Department, also followed.

On November 16, 1922, municipal council chairman Hardy Simms formally opened the new building to the public (figure 5.10). The complex occupied approximately two square acres within the city, with four hundred offices for a total foreign staff of eight hundred and a floor area of fifty thousand square feet, including the municipal council, the departments of public works, electricity, fire, health, and police, various volunteer clubs, the Shanghai Volunteer Corps as well as its drill hall. Even with the sacrifice of lavish interior decorations, 1.34 million taels were spent on the building's construction.[74] The project's nods to British civic architectural precedent revealed its primary audience, namely, its Shanghailander constituency. The façade borrowed extensively from English town hall precedent, with three clearly delineated stories, each articulated and bound together by an aggressive cornice, molding work, and decorative linear banding. Its steel frame windows were ordered from Birmingham, with interior tiling, a heating system, paneling as well as flooring all provided by British firms. Notably, however, the project was not celebrated as an emblem of British

FIGURE 5.10. Shanghai Municipal Council Offices, Robert Charles Turner, Shanghai, 1914–22. Reprinted from *Shanghai Municipal Council Report for 1922 and Budget for 1923*, Special Collections, University of Hong Kong Libraries.

industriousness. Rather, it was highlighted as a physical embodiment of the city's internationalism—the kind of collaboration specific to Shanghai's extra-territorial environment. English and Chinese newspapers noted its Suzhou granite finish and the use of Chinese laborers as evidence of the council's complex, bifurcated local and international identity.[75] With its carefully divided wings, each segmented into various municipal responsibilities, the building also offered a physical and organizational model council members imagined Chinese municipal institutions might one day emulate.[76]

Of particular signifying value in this respect was the involvement of Chinese carpenters in the project. Chinese contractors had once been publicly disparaged as an unfortunate necessity to living in Shanghai; they now embodied all that was both unique and vital to Shanghai's prosperity. As a *North-China Herald* editorial reminded its readers:

> Visitors from other lands will, perhaps, be more lavish of praise for the workmanship displayed than we are who are accustomed to the excellence of Chinese workmen. Cooperation between the East and West built Shanghai and the same cooperation produced the new building which fitly symbolizes the progress that has been made. . . . We must not forget that without the business acumen and energy of the Chinese merchants . . . found here, the success, which we signalize by the structure just opened, could not have been won. As it was in the past, so it must be in the future. Our interests are bound up with the well-being of the nation in which we sojourn.[77]

Such praise, itself a departure from foreign claims of Chinese building negligence just ten years earlier, signified the value foreign representatives placed on the act and symbolism of collaboration. Notably, the project's completion also came as the municipal council agreed, in 1921, to the formation of a Chinese advisory board organized to ensure that the voices of Chinese ratepayers were heard in relation to the settlement's administrative matters.[78] Architecture offered an ideal vessel through which an image of cooperation could be projected—a physical monument borne of cross-cultural design ingenuity and labor. "The building is a parable in stone commemorating the past and prophesying of an even better future," lauded the *North-China Herald*.[79] The municipal council offices figured as a prominent façade in the city's simulacrum of cosmopolitanism—visual, material, and procedural evidence of successful cross-cultural engagement that obscured the lack of genuine integration.

THE FRENCH CONCESSION'S WATERWORKS

If architecture presented one measure of esteem within the city, infrastructural engineering projected a slightly different countenance—an image of technological progress and economic prowess rooted in the performative aesthetics of process. By the end of the nineteenth century, foreign engineers had emerged as critical foot soldiers in the international struggle for territory and resources, not only in China but around the world. Railroad construction, telegraph lines, water systems, canals, and road building disciplined both territory and people in ways that, as Victor Hugo observed, "astonish the world by the great deeds that can be won without a war!"[80] Ironically, however, early international infrastructural projects such as the Panama or Suez Canals were considered so important to a nation's geopolitical standing that competition over their construction was often fraught with the risk of violence.[81]

Engineering represented one discipline to which France could make unrivalled claims of greatness. As Ingénieurs de l'État, France's colonial engineering corps were responsible for the shaping of a new international Francocentric imperial network. Architectural historian Tom Peters, for example, has noted that the superior quality of French civil engineering, which he attributes to the French educational system of Écoles d'application, in contrast to the equivalent British system in which students gained their engineering expertise informally through apprenticeships.[82] American engineers may have begun to master the construction of the skyscraper, but they had not yet demonstrated their technical prowess with works such as the Panama Canal, and most were considered of a lower intellectual order than either their British or French contemporaries.[83]

The proliferation of architectural and engineering monuments in Shanghai came at a time in which increasing evidence suggested that for all of the physical investment taking place in China, foreign commercial expansion there was not, in fact, proving profitable for any major European imperial power.[84] In 1899, for example, debate arose within the French Parliament over whether France's investment was paying any commercial dividends. Paul Henri d'Estournelles de Constant (1852–1924) made a prescient speech stating that while "Denys Cochin . . . has depicted the Chinese market as inexhaustible, a market for 400 million purchasers . . . I do not believe in them. The Chinese way of life and its resistance to outside influences are well known and should enlighten us on this point. The Chinese will copy and counterfeit European goods, but will not buy them. I see them, not as 400 million purchasers, but as 400 million producers."[85] If Europe were to succeed in transforming China into the world's largest market, new mechanisms for foreign production and distribution were needed to provide and promote goods on an unprecedented scale. Continued infrastructural engineering was considered important to these efforts.

As a multidimensional barometer of social standing, face also resonated within large-scale municipal infrastructural works undertaken in China at the time.[86] These projects were predicated less on the stylistic trappings of façade and more on the demonstration of control and efficiency. They were designed to convey authority over basic material resources—an essential component to both capitalism and the operation of specific forms of power.[87] Groundbreaking ceremonies were events intended to impress local audiences, and they featured local elite as well as businessmen from other countries with vested interests in China. "Enormous" crowds often gathered to watch the "strange spectacle of a spade thrust into the ground."[88] Many foreign observers believed that a foreign nation's prestige was dependent not merely upon how Qing or Nationalist officials may have viewed a particular project but upon how other nations respected it, and the extent to which such esteem would register with Chinese residents and officials. In Shanghai, engineering projects served similar purposes. Besides providing basic public services, infrastructural improvements also represented an opportunity to gain favor with Chinese residents and overshadow municipal rivals.

These rivalries came dramatically to light over the course of the French Concession's waterworks construction. French officials had long struggled to assert their own autonomy in the shadow of the International Settlement; of the 5,114 foreigners living in Shanghai in 1897, only 430 resided in the French-administered areas, and French trade accounted for only 114,609 of 3,887,000 total shipping tons entered at Shanghai in 1897. That same year, the French government announced plans to construct a new waterworks for the concession, which had heretofore been purchasing water from the International Settlement's Shanghai Waterworks Company, established in 1881. The project represented a chance for France to assert its own overlooked expertise in reshaping the physical environment. Land was purchased in Dongdajiu, a Chinese-administered area located south of the Chinese city along the Huangpu, and a route for pipes and conduits was prepared that would circumvent the Chinese city, thus preserving the concession's physical autonomy. Chief municipal engineer Chollot was asked to prepare designs for the waterworks' foundations.

The construction of the French waterworks represented Chollot's second major civic project in Shanghai following the completion of the new French consulate, and it came as France's limited political and commercial standing within the city still seemed a liability. In 1899, evidence of American and British efforts to expand the International Settlement's territory around the French Concession fanned French fears over its eroding its geopolitical and commercial status within the city.[89] Concession representatives demanded from the Qing government an extension of its boundaries as repayment for a second round of violent and costly Chinese protests centered around the Ningbo guild.[90] British and American officials in Shanghai protested the claim, arguing that neither the extent of French trade with China nor the number of their residents warranted such action.[91] French officials, meanwhile, were working off of intelligence from Beijing that their British and American counterparts were negotiating with local authorities to extend the International Settlement into two districts directly west and southwest of the French Concession.[92] Evidence of an American-British conspiracy only heightened suspicions between the two foreign areas, further stoking French paranoia over its reputation in China. An independent waterworks system would enable the French Concession to improve its reputation and expand its own physical boundaries while delivering the best, fastest water in the city—at least fifty liters per second, or double the current volume produced by the International Settlement's waterworks at the time.[93] In Asia, where "rivalries are so deep, and criticisms so shrill," such performance mattered. "English and German engineers have been delighted to prove to the Chinese, via practical demonstration, that the French and their engineers are incapable of seeing any enterprise through," lamented the French consul general to his supervisors in Paris.[94]

The French Municipal Council approved a project budget on the basis that all of the equipment for the construction be imported from France, per Chollot's insistence. However, it was soon determined that such an expense would double the project's initial cost estimate. Regardless, the Chinese contractor Ya Ji was hired for the job, with construction slated for that summer.[95] Chollot would not ultimately be present to supervise the waterworks' construction himself; in September, he returned to France on a one-year, council-approved leave of absence so that his two children might pursue their education at home while he researched industrial factory construction, the best conditions for water engineering, and various technological advancements. The following May, as the project took physical form, several British members of the council raised concerns over the project's quality and cost under the unsupervised Chinese contractor, prompting the council to demand Chollot's return. Amid the growing controversy, however, Chollot was promoted to the grade of Ingénieur Auxiliaire des Ponts et Chaussées by ministerial decision, while Ya Ji was given another commission within the concession to build its Quai des Fossés in July. In September 1899, Chollot was nominated for the Chevalier de l'Ordre of the Légion d'Honneur, which he received in 1907.

The project, formally opened in 1902, proved a disaster. By 1906, cracks had already developed in the waterworks' reservoirs. In an effort to cut down on expenses, Chollot had insisted that 1,000 metric tons of cement from France, mixed with Chinese lime, would be adequate, though other consulting engineers advocated for the use of at least 1,800 metric tons. Additional issues with other public works projects completed under Chollot's supervision emerged, including the inferior quality of the concession's macadam roads as compared to those of the International Settlement, and a Chollot-designed post office beset with numerous cracks in its walls and roof leaks.[96] In January 1907, a disgraced Chollot, one of the largest landholders and most influential residents in the French Concession, resigned as president of French Municipal Council, a post to which he had been elected earlier that year.[97] Eventually tried in French colonial court in Saigon as an employee of the state, Chollot initially blamed the reservoir's cracks on the impact of a typhoon in 1905, only to recant his testimony after being confronted with evidence that cracks had been detected in the purified water basin's apron three days before the storm.[98] Even more damning, and despite Chollot's assurances that the French waterworks would represent the latest in French engineering superiority, the system of filtration ultimately employed for the project was the very same one adopted throughout England and employed in the International Settlement's Shanghai Waterworks Company.[99] The court ultimately found Chollot guilty of negligence.

Despite the scandal, the French Concession's waterworks helped France expand its concession more than threefold, virtually enveloping the Chinese-administered section of Shanghai and disrupting the spatial politics at work in the city. It also served its purpose as a performance of French modernity. At the opening ceremony, Daotai Yuan Shuxun (1853–1922) was shown the system's pumping engines and filtering beds, and both he and Consul Ratard took the opportunity to publicly declare that with the Chinese city and French Concession being so geographically close to each other, it was necessary that they "be on the best of terms."[100] Yet the project also tested the performative premise upon which the concession and its administration was based. The waterworks scandal came amid growing scrutiny from Paris over the concession's administrative competency and concern over the costs of major public works projects there, which in addition to the waterworks included road expansion, telephone services, and a full-time police force.[101] It also further frayed relations between the multinational French Municipal Council and the French consular administration, with claims of "systematic hostility" made by Consul General Hervé Déjean de la Bâtie concerning the council's treatment of the French chief of police and police force itself. The consul temporarily dissolved the council in 1912 for showing a general "lack of respect" not only to the consul general but to the French Republic.[102]

THE CHINESE CITY AND ITS WALL

The perceived loss of China's "face" on the global stage proved a spark in mobilizing popular Chinese dissent over the course of the early twentieth century. The Boxer Rebellion of 1900 and Shanghai's Mixed Court Riot of December 1905, among other protests, highlighted dissatisfaction with the Qing government and its perceived failure to protect China's rights or its "national prestige" within the nebulous realm of transimperial diplomacy, even as Qing leaders were adopting the "modern technologies of governance" believed necessary to accommodate China's geopolitical reality.[103] In Shanghai, public anxiety fueled local gentry and guild-organized efforts to self-organize and establish public boards for the collection of taxes, postal and telephone services, the dredging of waterways, road and bridge construction, garbage and night soil removal, and manage a Chinese police force—the first embodiment of a municipal institution in the Chinese city.[104]

In December 1895, and with the support of Shanghai's county magistrate Huang Chengxuan, a road privately built by Chinese gentry materialized along the Huangpu River to the south of the French Concession. The avenue heralded the establishment of the South City Roadworks Board (Nanshi Malu Gongcheng Ju), which also assumed responsibility for its physical maintenance. In 1905, local gentry formed the General Works Board (Zong Gongcheng Ju) with the support of Daotai Yuan. Members included well-known merchants such as Li Zhongjue (1853–1922); Zhu Baosan (1848–1926); Wang Yiting (1867–1938), a comprador and president of the southern city's Chinese Chamber of Commerce; Cheng Ju, president of the general Chinese Chamber of Commerce and a leader of the 1905 anti–American goods boycott; and Zhu Yinjiang, Jardine Matheson's lumber comprador. Foreign residents considered the board to be a "purely Chinese municipal representative government."[105] It was followed, in 1906, by the creation of two other boards in Zhabei and Pudong, two subdistricts of Shanghai.

Like their non-Chinese counterparts, Qing elite and officials understood that public works offered more than simple apparatuses designed for municipal management. They also represented discernible signs of progress and bureaucratic maintenance, and a visual "resistance" to foreign infringement in response to the contested legitimacy of the Qing government, and the growing demands of localized interest groups, particularly in China's rapidly transforming urban areas.[106] In 1909, the Qing court, under duress by national calls for political change, published a series of regulations for the local self-government of cities, towns, and rural communities (*Cheng zhen xiang difang zizhi zhangcheng*) calling for the institution of autonomous local government offices to be controlled by the Qing government. Following the fall of the Qing government, however, the Jiangsu provincial assembly announced plans to divide Chinese-controlled Shanghai into local self-governed municipalities. Each would have its own Urban Self-Government Bureau (Cheng Zizhi Gongsuo), later identified as a town hall, or *shizhengting*.[107]

Although there is documentation detailing the managerial structure and responsibilities of these offices, and the kind of public architecture they commissioned, very little is known about the architectural qualities of the government buildings themselves.[108] It is unlikely permanent structures were ever completed; in 1914, Yuan Shikai (1859–1916), who wrested control over the new republic's presidency from Sun Yat-sen less than two months after his election, promulgated directions to abolish local self-government boards throughout the country over suspicions that they were influencing the course of increasingly unstable postrevolutionary political events.[109] Nevertheless, their influence

FIGURE 5.11. The city wall, Shanghai, nineteenth century. Archives du Séminaire des Missions étrangères, Paris (120).

survived in the physical changes they catalyzed in cities like Shanghai. Of these, the effort to destroy Shanghai's city wall is significant. As the most glaring physical impediment to the Chinese city's economic development and hygienic control, the wall had long represented a stubborn obstacle to modernization (figure 5.11).[110] Merchants located within the city's wall were unable to effectively interact with those businesses lying outside the wall, including foreigners, while Chinese merchants positioned beyond the wall's limits had grown dependent upon foreign business for their livelihood. Foreign officials objected to both the wall and its accompanying moat on the grounds that it represented a public health hazard; there existed particularly high risks of cholera outbreaks within the area between the wall and the moat, where hundreds of Chinese homes had been constructed against imperial Chinese regulations.[111]

Meetings to discuss the demolition of the wall first took place in 1906, with over two-thirds of the General Works Board and a number of other leading members of the city's gentry favoring the wall's destruction in order to improve communications in and around the city.[112] General Works Board member Li subsequently petitioned the Guangxu Emperor (1871–1908) for permission to tear down the wall. This was followed, in February 1907, by a request to the viceroy of Nanjing to replace the wall with a circular boulevard, which would help both in spurring local commerce while providing a location for leisure activities such as strolling.[113] While the viceroy promised to look into the situation, demolition advocates began to lobby the *daotai* to open gates on the city's north and east sides and two along its western boundary.[114] Ninety-two people signed the petition, including seven prior advocates of the wall's demolition and fifteen original opponents of the wall's demolition.[115] In October, one Chinese merchant offered US$500 to the Qing government to open up a subscription system whereby local elite could help pay for the opening of more gates in the city wall.[116]

Others began to campaign for the wall's preservation on the basis that it left the Chinese city exposed to the risks of piracy and undue influence from the foreign settlements.[117] The Wall Preservation Committee (Chengyuan Baocun Hui) launched a campaign blaming undue foreign influence for local perceptions that the wall required demolition.[118] Die-hard demolitionists subsequently began to fight a fierce and effective delaying action to stop any kind of compromise plan from securing adequate financial backing. This left the newly formed General Works Board confronting a potentially dramatic loss of face if provincial-level officials insisted that a compromise plan be carried out. In 1908, Daotai Cai Naihuang (1860–1916) brokered a compromise whereby the wall would remain intact but additional gates would be opened, with the General Works Board agreeing to take over funding and implement of the work itself. Over the next three years, the city's north, east, and little east gates were all opened to more traffic.[119]

Calls to tear down the wall persisted, however. In January 1912, Shanghai gentry member Yao Wennan sent a letter to the newly established Republican county government urging their support for demolition.[120] Project supporters argued that the wall's destruction would produce vast new swathes of land that could be auctioned off by the government for a profit. Demolition initially began around the city's western gate and the Dongdajiu waterworks under the leadership of Pan Kegong (1852–1917) in conjunction with a plan to link the city's west side to its east gate by a new tramline undertaken in cooperation with the French government (map 5.1).[121] Further financial difficulties caused by the continued revolution brought these efforts to another halt in February, however. In July, the discovery of several memorial tablets commemorating British heroes of the Small Swords Uprising stopped work again.[122] Plans were announced for the construction of a new circumferential boulevard on the wall's foundations in October. French and Chinese officials discussed how to link their respective road systems, eventually agreeing that any underground work not encroach beyond the boundaries of each respective power and that Chinese and French police work not transgress each jurisdiction's established borders.[123] The entire city wall was torn down by the end of 1914, and the new road, measuring four *zhang* (12.8 meters) wide and occupying territory within both the concession and the Chinese city, was completed in 1916 with the French

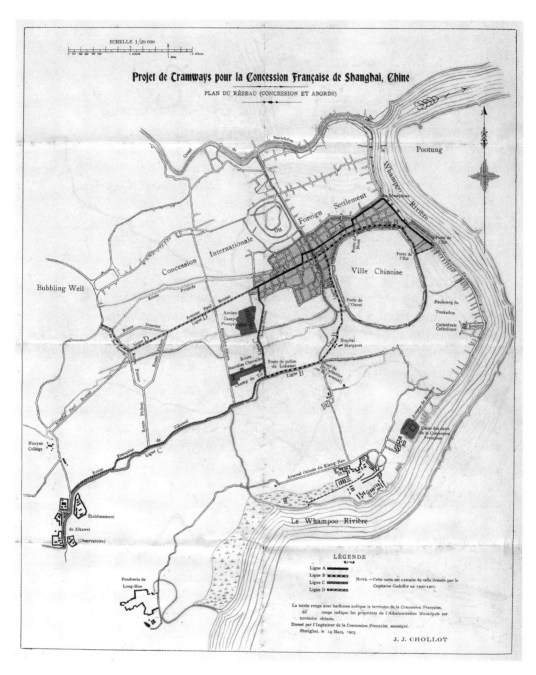

MAP 5.1. French Concession tramway scheme, Shanghai, 1903. Archives du Ministère des Affaires étrangères, Centre des Archives diplomatiques de Nantes, France, 635PO/B/65.

Municipal Council's approval.[124] Its construction offered an unobstructed link between the Chinese city, the French Concession, and the International Settlement for the first time.[125]

The destruction of Shanghai's wall signaled acquiescence to the new civic visions materializing around it. The Chinese city wall had long represented a particular manifestation of the Chinese state and a specific mode of governance. No longer could foreign critics deride the city for being "under the grip of the dead hand of their ancestors."[126] Shanghai was not unique in these efforts; between 1912 and 1916, campaigns were launched in Hangzhou, Guangzhou, and Beijing, among others, to tear down portions, if not all, of their ancient walls.[127] Collectively, these efforts speak to the rise of a new spatio-politics rooted in visibility. As spectacles of erasure, the disappearance of these walls forced residents and officials alike to confront that new system and its commercial and political implications for Chinese society.

Taken in combination with the proliferation of consulates, municipal offices, and public infrastructure taking place within Shanghai at the turn of the century, these efforts collectively prefigure the more familiar "visual politics" that later blossomed within republican cities through showy commercial architecture and culture over the course of the 1920s.[128] Physically, these earlier, more civic-minded projects connoted the active, and at times contradictory, negotiations taking place between municipal-level constituencies and the national representatives responsible for their well-being. As physical manifestations of extraterritorial spatial imagination, they document the erosion of the various physical, social, and cultural boundaries throughout the country; they also help to trace the organization of empowered, diverse, and competitive Chinese merchant communities seeking the progress these works seemed to signify.

In 1927, the International Settlement's municipal offices were featured on the cover of *Shanghai of To-day*, a locally produced compilation of Shanghai's most prominent architectural landmarks. As the new face of foreign administration, the edifice represented an architectural mnemonic reminding residents that "East is East and West is West and the two are so intimately bound together here in Shanghai that neither we nor the Chinese can prosper apart from each other."[129] It was in part through the discourse on face that general perceptions persevered of the city as somehow existing despite a chronic lack of municipal cooperation. Concerted efforts to project an aesthetics of governance left Shanghai straddling reality and fiction—both an idealized "wonder city of all Asia" and a functioning "real city."[130]

Underneath the illusion of syncretism, however, unpredictability remained. Shanghai still signified a battlefront in which numerous international powers remained committed to the shaping of modern China's political economy. The appearance of the city's architecture, which remained an assemblage of Chinese structures and styles imported from Europe, the United States, and other parts of Asia, reflected these competing interests. Gaps in general perceptions of architecture's physical and representational significance lingered, and an inability to govern taste within the city still figured as a municipal concern. In theory, the designer's participation in the construction of Shanghai's extraterritorial milieu offered a stabilizing force, with the potential to naturalize the odd legal and diplomatic incongruities at work. In practice, however, the exploitation of Shanghai's "patchwork and hand-to-mouth" system of development meant that "every architect is so much a law unto himself and every building presents a solecism in one particular or another," producing odd physical results with unsettling representational implications.[131] It was in reaction to this environment that the modern Chinese architect as well as the search for a modern Chinese architectural style took form.

CHAPTER 6

National Architects, National Architecture

S HANGHAI was influential in the shaping of early twentieth-century architectural culture in China. Chinese exposure to Western building techniques and materials often came through firsthand experiences with Shanghai, while a range of new objects, practices, and ideas also originated there before being disseminated to other parts of China via the city's expansive print culture.[1] China's first professional architectural firms were established in Shanghai, and the International Settlement's building regulations represented the country's first. By the 1920s, and over the course of the Nanjing Decade (1927–37), Shanghai figured as a primary destination for the select group of young, professionally trained Chinese architects returning from study in Japan, Europe, and the United States in search of design work. Nanjing was a popular destination, given its status as the country's new political capital, and treaty ports like Guangzhou and Tianjin figured as important crucibles for Republican-era architectural ideas.[2] It was in Shanghai, however, that a distinctive political agency relative to international capitalism and the act of design was most substantially forged.

The formation of the professional Chinese architect was taking place as the field of architecture was undergoing dramatic change around the world, particularly in relationship to industrialization. In Europe and the United States, growing evidence of an increasingly urbanized, interconnected planet fueled calls for equally universal forms of architecture. In 1925, Walter Gropius (1883–1969), founder of the Bauhaus and a pioneer of architectural modernism, urged architects to realize "that the economic utilization of time, space, materials, and money in industry and commerce decisively determines the features of the appearance of all modern building organisms."[3] The complex interpenetrations of economy and space demanded a new "international architecture" capable of responding to such forces.[4] Such themes resonated with architects around the world in different ways.[5] For many of China's first professionally trained architects, terms like architectural modernism (*xiandai jianzhu*) and internationalism, or the international style (*wanguo shi*), carried with them a perceived loss of cultural autonomy and conjured images of China's past humiliations at the hands of Western imperialists. Certain aspects of internationalism held immediate and obvious appeal, including the feelings of dynamic cosmopolitanism it seemed to engender, the use of innovative building materials such as glass, and the extent to which these new material and spatial conditions gestured toward a degree of democratization.[6] At the same time, however, the lure of an international architecture was tempered by the corrosive effects of extraterritoriality, which was understood as a uniquely international in nature, and on vivid display in treaty ports like Shanghai. There, Chinese architects witnessed an urban infrastructure built on the backs of an oppressed Chinese labor class and dominated by foreign imports and expertise, along with a fierce professional struggle comprising "a paid competition between American, British, French, and Spanish architects."[7] Internationalism's perceived benefits—easier access to goods, more efficient production methods, greater international communication—were offset by the fragmented, unjust environments left in internationalism's wake.

It was within the contested and pluralistic atmosphere of Shanghai's architectural offices, its governing committees, and professional associations and organizations, and throughout the treaty port more generally, that the Chinese architect was "invented."[8] More specifically, Shanghai was a prominent site where Chinese designers began to define their responsibilities in relation to the Chinese nation-state and the outside world. China's nation-building project was a physical exercise, and it required young Chinese professionals committed to the mission. Shanghai's international and competitive arena contributed to the development of modern Chinese architectural practice, discourse, and expression.

THE RISE OF THE CHINESE ARCHITECT

Beginning in the late nineteenth century, the self-strengthening efforts of the Qing government supported the education of China's first professionally trained designers in Europe, Japan, and the United States.[9] In Shanghai, Qing-sponsored technical educational initiatives included the Machinery Institute (Shanghai Jixie Xuetang) in 1867 as well as the Telegraphic Engineering Institute (Shanghai Dianbao Xuetang) in 1882. By 1903, further educational reform led to the creation of a formal engineering curriculum based upon

Japanese models that included courses in mathematics, building materials, as well as architectural history. A second, more substantial wave of Chinese students to the United States funded through the Boxer Indemnity Fund program transformed a handful of American universities, most notably the University of Pennsylvania but also including the University of Illinois, Columbia University, and the Massachusetts Institute of Technology, into influential hubs for Chinese architectural education. Perceived compositional similarities between imperial-era Chinese architectural and urban design methods and those offered by the Beaux-Arts curriculum—a shared emphasis on axiality, symmetry, and sequence, among other examples—inspired a select number of China's first professionally trained designers to promote the style back home.[10]

The Beaux-Arts' distinctive engagement with questions of governance represented another important if relatively underexplored explanation for its popularity in Republican China.[11] In Philadelphia, for example, the University of Pennsylvania's Department of Architecture chairman, Paul Philippe Cret (1876–1945), emphasized the value of architecture, not simply in supporting the role of government as well as cultural institutions, but in actively projecting key republican values to the population.[12] Cret's own built work also tended toward civic commissions such as the Pan American Union Building, completed in Washington, DC, in 1910, and the Folger Shakespeare Library, constructed in Washington between 1928 and 1932. These buildings aimed at encouraging greater public participation in the municipal realm by conveying the character and accessibility of the institution through the beauty of architecture.[13] Lessons concerning an architect's responsibilities to the political aspirations of his/her society would have resonated among China's first generation of architects, all of whom were bearing witness to political upheaval in China influenced, in part, by large-scale physical change.

It was foreign-educated Chinese designers who first published calls for their fellow architects to contribute to the nation building taking place in China. Identifying a uniquely Chinese architectural expression worthy of the country's aspirations and honoring local materials in the realization of such objects were components of these efforts. In one oft-cited example, William Chaund's 1919 essay "Architectural Effort and Chinese Nationalism," the author described the designer as "an indispensable servant to human evolutionary progress, and he urged China to develop a "vigorous" architecture with "Chinese" characteristics that might address pressing issues of modern urban growth and planning plaguing twentieth-century China.[14] Chaund, a graduate of Chicago's Armour Institute of Technology, understood that architecture, which was historically an art of secondary importance to China, required reevaluation as a new means of expression for the modern Chinese nation-state if the country was to represent itself effectively in international affairs. These themes resonated not only with other young Chinese architects but with the work of Chinese builders and other figures in the construction industry eager to contribute to a Chinese architectural renaissance.

THE CHINESE ARCHITECT IN SHANGHAI

The emergence of the professional Chinese design community took place as Shanghai's Chinese political and commercial elite struggled to reestablish some basic semblance of governance. A municipal office (*shigongsuo*) was established in 1924; this was followed, in March 1927, by the organization of a Congress of Shanghai Residents coordinated by local CCP leaders. The arrival of the Nationalist army in Shanghai later that month led to the establishment of a provisional municipal government on March 20, 1927. However, this body quickly became controlled by the city's localized Communist leadership, which challenged the Nationalist party's own claims on power. On April 1, 1927, the Nationalists established martial law throughout the city, which provided the necessary legal exception to launch the Shanghai massacre, a violent Nationalist-led attack on Shanghai trade union and CCP offices beginning on April 12 that consolidated the Nationalist grip on municipal and national power. A new, Nationalist-led Shanghai municipal government was founded on July 7, 1927.

The stabilization of Shanghai's Chinese government during the Nanjing Decade presented opportunities for the city's young architectural elite. Chiang Kaishek (1887–1975), the charismatic Nationalist leader and ideological heir to Sun Yat-sen, understood the value of technology to his fledgling regime, and he promoted a strong centralized government staffed by a new generation of well-educated and technocratic cadres. Nationalist leaders, many having witnessed years of foreign dominance in cities like Shanghai, understood the political value of fields like civil engineering and architecture, which could help to build public support through impressive feats of physical construction.[15] Yet the existence of treaty ports like Shanghai also posed questions about the origins of modern architecture in China, and the nature of the modern Chinese state, particularly in relation to the country's international relations and sovereignty. By the late 1920s, foreign and Chinese scholars began to identify the international treaty port as the origin point of "modern style" architecture in China, which informed debate as to the cultural and political origins of a modern Chinese architecture.[16] Distinctions between "foreign" and "Chinese" building forms, which historically had been used to limit perceived uncontrolled Chinese architectural production, took on new, nationalistic meaning under a centralized Chinese authority. Similarly, the roles of the foreign architect and Chinese builder in defining a modern Chinese architecture began to take on a distinctly political hue as well. These debates prompted architects, builders, and politicians alike to reconsider how to best embody China's nationhood in architectural terms in contribution to the cause.

Between 1926 and 1933, the number of Chinese architects working within the city climbed from seven to more than fifty, though opportunities for professional advancement were few. Some established their own firms; Shanghai's first Chinese-run firm, the Huahai Architectural Office (Huahai Jianzhushi Shiwu-suo), was established in 1923 by Tokyo Polytechnic–trained architects Liu Shiying (1893–1973), Liu Dunzhen (1897–1967), and Wang Kesheng.[17] Another well-known firm in Shanghai was Zhao and Chen Architects (Zhao Shen Chen Zhi jian-zhushi shiwusuo), established in 1931 by two graduates of the University of Penn-sylvania, Zhao Shen (1898–1978) and Chen Zhi (1902–2002).[18] Others broke into the city's architectural industry as draftsmen for foreign architects, particularly Henry Murphy, including Dong Dayou (1899–1973), the architect responsible for the Greater Shanghai Plan's major administrative buildings; Lü Yanzhi (1894–1929), who designed both the Sun Yat-sen Mausoleum in Nanjing as well as the Sun Yat-sen Memorial Hall in Guangzhou; and Li Jinpei (1900–1968), whose works included the city's Chinese YMCA, completed in 1929 (figure 6.1).[19]

Calls for a new Chinese architecture came as Shanghai's physical environ-ment began to change. Until 1920, deep-verandahed compounds had given the foreign settlements "the appearance and characteristics of a colonial city."[20] The Chinese city, meanwhile, remained in a state of gradual physical decline, due in large part to the absence of any sustained, centralized municipal leadership. Over the course of the 1920s, however, new technological innovation and increased real estate prices helped to trigger a new era in Shanghai's architectural development. This activity initially emerged within the foreign-administered zones, where a "modern style . . . common to most of the high-class buildings of the West" began to take root.[21] The introduction of larger-scale, multistoried buildings were understood as emblematic of this modern style and distinctly "American" in nature.[22] These impressions derived from the use of American technology in their construction and the influence of high-rise construction in places like Chicago and New York City, but they also illuminate the ways in which Shanghai was understood to possess a uniquely adaptive environment capable of absorbing influence from all around the world. The ubiquity of foreign products, which accounted for at least 50 percent of China's building materials industry, was another factor. Chinese construction materials were widely con-sidered inferior to foreign goods, a legacy, in part, of concerted foreign efforts to sell their own products while diminishing Chinese architectural culture. As a result, Chinese builders and architects had little choice but to embrace foreign building materials in the city, which in turn contributed to popular impressions of the city as a global, as opposed to localized, environment. A house with "bricks [which] may be American, tiles [which] may be English, cement [which] may be German, and steel [which] may be Italian" represented something "able to last 100 years without moving one fraction," while buildings constructed with Chinese material would be "presumed to fall down immediately."[23]

FIGURE 6.1. Chinese YMCA, Li Jinpei, Fan Wenzhao, Zhao Shen, Shanghai, 1929–31. Reprinted from *Zhonghua tuhua zazhi*, no. 19 (1933), Special Collections, Shanghai Library.

Nascent notions of the modern also emerged in relation to Chinese architecture through the work and writings of a number of foreign architectural advisors practicing in China at the time, including Murphy and Harry Hussey. Both figures had long advocated for the integration of foreign and Chinese motifs, which they felt both suited the demands of the state's architectural program while also engendering a constructive sense of mutual cultural cooperation that boded well for a continued foreign presence in China. Murphy in particular worked with his younger Chinese staff to distill his interpretation of China's architectural uniqueness into key aesthetic, spatial, and structural elements, including the progressive delineation of space on display in the Forbidden City and the specific structural and decorative aspects of *dougong*, or bracketing sets, roofs, and the use of color. These principles formed the basis for what he termed to be an "adaptive architecture" to be propagated around China—a style that might employ modern building material and technologies while remaining referential to what he determined to be key traditionally Chinese architectural elements.[24]

ORGANIZING DESIGN

Shanghai was an important hub for professional associations in China, not only in relationship to architecture but for all forms of cultural production.[25] Over the course of the late 1920s and 1930s, Shanghai-based architects, builders, engineers, and manufacturers relied upon these networks to organize themselves with the broader interests of stabilizing the Chinese nation-state and its building industry in mind.[26] Over time, their efforts became associated with the construction of a modern Chinese architecture and, by extension, a modern China. Architectural student organizations established in the United States, for example, provided foundational relationships through which China's returning architects and engineers first organized themselves.[27] In 1924, the Chinese Architects' Society (Zhongguo Jianzhushi Xuehui) was founded in Shanghai with the aim of "bringing together researchers and developers from the architecture profession to benefit and promote the improvement of city government" and helping each major Chinese municipality hire at least four professionally trained people to organize and create rules to which architects could adhere.[28] The perception of shared national interests across industry and profession helped to strengthen professional ties between China's young architects, contractors, and builders. The Shanghai Builders' Union (Shanghai Shi Yingzaochang Tongye Gonghui) was founded in 1930 by native Shanghainese construction workers through the merger of two of the city's oldest construction guilds.[29] These groups offered platforms through which the city's various Chinese architectural interests could begin to address the pressures of international competition while advocating for greater self-preservation, higher salaries, improved working standards, and better communication across respective industries. Corruption and fraud also figured as mobilizing concerns among Chinese builders and designers alike.[30]

Adult educational programs rivaling those offered by those within the International Settlement equipped Chinese builders with the skills necessary to compete in the city's competitive construction field. In the autumn of 1930, for example, a Chinese night school for Shanghai's construction community was launched with courses ranging from mathematics to engineering to Chinese literature to English. The program was overseen by a collection of architects, builders, and public officials, including Tang Jingxian; Jiang Zhanggeng; He Jingdi; Jiang Shaoying, an engineer from Tangshan Xiaoda Public Works Department; Shen Wenhong, a local college literature student; and Yuan Song-yao, a graduate of the Fudan Business School. By 1934, the school had expanded, and plans were made to establish a two-year formal architectural educational training program with the assistance of the Chinese Architects' Society and Hujiang University. Wang Huabin, Ha Xiongwen, and Luo Bangjie were hired as the program's professors, and Zhang Jun and Dong Dayou prepared campus designs, though these were never constructed.[31]

The Shanghai Architectural Society, established in 1927 by a collection of Shanghai architects, engineers, and contractors led in part by Du Yangeng (1896–1961), was one of the largest and most influential professional groups in the city (figure 6.2).[32] Du was a pioneering young architect and teacher interested in promulgating modern architectural development around China. He came from a family of carpenters based in Chuansha, and his motives to establish such an organization were fueled by his experience trying to realize his own designs for a seven-story office building eventually completed in Shanghai in 1927. Dealing with an "incredibly arrogant and overbearing" Western foreman prompted Du, in part, to abandon architectural practice and focus on how to improve construction industry conditions within the various factions of the Chinese building community, where he saw a desperate need to update its own archaic practices.[33]

The society's first formal organizational meeting was held in February 1931 and was attended by more than three hundred people, including Shanghai political leaders such as Li Dazhao, director of the city's Education Bureau, and Shen Yi, Public Works director.[34] Du drafted the organization's regulations and manifesto, which urged Chinese architects to remember that "Western architectural and artistic development in China continues to improve and thrive more each and every day. . . . If things continue like this we will miss an opportunity, and our power will subsequently diminish. It is important to examine our national conscience and continue the legacy of Asian architecture by combining Western materials with China's ancient cultural spirit."[35] Like the Qing-era custom of bound feet, Du considered China's architectural traditions to

FIGURE 6.2. Fourth general assembly meeting of the Shanghai Architectural Society (Shanghai Shi Jianzhu Xiehui), 1936. Reprinted from *Jianzhu yuekan* 4, no. 9 (1936), University of Hong Kong Libraries.

represent a classical form of beauty rendered obsolete by modernity.[36] Other organizational goals included the promotion of national products in the country's building materials industry, the designing and improvement of modern architectural methods that could be replicated throughout China, and the promotion of architecture-related topics to the Nationalist Party. Society members began to encourage the compilation of various statistics concerning Shanghai's building industry and to advocate for the improvement of the lives of China's construction laborers and the establishment of an architectural library for members, among other initiatives.[37] Through a systematic reconfiguring of China's building industry, leaders hoped a new, modern architectural culture would emerge capable of producing an architectural vocabulary that could both garner foreign attention and signify the country's new political trajectory.

Architects' self-organization mirrored steps toward professional registration at the national level. Debates over the need for a professional certification process among Chinese construction workers and designers echoed those that had taken place within the International Settlement decades prior. In fact, by the early 1930s, the issue of professional registration had become even more problematic in Shanghai, where its tripartite governing structure left three different types of registration and various building standards uncoordinated and complicated.[38] Shanghai's Chinese political leadership worked to establish a rational system of municipal administration based upon both the principles at work within the foreign settlement as well as the bureaucratic organizations already established in other Republican cities such as Guangzhou.[39] In 1933, broader, nationwide efforts to standardize the profession were pioneered by a National Architectural Curriculum Conference, attended by the Chinese architectural historian Liang Sicheng (1901–1972), the architect and Chinese garden specialist Tong Jun (1900–1983), and architects Liu Futai and Guan Songsheng, among others. That same year, a professional architects' registration drive was launched in Nanjing before expanding to Shanghai, where the Greater Shanghai government had already begun attempts to remedy a divergence of building quality within the city through municipality-wide initiatives aimed at improving overall education and inspection standards for builders.[40] Through these efforts, the architect began to take on definition in Chinese society as a professional with the creative and technical expertise needed to secure China's participation in the modern world order.

PUBLICIZING THE CHINESE ARCHITECT

In 1932, Du published the first issue of the *Builder* (Jianzhu yuekan), which along with *Chinese Architecture* (Zhongguo jianzhu), the official publication of the Shanghai Architectural Society, represented China's first professional architectural journals (figure 6.3). Amid growing coordination among the professions of building, engineering, and architecture within Shanghai's Chinese community, there existed a need to better articulate the professional role of the architect vis-à-vis these other fields. Historical overlaps between Chinese contractors, engineers, and architects clouded the public's understanding of the Chinese architect's role in society, his/her professional responsibilities, and his/her position vis-à-vis traditional Chinese carpentry and modern engineering. New forms of media offered conduits through which the country's Chinese architectural community could begin to communicate with each other while promoting their work to a broader audience. Journals like the *Builder* contributed to public perceptions of the architect as a new and important professional figure in China. Although the publication was not well-circulated, it offered an important new resource for construction laborers, engineers, and architects in certain parts of the country by facilitating collaborative discourse within the industry and offering a forum within which young builders and designers could learn and debate contemporary disciplinary issues.[41]

Chinese efforts to empower the architect echoed campaigns in other parts of the world to promote the profession amid growing challenges from the fields of engineering, planning, and real estate concerning the value of architectural expertise to modern society.[42] In China, as elsewhere, modernizing the architectural profession took on a particular nationalistic fervor. Unlike other parts of the world, however, the history of professional design in China, and with it, a specific strain of architectural modernism, could be traced back to the Opium War, leaving notions of a modern Chinese architecture and the Chinese architect fraught with conflicted feelings of resignation and shame. Over the course of the late 1920s and 1930s, architecture-affiliated organizations and the state collectively began to channel these emotions into productive service. The Chinese architect was understood as an expert, equipped not simply with international training or experience but with a specific moral imperative to contribute to the making of the Republican Chinese state. The act of design was promoted as a public service in the reconstruction and preservation of Chinese society and its norms. For example, the *Builder* encouraged young architects and builders to avoid indiscriminately adopting foreign goods and practices in favor of preserving some aspects of Chinese architectural tradition while employing Western technological advancements for the betterment of China. "Architecture for the health of mankind"—a common ideological refrain of modernists in Europe and

FIGURE 6.3. Cover, *The Builder* (Jianzhu yuekan) 1, no. 1 (1932), University of Hong Kong Libraries.

elsewhere—resonated in China, where it spoke to the need to alleviate China's poor housing situation and improve the lives of Chinese citizens.[43] Not coincidentally, Shanghai was also the epicenter of China's National Products Movement, a Nationalist-inspired propaganda effort that had an impact upon the city's construction industry throughout the 1920s and 1930s.[44]

In 1932, a regular Chinese-language architectural column began to run in Shanghai's *Shenbao*, one of the country's most widely read Chinese newspapers. Though the feature would run for only three years, it offered news and editorials that defined and expanded architecture's participation in Chinese society. Articles devoted to China's architectural heritage, modern architecture, and new building materials, among others, further influenced public impressions of architects and their work. Through these and other publications, a new generation of Chinese citizens understood the architectural profession as a discipline committed to social change through spatial and technological innovation on behalf of the Chinese people.[45] These efforts also echoed broader Nationalist-organized campaigns such as the New Life Movement, which promoted a standard set of cultural values capable of crafting the modern Chinese citizen.[46] A culture of professional responsibility and public service within the city's Chinese building industry began to take hold that redefined the architect's duties as somehow analogous to that of the banker, lawyer, or doctor. Architecture even became the subject of children's books; like other skilled white-collar fields, design depended upon ambitious and educated students capable of contributing to the modernizing Chinese nation (figures 6.4 and 6.5).[47] New China deserved a new architecture. As one Chinese children's book cautioned, "old buildings are simple, crude and coarse, while new buildings are beautiful and sturdy!"[48]

As foreign threats continued to imperil Republican China's sovereignty, the role of the architect shifted from public servant to militarized visionary. Japan's invasion of Manchuria in September 1931, followed by its redefinition as an independent state to be led by the former Qing emperor Pu Yi with complicit Japanese military protection, shocked China's fragile political system and threatened China's very existence as a nation-state.[49] Nationalist diplomats appealed to the League of Nations for diplomatic intervention, to no avail.[50] This was followed, on January 18, 1932, by an outbreak of war between Japan and China in Zhabei, a contested district located north of the International Settlement. The battle was triggered when five Japanese residents, including two Buddhist monks, were attacked by a group of fifty to sixty Chinese residents. Approximately twenty-six thousand Japanese residents lived within the settlement boundaries, while an additional six thousand residents lived beyond the borders in the contested area. Japanese residents retaliated by lighting fire to a towel factory in which it was believed the Chinese assailants worked, prompting the escalation between Japanese and Chinese troops.[51] Officials declared a state of emergency, and the various forces responsible for the settlement's defense, including British soldiers, American and Japanese marines, and the Shanghai Volunteer Corps, all took preassigned positions along the border. Fighting lasted until May, when a force of fifty thousand Japanese troops pushed the Chinese army twelve miles away from the settlement and a formal truce was subsequently signed.

These events temporarily transformed Shanghai's architectural community into a volunteer army of more than five hundred architects, builders, and engineers mobilized to work on several engineering projects following the bombing, including the reconstruction of a bridge.[52] The physical and psychological damage resulting from both incidents temporarily stunted the country's blossoming construction industry, but by 1933, architectural and urban development throughout Nationalist-controlled areas of China had begun to recover. The Nationalist government declared 1933 the Year of National Products, and architects and builders were asked to help improve the reputation of Chinese construction materials by privileging them for any and all construction projects. Zhong Qin, a pseudonymous contributor to *Shenbao*, argued that "prior to foreign arrival in the city, or the introduction of materials like steel and concrete, we still built houses, and they didn't immediately collapse. There is no evidence that our ancestors were crushed to death by homes made of Chinese products. This tendency to fetishize Western thinking (*shang yang sixiang*) is despicable."[53] Meanwhile, major civic improvements ranging from road paving, the installation of public lighting and telephone systems, and the replacement of old tiled-roof buildings by more modern facilities offered physical embodiments of the Republican government's efforts to improve the country.[54]

A 1933 call to Chinese architects published in *Shenbao* captured the era's martial urgency: "Architects! Raise your heads and look at this country with 5,000 years of history, lower your heads and look at the surge of this scientific world; we are at the time when we can see the rejuvenation of Asian art and the rise of Western science. Right now, you bear a heavy burden, will you take this journey?"[55] For all of the impressive

FIGURE 6.4. Cover, *How Do You Build a House?* (Zenyang jianzhu fangwu), 1933, Special Collections, Shanghai Library (120097).

physical and political mobilization taking place, however, by the mid-1930s the Nationalist government's continued struggles to retain control over the country began to strain its partnerships with members of China's architectural elite. The architectural profession had emerged as an important political force in China, and Nationalist Party leaders struggled to subsume the movement within their own corporatist vision.[56] For some designers seeking to effect a broader mobilization of the country's building community, communism carried particular appeal.[57] More generally, politics seemed to inform a number of the debates taking place within the country's architectural profession, from regulation and professionalization to issues of architectural representation.[58] Each issue gave new definition and contour to the notion of a modern Chinese architecture.

THE POLITICS OF DESIGN

In 1929, Hua Nangui (1875–1961), vice president of the Chinese Institute of Engineers as well as director of Beijing's Bureau of Public Works, argued in front of

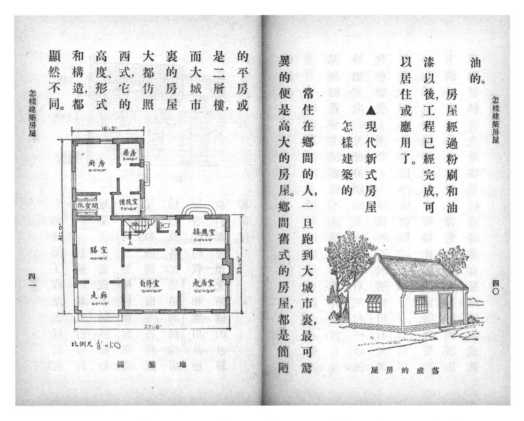

各欄（右頁四○）

油的。

房屋經過粉刷和油漆以後，工程已經完成，可以居住或應用了。

怎樣建築的

▲ 現代新式房屋

常住在鄉間的人，一旦跑到大城市裏，最可驚異的便是高大的房屋。鄉間舊式的房屋，都是簡陋

落成的房屋

的平房，或是二層樓，而大城市裏的房屋大都仿照西式的，它的高度、形式和構造，都顯然不同。

厨房

茶房

休食間

懷孕室

膳室

接應室

走廊

自外室

起居室

上

比例尺　⅛″=1:0

地　盤　圖

FIGURE 6.5. Detail, *How Do You Build a House?* (Zenyang jianzhu fangwu), 1933, Special Collections, Shanghai Library (120097).

an international audience at the Tokyo World Engineering Congress that "Chinese architecture is not purely Chinese, but is mingled with the designs of other nations. The Chinese are susceptible to absorbing the civilizations of those nations coming into contact with them."[59] Titled "The Value of Chinese Architecture in the Past and in the Future," Hua's talk represented a thinly veiled promotion of continued foreign and Chinese architectural collaboration that underscored the Nationalists' recognition that further Chinese knowledge of Western building trends would help quicken the country's modernization, even as it risked blunting Chinese architects' ability to explore design's representational possibilities. Architectural hybridity, once the scourge of International Settlement building inspectors, took on new semiotic meaning in light of China's efforts to improve itself relative to a dominant Euro-American world order. Nationalist leaders understood the need for continued international cooperation, even as they sought to instill national pride in the fractured Chinese populace, and architecture offered a vessel through which forms of compromise could be expressed that would both honor China's cultural autonomy while acknowledging its international ties.

Many young Chinese designers may have disagreed with the political values promoted by the Nationalist Party. Nevertheless, frustration with perceptions of China's perpetual weakness at the hands of its foreign aggressors fed Nationalist-inspired sentiment that only through more disciplined Chinese efforts would a truly modern yet uniquely Chinese architecture capable of embodying an advanced yet autonomous Chinese state materialize. For some Chinese architectural professionals such as Liang Sicheng, a more rigorous study of China's architectural history was necessary to feed design innovation. Liang considered foreign appropriations of Chinese architecture unsightly and ill-suited to the particular ideological needs of modern China, whereas Chinese appropriations of foreign building material and technologies that drew on the beauty of China's classical palace architecture were acceptable.[60] Other Chinese designers were more amenable to the influence of "International Style" architecture and its promises of efficiency and functionalism.[61] For some, aesthetic choices depended upon the nature of the project itself.[62] The spectrum of interpretations as to the meaning and roots of China's architectural modernity, each characterized to varying degrees by themes of cultural homogenization and standardization, and akin to the contemporaneous designation of an official language, ushered in a new era in China's architectural production.

It also helped to fuel a "new spirit in municipal administration" for the young republic.[63] Linking these efforts together was the desire to identify the most appropriate architecture for the new Chinese nation-state. Shanghai presented a major front in this battle. Primary among the new Chinese municipal government's aims was the construction of new Chinese-administered spaces that would challenge foreign hegemony within the city and, in turn, reassert China's political authority.[64] "A group of young students went to America and Europe to study the fundamentals of architecture," explained Dong Dayou (1899–1973), Columbia University graduate and designer of the Shanghai Civic Center, among other projects. "They came back to China filled with ambition to create something new and worthwhile. They initiated a great movement, a movement to bring back a dead architecture to life: in other words, to do away with poor imitations of western architecture and to make Chinese architecture truly national."[65] For many, the search for a contemporary Chinese architectural style had come to exemplify the much broader pursuit of an ideal Chinese state.

CHAPTER 7

A Contested Municipality

THE imposition of extraterritoriality upon China ensured that for subsequent generations of Chinese people, modernity was understood first and foremost as a political condition. To become modern meant access to new experiences, new objects, and the world at large, but it also meant being able to govern oneself as a nation equal to other nations. For Republican Chinese officials and designers alike, municipal architecture thus figured as the logical medium through which distinctive architectural icons of China's modernity would take shape. Lady Dorothea Hosie (1885–1959), the Ningbo-born daughter of a well-known China expert at Oxford, noted that when Chinese cities like Guangzhou began to conceive of themselves as "modern," they "started with [their] administration buildings. Beauty in public architecture lifts the soul of a city to hope and self-respect."[1] Public buildings and city-planning schemes were emblems of the new Republican regime—evidence that under modern Chinese leadership, the country could defend itself while absorbing foreign technologies in ways that would make China autonomous and universally legible and admired.[2]

The Greater Shanghai Plan, announced shortly following the Nationalist Party's consolidation of political power within the Chinese city, represents a culmination of Nationalist efforts to consolidate its own grip on Shanghai by reimagining a new physical center for the treaty port.[3] The scheme aimed to reorganize Shanghai's various foreign and Chinese administrative districts around a new civic center (*shi zhongxin*)—a Chinese-controlled locus of administrative, commercial, cultural, and social activity in an area located miles north of Shanghai's preexisting urban core (map 7.1). To do so, the Chinese government proposed the construction of a new deepwater port, new train and road

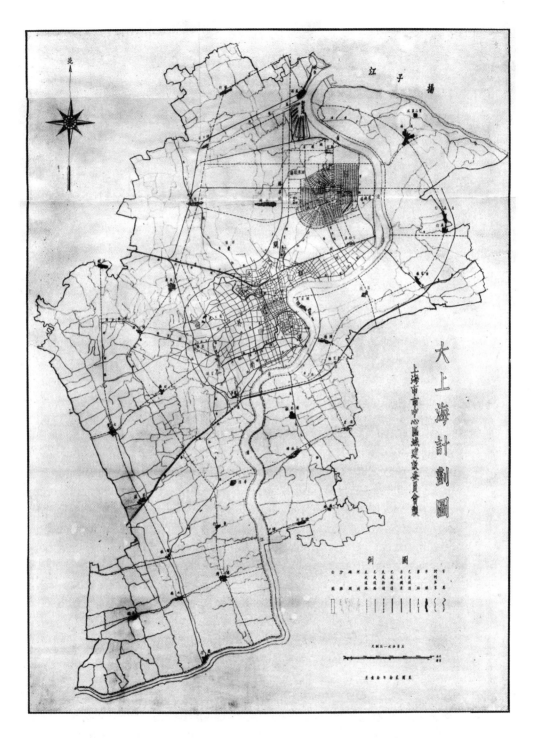

MAP 7.1. Shanghai, 1935, showing the location of the Greater Shanghai Plan vis-à-vis the preexisting urban landscape. Reprinted from Tang Liangli, *Reconstruction in China: A Record of Progress and Achievement in Facts and Figures* (Shanghai: Chinese United Press, 1935). Courtesy of the Virtual Shanghai Project.

systems, a mayor's building, museum, library, and stadium, and series of housing units. Although the plan was initially overlooked in the history of China's modern architectural and urban development, it has been rightfully exhumed and reframed as a monumental undertaking comparable to other extensive urban reimaginings of the past three hundred years such as Haussmann's nineteenth-century Paris, Wren's seventeenth-century plan for London, and early twentieth-century imperialist visions in Canberra and New Delhi.[4]

What remains unexamined in the Greater Shanghai Plan's history is its effect upon subsequent civic architectural and urban proposals in both the International Settlement and French Concession. In March 1931, three months prior to the laying of the foundation stone for the Greater Shanghai's Mayor's Building, International Settlement resident and Englishman Ernest F. Harris led public efforts to purchase the Majestic Hotel, located within the settlement's western district, and convert it into public gardens and a new civic center, including a concert hall, public library, open-air cinema, and new municipal offices (figure 7.1). Eight months following the completion of the Greater Shanghai Mayor's Building, in June 1934, the French Municipal Council announced its own plans for a new French municipal center (figure 7.2). Designed by the Shanghai-based French architectural firm of Léonard, Veysseyre, and Kruze, the complex was to be built near the concession's western boundary along Avenue Joffre, and was envisioned as a seven-story conglomeration of tax-collection

FIGURE 7.1. The Majestic Hotel, Lafuente and Yaron, Shanghai, 1922. Courtesy of the Hong Kong Heritage Project, HSH, vols. 1–3.

offices, a public works department, general municipal administration, consular affairs and central police headquarters.

Efforts to realize three monumental and ambitious projects within several years of each other, amid an anxious era fanned by ongoing Chinese administrative dysfunction, growing Japanese aggression, and turbulent economic development, culminate the history of municipal construction in Shanghai. In each project, decisions made with respect to site, scale, and architectural style reveal subtle but important clues into each municipal stakeholder's vision for Shanghai's uncertain future. Each embodied a different iteration of modern architecture as well as governance at work within the city. As imagined systems of administrative, social, and spatial organization, they give physical form to the various fissures and alliances within Shanghai's cosmopolitan community just prior to World War II.

FIGURE 7.2. French municipal center (proposed), Léonard, Veysseyre, and Kruze, Shanghai, 1934. Reprinted from *Le Journal de Shanghai*, December 13, 1936, Bibliothèque nationale de France.

THE GREATER SHANGHAI PLAN

Following the establishment of a new Chinese government by the country's ruling Nationalist Party in Nanjing in April 1927, Nationalist officials quickly set about reestablishing a Chinese governmental structure in Shanghai. Decades of extraterritorial governance had generated a palimpsest of political, economic, and spatial ambiguities that left the city physically fragmented, poorly managed, difficult to navigate, and synonymous with nefarious international intrigue and illicit activity. An initial set of regulations attempted to redefine the physical boundaries of the municipality and establish a centralized municipal administration to govern it, including the appointment of a mayor and an administrative council, as well as the establishment of a municipal council through public elections. However, disagreement between local and provincial officials complicated these efforts, leading to the postponement and nullification of some provisions, and resulting in a governing structure shaped by national, as opposed to municipal, considerations.[5]

Of foremost concern to Nationalist officials was regaining political control over the foreign influences at work in Shanghai. By 1932, Shanghai was home to an estimated 3,063,985 Chinese residents and 69,797 foreigners. Nevertheless, foreigners continued to dominate the city's economy and its skyline. "The Shanghai as it exists now is a foreign Shanghai, and it is an embarrassment," lamented Du Yangeng in the pages of the *Builder*.[6] Consolidating power proved difficult in a city compromised by divisions of class, race, political allegiance, and origin, however. Town planning emerged as one early and important priority.[7] In July 1929, Nationalist officials announced plans for new urban center to be built in Jiangwan, an undeveloped area located northeast of the International Settlement and south of Wusong, a potential destination for the new deepwater port. Inspired in part by a 1925 proposal put forward by Sun Yat-sen to transform Shanghai into the largest port in Asia, the Greater Shanghai Plan aimed to liberate the government from the constraints of the preexisting city and reorganize the municipality around a new physical center zoned for administrative, business, industrial, and residential purposes.[8] The city's administrative council organized a Civic Center Building Committee (Shanghai Shi Shizhongxin Quyu Jianshe Weiyuanhui), which was responsible for organizing China's second-ever international architectural competition following the Sun Yat-sen Mausoleum in Nanjing. By February 1930, more than fifty submissions were winnowed down to nine final schemes.[9]

One of the competition organizer's major concerns—indeed, one of the key debates within China's architectural community at the time—concerned how design could reassert Chinese administration into the city's management. On December 28, 1929, as the civic center proposals were being evaluated, the Nationalist government announced an abolishment of extraterritoriality from the city beginning January 1, 1930.[10] It was a symbolic and ultimately unsuccessful gesture, but it reflected Nationalist desire to reorganize the city on their own terms. Architecturally, such assurance took physical form in the cruciform that dominated each of the plan's final competition entries. Although the cruciform was not a stated prerequisite in the competition guidelines, its use reflects the prevalence of Beaux-Arts design methods in China at the time, particularly the perception that compositional qualities based on axiality, symmetry, and an overall architectural coherence could allow China to acquiesce to international planning standards while remaining true to imperial-era Chinese planning traditions. Moreover, the cruciform also represented a popular trope for Shanghai itself. The city had long been depicted in foreign and Chinese media as representing a kind of crossroads between China, Asia, and the world, charging the form with additional geopolitical import. This excerpt from a 1906 Shanghai guidebook describes the International Settlement as a kind of fulcrum between Europe and North America: "When you stand upon the Shanghai Bund and look westward, you have the whole of the Old World before you, the largest extent of land on the globe. Between you and the most westerly point of Europe, a distance of over 7000 miles, there is nothing but land. If you turn to the east, you face the greatest ocean of the world, and you can go direct to San Francisco or to Vancouver, a distance of 6000 miles."[11] In appropriating this imagery and rendering it in literal, physical terms, Chinese architects hoped to domesticate the cruciform and subsume it within China's own emerging modern architectural vocabulary.

The competition's winning scheme was designed by the University of Pennsylvania–trained Chinese architect Zhao Shen (1898–1978) in collaboration with his

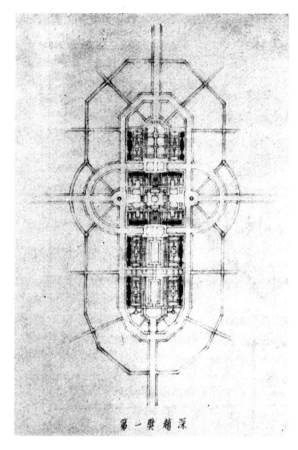

FIGURE 7.3. First-prize entry, Greater Shanghai Plan, Zhao Shen and Zhao-Sun Ximing, 1929. Reprinted from Shanghai shizhongxinqu chengjianshe weiyuanhui, *Jianzhu Shanghai shi zhengfu xin wu jishi* (1934), University of Chicago Library.

wife, Zhao-Sun Ximing (figure 7.3). The couple proposed a series of buildings clustered around the intersection of two major avenues: one running east to west linking the city's new railroad with Wusong, and a second route stretching north to south connecting the new urban center with the preexisting city. A system of circumferential roads accentuated the cruciform pattern while linking the zones to the proposed city center, which was itself divided into four quadrants by three secondary east-west boulevards. The framework of new roads would also help to stitch the plan into the city's preexisting urban systems. Opportunities for improved communication and contact between the new city government's own new vision of Shanghai and the preexisting urban core would eventually be triggered by this new network of roadways. The names of the proposed roads, including Good Government Road (Zhengtong Lu) and National Sovereignty Road (Guoquan Lu) underscored the fierce nationalist spirit and ideological aims intertwined within the physical proposal itself.[12] The physical meeting point of the center's circulation system formed a natural nexus for the city's future administrative district, to be composed of various government agencies and offices and outlying residential, commercial, and recreational zones, and to be anchored by a massive administrative complex designed in an imperial-era Chinese aesthetic with advanced building materials such as steel and reinforced concrete. Additional government buildings abutted the roads to both the north and south, with two pagodas located to the east and west of the main structure along the scheme's cross-axis.

Despite pains taken by the architects to create an appropriately dramatic and sufficient municipal setting, however, the jury did not find the scheme's monumentality particularly "effective," and its architecture was dismissed as an unsatisfying pastiche of East and West that diminished from the plan's overall composition.[13] Control over the project was passed to Dong Dayou (1899–1973), then serving as the search committee's secretary. Dong reduced the architectural scale of Zhao's proposed government building clusters and inserted more public space into the composition, thereby providing a greater sense of openness and inclusivity (figure 7.4). Dong also oversaw the expansion of the site's main boulevards, the repositioning of the Mayor's Building north of the plan's physical center, and the addition of a memorial temple to Sun Yat-sen located just behind it. Each decision helped to generate a more linear, rather than centripetal, hierarchy within the plan in keeping with both Chinese precedent and Beaux-Arts notions of progression and balance. The crossing of the plan's major north-south and east-west axes now consisted of an open, public space to be crowned by a 55-meter-tall central pagoda (figure 7.5). Then the tallest Chinese-designed and built structure in the city, the pagoda and its placement, as a physical marking of the city's central square as a public, albeit Chinese-controlled, space, seemed to seek a balance between a sense of civic inclusion and hierarchy. In this respect, the scheme attempted to resolve a tangled administrative system shaped by legal and diplomatic ambiguity.

As a monument to the Nationalist regime, the Greater Shanghai Plan signified a complex Chinese-run municipal system designed to reposition the young Chinese nation-state within an interconnected, increasingly technocratic world order. In both its scale and complexity, the plan aimed to counter preexisting, competing, and relatively autonomous systems of governance in both the city's International Settlement and French Concession. Foreign officials in both areas had long rationalized the extraterritorial system and its architecture necessary on the grounds that Qing China's ancient legal system did not adhere to a universal standard. The first structure completed on the site, the Mayor's Building, offered a striking physical counter (figure 7.6). The edifice consisted of a four-story reinforced concrete structure clad in imperial-era Chinese architectural motifs, including decorative *dougong*, a tiled roof, and broad, overhanging eaves. The building's aesthetics sought to marry imperial-era Chinese detailing to the

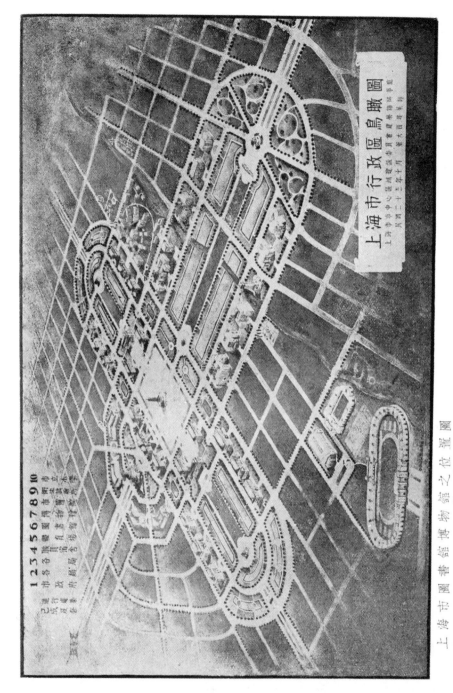

上海市行政區區鳥瞰圖
上海市中心區域設計委員會民國二十三年五月繪大略概歷

General View of the Civic Centre of the Municipality of Greater Shanghai
1. Municipality Administration Building
2. The Bureaus
3. The Bureaus
4. Staff Quarters
5. Recreation Ground
6. Library
7. Museum
8. Public Hospital
9. Sanitary Research Building
10. Primary Public School

上 海 古 圖 書 館 博 物 館 之 位 置 圖

1 2 3 4 5 6 7 8 9 10
市令各職辦國得市衙市
政行各有上待市立立
及建府局局場發普每察分
各業所局舍每汙察普著學

FIGURE 7.4. Administrative District, Greater Shanghai, Dong Dayou, 1930–35. Reprinted from *Jianzhu yuekan 2*, nos. 11 and 12 (1934), University of Hong Kong Libraries.

progressive and technocratic program of civic governance. Internally, too, advanced technological features like indoor plumbing and central electricity were juxtaposed with the ceremonial spaces and aesthetics deemed essential for China's political legitimacy. Importantly, much of its technology, including electric lights, elevators, water heaters, plumbing fixtures and other assorted building materials were all produced in China, while its concrete and tile were manufactured by the Qixin Cement and Guangzhou Tile companies, respectively.[14] The

FIGURE 7.5. Greater Shanghai Plan commemorative (jinian) pagoda (proposed), Dong Dayou. Reprinted from Shanghai shi zhongxin qu cheng jianshe weiyuanhui, *Jianzhu Shanghai shi zhengfu xin wu jishi* (1934), University of Chicago Library.

FIGURE 7.6. Mayor's Building, Greater Shanghai, Dong Dayou, 1933. Reprinted from Shanghai shi zhongxin qu cheng jianshe weiyuanhui, *Jianzhu Shanghai shi zhengfu xin wu jishi* (1934), University of Chicago Library.

FIGURE 7.7. Interior, Mayor's Building, Greater Shanghai, Dong Dayou, 1933. Reprinted from Shanghai shi zhongxin qu cheng jianshe weiyuanhui, *Jianzhu Shanghai shi zhengfu xin wu jishi* (1934), University of Chicago Library.

FIGURE 7.8. Sapajou, "A Vision of a Future Ambition," *North-China Daily News*, May 10, 1926, Special Collections, University of Hong Kong Libraries.

mayor's office itself, located on the structure's third floor, aimed to balance the ornate, ceremonial prestige of China's past with modern mechanisms of governance, symbolized by an exquisite executive desk (figure 7.7). An accounting department, a general management office, a municipal archive, research center, banquet halls, and meeting rooms were organized around the office.

The Greater Shanghai Plan's scale and implementation schedule were designed to compete not only with rival municipal administrations in the International Settlement and French Concession but with international cities like New York, London, and Paris (figure 7.8). Following the completion of the Mayor's Building and its inaugural ceremony in October 1933, the city's Public Works Department relocated to the civic center in late December 1933.[15] A stadium and gymnasium were both completed in time to host the sixth national athletic games in October 1935.[16] Other governmental departments, built along the plan's major north-south axis, included a municipal museum and library, completed in June 1936. Collectively, these buildings embodied the new physical and administrative infrastructure for a modern, Chinese-controlled Shanghai—an image of order noted by observers such as Liang Sicheng, who admired the scheme's grand and imposing spirit.[17] Privately, however, and throughout the civic center's construction, Chinese government officials worried that the public had become distracted by a perceived lack of visible progress on the scheme's more symbolic civic structures in relationship to the city's other two municipal administrations, and was failing to grasp the enormity of the entire planning scheme.[18] This disjuncture between public reception of the project and official fears over its own ambition is important, insofar as it underscores the utopian impulses driving the plan from its inception; namely, the smooth reconfiguration of Shanghai as a modern, progressive, and Chinese-controlled metropolis amenable but not beholden to foreign cohabitation.

The Greater Shanghai Plan was designed to structure and organize the city into a singular civic entity for the first time in its nearly one-hundred-year history as an international treaty port. In this hopeful projection of completeness, however, the minute details of administrative functionality remained unsettled. In 1934, the British planner, educator, and writer Jacqueline Tyrwhitt (1905–1983) toured the site during a trip to Shanghai to visit her brother. There, she found "a very fine, if rather grandiloquent, plan of a future Chinese city."[19] The Mayor's Building itself was "a fine building and cannot fail to impress all beholders," though evidence of malfeasance was inscribed throughout the completed structure. "The only thing entirely without flaw is the beauty of the design," lamented Tyrwhitt:

> The Chinese system of "squeeze," the local term of graft, has allowed very little of the materials originally planned to actually be employed upon the building. As we walked around it we saw red paper on the ground attached to flakes of plaster. Frost had peeled this off from the lacquer columns. Much of the carved woodwork betrayed in the same way that it had a plaster origin and the stone was mostly cement. We could not test the bronze doors, but it was most unlikely that they would prove to have more than a bronze finish on the outside.[20]

The government's efforts to complete the project in the face of budget limitations and armed conflict were inscribed in the civic center's architectural quality. Such shortsightedness extended outward to imbue the entire scheme with an improvised, unfinished air. The plan's road system "radiates from the Centre," admired Tyrwhitt, "but, [the roads] for the most part go nowhere as yet. They travel for a certain distance and then abruptly terminate."[21] Focus on the aesthetic of governance aimed to overcome civil strife and foreign aggression, leaving the Greater Shanghai Plan haunted by its own potential. It also dogged two projects inspired by the Chinese scheme, including the French Concession's municipal center scheme as well as the International Settlement's proposed town hall—prominent structures of striking physical form incapable of inducing the kind of dramatic political action needed within the city.

THE INTERNATIONAL SETTLEMENT'S TOWN HALL

Over the course of the 1920s, segments of Shanghai's foreign population sought to stabilize their legacies within the city amid increasing pressure from home governments to rescind foreign extraterritoriality, and continued political uncertainty in China. In 1924, for example, members of the American Legion Post, working in coordination with Chinese officials, unveiled a monument to Frederick Townsend Ward at his grave designed to refresh his legacy and the long history of foreign influence it represented.[22] Following the announcement of the Greater Shanghai Plan, a number of smaller-scale public building proposals within both the International Settlement as well as the French Concession each attempted to visualize "the future of the foreigner in China," and Shanghai in particular.[23] For example, the Shanghai Municipal Council began to deploy a distinctly European modernist aesthetic paradigm for major public edifices, including markets, schools, and police stations. Cloaked in an aesthetic of rationalism marked by unadorned façades, horizontally banded windows, and modern building materials such as steel and concrete, these structures—and by extension, the administrative authority behind them—exuded an aura of efficiency, progress, and hygienic superiority that stood in stark contrast to the Greater Shanghai Civic Center's more localized, distinctly Chinese modernist style (figure 7.9).

Another segment of the settlement's population pined for a civic space capable of addressing the uncertainties of Shanghai's future—one rooted not in the austere aesthetics of internationalism per se but in forms of cross-cultural social engagement specific to the place of Shanghai itself. In March 1931, Ernest Harris, a British national then living in Shanghai, publicly advocated for the purchase of the settlement's most prestigious hotel, the Majestic, which had been recently put up for sale, with the goal of converting it into public gardens and a new civic center. In Harris's estimation, the building would finally provide Shanghai with

FIGURE 7.9. Police Station, Public Works Department, Chengdu Road, Shanghai, 1930. Shanghai History Museum (C015-1-1-F).

a civic facility that could be found in "all cities of importance."[24] Harris believed the building, located along Bubbling Well Road and converted in 1924 from a private residence into a hotel by the Shanghai-based foreign firm Lafuente and Yaron, could easily be renovated again to accommodate a concert hall, public library, open-air cinema, new municipal offices, as well as an exhibition hall celebrating the settlement's history and industry.[25] The showy Renaissance-style monument was considered "almost beyond imagination beautiful" and included an elaborately decorated winter garden, ballroom, extensive sitting rooms, and lounges (figure 7.10).[26] The ballroom was capable of hosting 1,800 people; it featured a gold-leaf and marble floor in the shape of a four-leaf clover, an elaborate water fountain, and murals painted by artists hired from Italy and France.[27]

Like the Greater Shanghai Plan, the proposal to purchase the Majestic gestured toward a form of cross-cultural civic diplomacy rooted in the design of space. In contrast to the Chinese government's proposal, however, proponents of the International Settlement's town hall scheme saw the benefits of relying upon a preexisting architectural icon to capitalize on its established social spheres and the public nostalgia associated with the building to soothe hostilities between Chinese and foreign residents.[28] A new kind of modern civic space beckoned—one shaped not by the utopian imaginings of an ambitious Chinese government but by a naive urban elite interested in preserving an endangered

FIGURE 7.10. Interior, Winter Garden, Majestic Hotel, Lafuente and Yaron, Shanghai, 1922. Reprinted from *The China Architects and Builders Compendium* (Shanghai: North-China Daily News, 1924), Special Collections, University of Hong Kong Libraries.

way of life. The formal designation of a social space to be shared by foreign and Chinese residents was a response to the question of the settlement's long-term survival. The hotel, particularly its ballroom, was a popular cross-cultural social domain for foreign and Chinese residents. It had also been used as a de facto meeting ground for municipal council members and the city's Chinese elite to discuss the social ills of the day—sessions that were hailed as "milestone[s] in the history of Shanghai," and "the first time in the history of this municipality when any such gathering has taken place."[29] Its status as the site of Generalissimo Chiang Kaishek's "world famous" wedding in 1927, too, suggested a value that transcended the city's local politics by feeding into "emerging recognition of the 'world view' of Shanghai while offering a common meeting ground between Foreigners and Chinese."[30] Proposal supporters capitalized upon these facts to argue for the building's civic significance, arguing that the scheme could become a civic center in keeping with "modern Town Planning" standards, thereby making it a strategic intercultural investment in the city's future.[31]

Many foreign taxpayers, including the settlement's Japanese residents, remained opposed to the scheme, however, making the support of its Chinese community—a group who collectively represented 97 percent of the zone's population and two-thirds of its tax income base—vital to its potential success.[32] Their endorsement hinged upon the building's proposed transformation into a hub of social activity and entertainment, with several prominent Chinese residents expressing interest in the Majestic's ballroom as a nexus for organized, social interaction.[33] On March 20, the Shanghai Land Investment Company formally submitted an offer to sell the Majestic Hotel property to the municipal council for 3.5 million taels, though council and Public Works Department members could not reach an agreement on the project's specifics. It was agreed to delay the decision as to the type of building to be constructed or purchased in part due to the "uncertain future status of the Settlement."[34]

Two years later, in April 1933, a second resolution was brought before International Settlement taxpayers proposing the purchase of land for the construction of a new town hall. This proposal was also rejected. New plans subsequently resurfaced in May for a town hall to be built within the Public Gardens along the Huangpu River. The site represented a marked retreat from the settlement's contested western boundaries toward a more easily defensible, reassuring location along the Bund, which remained the preeminent symbol of the city's dominance at the hands of foreign political and commercial powers. In the end, however, ratepayers also voted it down.

THE FRENCH CONCESSION'S MUNICIPAL CENTER

In January 1932, Japan's bombing of Shanghai's Zhabei district inflamed the city's ill-defined borders, turning neighborhoods long since fractured along fissures of nationality and socioeconomic status into literal battlegrounds. The violence damaged the new civic center in Jiangwan, but it did not derail efforts at civic center construction within any of the city's three municipalities. On June 17, 1934, the French Concession's old municipal headquarters, located on the rue du Consulat, were demolished in anticipation of the construction of a new municipal center, to be built within the concession's western district along avenue Joffre. French efforts to build a new municipal town center can be traced back to 1923, when the French Municipal Council approached then consul general Henry Auguste Wilden (1879–1935) with a proposal to replace the concession's municipal offices and consulate, completed in 1866 and 1894, respectively, and combine them into one facility.[35] Nothing was built, however, and the project went unrealized until 1934, when temporary municipal offices were built on avenue Joffre and rue de Say-Zoong. An invitation was transmitted exclusively to French architects living in France, French colonies in southeastern Asia, and Shanghai to submit plans for new municipal offices.[36]

The French architectural firm, Léonard, Veysseyre, and Kruze took first and second places. The three French architects, each trained at the École des Beaux-Arts, operated a prolific regional practice with offices in Shanghai and Saigon.[37] Their first-place entry featured a seven-story structure with a stark granite-faced façade accentuated by a public garden to the building's south (figure 7.11). The main structure held offices for the concession's tax collection bureau, general administration, public works, judicial offices, and land registry. It was crowned by the consul general's office, a spatial articulation of the imperial power wielded by the French national government. Positioned behind the main building was a smaller police station, separated by a semi-private courtyard to be used for public assemblies, police drills, and exercises. Public access to the building was designed to be from avenue Joffre to the south, requiring passage through a Court of Honor highlighted by a series of monuments in honor of the French Republic.

The decision to appeal to French architects represented continued efforts on the part of Shanghai's French officials to solidify the French Concession's autonomy through built form. The French government had long felt dominated by the International Settlement's commercial and political clout, and French residents continued to comprise only a tiny percentage of the concession's diverse population—1,208 people out of a total of 462,342, and smaller than the number of Chinese, Americans, British, or Russians within the city.[38] Growing Chinese unrest within the French Concession, including a 1931 strike by 2,500 Chinese municipal workers, also unnerved French representatives.[39] The French-built municipal center was thus imagined as a visual and spatial mnemonic of French administrative control amid a sea of non-French residents. Limiting the competition to French architects, and ultimately selecting the most prolific French firm in Southeast Asia, helped to reinforce the French Concession's desired

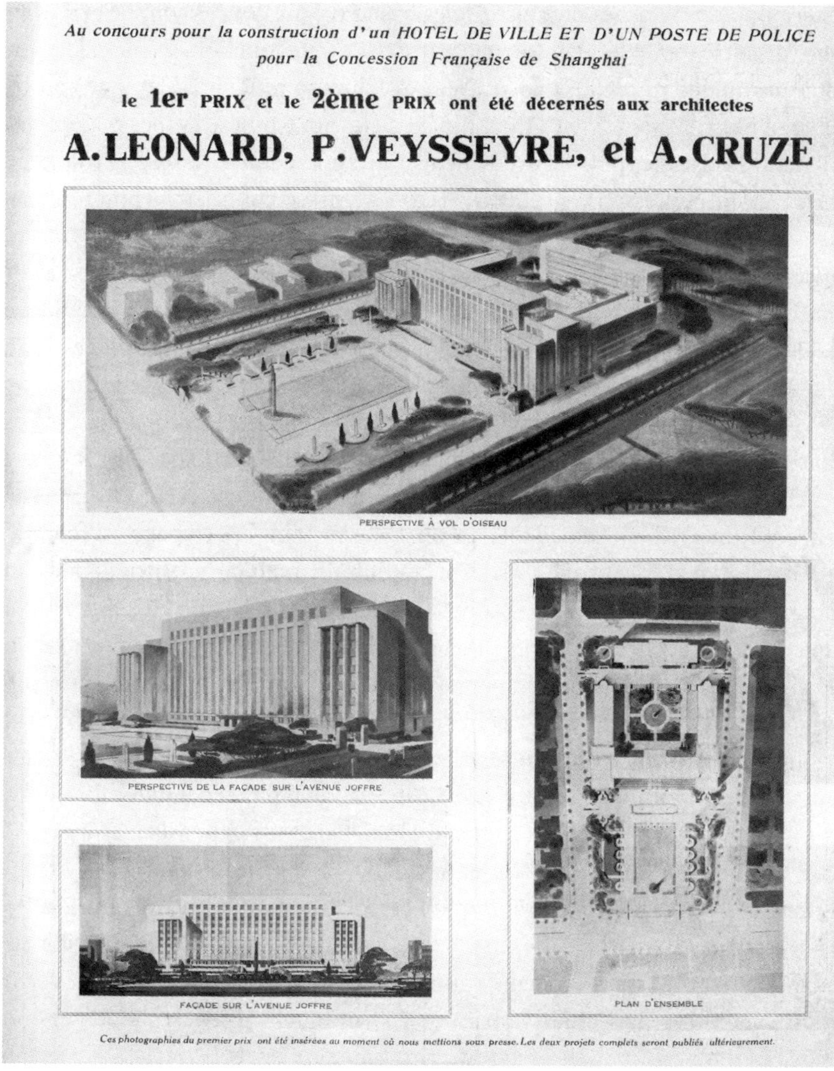

Au concours pour la construction d'un *HOTEL DE VILLE ET D'UN POSTE DE POLICE* pour la Concession Française de Shanghai

le **1er** PRIX et le **2ème** PRIX ont été décernés aux architectes

A. LEONARD, P. VEYSSEYRE, et A. CRUZE

PERSPECTIVE À VOL D'OISEAU

PERSPECTIVE DE LA FAÇADE SUR L'AVENUE JOFFRE

FAÇADE SUR L'AVENUE JOFFRE

PLAN D'ENSEMBLE

Ces photographies du premier prix ont été insérées au moment où nous mettions sous presse. Les deux projets complets seront publiés ultérieurement.

FIGURE 7.11. French municipal center (proposed), Léonard, Veysseyre, and Kruze, Shanghai, 1934. Reprinted from *Le Journal de Shanghai*, July 28, 1935, Bibliothèque nationale de France.

position within a broader French colonial sphere, despite the fact that the concession itself remained leased land.

The proposal was part of a larger scheme to rezone the entire concession. As in both the Greater Shanghai Plan and the Majestic Hotel scheme, it targeted a site located within proximity to the city's less developed, contested western boundaries in an attempt to regain some degree of spatial control from the city's other, more crowded areas. Shifting the municipal center westward represented a retreat from the concession's Chinese-dominant eastern sector and the International Settlement's Bund, with all of its architectural connotations of British imperial power. A series of zoning laws based on the concession's preexisting police districts was to be enacted whereby a building's function, style, and height would be predetermined by its location. A Chinese residential zone would be enforced near the border with the Chinese city, with Chinese homes required to be at least two stories tall. A government affairs and commercial zone would be located in the concession's northeast section, a mixed commercial and residential zone farther to the west, and to the far west, an exclusive residential zone within which Chinese constructions were prohibited. Any skyscrapers, then seen in Shanghai as buildings of ten to twenty stories in height, would be allowed, though stylistically, they would need to blend with the concession's other tall buildings to form a dignified and uniform architectural ensemble.[40]

Visibility, as in both the Greater Shanghai Plan and the International Settlement's Town Hall, was crucial to the project's anticipated success. The new French municipal offices' position along avenue Joffre was accentuated by the Court of Honor, which helped to maximize the building's "perspectival effect."[41] This public square featured a series of fountains, manicured shrubbery, and statuary that commemorated France's unique position within the city. At the same time, however, the building's relatively unadorned exterior seemed to echo debate over the nature of contemporary French architecture and its relationship to the state. In 1934, the socialist politician André Morizet (1876–1942) published an editorial in *Architecture d'aujourd'hui* calling for public buildings in France that resembled "municipal factories."[42] The Shanghai project employed ostensibly modernist architectural elements in Shanghai at the expense of any particularly Chinese building tradition or aesthetic—a shift in visual strategy from the formal colonial building programs of association on display in French Indochine and North Africa at the time.[43] The jury, composed of French residents and officials, noted in the scheme's simplicity, regularity, and absence of decoration something particularly striking and uniquely "French," a perception echoed by Chinese analysis of architectural modernism.[44] Léonard, Veysseyre, and Kruze were also celebrated for their interpretation of "nationalist spirit" and lauded as proof against stereotypes of French architects and engineers as uncooperative individualists whose projects lacked the scale and scope of those of the American engineering profession, for example.[45]

Shanghai's French municipality lacked the trappings of a traditional and comprehensive colonial infrastructure, and the proposed designs for Shanghai's new French municipal center sought to strengthen the extraterritorial concession's ties to the French *métropole* itself through decisions made with respect to scale, material, as well as slight but detectable decorative flourishes such as statuary. In doing so, the selected proposal echoed debates within France's own architectural community over modern architecture's value as a "national" style at the time.[46] The subsequent construction of the concession's largest and first "modern" police station upon the former Municipal Council grounds, too,

FIGURE 7.12. Police headquarters, Léonard, Veysseyre, and Kruze, Shanghai, 1936. Courtesy of the Virtual Shanghai Project.

underscored efforts to appropriate the aesthetics of modernism as a distinctly French municipal design approach (figure 7.12). There, a public plaza centered around the concession's preexisting Admiral Protet sculpture grounded the structure in the history of French municipal governance in Shanghai.

BUILDING FOR AN EXTRATERRITORIAL COMMUNITY

Plans for each project ended with the Japanese invasion of the city in August 1937. Over the course of 1938 and 1939, a Japanese-controlled "Great Way" government center materialized that was modeled on the Greater Shanghai Plan and partially built upon the original site of the proposed civic center.[47] Like its predecessor, the project featured two major axes and a proposed series of administrative structures. Its construction was literally pieced together from the physical rubble of the previous Chinese administration.[48] For all of the devastation and disappointment associated with this era, however—in particular the inability of Shanghai's three municipalities to fully realize these works—this period in Shanghai's civic architectural history remains significant for several reasons. Paradoxically, civic architectural development reached its most active and dynamic state of engagement, both with the public and between each of its municipal authorities, at the very moment that Shanghai's nonviability as an international treaty port became undeniable.

Each of these projects remains linked by a resolute utopianism. A delusional, almost messianic fervor took root within sections of the city's Chinese and foreign communities around these projects that reveals the latent power of public architectural form in fueling imaginaries capable of transcending harsh geopolitical and socioeconomic realities. The less certain each project's realization became, the more ethereal the imagery used to describe it—a tacit acknowledgment of each project's impossibility in the face of the city's tenuous political condition. In 1933, the Chinese city's mayor, Wu Tiecheng (1888–1953), compared the Greater Shanghai Plan to El Dorado, with an enchanting power that would prove so intoxicating residents would never want to leave.[49] By 1935, Dong Dayou described the plan as "a new city is arising like magic upon the once open lands."[50] Similarly, the Chinese architectural critic Du Yangeng remarked that the Greater Shanghai Plan represented a means "of saving not only the city, but the entire country."[51] Both the Majestic Hotel proposal and the French Concession scheme were propelled by similar, redemptive rhetoric. An anonymous Chinese resident living within the International Settlement, for example, was quoted as describing the Majestic Hotel as an architectural means by which a "spirit of common citizenship between the Foreigners and the Chinese" would be engendered that "would lengthen the life of this Settlement by at least 10 years and might prolong it indefinitely."[52]

The Greater Shanghai Plan was the most ambitious of these schemes, given its efforts to simultaneously accommodate and hasten the imminent unraveling of Shanghai's administrative framework through the fusion of modern building materials and imperial-era Chinese decoration (figure 7.13). Over time, however, and in the face of increasingly insurmountable financial and logistical obstacles, Chinese officials acknowledged the plan's ambitious and ultimately unrealistic goals. Dong publicly suggested that the value of the project's visibility transcended its ability to function: "The appeal to the eye is not to be ignored. The pride of the citizen is stirred as his city rises above the commonplace. The interest of the visitor is won by the dignity and distinction as revealed by its appearance."[53] The emphasis placed on image did not go unnoticed by foreign residents; one year earlier, in 1934, O. M. Green, editor of the *North-China Daily News*, used the project's optics to reiterate an ironic litany of claims he had first made in 1930 that the new Chinese government and its new plan remained an arbitrary, nonrepresentative entity. In an editorial first published in his own paper and subsequently reprinted in the city's *Journal de Shanghai*, Green described the Greater Shanghai Civic Center as a transparent attempt to legitimize the new government through "an outward appearance . . . so grandly imposing" that the foreign administrations would feel compelled to acquiesce to an overarching Chinese municipal authority.[54] As an exercise in legitimization, however, the Greater Shanghai Plan represented the culmination of decades of visual politics on display in the city, and an ambitious effort to instill a specific aesthetic and spatial expression of order.

FIGURE 7.13. New civic center, Shanghai, 1937. Reprinted from Shanghai shi gongwu ju, *Shanghai shigongwuju zhi shinian* (1937), Special Collections, Cornell University Library and Cornell Digital Consulting and Production Services.

Collectively, then, these projects speak to the broader semiotic obstacles posed by extraterritoriality and the project of modernity purportedly at its heart—an ideality rooted in the purported benefits of exchange and expressed most vividly through physical infrastructure designed to facilitate trade.[55] By the 1930s, it was clear some new iteration of the modern had taken shape in China, with architectural ideals rooted not simply in material and programmatic tropes of efficiency and functionalism, but in capable, stable governance. These goals lay at the heart of all three civic projects, though each was proposed with different political goals and distinctive, as yet unseen Shanghai futures, in mind. In this respect, these projects should be seen as part of a much larger cultural movement taking shape in the city at the time over Shanghai's possible fate. In a slim volume titled *Shanghai's Future* (Shanghai de jianglai) and published in 1934, seventy-nine Chinese intellectuals, writers, and officials, including Mayor Wu, debated the city's trajectory, and whether the extraterritorial city should—or could—even have one.[56] It was a moment for architecture, an anticipatory discipline by nature, to demonstrate its agency in effecting change. Ultimately, however, these projects could not resolve the domestic and international challenges posed by the treaty port system. Architecture's transformative capacity had limits rooted in the idealized mechanisms of power to which each project respectively aspired.

CHAPTER 8

Exhibiting a Modern Chinese Architecture

L IKE the treaty port, the international exposition was another consequential
site in the relationship between China's governance and questions of architectural representation—one designed for commerce and rooted in extraterritoriality's institutional framework, yet operating largely independently of the
system's particular physical or diplomatic restraints. Translated into Chinese as
wanguo bolanhui, or ten thousand nations' exhibitions, international exhibitions were important cogs for communication and exchange in a massive international bureaucracy. They introduced new technologies and manufactured
goods from around the world to potential consumers; they were also elaborate
cultural spectacles in which international audiences could digest imperial narratives carefully rendered through a selection of artistic and architectural
objects from around the globe.[1]

Through the exhibitionary format, the extraterritorial system did more than
compromise the Qing government's capacity to control its own domestic affairs.
It also contributed to the shaping of foreign perceptions of China abroad. As
conduits through which European and North American images of China, and
non-Western people in general, were disseminated to a broader international
public, exhibitions and fairs were influential in the construction of a modern
Chinese architecture and, by extension, the modern Chinese state both inside
and outside China's contested borders. The Imperial Maritime Customs Service,
founded in 1854 in the wake of the Small Swords Uprising, initially supervised
much of this circulation. In addition to monitoring all duties and dues levied on
trade and shipping in and out of China, customs superintendents in Beijing,

Shanghai, and Guangzhou were tasked with designing China's displays and selecting the objects to be included; theirs was a position from which they exercised power over not only Chinese trade exports but international perceptions of China. Such fairs did not appeal to Qing leaders, who read in them a kind of coerced multilateral engagement that, like the empire's forced opening to foreign commercial expansion in 1843, seemed to offer China little but exploitation at the hands of foreign organizers.[2] However, foreign advisors saw commercial and diplomatic benefits to such showcases, and Qing China was officially involved in at least six international exhibitions between 1873 and 1904.

The establishment of the Republic of China in 1912 promised a shift in how China would defend its sovereignty and image domestically and internationally. The country's leaders took greater interest in promoting the "new" China, even as they understood the constraints imposed upon them by the modern world order. Republican officials recognized international expositions presented opportunities to learn from other parts of the world, particularly in relationship to architecture, and over the course of the early twentieth century, international expositions served as prominent forces in shaping Chinese conceptualizations of internationalism and modern architecture beyond China's borders. By the mid-1930s, several of the country's professionally trained designers became involved in these events as well, experiencing the imbalances of power at work in international exhibitions firsthand. Redressing the state of China's compromised architectural image both at home and abroad became a rallying cry for Chinese architects. Their collective efforts culminated in a 1936 architectural exhibition held in Shanghai, which marked a consequential moment of consolidation in China's approach to modern architecture and its cultural self-representation.

CONSTRUCTING "CHINA" ABROAD

The 1873 Vienna International Exhibition was the first fair in which China participated in an official capacity. Coordination of the display fell to Robert Hart (1835–1911), an English-Scottish member of Britain's consular service born in Northern Ireland. In fact, the initial impetus for Chinese participation in these fairs largely originated with Hart, who saw tremendous benefit in promoting China to foreign audiences.[3] Following the Vienna exhibition and extending through the 1890s, Hart's team was responsible for assembling six Qing displays, including events in Philadelphia, London, and Paris. Each featured elaborately carved *pailou* and an assortment of Chinese porcelain, furniture, paintings, and miscellaneous objects, with displays constructed by Chinese laborers per customs officials' demands. In addition to numerous logistical and budgeting challenges, Hart also had to grapple with foreign preconceptions of China itself. "The English idea of the Chinese Tea-House and Chinese

Restaurant has nothing corresponding to it in China except the fact that there are buildings in which people can buy and eat food and drink tea," vented Hart to his London-based agent and friend James Duncan Campbell in 1884. "If we could supply you with one of them bodily, you would indeed have a slice out of the real life of China, but English sightseers would neither eat in it nor sit in it."[4] The pressures of audience expectations and cost resulted in essentializing juxtapositions of everyday Chinese objects and precious imperial art. These displays left visitors with impressions of China as a land of impossible extremes and seemingly irresponsive to the changes being effected within the country through foreign exchange.

Following the collapse of the Qing regime, the San Francisco's 1915 Panama-Pacific International Exhibition presented the Republican government's first opportunity to project an image of the new Chinese nation-state abroad. The Chinese pavilion grounds, which included a simplified, scaled replica of the Forbidden City's Hall of Supreme Harmony flanked by two teahouses for public concessions, were met with a mixed international response (figure 8.1). At least one Western editorial applauded the "modern" and "democratic" decision made by the Chinese government in reappropriating one of the Qing dynasty's most sacred political monuments for the purposes of widespread public consumption. Chinese American observers, by contrast, found the display "extremely inferior" and "shameful" and its workmanship, undertaken by Chinese carpenters sent to San Francisco for the occasion, "entirely insufficient to represent China's progress."[5] Such equivocality portended the Republican government's challenges in rendering new national aspirations legible to an international audience.

The 1933 Chicago World's Fair, titled "A Century of Progress," was the first international exposition organized after the Nationalist government's reunification of China. Following years of civil strife and factionalism, Chicago's inclusive, forward-thinking theme resonated with a Republican Chinese leadership eager to promote the country's political and economic advancements abroad. The Chicago fair also took shape as another well-known exhibition, the Museum of Modern Art's *The International Style*, helped bring the collective attention of China's architectural community to the idea of an international architecture—alternatively translated as "ten thousand nations' style" (wanguo shi) or "international style" (guoji shi)—without historical or traditional precedent.[6] Stimulating and promoting an inclusive, more liberally defined modern architectural idiom "not only in America but in the world at large" represented a major imperative of the Chicago fair.[7] Foreign participants were assured that Chicago's architectural committee would not "tell our friends representing other governments what their exhibitions shall be"; rather, they were instead encouraged to create an "attractive" display with information concerning "the manner in which other people live and meet the daily problems of existence."[8] For a Chinese architectural community seeking out models for a modern

FIGURE 8.1. Chinese Pavilion, Panama-Pacific International Exposition, San Francisco, 1915. San Francisco History Center, San Francisco Public Library (AAZ-0926).

Chinese architectural language, the fair was an opportunity to test a physical articulation of the developing Chinese nation-state on foreign soil while learning from other parts of the world.

China was eventually represented by two structures at the fair: a hastily constructed Chinese-courtyard-style pavilion financed by a group of Shanghai businessmen, and a replica of an eighteenth-century Tibetan Buddhist shrine, the Golden Temple of Jehol. An exaggerated interpretation of a Shanghai neighborhood titled "Streets of Shanghai" was added to the fair in 1934. None of these constructions presented a particularly satisfying embodiment of modern China, and the country's participation in the fair was largely considered a failure.[9] Nevertheless, Chicago helped to illuminate the role played by international fairs, exhibitions, and curatorial activity in producing diverging definitions of the modern in relationship to China's architectural image around the world. The exposition also laid bare the empowering and restrictive aspects of political and cultural systems both inside and outside the country. The asymmetries of knowledge and power on display in Chicago left Chinese participants, which included designers like Guo Yuanxi (1904–2005), Tong Jun (1900–1983), Wu Jingqi (1900–1943), and Xu Jingzhi (1906–1983), frustrated and conflicted as to the role of architectural modernism in a modernizing Chinese society. Nevertheless, these and other members of China's architectural community recognized the exhibition as a medium through which they could address perceptions of their country's backwardness and attempt to regain control over the narratives long used to depict China's architectural past, present, and future in compromised and restrictive ways.

THE SHANGHAI ARCHITECTURAL EXHIBITION, 1936

Following the Chicago fair, Chinese debate over modernism and the International Style focused on how a so-called "international" architecture could meet the needs of a nation-state struggling against the demands imposed upon it, in part, by global capital. These discussions also concerned the implications of architectural internationalism for China's architectural history. Chinese architects looked at the country's largest treaty ports and saw nearly one hundred years of what they considered to be forms of international architecture on display that ignored the country's rich imperial-era architectural culture while contributing little to the development of the Chinese nation.[10] Amid questions as to how an international architecture might address the specific needs of the modern Chinese citizen, Chinese architects set about fomenting a new architectural movement—one driven by nationalism and broader concerns regarding the manipulation of China's cultural identity through architectural expression.

A series of essays and exhibitions published and promoted in the country's most notable architectural journals spurred debate forward. In February 1934, a *Shenbao* article titled "The Relationship between Traditional Chinese Architecture and Modern Architecture" posited spatial simplicity, color, and the shared verticality of pagodas and skyscrapers as potential junctures between contemporary architectural design and China's own building history. A February 1934 exhibition in Shanghai sponsored by Fan Wenzhao and Carl Lindbohm focused on Spanish residential architecture.[11] Eliel Saarinen's work also began to be publicized in Shanghai's architectural circles.[12] The Finnish designer's inquiries concerning modern architecture's ability to adapt to local conditions as well as customs resonated in China, where the ideological significance of resuscitating China's architectural past remained strong. Professional organizations also helped in shaping such discourse. For example, through their official bulletin, Liang Sicheng and the work of the Society for the Research of Chinese Architecture (Zhongguo Yingzao Xueshe) directed the attention of the Chinese architectural community to the representational virtues of traditional Chinese architecture, even as their findings occasionally contradicted dominant political narratives regarding China's cultural singularity.[13] Nevertheless, such work produced a theoretical foundation upon which Chinese architects could begin to reframe internationally acknowledged weaknesses in Chinese architecture, including its imperviousness to change and perceived structural fragility, as conceptual virtues.[14] Such efforts also coincided with the work of Chinese art historians to produce new art and architectural histories that organized the development of the country's cultural production along an unbroken and progressive trajectory through time.[15]

Raising public awareness to the profession's concerns required a public event of some magnitude capable of addressing China's architectural past in a more sysfematic and clinical fashion than had previously been attempted. Public exhibitions and museums were important mechanisms for mass education and nation building in Republican China, particularly during the Nanjing Decade.[16] The 1929 National Art Exhibition held in Shanghai, for example, was an ambitious event featuring a total of 2,328 artworks and more than eight hundred artists from China, Japan, Europe, and the United States. Aimed to educate the modern Chinese citizen regarding the value of art in constructing the Chinese nation, the event was also not without controversy, particularly in relation to debate over modernism and appropriate national forms of artistic representation in China.[17] By contrast, architecture had never before been the subject of any large-scale museum display in China, though buildings had formed key components of several industrial expositions organized in China, such as the Nanyang Exposition of 1910 (Nanyang Quanye Hui). Through the exhibitionary format, leaders of China's architectural community began to craft an architectural narrative for China that elevated the study, practice, and history of architectural design above the act of industrialization itself.

One of the first and most ambitious public expositions to include contemporary architectural materials in China was held in Shanghai, October 10–30, 1935. It signaled an important step toward the legitimization of Chinese building materials and, by extension, Chinese architectural design quality.[18] Organized by Dong Dayou, Mo Heng, Xue Ciwei, and others, with help from the Shanghai Workers Guild and the Chinese Engineering Society, the event aimed to counter perceptions that Chinese construction materials were inferior to imported or foreign-produced material. The event also featured a selection of blueprints detailing current projects in the city, including the Shanghai stadium, pool, and gymnasium. Following that show, Shanghai public works director Shen Yi, Du Yangeng, and other members of the Shanghai Architectural Society met in November 1935 to discuss the possibility of staging a larger, more substantive exhibit devoted to historical and contemporary Chinese architecture.[19]

There appears to have been little debate over where such an exhibit would be held. All of the event's initial organizers were based in Shanghai, and the city's newly constructed museum, both the country's largest and most modern curatorial facility at the time, was set to open in 1936 (figure 8.2). Shanghai's status as one of the largest cities in the world also likely figured as a consequential factor in bringing long overdue attention to Chinese architectural culture and modern urban development. As the country's fulcrum of Chinese-Western interaction and perhaps the only city in China capable of "attracting the world's attention," Shanghai was considered a prominent global metropolis, even as its

FIGURE 8.2. Shanghai Museum, Dong Dayou, Shanghai, 1936. Reprinted from *Jianzhu yuekan* 4, no. 3 (1936), University of Hong Kong Libraries.

position within China remained ambiguous.[20] Shanghai's perceived proximity to the rest of the world imbued architectural form, practice, and construction there with a degree of international currency other Chinese cities such as Beijing, the former imperial capital, or Nanjing, the government's new model capital, did not possess. These factors also made Shanghai a target for criticism among Chinese architects; at least one Guangzhou-based designer, for example, chastised Shanghai's Chinese architects for focusing on the speculative and spectacular in Shanghai rather than on the needs of the city's impoverished Chinese population.[21] Indeed, Shanghai was a place constructed through years of unheralded Chinese labor and during an era in which China's architects and builders had found themselves consistently ignored, ostracized, and discriminated against by many within the foreign building community. This exhibition would, in theory, shed light on those figures. Finally, Shanghai's status as an important destination for young designers made it a useful platform for the recruitment of young people to the discipline of architecture and engineering—key fields for China's future development. Shanghai was also perceived as lacking history, in particular, physical evidence of centuries-long development of China's architectural culture over time.[22] The exhibition would provide that history, enriching both public perceptions of the city's contemporary growth and contributing to it a narrative that would detail the various contours of the country's architectural identity.

In March, a steering committee that included several members of China's 1933 World's Fair commission was quickly compiled, suggesting a desire to apply both the political and curatorial lessons learned from Chicago. The group featured twelve Shanghai-based architects, engineers, contractors, and key government officials, including the artist Ye Gongchuo (1881–1968) and Mayor Wu Tiecheng, who were named the event's president and honorary president, respectively. Ye played a key organizational role in the First National Fine Arts Exhibition of 1929, and he was a proponent of developing national-level cultural societies capable of promoting Chinese arts within the country and abroad.[23] A coalition of industry and cultural figures coalesced around them. By early April more than fifty-two organizations were involved in the event's planning, including the Greater Shanghai Municipality, the Beijing Municipality, Zhongda, Jiaoda, and Fudan Universities, numerous Shanghai-based labor, architectural, and engineering organizations, various firms, building material and construction companies from around the country, as well as the Society for Research of Chinese Architecture.[24] The event's financial support and marketing, including the publication of a commemorative booklet, was an early concern.[25]

By the end of March, a rough picture of the exhibition's contents and overall scope began to emerge. Proposed items included numerous examples of imperial and recent Chinese architectural and engineering projects represented through photographs, models, and plans. Various accoutrements of both traditional and contemporary building practice in China were also displayed, including job contracts, construction tools, and diagrams of various building techniques. Given the event's goal to produce a constructed experience of architectural and national solidarity, inclusivity was a major curatorial concern. The exhibition eventually included approximately two thousand objects donated by numerous builders and designers around the country, various organizations, as well as the Beijing National Library. Organizers decided to divide the exhibition between the Shanghai Museum and the nearby China National Aviation Association Building. Objects were eventually divided into six main categories; these included blueprints, models, tools, physical building materials, photographs, and literature.

The exhibition's opening, originally scheduled for April 9, 1936, was ultimately pushed back until April 12 due to logistical delays (figure 8.3). Nevertheless, it managed to attract several thousand people, thanks in part to a fairly comprehensive multilingual advertising campaign.[26] The exhibition concluded one week later with a roundtable discussion of twenty participants, including Liang Sicheng, Zhu Qiqiao, Shen Yi, Ye Gongchuo, Li Dazhao, Guan Gongsheng, and Dong Dayou. It was estimated that more than four thousand people visited the exhibition each day, making it both a popular and financial success.[27] Unfortunately, existing visual evidence of the exhibition is limited to a pictorial overview provided by an April 1936 issue of the *Builder*. Through its limited collection of photographs, one can still discern the wide temporal and typological variety of architecture-related objects and images included (figure 8.4). Imperial architectural examples ranged from a collection of Zhou-era roof tiles to a number of individual architectural monuments in Beijing, including the Tiantan Altar, several South Lake Fengyue pavilions, as well as the Forbidden City's Qianqiu Pavilion and a sample Palace Corner Tower. Drawings and models helped to re-create for visitors an array of imperial-era architectural treasures few had been able to visit. Juxtaposed with these was Republican-era material, including a model of concrete equipment provided by the Fuji Construction Company and a number of renderings of Nanjing's most recent or planned constructions, including its stadium, museum, and an electricity-generating factory. An image of at least one foreign-designed building, F. G. Ede's Pudong Guild Headquarters, suggests the event was not restricted to Chinese-designed projects.

FIGURE 8.3. Cover, *Chinese Architectural Exhibition Proceedings* (Zhongguo jianzhu zhanlanhui huikan) (1936), Special Collections, Shanghai Library ([2019] 1057).

Reviews of the exhibition from the time offer experientially based accounts that allow for a partial reconstruction of its general layout and format.[28] Upon entering the museum, visitors were greeted by a model of the Dule Monastery, a Liao-era wooden construction located in Hebei. The model was flanked on either side by models of Zhou and Qin dynasty roof tiles, glass tiles, and Longwen water pipes. Adjacent to them were hung the extensive results of the Society for Research of Chinese Architecture's comprehensive field surveys, including blueprints, photographs, and various elevations of the Yingxian pagoda in Shanxi, Hangzhou's Liuhe pagoda, the Summer Palace in Beijing, and the Dingxing stone column and Anji bridge, both located in Hebei, among other examples. Alongside these archaeological findings were displayed contemporary building projects by the Tushui and Jitai engineering companies. Beyond these were positioned several previously noted models of Beijing's best-known imperial landmarks.

The second floor featured architectural models and blueprints of the Greater Shanghai Plan, including the Mayor's Building, Zhongshan Hospital, the city library, museum, a model housing village, and the airport expansion plans at Longhua. Visitors could also study various blueprints and photographs of

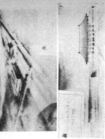

中國建築展覽會特刊

FIGURE 8.4.

Objects from an architectural exhibition, Shanghai, 1936. Reprinted from *Jianzhu yuekan* 4, no. 3 (1936), University of Hong Kong Libraries.

projects undertaken by members the Society of Chinese Architects, including the aforementioned Pudong Guild Headquarters as well as designs for a new apartment building on Tibet Road. Images of the Shanghai-Hangzhou and Nanjing-Shanghai railroads, too, were displayed there. A miscellaneous variety of projects sent in from architects and engineers around the country filled another room located off of the building's second-floor lobby, including photographs of the Tsinghua and Dongbei University campuses, for example, as well as several buildings constructed in Hankou. The exhibition highlighted several books detailing modern interior design as well as classic styles of Chinese architecture, along with examples of building products manufactured by China's largest architectural and engineering firms, including the Huaxin Cement Company, Dazhong Brick and Tile, and Xingye Steel.[29]

Inclusivity and equivocality, of a professional, thematic, geographic, stylistic, as well as temporal nature, marked the event as an unprecedented and encyclopedic synthesis of what organizers imagined as China's architectural history. The breadth of the collection was essential to its meaning, both as spectacle and narrative. More than three hundred photographs, elevations, and sections, ten models, and sixty blueprints of imperial Chinese architecture, collected by the Society for Research of Chinese Architecture, composed the exhibit. Interspersed within them was a spectrum of contemporary works donated by members of the Shanghai Architectural Society, the Society of Chinese Architects, and the Chinese Engineering Society, among other organizations. Republican public housing projects coexisted with Qing-era imperial treasures, with no apparent prioritization concerning objects or their broader organization into any kind of perceptible hierarchy.[30] There is little evidence to suggest there was any overarching thematic, formal, or chronological synchronicity binding the exhibition together apart from a shared place of origin—China.

This common thread rendered the event a curatorial exercise in state building. As the first major museum exhibition in China devoted exclusively to architecture, the event helped to reframe architecture as an essential tool in the literal and metaphorical construction of the nation. Following decades in which selected images and objects of China circulated abroad to illustrate the country's history and market its commercial opportunities, Shanghai's architectural exhibition laid claim over the entire trajectory of China's architectural history and, with it, Chinese architectural production in general. In this respect, the show's legacy is distinct from those of other national exhibitions such as the 1929 *National Art Exhibition*, for example.[31] In architecture, to be modern implied a degree of abstraction and universalism, but it also connoted themes of technical advancement and progress considered essential to the state's development. Pairing selected examples of aesthetic, formal, and spatial antecedents in China's architectural history with current Republican building construction presented Nationalist building efforts as a worthy and natural successor to an architectural heritage in the process of being unearthed by loyal Republican architects, academics, and scholars. More generally, it produced a progressive, uninterrupted trajectory of China's architectural past, present, and future.

The event also made clear that China's architectural community had little choice but to pursue the Nationalist agenda, particularly in relation to the government's efforts to rejuvenate Chinese society through the New Life Movement.[32] As Du Yangeng argued in the exhibition's catalogue: "At a time in which the will and spirit of the people is depressed, reinvigorating ancient Chinese culture enlivens the idea of the Chinese people. . . . Using either Western or traditional architecture won't change the dishonor that has befallen China. What is needed is the preservation of China's cultural essence in combination with the pursuance of particular international trends. That is the only proper way."[33] Organizers hoped visitors would converge upon the displays highlighting China's own architects and engineers, recognize their unsung contributions to society, and leave inspired and cognizant of a Chinese architectural history denied them by the Orientalist undertow of events such as the Chicago World's Fair. In a pamphlet promoting the event, National Central University's Architecture and Engineering Department underscored the revisionism at the event's heart: "Solemn and majestic, not inferior to Europe; architecture has not always been valued as a topic of study, and associated with the construction worker's life of toil. But the architectural object's realization depends upon the architect's skillful plans."[34] In a country hampered by political and social fragmentation, the exhibition presented an expanded spatial and visual continuum through which China could be seen as inviolate and whole, with the architect positioned as an essential contributor to the effort.

CURATING THE PAST, ENVISIONING THE FUTURE

The impulse to craft a unified Chinese architectural narrative through the exhibitionary format was more than simply a by-product of some collective desire within China's architectural community to organize themselves and honor the country's building industry. It was an active effort to consolidate competing conceptions of China and its architecture around a shared set of architectural, and by extension national, values. A 1936 article coauthored by Wu Jingqi and Lu Qianshou several months after the exhibition contributed to these efforts by mapping the emergence of three distinct design strategies in China, the roots of which were based upon the architectural antecedents displayed in Shanghai. The first, known as a "return to tradition" (*fugu*), represented a call for a greater understanding of imperial Chinese architecture prior to the experimentation advocated by figures like Liang. This approach recognized the inherent contradictions in the transnational claims made by foreign-derived exhibitionary and modernist praxes. This position was exemplified by

Xu's own winning proposal for the Nanjing Capital Museum, which relied extensively on strict Liao- and Song-era architectural ratios and measurements, evoking the mimetic attention to China's architectural past evidenced in the Golden Temple's reconstruction. It seemed to emphasize the overarching significance of cultural nationalism at the expense of any particularly modernist, socially progressive agenda.

The "search for the new" (*qiuxin*) represented a more substantive engagement with architectural modernism and eventually was embraced by designers like Fan Wenzhao, Guo Yuanxi, and Tong Jun. In June 1934, for example, a Guo-penned article lamented the superficial application of Chinese ornament to otherwise utilitarian structures like factories, shops, and public housing projects in favor of more economic, rational means of expression.[35] In a famous 1937 polemic, Tong exhorted Chinese architects to reconcile themselves to the flat roof, declaring that "the temple roof definitely has had its day. At present, classical Chinese architecture has nothing to offer to the modern building except surface ornamentation, and as the enduring and sublime qualities in architecture rest with structural values alone, it requires little imagination to foresee the rapid and universal adoption of the international (or modernistic) style in steel and concrete."[36] Although this faction's predilection for the formal aspects of modernism may have implied a rejection of the Nationalist government, Guo and Tong each would go on to write modern histories of Chinese architecture that attempted to reconcile the modern principles with traditional Chinese building practices.[37] Even in their embrace of modernism, these figures could not completely ignore a collective vision of the nation.

A "compromise" (*zhezhong*) of architectural eclecticism advocated by Wu represented the most politically palatable option.[38] It offered an amalgamation of modern materials and Chinese ornament not unlike earlier fusions of Beaux-Arts and Chinese architectural traditions. The position also acknowledged the nationalist ideology upon which the government's authority seemed to hinge while seeking new opportunities for international engagement and uniquely Chinese expressions of modernity. Ultimately, however, this path attempted to subsume modernism within the overarching project of nationalism, even as its capitulation to dominant architectural trends in Europe, North America, and Japan also exposed theoretical roots of China's modern architectural identity in conflicted feelings of inadequacy and failure.[39] Collectively, these three positions would continue to define the theoretical parameters of China's architectural discourse until the Japanese invasion of Shanghai on July 7, 1937.

Both the exhibition and the discourse that followed remain as artifacts of consolidation in the modern history of Chinese architecture. As forms of architecture, they evince belief on the part of China's architectural community in the discipline's ability to usher the country into a notion of modernity at a time in which the state appeared unable to do so. What that modernity looked like in architectural terms remained contested, though it was clear that China's architects were working to identify a normative expression acceptable both to China and the world at large—an architecture that would transcend the country's immediate extraterritorial history without abandoning China's architectural past or the modern world order.

In their efforts to authoritatively define and limit Chinese architecture's aesthetic and discursive possibilities, China's architectural community sought to buttress an embattled Chinese nation and its image through a more determined articulation of the cultural, spatial, and legal contours of the state. Identifying a univocal architectural articulation for China thus contributed to the literal and figural construction of the state itself. Extraterritoriality, and the architectural objects it produced, was a central motivating factor in this endeavor. Those architects who rejected modernism as inappropriate for China did so on the basis of its foreignness relative to China's own imperiled architectural traditions, fragments of which they worked to assemble into a new yet familiar aesthetic through occasions such as the Shanghai exhibition and their own design work. Even Chinese advocates of modernism felt compelled to qualify and distance this new, liberative kind of international architecture from the exploitative realities of the international treaty port experience. Desire to address the visual, and by extension, physical discordance of the treaty port through a more legible architectural aesthetic linked these distinctive groups together. Building for China a new reality that would transcend the country's historical failures and humiliations was paramount. It proved an unsuccessful dream under the Republican regime, but one that, with its impulses toward control and collectivity, anticipated the eventual emergence of another, new China.

Epilogue

A RETURN TO ORDER

FOLLOWING World War II, and over the course of the 1940s, Shanghai's charged extraterritorial energy was gradually drained and replaced with a new revolutionary vigor. The Shanghai Municipal Council continued to operate within the International Settlement until 1942, when its Allied-affiliated members resigned their seats in the face of Japanese control. On January 11, 1943, representatives from the British and American governments signed the Treaty for the Relinquishment of Extraterritorial Rights in China, and the Regulation of Related Matters in Chongqing and Washington, DC, respectively. Vichy France handed over the French Concession to Japan's Wang Jingwei–led puppet Nationalist government on June 5, 1943. Collectively, these events signaled the end of one hundred years of judiciary exceptionalism in China and the principles of laissez-faire capitalism in whose name the system had been rationalized.

Ideas about governance dominated postwar Republican-era architectural discourse in China. Prior to the war, figures like Liang Sicheng and Tong Jun relied upon characterizations of China's treaty ports as visually and spatially chaotic to advocate for the establishment of a new and necessary architectural order in China. In a 1938 essay tracing a broad history of foreign influence on Chinese architecture, for example, Tong Jun, an advocate of modernism himself, noted that "the 'foreign' buildings or *Yang lou*, as Yuan Mei [1716–1797] called it in one of his poems on Canton, ceased to be a curiosity and became a familiar sight after the 'treaty ports' had been thrown open to foreigners. Gradually foreign architects came to plan and supervise foreign-owned buildings in these ports, while the Chinese craftsmen served merely as builders and laborers. Large Chinese cities, Shanghai particularly, present a riotous spectacle of architectural styles of all nations and all periods—a phenomenon that greatly confuses the observer today."[1] Following the war, however, Liang, Tong, and others began to reevaluate the conceptual value of a singular visual expression of modern Chinese architecture, particularly in relationship to public architecture.[2] Prewar emphasis placed on a building's aesthetics had overshadowed basic necessities of governing through design, including proper consideration as to where to place particular edifices, the imposition of height limits, the relationship between buildings and public space, and land tax collection. Implicit in each of these concerns was the need for greater state control over society and the economy in the wake of a devastating world war and the influence of ongoing civil strife between the country's Nationalist and Communist factions.

Modernization remained an elusive goal as the country continued its search for a new national architecture amid postwar rebuilding efforts, economic crisis, and looming civil war. In Shanghai, reconstruction was hampered by a lingering sense of physical and administrative fragmentation. "Shanghai now lacks the force, derived from a common purpose and from common principles, that a city must have if it is going to amount to anything," wrote Christopher Rand in the *New Yorker* in 1948. "If things keep on as they are, Shanghai can look forward to more lawlessness, more riots, more traffic snarls, more Eastern scorn for Western gadgets, more confusion over whether speech is free or not, more recriminations, more chaos, and more decay. Barring a return of foreign control, which is unlikely, this train of dissolution may possibly continue until the city is ruined and deserted."[3] Of course, Shanghai was never deserted, and just one year later, following the formal establishment of the People's Republic of China on October 1, 1949, a single political authority finally claimed undivided rule over the city. The Communist government appropriated fifteen thousand foreign properties in the city; some but not all were nationalized in the name of China's socialist liberation. Key architectural landmarks, particularly along the Bund, were transformed into Chinese Communist Party (CCP) offices. A series of new urban plans introduced in 1950, 1951, 1953, and 1956, 1958, and 1959 sought to impose new, socialist-inspired discipline upon the city.[4]

Despite these changes, some still detected in Shanghai a hint of its extraterritorial atmosphere. Dick Wilson, former editor of the *Far Eastern Economic Review*, was surprised to discover "a relatively relaxed atmosphere" existing within the city upon his arrival in 1964, with at least six hundred foreign freighters docking at the port every year.[5] Communist overseers, meanwhile, worked hard to purge the city of its extraterritorial specter. Speaking at a 1954 speech at an International Meeting of Architects sponsored by the Association of Polish Architects, the Penn-trained Chinese architect Yang Tingbao (1901–1982) derisively referred to Shanghai as a "a city of another type" within the history of Chinese urbanism that "developed blindly, in a spontaneous and unorganized manner . . . with no connection between the communal management of these three zones. The plan of the roads was different. . . . Even the electrical current was different: 220 volts and 110 volts. . . . Although in some places particular buildings are well planned, nevertheless as a result of a lack of unified planning the town as a whole does not, from the urbanistic point of view, constitute a totality and is in a state of chaos."[6]

Treaty port–era Shanghai was one of the most populous and dynamic cities of the twentieth century, yet it maintains a phantom-like presence in the history of modernism, in large part because it has historically been considered little more than a disorganized, chaotic environment shaped by imperialistic greed and opportunism. For example, Le Corbusier's visionary 1929 modernist polemic *The City of To-Morrow* includes several maps of imperial-era Beijing but none of Shanghai's extraterritorial landscape. Ironically, Le Corbusier used Beijing's plan to subvert the ideological aim of extraterritoriality and the treaty port system. "Compare this plan [of Beijing] with that of Paris, a little further on," Le Corbusier urged his readers. "And we Westerners felt called on to invade China in the cause of *civilization!*"[7] Le Corbusier, like his eighteenth-century forebears, was entranced by the formal regularity and spatial discipline on display in the imperial Chinese capital and the possibilities it held for modern, rational city planning.[8] Architects and planners around the world were certainly aware of Shanghai, and a number of projects proposed or completed there were featured in well-known architectural journals around the world over the course of the 1930s and 1940s, including *Architectural Forum*, *Progressive Architecture*, *Kokusai-Kentiku*, *Journal of the Royal Institute of British Architects*, *Architecture d'aujourd'hui*, and *Architect and Building News*, among others.[9] Nevertheless, Shanghai did not grab the imagination of international design vanguards in the same way as Beijing. In many respects, Shanghai's fragmented palimpsest of national and ethnic interests seemed to offer a disorienting glimpse of the kind of fragmented urbanism European and North American architects and planners wanted to avoid—a sprawling metropolis without a plan, propelled unpredictably outward by the forces of internationalism, industrialization, and capitalism. "Shanghai has often been discussed as a city without a past," explained the social activist Bruno Lasker of the American Council Institute of Pacific Relations in 1940. "Today it may seem to have no future. . . . A city is the fixed abode of most of those who inhabit it, and its first function is to provide for their safety and the order conduct of their affairs. But it remains an armed camp if it does not include also the concentration of economic, administrative, and cultural functions for an area extending at least over a radius equivalent to a convenient day's journey."[10]

Shanghai's extraterritorial environment has taken on new significance in light of the crises within which modern, postmodern, and contemporary architecture and urbanism seem continually mired, particularly in relationship to international capital.[11] In 1949, the Republican Chinese government fled its Communist rival for Taiwan, where it eventually established one of the world's first export processing zones (EPZ) in Gaoxiong in 1966 designed to promote export-oriented industries from foreign countries by offering a relatively unregulated climate for industrial production.[12] The CCP later embraced a similar strategy beginning in 1980 when, facing imminent ideological as well as financial bankruptcy, it loosened its grip on a handful of carefully selected ports along its southeastern coast in the interest of economic liberalization. These four special economic zones—Shenzhen, Zhuhai, Xiamen, and Shantou—were imagined as new urban environments where unprecedented forms of socialist Chinese-foreign market experimentation could take place. More recently, China has begun to export these urban economic zoning models around the world, including Southeast Asia, the Middle East, South America, and the African continent. China is certainly not alone in employing this paradigm; the free zone embodies the "world-city template" de rigueur through which developing economies attract local and foreign investment by offering favorable tax policies for which most of the country's residents are not eligible.[13] Yet China promotes its own "economic cooperation" zones as distinctive insofar as they are somehow less intrusive and more responsive to the needs of their less developed partners. More generally, the Chinese government continues to promote a general principle of political "noninterference" in its dealings with the African continent to ensure that China's presence does not disrupt preexisting systems of governance, though determining the particular legal and spatial dimensions of such noninterference remains difficult.[14] Architecture's role in these spaces is also an open question.

The jurisdictional and spatial exceptionalism in Shanghai looms large in today's post-9/11 world, when perceptions of crises have compelled governments to establish what the Italian philosopher Giorgio Agamben has theorized as "the state of exception"; a paradigm of rule that is "neither external nor internal to the juridical order, and the problem of defining it concerns precisely a threshold, or a zone of indifference, where inside and outside do not exclude each other but rather blur with each other."[15] Shanghai epitomized these kinds of urban conditions, and its architectural history may be best understood as a series of individualized architectural parts in perpetual dialectical relation to the uncertain shifts of a new global order. Architectural analysis reveals a uniquely contested kind of civic experience in Shanghai—a distinctive urban geography fashioned by local and international forces, with particular sets of economic as well as diplomatic considerations behind them. Compromised by struggles not only between indigene and foreigner, but between sojourning nationals and the broader governmental interests working to adapt to shifting interpretations of the state, Shanghai illuminates the intersections between architecture, urban space, and international law, and the subjectivities and temporalities at work in sovereignty as both a modern political and spatial project.

The legacy of extraterritoriality continues to echo in China's architectural and political economic discourses today. Chinese Communist Party leaders routinely invoke the importance of national sovereignty to China's success amid the perceived constraints of international law, in particular the calls made to the country's political establishment to acknowledge certain theoretically universal human rights. Architecturally, monuments rooted in abstracted imperial-era Chinese forms, including overscaled roofs and courtyard-like aggregations of buildings, strain to reinforce China's political and cultural autonomy. Yet architecture also gives form to the ambiguous and, at times, accidental space produced through international engagement. As current perceptions of the relationship between physical territory and political sovereignty continue to change in China and around the world, architecture will remain an important means by which the formal and conceptual parameters of these as yet unseen conditions may be measured and understood.

NOTES

INTRODUCTION

1   Medhurst, *General Description of Shanghae and Its Environs*, 147.

2   Medhurst, *General Description of Shanghae and Its Environs*, 148.

3   Archer, "Character in English Architectural Design," 339–71.

4   Over the course of the mid- to late nineteenth and early twentieth centuries, more than one hundred ports and landlocked cities in China, Japan, and South Korea found themselves reimagined as treaty ports pried open for international commercial exchange by unequal treaties and controlled by the ever-present threat of foreign military action (Nield, *China's Foreign Places*, 1–22).

5   One of the most persistent myths concerning Shanghai's establishment as a treaty port was the transformative significance of British merchants to its development from a small fishing village into an international trading hub (see, for example, *All about Shanghai and Environs*, 1).

6   The French Concession adopted the same system as the International Settlement for additional territory acquired in 1899 and 1914 (Mou, "Land, Law and Power," 297).

7   Fishel, *The End of Extraterritoriality in China*, 5; Yuan, *Jindai Zhongguo zujie shigao*, 1–20.

8   "Homicides in China," 38.

9   For a history of the *huiguan*, see Belsky, *Localities at the Center*.

10 Hevia, *Cherishing Men from Afar*, 29–56.

11 Here, I am indebted to Dell Upton's analysis of the "republican spatial imagination" at work in early nineteenth-century America (Upton, *Another City*).

12 Scully, *Bargaining with the State from Afar*, 11.

13 Wakeman and Yeh, eds., *Shanghai Sojourners*, 267–68.

14 Zhang, ed., *Jindai Shanghai chengshi yanjiu*, 19–27.

15 Goodman, *Native Place, City, and Nation*, 50. See also Liang, *The Shanghai Taotai*, 146; Bickers, "Shanghailanders," 161–211; Scully, "Prostitution as Privilege," 855–83; Zhang, *The City in Modern Chinese Literature and Film*.

16 See Goodman and Goodman, "Introduction: Colonialism and China," 1–22; Jackson, *Shaping Modern Shanghai*, 2; Osterhammel, "Semi-colonialism and Informal Empire

in Twentieth-Century China," 290–314; Shih, *The Lure of the Modern*; and Rogaski, *Hygienic Modernity*, 18–21.

17 Nield, *China's Foreign Places*, 6–9.

18 Cited in Mitchell, *Colonising Egypt*, 33.

19 Cassel, *Grounds of Judgment*, 6.

20 Huber, *Channelling Mobilities*, 73.

21 Wilson, *The Domination of Strangers*, 8–9.

22 See, for example, Denison and Guang, *Building Shanghai*; Qian, *Bainian huiwang*; Wu, *Shanghai bainian jianzhu shi, 1840–1949*; and Xue, *Waitan de lishi he jianzhu*.

23 Rogaski, *Hygienic Modernity*; Wu, *Shanghai bai nian jianzhu shi, 1840–1949*; Henriot, *Shanghai, 1927–1937*, 229–41.

24 See, for example, Denison and Guang, *Modernism in China*; Kuan and Rowe, *Architectural Encounters with Essence and Form in Modern China*; Cody, Steinhardt, and Atkin, eds., *Chinese Architecture and the Beaux-Arts*; and Liang, *Mapping Modernity in Shanghai*.

25 See Yue, *Shanghai and the Edges of Empires*.

26 Hay, "Painting and the Built Environment in Late-Nineteenth-Century Shanghai," 90.

27 Brewer and Hellmuth, *Rethinking Leviathan*, 21.

28 Shih, *The Lure of the Modern*, 35.

29 Wasserstrom, "Cosmopolitan Connections and Transnational Networks," 206–24.

30 Hyde, *Constitutional Modernism*, 13–14.

31 For a history of the Qing dynasty's segregation of Beijing, for example, see Naquin, *Peking*, 287–301.

32 Cassel, *Grounds of Judgment*, 15–38.

33 Johnson, *Shanghai*; Esherick and Rankin, *Chinese Local Elites and Patterns of Dominance*.

34 Agamben, *What Is an Apparatus? And Other Essays*; Foucault, *The Foucault Effect*; Hevia, *The Imperial Security State*; Mehta, *Liberalism and Empire*; Wilson, *The Domination of Strangers*.

35 Aihwa Ong has employed the term *variegated sovereignty* to describe the new kinds of economically and politically integrative strategies at work in China today (Ong, "The Chinese Axis," 69–96).

36 Walzer, "On the Role of Symbolism in Political Thought," 198.

37 Fu, Guo, Liu, Pan, Qiao, and Sun, *Chinese Architecture*, 1–9.

38 Wheatley, *The Pivot of the Four Quarters*; Steinhardt, *Chinese Imperial City Planning*; Xu, *The Chinese City in Space and Time*.

39 Nieuhof et al., *An Embassy from the East-India Company of the United Provinces*, 157.

40 Nieuhof et al., *An Embassy from the East-India Company of the United Provinces*, 203. See also Markley, *The Far East and the English Imagination, 1600–1730*, 110–20.

41 Le Comte, *Memoirs and remarks*, 56, 72.

42 Abramson, *Building the Bank of England*, 17–18; Shoemaker, "The London 'Mob' in the Early Eighteenth Century," 273–304; Ziskin, *The Place Vendôme*, 94; Ottenheym, "Amsterdam 1700," 119–20.

43 Du Halde, *Description géographique*, 34. See also Navarrete, *The Travels and Controversies of Friar Domingo Navarrete*.

44 Jenkins, *A Taste for China*; Porter, *Ideographia*.

45 Defoe, *The Farther Adventures of Robinson Crusoe*, 164.

46 Appleton, *A Cycle of Cathay*, 96. See also Attiret, *A Particular Account of the Emperor of China's Gardens near Pekin*, 6.

47 Chambers, *Designs of Chinese Buildings*, preface.

48 Fairbank, *Trade and Diplomacy on the China Coast*, 39–53.

49 Smith, *An Inquiry into the Nature and Causes of the Wealth of Nations*, 59.

50 Carter, *The Builder's Magazine*, 199. See also Soane and Watkin, *Sir John Soane*, 149–50; Legh, *The Music of the Eye*, 7; and Fergusson, *A History of Architecture in All Countries*.

51 Freeman, *A History of Architecture*, 51.

52 Barrow, *Travels in China*, 93, 101. See also Gützlaff and Reed, *China Opened*.

53 Porter, *Ideographia*, 235.

CHAPTER 1: THE ARCHITECTURE OF EXTRATERRITORIALITY

1 "Success in Afghanistan and China," *Times* (London), November 23, 1842, 5.

2 Davis, *The Chinese*, 2:21, 23.

3 "Notices of Shanghai," 468.

4 Chambers, *A Treatise on Civil Architecture*, i.

5 Keay, *The Honourable Company*. For a history of the Company's dealings in China and its impact upon Anglo-American trade, see Fichter, *So Great a Proffit*.

6 King, *The Bungalow*, 18.

7 For a comprehensive architectural history of the Factories in Guangzhou, see Farris, *Enclave to Urbanity*. See also Garrett, *Heaven Is High*.

8 Tiffany, *The Canton Chinese*, 214.

9 Wong, *Global Trade in the Nineteenth Century*, 28–29.

10 Wong, *Global Trade in the Nineteenth Century*, 84–88.

11 Phipps, *A Practical Treatise on the China and Eastern Trade*, 105.

12 Carroll, "Slow Burn in China," 35–55.

13 Davis, *The Chinese*, 2:22.

14 Hunter, *The "Fan Kwae" at Canton before Treaty Days, 1825–1844*, 26.

15 Robert Thom to William Jardine, March 11, 1836, cited in Yorke, "The Princely House," 18. In referring to the firm as "Jardine Matheson," I conform to the company's archival nomenclature, though shifting branding strategies and legal definitions of the term partnership prompted several English- and Chinese-language variations of the firm's name over time (Wong, *Global Trade in the Nineteenth Century*, 166–67, 170–72).

16 Yorke, "The Princely House," 18.

17 Slade, *Narrative of the Late Proceedings and Events in China*, 99–100.

18 Wood, *Sketches of China*, 69.

19 Cited in Blake, *Jardine Matheson*, 123.

20 See "Opium War with China," *Times* (London), April 25, 1840, 5; and Blue, "Opium for China: The British Connection." 30–47.

21 Macaulay, *Speeches by the Rt. Hon. Thomas Babington Macaulay*, 371.

22 Downing, *The Fan-qui in China*, 2:53.

23 Ouchterlony, *The Chinese War*, preface.

24 Pottinger to Lord Aberdeen, November 3, 1843, in Jarman, *Shanghai Political and Economic Reports, 1842–1943*, 1:450.

25 "Treaty with China," *Times* (London), November 23, 1842, 4.

26 Port, *The Houses of Parliament*, 21–22.

27 Ouchterlony, *The Chinese War*, 304.

28 Skinner, *The City in Late Imperial China*; Xu, *The Chinese City in Space and Time*.

29 See Cao, "Yihuan beichang ji"; and "China and Afghanistan," *Times* (London), November 25, 1842, 3.

30 Pottinger to Lord Aberdeen, June 9, 1843, in Jarman, *Shanghai Political and Economic Reports*, 1:337.

31 Smith, "Ritual in Ch'ing Culture," 281–310.

32 Xu, *The Chinese City in Space and Time*, 86.

33 Liang, *The Shanghai Taotai*, 8.

34 Ayscough, "Cult of the Ch'eng Huang Lao Yeh," 143. See also Liu, *Shanghai cheng-huang miao daguan*.

35 The magistrate was also known to clear the City God Temple of all people on occasion, enter the compound by himself, and pass the night there praying for divine advice concerning particularly difficult administrative decisions (Ayscough, "Cult of the Ch'eng Huang Lao Yeh," 153).

36 Zito, "City Gods, Filiality, and Hegemony in Late Imperial China," 334; Pan, *Shanghai fosi daoguan*. For a history of temples and their role in Qing-era urbanism, see Naquin, *Peking: Temples and City Life*, 622–78.

37 Wheatley, *The Pivot of the Four Quarters*; Freedman, "Geomancy," 5–15; Meyer, "Feng-Shui of the Chinese City," 138–55.

38 Cummins, *A Question of Rites*, 224–51; Liang, *Xu Guangqi nianpu*.

39 Johnson, *Shanghai*, 126.

40 Johnson, *Shanghai*, 202–6.

41 Medhurst, *General Description of Shanghae and Its Environs*, 110.

42 Fortune, *Three Years' Wanderings in the Northern Provinces of China*, 108.

43 Medhurst, *General Description of Shanghae and Its Environs*, 48–49. See also Goodman, *Native Place, City, and Nation*, 18–20.

44 Nyíri, "Extraterritoriality." For an analysis of the relationship between legal states of exception and political standards of sovereignty, see Agamben, *State of Exception*, 1–31.

45 See Cassel, *Grounds for Judgment*, 67; Dillon, *China's Muslim Hui Community*, 11–26; and Shih, *Extraterritoriality: Its Rise and Its Decline*, 80–81.

46 Shih, *Extraterritoriality: Its Rise and Its Decline*.

47 "Senex," *Canton Miscellany* 1, no. 2 (January 1831): 67, 73.

48 Mitchell, *Rule of Experts*, 78.

49 Fishel, *The End of Extraterritoriality in China*, 3; Keeton, *The Development of Extraterritoriality in China*, 155–72.

50 Cassel, *Grounds of Judgment*, 54.

51 The United States agreed upon terms with China for consular jurisdiction on August 11, 1848, followed by Belgium in December 1851; France in July 1852; Spain in November

1854; the Netherlands in July 1871; Denmark in February 1895; Japan in 1899; Norway in March 1906; and Sweden in June 1909 (Cassel, *Grounds of Judgment*, 6).

52 Cassel, *Grounds of Judgment*, 47.

53 Home, *Of Planting and Planning*, 9–37.

54 Glover, *Making Lahore Modern*, 28.

55 Pottinger to Lord Aberdeen, June 24, 1842, in Jarman, *Shanghai Political and Economic Reports*, 1:232. For histories of British colonial urban policy in South Asia, see Perera, *Decolonizing Ceylon*, 45–48; Glover, *Making Lahore Modern*, 17–25; and Kidambi, *The Making of an Indian Metropolis*, 33.

56 Balfour to Pottinger, March 29, 1844, in Jarman, *Shanghai Political and Economic Reports*, 1:593.

57 Staunton, *Remarks on the British Relations with China*, 42.

58 Montalto de Jesus, *Historic Shanghai*, 24.

59 Davis, *The Chinese*, 2:26–27.

60 At least one American resident in Shanghai would later identify the treaty port as representing "the New Orleans of the Empire" (Taylor, *The Story of Yates the Missionary*, 46).

61 Pottinger to Lord Aberdeen, June 24, 1842, in Jarman, *Shanghai Political and Economic Reports*, 1:232.

62 Balfour, *Memorandum of the Services of Captain Now Major George Balfour*, 3–6.

63 Note, Robertson, June 12, 1878, F.O. 17/789, National Archives, Kew.

64 Johnson, *Shanghai*, 187.

65 Medhurst, "Reminiscences of the Opening of Shanghai to Foreign Trade," 81.

66 Lang, *Shanghai Considered Socially*, 18.

67 Lane-Poole and Dickins, *The Life of Sir Harry Parkes*, 122.

68 Montalto de Jesus, *Historic Shanghai*, 30.

69 Johnson, *Shanghai*, 192.

70 Johnson, *Shanghai*, 191. One *mu* is equivalent to .06 hectares.

71 Balfour to Pottinger, December 21, 1843, in Jarman, *Shanghai Political and Economic Reports, 1842–1943*, 1:574.

72 Godfrey, "Some Notes on Tenure of Land in Shanghai," 49.

73 Maybon and Fredet, *Histoire de la Concession Française de Changhai*, 16.

74 Tiffany, *The Canton Chinese*, 225.

75 Montalto de Jesus, *Historic Shanghai*, 36.

76 Heard to Heard, January 30, 1855, "Heard Family Business Records, 1754–1898," Baker Business Historical Collections, *Mss: 766 1754–1898, Harvard University.

77 Lanning, "Names and Nicknames of the Shanghai Settlements," 91.

78 Medhurst, "Reminiscences of the Opening of Shanghai to Foreign Trade," 83.

79 Cunynghame, *The Opium War*, 40. See also Herbert, *Pioneers of Prefabrication*, 40–74; King, *Colonial Urban Development*, 90; and White, *Prefabrication*, 12–20.

80 King, *The Bungalow*, 15.

81 The shipping of prefabricated iron warehouses from London to Africa, the West Indies, as well as California dates back to the 1840s (Hitchcock, *Early Victorian Architecture in Britain*, 516).

82   Heard to Heard, March 29, 1856, "Heard Family Business Records, 1754–1898," Baker Business Historical Collections, *Mss: 766 1754–1898, Harvard University.

83   Chattopadhyay, "Blurring Boundaries," 165.

84   Maynard, *Architecture in the United States, 1800–1850*, 167–218.

85   Nelson, *Architecture and Empire in Jamaica*, 79–88.

86   Chattopadhyay, "Blurring Boundaries," 154–79; Metcalf, *An Imperial Vision*, 6; Victoir, "Hygienic Colonial Residences in Hanoi," 231–50.

87   Nilsson, *European Architecture in India, 1750–1850*, 180–82.

88   In 1850, for example, the roof of the settlement's first Trinity Church collapsed after its supporting brickwork gave way, weakened by a constant deluge of waste rainwater pouring upon the structure's main beam from a misplaced waterspout ("Falling in of the Roof of Trinity Church," *North-China Herald [NCH]*, August 3, 1850, 1). Subsequent notes will refer to both the *North-China Herald and Market Report* (1867–69) and the *North-China Herald and Supreme Court and Consular Gazette* (1870–1941) as *NCH*.

89   Walker to Woodgate, June 8, 1857, FO 17/271, National Archives, Kew.

90   In 1929, F. L. Hawks Pott noted that Shanghai's earliest structures "were adapted to a tropical climate, and the builders seemed to have had only the four months of hot weather in mind, and to have overlooked the need of sunshine in their homes during the rest of year" (Pott, *A Short History of Shanghai*, 22).

91   Memorandum on repairs required for the Consular Buildings at Shanghai, July 11, 1857, FO 17/271, National Archives, Kew.

92   See Lanning and Couling, *The History of Shanghai*, 252; and Macpherson, *A Wilderness of Marshes*, 23.

93   Minutes of Public Meeting of Foreign Renters of Land, July 11, 1854, "Collection of pamphlets relating to Land Tenure in the Foreign Concessions, 1845–1883," Special Collections, University of Hong Kong Libraries. Years later, Theodore Sopher, a resident expert on Shanghai real estate and local newspaper columnist within the city in the 1920s and 1930s, noted that "Shanghai encouraged enterprising merchants to build solid, modern, English, Greco-styled edifices for the purpose of providing luxurious offices and flats. These massive structures, of fortress-like thickness, were in fact too durable, and, with the rapid progress of modern science and invention, suffered from obsolescence and inefficiency" (Sopher and Sopher, *The Profitable Path of Shanghai Realty*, 320).

94   Maybon and Fredet, *Histoire de la Concession Française de Changhai*, 16.

95   Hancock, *Citizens of the World*, 102–3.

96   In 1847, for example, Arthur Dallas, Shanghai representative for Jardine Matheson & Company, was asked by the Alliance Fire Assurance Company to provide sketches of his newly constructed compound for the purposes of fire insurance. Dallas promised that "The buildings are all detached of solid brick work with tiled roofs and generally in spacious compounds, some few of the buildings have wooden pillars built in the walls. I look upon both houses and godowns in Shanghai as safe risks" (Dallas to Agents' Alliance Fire Assurance Office, September 9, 1847, JM/C43, Volume 1, General Letters, Shanghai to Hong Kong, Jardine Matheson Archive, Cambridge University Library).

97 Henriot, "The Shanghai Bund in Myth and History." 11–13; Politzer, "The Changing Face of the Shanghai Bund," 64–81.

98 Mathur, *India by Design*, 80–108; Eaton, *Mimesis across Empires*.

99 Alcock to Davis, March 10, 1848, in Jarman, *Shanghai Political and Economic Reports*, 2:237.

100 Morse, *International Relations of the Chinese Empire*, 1:355.

101 Balfour to her Britannic Majesty's Subjects, notification, December 5, 1844, in Jarman, *Shanghai Political and Economic Reports*, 1:641.

102 Land Regulations, November 29, 1845, "Collection of pamphlets relating to Land Tenure in the Foreign Concessions, 1845–1883," Special Collections, University of Hong Kong Libraries.

103 Kotenev, *Shanghai, Its Mixed Court and Council*, 4–5.

104 Cassel, *Grounds of Judgment*, 15–39.

105 Henri Brunschwig has argued that following Napoleon's defeat at Waterloo in 1815, France came to see colonization as a "vital element in its national prestige, particularly in the power-relationship with Britain" (Brunschwig, *French Colonialism, 1871–1914*, 182).

106 Maybon and Fredet, *Histoire de la Concession Française de Changhai*, 62.

107 Bergère, *Shanghai*, 12.

108 "Heard Family Business Records, 1754–1898," Baker Business Historical Collections, *Mss: 766 1754–1898, Harvard University. The practice was also evident in Guangzhou, where independent British traders working with the British East India Company occasionally reappeared within the city as representatives of other countries (see Keay, *The Honourable Company*, 453).

109 Johnson, *Shanghai*, 238.

110 "History of the Northern Lodge of China, No. 570, E. C." See also Gratton, *Freemasonry in Shanghai and Northern China*.

111 *NCH*, December 4, 1852, 70.

112 Ma, *Shanghai xinwenshi (1850–1949)*, 14.

113 Jarman, *Shanghai Political and Economic Reports*, 2:418.

114 For example, the premises provided no married quarters for the vice consul or interpreter. The interpreter was also required to share a toilet with his servants (Coates, *The China Consuls*, 93).

115 *NCH*, March 6, 1852, 126.

116 Morse, *The International Relations of the Chinese Empire*, 356.

117 *NCH*, March 6, 1852, 126.

118 Morse, *The International Relations of the Chinese Empire*, 1:349.

119 Robertson estimated that ten years in Shanghai's climate did the damage of "thirty to forty years" in more temperate regions ("Memorandum on repairs required for the Consular Buildings at Shanghai, July 11, 1857," FO 17/271, National Archives, Kew). British interpreter T. T. Meadows (1851–1868) would also complain that the consul's furnishings, which included an iron safe, an iron money-chest, a writing table, three "nearly worn out" rattan chairs, and a clock, left the premises below the standard considered "decent in the most mercantile establishment" (Coates, *The China Consuls*, 93).

120 "The S.V.C. Parade," *NCH*, December 28, 1870, 464; "A Plea for Light and Air—Letter to Editor," *NCH*, 3 August 3, 1912, 336.

121 Alcock to Davis, June 14, 1847, in Jarman, *Shanghai Political and Economic Reports*, 2:152.

122 Taylor, *The Story of Yates the Missionary*, 46; Platt, *Autumn in the Heavenly Kingdom*, 74.

123 Medhurst, *General Description of Shanghae and Its Environs*, 49.

124 Medhurst, *General Description of Shanghae and Its Environs*, 49.

CHAPTER 2: COMMEMORATION AND THE CONSTRUCTION OF A PUBLIC SPHERE

1 See Cranston, "Shanghai in the Taiping Period," 151.

2 Taylor, *The Story of Yates the Missionary*, 90.

3 Reilly, *The Taiping Heavenly Kingdom*.

4 Platt, *Autumn in the Heavenly Kingdom*, 358.

5 Scarth, *Twelve Years in China*, 238.

6 Morse, *In the Days of the Taipings*, 181.

7 Parkes to Wade, December 24, 1864, in Jarman, *Shanghai Political and Economic Reports*, 5:226–34.

8 Alcock, *The Capital of the Tycoon*, 38.

9 Johnson, *Shanghai*, 279–91.

10 Montalto de Jesus, *Historic Shanghai*, 60. See also Johnson, *Shanghai*, 286–91.

11 Following the Chinese imperial army's assault of three foreign residents, American and British merchants ignored their consuls' respective orders and joined forces to create the Shanghai Volunteer Corps. On April 3, 1854, the battalion clashed with Qing troops in the much-mythologized and diplomatically embarrassing Battle of Muddy Flat ("Three Letters from H. E. the Taoutae to the Foreign Consuls," *NCH*, April 5, 1854, 1; see also Alcock to Bonham, April 5, 1854, in Jarman, *Shanghai Political and Economic Reports*, 3:255–62).

12 See Fortune, *Three Years' Wanderings in the Northern Provinces of China*, 127; Smith, *A Narrative of an Exploratory Visit to Each of the Consular Cities of China*, 153.

13 Morse, *In the Days of the Taipings*, 150–51.

14 "China," *New York Daily Tribune*, January 14, 1854, 6.

15 Wang, Sheng, and Shanghai tongshe, *Taiping jun, xiaodaohui luan hu shiliao*, 151.

16 Maybon and Fredet, *Histoire de la Concession Française de Changhai*, 133; *NCH*, October 27, 1855, 50.

17 "The Present Aspect of the City of Shanghae and Its Suburbs," *Friend of China and Hong Kong Gazette*, March 14, 1855, 83.

18 Wang, Cao, and Shanghai tongshe, *Taiping jun, xiaodaohui luan hu shiliao*, 155–56.

19 Alcock to Bowring, June 5, 1854, in Jarman, *Shanghai Political and Economic Reports*, 3:400.

20 Alcock to Bowring, June 5, 1854, in Jarman, *Shanghai Political and Economic Reports*, 3:400.

21 *NCH*, June 3, 1854, 174.

22   Montalto de Jesus, *Historic Shanghai*, 103.

23   Marshall to Marchy, July 26, 1853, "Despatches from U.S. Ministers to China," R59 M92, National Archives and Records Administration, College Park, MD.

24   Minutes, "Public Meeting of Foreign Renters of Land," July 11, 1954, in Jarman, *Shanghai Political and Economic Reports*, 3:412.

25   Alcock to Bowring, July 30, 1852, in Jarman, *Shanghai Political and Economic Reports*, 2:690.

26   Other consular representatives on the council included David Olyphant King of the British firm Smith, King and Company and consular representative for Prussia; Thomas C. Beale, British founder of Dent, Beale and Company and consular representative for Portugal; and William Hogg, British merchant with Lindsay and Company and the consul for Hamburg (see Minutes, "A Public Meeting of Foreign Renters of Land," July 11, 1854, in Jarman, *Shanghai Political and Economic Reports*, 3:541).

27   Minutes, "A Public Meeting of Foreign Renters of Land," July 11, 1854, in Jarman, *Shanghai Political and Economic Reports*, 3:541.

28   Maybon and Fredet, *Histoire de la Concession Française de Changhai*, 134.

29   "Notice," *NCH*, August 1, 1857, 2.

30   *NCH*, January 3, 1857, 90.

31   Robertson to Bowring, dispatch, December 31, 1855, in Jarman, *Shanghai Political and Economic Reports*, 3:662.

32   Alcock to Bowring, dispatch, May 6, 1854, in Jarman, *Shanghai Political and Economic Reports*, 3:302.

33   Shanghai's first Board of Inspectors comprised Arthur Smith, translator for the French consulate; Thomas Francis Wade, British vice consul to Shanghai; and Lewis Carr, of the American legation (see Hart and Bruner, *Entering China's Service*, 161–68).

34   Robertson to Bowring, dispatch, September 4, 1855, in Jarman, *Shanghai Political and Economic Reports*, 3:656.

35   "Minutes of Meeting of *Daotai* and the three Treaty Power Consuls," June 29, 1854, in *Documents Illustrative of the Origin, Development and Activities of the Chinese Customs Service*, 50.

36   Hay, "Painting and the Built Environment in Late-Nineteenth-Century Shanghai," 70.

37   Meadows to Lord Russell, dispatch, February 19, 1861, in Jarman, *Shanghai Political and Economic Reports*, 4:334.

38   British consul Robertson and American consul Murphy were both apparently amenable to the scheme, but it was denied by Daotai Lan (Letter, Heard to Heard, April 30, 1855, "Heard Family Business Records, 1754–1898," Baker Business Historical Collections, *Mss:766 1754–1898, Harvard University).

39   *NCH*, August 25, 1866, 134.

40   Platt, *Autumn in the Heavenly Kingdom*, 151.

41   Flynt, *Taking Christianity to China*, 295.

42   Medhurst to Bruce, June 26, 1861, in Jarman, *Shanghai Political and Economic Reports*, 4:420.

43   Wang, *Yingruan zazhi*, 6:7a–b.

44   Report, Bruce, January 22, 1863, in Jarman, *Shanghai Political and Economic Reports*, 5:18.

45 Liang, "Where the Courtyard Meets the Street," 484.

46 Cody, "Minguo shiqi Shanghai de zhuzai fandgi chanye," 263–74.

47 Medhurst to Bruce, June 26, 1861, in Jarman, *Shanghai Political and Economic Reports*, 4:420.

48 Report, Bruce, January 22, 1863, in Jarman, *Shanghai Political and Economic Reports*, 5:18.

49 See Des Courtils, *La Concession Française de Changhaï*, 10.

50 Seward to Davis, May 25, 1874, "Consular Dispatches, 1847–1906," RG 59 M112, National Archives and Records Administration, College Park, MD.

51 Committee of Landrenters to Bruce, June 12, 1863, in Jarman, *Shanghai Political and Economic Reports*, 5:93.

52 Medhurst, "Memorandum on the naming of the Shanghae streets," *NCH*, May 24, 1862, 85. Consulate Road became known as Beijing Road; Park Lane was renamed Nanjing Road; Rope Walk Road became Jiujiang Road; and Customs House Road was called Hankou Road. Bridge Street was renamed Sichuan Road; and Barrier Road became Henan Road.

53 Ge, *Shanghai fanchang ji*, 89.

54 Burlingame (quoting Cunningham) to Seward, June 25, 1863, "Despatches from U.S. Ministers to China," RG 59 M92, National Archives, College Park, MD

55 Savage, *Standing Soldiers, Kneeling Slaves*, 4–7. See also Musgrove, *China's Contested Capital*, 20–21.

56 Meyer-Fong, *What Remains*, 188.

57 Bickers, "Moving Stories," 829.

58 Maybon and Fredet, *Histoire de la Concession Française de Changhai*, 129.

59 Morse, *In the Days of the Taipings*, 155.

60 See, for example, Moore, *La Mortola*, 54.

61 "Interment of French Officers and Marines in the New Mausoleum," *NCH*, March 17, 1855, 131.

62 Vidler, "X Marks the Spot: The Obelisk in Space," 221–32.

63 "La France en Chine," *L'Illustration*, July 5, 1856, 15–17.

64 French officials attributed the slight to the fact that evidence of French assistance in the conflict did not conform to the "dignity" of the Qing Empire (see Maybon and Fredet, *Histoire de la Concession Française de Changhai*, 136).

65 See, for example, *NCH*, December 24, 1864, 105. See also "The Civil War in China," *New York Times*, August 15, 1864, www.nytimes.com/1864/08/15/news/the-civil-war -in-china.html.

66 Carr, *The Devil Soldier*, 300–302.

67 Li, *Li Hongzhang quanj*, 1:97–99.

68 Li, *Li Hongzhang quanj*, 1:491–92.

69 Li, *Li Hongzhang quanji*, 2:18–19.

70 *NCH*, August 25, 1866, 134.

71 *NCH*, August 25, 1866, 134.

72 *NCH*, August 25, 1866, 134.

73 Bickers, "Moving Stories," 831.

74 In his famous 1905 serial short story *A Flower in a Sinful Sea* (Niehai Hua), for example, Zeng Pu (1872–1935) describes a horse carriage of Chinese visitors looking "over
to the bronze statue of Gordon, on the further bank of the river, and then they went
on until they came to a tablet of stone which they realized must be the Obelisk." In
fact, they likely saw the statue of Sir Harry Smith Parkes (1828–1885), which was
erected in 1890 (see Zeng, *Niehai hua*, 8).

75 "Notification," March 27, 1863, in Jarman, *Shanghai Political and Economic Reports*, 5:17.

76 "Notification," March 27, 1863, in Jarman, *Shanghai Political and Economic Reports*, 5:17.

77 Winchester to Alcock, March 24, 1866, in Jarman, *Shanghai Political and Economic
Reports*, 5:504.

78 *NCH*, November 26, 1864, 190.

79 "Meeting of Foreign Consuls to discuss measures for security of the Foreign Settlements, Shanghai," November 20, 1863, in Jarman, *Shanghai Political and Economic
Reports*, 5:154–55.

80 "Meeting of Foreign Consuls to discuss measures for security of the Foreign Settlements, Shanghai," November 20, 1863, in Jarman, *Shanghai Political and Economic
Reports*, 5:154–55.

CHAPTER 3: BUILDING A SHANGHAI PUBLIC

1 Yeh, "Where Is Shanghai?," 506–11. See also Wasserstrom, *Global Shanghai, 1850–
2010*, 38–39.

2 Metcalf, *An Imperial Vision*, 2.

3 Banno, *China and the West, 1858–1861*.

4 See, for example, Wright, "John Fryer and the Shanghai Polytechnic," 1–16.

5 *Chouban yiwu shimo-Tongzhi*, vol. 419: 396a.

6 In 1861, for example, Zeng implored the Xianfeng Emperor to purchase foreign
steamships not simply to improve waterborne traffic but to acclimatize Chinese people to the new technology with the aim of denying British and French militaries their
perceived superiority (*Zeng Guofan quanji*, 3:948a).

7 Kennedy, "Li Hung-Chang and the Kiangnan Arsenal, 1860–1895," 198.

8 Elman, "Naval Warfare and the Refraction of China's Self-Strengthening Reforms
into Scientific and Technological Failure, 1865–1895," 291.

9 Yu, *Chongxiu Shanghai xianzhi*, 1:39.

10 Li, Guo, and Dai, *Li Hongzhang quanji*, 1:630–31.

11 *Gezhi huibian* 5, no. 1 (Spring 1890): 1.

12 Wright, *The Last Stand of Chinese Conservatism*, 211–12.

13 Wright, "John Fryer and the Shanghai Polytechnic," 6.

14 Pong, "Keeping the Foochow Navy Yard Afloat, Government Finance and China's
Early Modern Defence Industry," 121–52. See also Elman, *On Their Own Terms*,
359–77.

15 Giquel, *The Foochow Arsenal, and Its Results*, 14–15.

16 "Correspondence," *NCH*, March 12, 1874, 225.

17 "Object Lessons," *NCH*, April 30, 1870, 301.

18   Organizers hoped a "small Crystal Place" would be erected on open space outside the completed building ("Opening of the Shanghai Polytechnic Institution," *NCH*, June 24, 1876, 617; "The Polytechnic," *NCH*, October 14, 1875, 378).

19   Wright, "John Fryer and the Shanghai Polytechnic," 9; Biggerstaff, "Shanghai Polytechnic Institution and Reading Room," 136–38.

20   Cassel, *Grounds of Judgment*, 64.

21   Kotenev, *Shanghai*, 75.

22   Stephens, *Order and Discipline in China*, 44.

23   "Public Meetings: The Polytechnic Report," *NCH*, Oct. 14, 1875, 378.

24   Maybon and Fredet, *Histoire de la Concession Française de Changhai*, 245.

25   Freemasonry was an important factor in the domination of British architecture and engineering in treaty ports like China. Early participants in Shanghai's construction included Freemasons like Thomas Walker and George Strachan, employees of Jardine Matheson in Hong Kong. Strachan was responsible for, among other buildings, the Hong Kong Club (1845), Jardine Matheson's first Shanghai compound (1849), Shanghai's first British Consular Offices (1852), and Shanghai's first Masonic Hall (1852) ("History of the Northern Lodge of China, No. 570, E.C.").

26   Conseil d'administration municipale de la Concession Française à Shanghai, ed., "Compte rendu de la gestion pour l'exercise, 1866–7, et budget, 1867–8," PER 373, Les Archives diplomatiques du Ministère des Affaires étrangères, Nantes. See also Shanghai jianzhu shigong zhiweihui, *Dongfang "Bali,"* 66–69.

27   Kowsky, "The Architecture of Frederick C. Withers (1828–1901)," 83–107; Van Zanten, "Second Empire Architecture in Philadelphia," 9–24.

28   "The Hotel Municipal," *NCH*, February 13, 1934, 250.

29   Macgowan, "Modes of Keeping Time Known among the Chinese," 607–12.

30   Adas, *Machines as the Measure of Men*, 248–49.

31   Ye, *Dianshizhai Pictorial*, 72–73. As early as 1852, public subscriptions were collected to purchase a turret clock in the British Settlement ("Notice," *NCH*, July 28, 1854, 220).

32   Ge, *Shanghai fanchang ji*, 90.

33   Ge, *Huyou zaji*, 56.

34   "The French Municipal Council Report," *NCH*, May 28, 1870, 375.

35   Maybon and Fredet, *Histoire de la Concession Française de Changhai*, 245.

36   Gordon and Mossman, *General Gordon's Private Diary of His Exploits in China*, 72. See also Platt, *Autumn in the Heavenly Kingdom*, 285.

37   "Inauguration of a Statue to Admiral Protet," *NCH*, December 13, 1870, 427–28.

38   "Inauguration of a Statue to Admiral Protet," *NCH*, December 13, 1870, 427–28.

39   Zhang, *Dianshizhai huabao*, 13:146.

40   Maybon and Fredet, *Histoire de la Concession Française de Changhai*, 209.

41   Ge, *Shanghai fanchang ji*, 90.

42   Two wings were subsequently added by the Chinese construction company Wangsong Ji, including five rooms and kitchens for the employees of the Municipal Engineer and Secretary in 1877 (see Conseil d'administration municipale de la Concession Française à Shanghai, ed., "Compte rendu de la gestion pour l'exercise, 1877, et budget, 1878," PER 373, Les Archives diplomatiques du Ministère des Affaires étrangères, Nantes).

43 The decision seems to have been primarily motivated by financial considerations, as Kingsmill and Whitfield were charging more than one hundred thousand taels for their work (see Maybon and Fredet, *Histoire de la Concession Française de Changhai*, 303).

44 Qtd. in Kingsmill's report, March 18, 1867, "Hôtel consulaire: Construction du premier hôtel consulaire, 1863–1867; Reconstruction de l'hôtel consulaire, 1894–1896," Series B, Carton 28, Conseil d'administration municipale de la Concession Française à Shanghai, Les Archives diplomatiques du Ministère des Affaires étrangères, Nantes. See also Maybon and Fredet, *Histoire de la Concession Française de Changhai*, 303.

45 See Schmidt to consul general, October 12, 1865, "Hôtel consulaire: Construction du premier hôtel consulaire, 1863–1867; Reconstruction de l'hôtel consulaire, 1894–1896," Series B, Carton 28, Conseil d'administration municipale de la Concession Française à Shanghai, Les Archives diplomatiques du Ministère des Affaires étrangères, Nantes.

46 Bonneville to Brenier de Montmorand, March 10, 1867, "Hôtel consulaire: Construction du premier hôtel consulaire, 1863–1867; Reconstruction de l'hôtel consulaire, 1894–1896," Series B, Carton 28, Conseil d'administration municipale de la Concession Française à Shanghai, Les Archives diplomatiques du Ministère des Affaires étrangères, Nantes.

47 Kidner's report, March 11, 1867; Kingsmill's report, March 18, 1867, "Hôtel consulaire: Construction du premier hôtel consulaire, 1863–1867; Reconstruction de l'hôtel consulaire, 1894–1896," Series B, Carton 28, Conseil d'administration municipale de la Concession Française à Shanghai, Les Archives diplomatiques du Ministère des Affaires étrangères, Nantes.

48 Jackson, *Shaping Modern Shanghai*, 4.

49 "Correspondence Regarding Municipal Government," *NCH*, January 12, 1867, 7.

50 Jackson, *Shaping Modern Shanghai*, 63.

51 "The Landrenters' Meeting," *NCH*, September 3, 1864, 143; "Landrenters' Meeting," April 25, 1865, in Jarman, *Shanghai Political and Economic Reports, 1842–1943*, 5:298. In 1862, several residents had put forth a proposal to declare Shanghai as an independent "free city" under the protection of Great Britain, France, the United States, Russia, and China (Kotenev, *Shanghai*, 12).

52 "Landrenters' Meeting," April 25, 1865, in Jarman, *Shanghai Political and Economic Reports, 1842–1943*, 5:298.

53 For a history of the International Settlement's waterworks, see Macpherson, *A Wilderness of Marshes*, 98–104.

54 "The Municipal Council," *NCH*, September 10, 1864, 146.

55 "The Municipal Budget," *NCH*, July 16, 1864, 115.

56 Kingsmill arrived in Shanghai via Hong Kong and Guangzhou, where he had designed a number of buildings, including Christ Church (1862) and the British consulate (1865), both with Carl Brumstedt. In Shanghai, Kingsmill designed the Royal Asiatic Society building, eventually completed in 1872. Kingsmill was also actively involved in Freemasonry. He first joined the Masons in Shanghai in 1865 and subsequently served in a number of positions within the organization, including Past Master of the Northern Lodge of China in 1870, a First Principal in the Zion Royal

Arch Chapter in 1875 and 1879, and a Deputy District Grand Master from 1886 to 1893. Kidner was a Scottish designer who arrived in Shanghai in 1864 to realize George Gilbert Scott's plans for the Holy Trinity Cathedral. He became a Freemason in 1865 and worked as a building inspector for the Shanghai Municipal Council in 1869. He was elected a Royal Institute of British Architects (RIBA) Fellow in 1876 (see Denison and Yu, *Building Shanghai*, 52; and Gratton, *Freemasonry in Shanghai and Northern China*, 85–88, 146–50).

57 Kidner remained the most vocal proponent of the public competition and insisted that he did not speak from any "selfish motive." Others doubted a local architect would be willing to produce drawings for so large a building without charging an excessive amount ("Shanghai Municipal Council Report for the Year Ending March 31, 1866, and Budget for the Year Ending March 31, 1867," 20–21).

58 See, for example, Coomans, "A Pragmatic Approach to Church Construction in Northern China at the Time of Christian Inculturation," 89–107.

59 Wright and Cartwright, *Twentieth Century Impressions of Hongkong, Shanghai, and Other Treaty Ports of China*, 378.

60 The tael was the standard Qing silver currency equivalent to one Mexican silver dollar. Minutes of Annual Meeting of Subscribers to the British Episcopal Church, January 25, 1866, F.O. 17/454, National Archives, Kew.

61 Minutes of Annual Meeting of Subscribers to the British Episcopal Church, January 25, 1866, F.O. 17/454, National Archives, Kew.

62 Denison and Yu, *Building Shanghai*, 52.

63 Cohn, "Representing Authority in Victorian India," 47–69.

64 Minutes of Annual Meeting of Subscribers to the British Episcopal Church, January 10, 1866, F.O. 17/454, National Archives, Kew. Over the course of Scott's career, he was responsible for the designs and/or construction of the exterior of London's Foreign and India Offices in 1858, its Colonial Office (1870–74), as well as its Home Office (1870–75). See also Port, *Imperial London*, 2–3; and Bremner, *Imperial Gothic*, xiii, 203.

65 Bremner, "Nation and Empire in the Government Architecture of Mid-Victorian London: The Foreign and India Office Reconsidered," 703–42.

66 "How Shanghai Strikes a Stranger," *NCH*, November 16, 1887, 541.

67 Bailey, *Leisure and Class in Victorian England*, 77.

68 See "History of the Northern Lodge of China, No. 570, E.C."

69 "Notice," *NCH*, July 7, 1870, 5.

70 Gratton and Ivy, *The History of Freemasonry in Shanghai and Northern China*, 1.

71 Medhurst to Underwood, March 4, 1863, in Gratton, *Freemasonry in Shanghai and Northern China*, 4–5.

72 "Notice," *NCH*, July 7, 1870, 5.

73 "Laying the Foundation Stone of the New Masonic Temple at Shanghai," *Illustrated London News*, November 18, 1865, 487.

74 "The New Masonic Hall," *NCH*, September 28, 1867, 272.

75 Winchester to Alcock, April 3, 1867, report, F.O. 17/480, National Archives, Kew.

76 "Shanghai," *NCH*, July 5, 1867, 142.

77 Merchants in China to Secretary of State, August 1, 1863, RG 59 M92, National Archives and Records Administration, College Park, MD. A subsequent report issued

in 1867 by American Consul Seward reinforced a perceived correlation between the lack of American influence in the country and its disorganized consular service (see George F. Seward and United States Consulate, *The United States Consulates in China*).

78   Sun and Chen, "Cong minzu taidu kan Wusong tielu de xingfa," 60–71. See also Pong, "Confucian Patriotism and the Destruction of the Woosung Railway, 1877," 647–76.

79   Hübner, *Promenade autour du monde*, 190.

80   Hübner, *Promenade autour du monde*, 190.

81   Hübner, *Promenade autour du monde*, 191–92.

82   Li, *Memoirs of Li Hung Chang*, 305.

83   Lang, *Shanghai Considered Socially*, 25.

84   Medhurst to Underwood, March 4 1863, in Gratton, *Freemasonry in Shanghai and Northern China*, 4–5.

85   "Shanghai Volunteer Corps," *NCH*, September 8, 1870, 182.

86   Shanghai General Chamber of Commerce to Granville, September 30, 1870, RG59 M112, National Archives and Records Administration, College Park, MD.

87   Andrews to Wells, November 6, 1877, RG59 M112, National Archives and Records Administration, College Park, MD.

88   "Concessions de Changhai, Juillet-Decembre 1874," Series 260, Ministère des Affaires étrangères, Missions étrangères, Paris. See also "Riot on the French Concession," *NCH*, May 9, 1874, 406.

CHAPTER 4: REGULATION, PROFESSIONALIZATION, AND RACE

1   See, for example, King, *Colonial Urban Development*; and Dutta, *The Bureaucracy of Beauty*.

2   Issar, "Codes of Contention," 164–88.

3   Wright, "Tradition in the Service of Modernity," 291–316; Stoler, "Rethinking Colonial Categories: European Communities and the Boundaries of Rule," 134–61; Bhabha, "Of Mimicry and Man," 152–62.

4   Yue, *Shanghai and the Edges of Empires*.

5   Michie, *The Englishman in China during the Victorian Era*, 1:256.

6   "Foreign v. Chinese Homes," *NCH*, September 22, 1871, 710.

7   See Andrews, "On the Slopes of an International Volcano," *New York Times*, November 11, 1906, SM3.

8   In 1910, more than nineteen thousand rats were exterminated within the International Settlement alone (Shanghai jianzhu shigong zhiweihui, *Dongfang "Bali,"* 39).

9   Shanghai was not alone in this respect; similar laws were implemented in Hong Kong over roughly the same period (Bremner and Lung, "Spaces of Exclusion," 235–45).

10   See "Minutes of the Public Meeting of Foreign Renters of Land," July 11, 1854, in Jarman, *Shanghai Political & Economic Reports*, 3:537.

11   Parkes to Wade, December 24, 1864, in Jarman, *Shanghai Political & Economic Reports*, 5:233.

12   Tang, Shen, and Qiao, *Shanghai shi*, 219.

13   Kotenev, *Shanghai, Its Mixed Court and Council*, 14.

14 "Land Renters' Meeting," *NCH*, April 29, 1865, 66. Settlement officials initially passed a 20 percent tax on house rentals, which was later revised to 16 percent. The collected revenue was divided between the settlement and the Qing government until the end of the Taiping hostilities in 1866, at which point the Qing government no longer taxed Chinese residents living within the International Settlement ("Retrospect of the Year," *NCH*, January 16, 1864, 11).

15 Following one devastating fire in September 1860, a *North-China Herald* editorial suggested that foreign and Chinese entrepreneurs not be allowed "to build wooden tenements which are a standing danger to human life, simply because they pay better and are built cheaper than houses made after the European model of brick or stone" (*NCH*, October 13, 1860, 162).

16 "Retrospect of the Year," *NCH*, January 16, 1864, 11.

17 Jackson, *Shaping Modern Shanghai*, 29. Between 1866 and 1870, it was estimated 463 Chinese homes had been on fire versus thirteen foreign houses. In one 1881 blaze, more than one thousand Chinese homes were destroyed in the French Concession despite the efforts of a volunteer fire brigade in 100-degree temperatures (Shanghai shidang'anguan, ed., *Gongbu ju dongshihui huiyi lu*, vol. 3, *1867–9*, 39; Pott, *A Short History of Shanghai*, 37; see also Smedley, "Chinese Buildings," 155).

18 "Foreign v. Chinese Homes," *NCH*, September 22, 1871, 710.

19 Shanghai zujie zhi bian zuan weiyuanhui et al., *Shanghai zujie zhi*, 565.

20 Shanghai Municipal Council, "Shanghai Municipal Council Report for the Year Ending December 31, 1878, and Budget for the Year Ending December 21, 1879," 11.

21 "Miscellaneous: Proposed Building Regulations," *NCH*, February 21, 1878, 188.

22 Shanghai Municipal Council, "Shanghai Municipal Council Report for the Year Ending December 31, 1899, and Budget for the Year Ending December 31, 1900," 185.

23 Shanghai zujie zhi bian zuan weiyuanhui et al., *Shanghai zujie zhi*, 565.

24 "Shanghai Municipal Council Report for the Year Ending December 31, 1903, and Budget for the Year Ending December 31, 1904," 340.

25 Yule, *Hobson-Jobson*, s.v. "Compradore," 243–44. See also Kingsmill, "Early Architecture in Shanghai," *NCH*, November 24, 1893, 825.

26 Michie, *The Englishman in China during the Victorian Era*, 1:246.

27 See Elvin, introduction to "The Gentry Democracy in Shanghai, 1905–1914," 1–16; and Carroll, *Between Heaven and Modernity*.

28 Hay, "Painting and the Built Environment in Late Nineteenth-Century Shanghai," 77; Yeh, *Shanghai Love*, 21–95.

29 Yeh, *Shanghai Love*, 46–47.

30 Wallpaper, for example, may have in fact originated in China (see Wisse, "Manifold Beginnings," 8–21).

31 Meihua'anzhu, *Shenjiang shengjing tushuo, juan xia*, 12–15.

32 "Shanghai Nanjing lu shangdian zhi zhuangkuang," 2.

33 "Shanghai Nanjing lu shangdian zhi zhuangkuang," 2.

34 Korigan, "Metiers chinois: Maçons et maçonnerie," *L'Echo de Chine*, December 23, 1909, 1.

35 "Building: Primitive Sanitation and the Vice of Comfort," *Shanghai Mercury*, April 17, 1929, 25.

36   "Shanghai Construit," *L'Echo de Chine*, July 23, 1903, 763. Prior to 1905 and the construction of the five-story Whiteway Laidlaw & Company headquarters, all of the buildings along Nanjing Road were approximately two to three stories. The first publicized mention of air-conditioning in Shanghai occurred in 1912 ("'Shanghai's Damp Atmosphere' from 'Christian Scientist,'" *NCH*, August 3, 1912, 319; see also "A Plea for Light and Air—Letter to Editor," *NCH*, August 3, 1912, 336).

37   A 1923 brochure asked potential tourists, "Do you know the city with two souls—the city where you can live in all the comfort and safety of the West, with the sound and the color and the mystery of the East, right around the corner?" (*Do You Know Shanghai?*).

38   *The Palace Hotel Guide to Shanghai*, 20.

39   Coomans, "Indigenizing Catholic Architecture in China," 125–44.

40   Wong, *Low Library*, 1–4. Buildings like Schereschewsky Hall were also imagined as models for other mission colleges and educational buildings around the country (*Sheng Yuehan daxue wushi nian shilüe, 1879–1929*, 10).

41   "Shanghai Municipal Council Correspondence, February-March 1907," U1-2-1207, Shanghai Municipal Archives.

42   See Mayne to Leveson, March 14, 1907, "Shanghai Municipal Council Correspondence, February-March 1907," U1-2-1207, Shanghai Municipal Archives.

43   Crinson, *Empire Building*, 10. For a broader discussion of race within the United States at the beginning of the twentieth century, see Guterl, "The New Race Consciousness," 307–52.

44   See Viollet-le-Duc, *Discourses on Architecture*, 473.

45   Robinson, *Architectural Composition*, 68.

46   Irving, *Indian Summer*, 42, 100–102.

47   See "A Closed Area for Foreigners," *NCH*, May 16, 1914, 547. See also Shanghai Municipal Council, "Shanghai Municipal Council Report for the Year Ending December 31, 1915, and Budget for the Year Ending December 31, 1916," 3B.

48   Bard to French Municipal Council, February 3, 1898, Conseil d'administration municipale de la Concession Française à Shanghai, ed., "Compte rendu de la gestion pour l'exercice, 1898, et budget, 1899," PER 373, Les Archives diplomatiques du Ministère des Affaires étrangères, Nantes.

49   Zheng, "Shanghai 'huayuan yangfang' qu de xingcheng he lishi tese," 34. See also Cherpitel, "Questions Municipale: L'Architecte," *L'Echo de Chine*, January 11, 1913, 1. In 1921, the Concession's Public Works Department restricted construction on Gong-guan ma, Aiduoya, Xiafei, Fuxu, and Bei'an Roads to Western-style buildings only.

50   Sabard, "L'Esthetique Shanghaienne," *L'Echo de Chine*, July 6, 1912, 197.

51   See Clear, "Presidential Address," 12.

52   Scully, *Bargaining with the State from Afar*, 152.

53   Cody, "The Woman with the Binoculars," 262–63.

54   See Gratton, *Freemasonry in Shanghai and Northern China*.

55   The 1903 Municipal Council's Annual Report stated that the new "foreign" building rules would restrict unregulated Chinese building activity and would "undoubtedly very much improve the character of buildings generally, more especially those erected under the supervision of Chinese" ("Shanghai Municipal Council Report for

the Year Ending December 31, 1903, and Budget for the Year Ending December 31, 1904," 182; see also "Société des Ingenieurs et Architectes," *L'Echo de Chine*, August 15, 1907, 1261).

56   Landale to Siffert, June 16, 1909, "Shanghai Municipal Council Correspondence, 1903–1938," U1-2-5857, Shanghai Municipal Archives.

57   See "Architects' Registration," *Journal of the Royal Institute of British Architects* 24 (1906): 1; and Levy, "The Professionalization of American Architects and Civil Engineers, 1865–1917."

58   Morrison, "Inaugural Address by President," 19.

59   "The Shanghai Society of Engineers and Architects: Rules Hong Kong," *NCH*, August 16, 1907, 370.

60   In 1911, the Society formally changed its name, asserting that "the architects of Shanghai have not supported this Society to the same extent that its engineers have" ("Annual General Meeting," 242–43). The Institute of Architects in China, meanwhile, was formed by seven original members, including William Dowdall, president; Walter Scott and Arthur Dallas, vice presidents; with A. E. Algar, I. Ambrose, Gilbert Davies, and R. B. Moorhead all serving as members.

61   "Shanghai Municipal Council Report for the Year Ending December 31, 1907, and Budget for the Year Ending December 31, 1908," 146.

62   Municipal Engineer's Report, June 12, 1907, "Shanghai Municipal Council Correspondence, 1903–1938," U1-2-5857, Shanghai Municipal Archives.

63   Siffert to Landale, April 19, 1909, "Shanghai Municipal Council Correspondence, 1903–1938," U1-2-5857, Shanghai Municipal Archives. Shanghai's consular authority subsequently advised that three non-British foreign architects be added to the group prior to the redrafting of any proposed rule changes, including Modest Marti, an architect of purported Spanish descent; C. Becker, a German engineer; and Chollot, the French Concession's municipal engineer. Rules for registration were eventually established in June 1908, with the Shanghai Municipal Council's approval occurring later that July. At a subsequent Consular Body meeting, however, it was determined any proposed changes to the Land Regulations, particularly with respect to professional registration, still constituted a potential British monopoly (Siffert to Landale, April 29, 1909, "Shanghai Municipal Council Correspondence, 1903–1938," U1-2-5857, Shanghai Municipal Archives).

64   See Carmichael to Shanghai Municipal Council Chairman, July 31, 1907, "Shanghai Municipal Council Correspondence, June–October 1907," U1-2-319, Shanghai Municipal Archives.

65   See "'Registration of Architects' Letter from 'Qualified,'" *NCH*, December 28, 1912, 883.

66   "'Registration of Architects' Letter to Editor," *NCH*, July 3, 1909, 57.

67   Secretary of Shanghai Municipal Council to Dowdall, April 5, 1913, "Shanghai Municipal Council Correspondence, 1903–1938," U1-2-5857, Shanghai Municipal Archives. The issue would again be raised in 1931, however, when it was proposed that a technical board be established by the Shanghai Municipal Council in consultation with the city's various technical and architectural societies, Chinese and foreign, to maintain and publish a yearly register of practicing civil engineers and architects in the

city (Berents to Harpur, March 20, 1931, "Shanghai Municipal Council Correspondence, 1903–1938," U1-2-5857, Shanghai Municipal Archives).

68 "Engineering Standards," *NCH*, December 23, 1904, 1424.

69 China eventually announced its adoption of the metric system in 1912, though it would not be implemented nationwide until after 1949 (Alder, *The Measure of All Things*, 339). For a history of China's imperial measurement systems, see Yang, *Zhongguo lidai chidu kao*.

70 Godfrey, "Registration of Architects and Civil Engineers," March 18, 1913, "Shanghai Municipal Council Correspondence, 1903–1938," U1-2-5857, Shanghai Municipal Archives.

71 See Hoang, *Notions Techniques sur la propriéte en Chine*, 9, 58.

72 For a brief account of the development of Shanghai's carpentry guilds, see Deng et al., *Shanghai bainian lueying*, 34.

73 Huang, "Songnan mengying lu," 111.

74 In 1868, for example, disagreement broke out among the city's Shanghai, Shaoxing, Ningbo, and Suzhou construction workers over the issue of salary standards within each building guild (Xue, *Shanghai waitan diming zhanggu*, 330). An agreement and merger was subsequently brokered by official Qing carpenter Zhu Bingshi, who became chairman of the newly integrated guild, though it would not last.

75 See "Yang Sisheng," *Sichuan xuebao* (July 1907): 5–6; "Yang Sisheng xuanbu Dongpu zhongxue zongzhi shu," *Sichuan xuebao* (July 1907): 5–7; Zhang, "Yang Sisheng xiaozhuan," *Shaonian* (June 1911): 19–21; "Gongjie huaren sishi," *Shenbao*, May 1, 1908, 3; Huang, "Xu Yang Sisheng xiansheng yanxing ji," *Shenbao*, May 11, 1908, 1; Xiang, "Ren jieke xie Yang Sisheng shengshuo," *Shenbao*, June 11, 1908, 7–10; Shen Enfu, "Chuansha Yang Sisheng muzhiming," *Zhonghua xuesheng jie*, June 25, 1915, 1–3. See also Huang, ed., *Yang Sisheng, Ye Chengzhong, Xiansheng Hezhuan*.

76 Huang, "Xu Yang Sisheng xiansheng yanxing ji," *Shenbao*, May 11, 1908, 1.

77 Rujivacharakul, "Architects as Cultural Heroes," 133.

78 Huang penned Yang's obituary, which was featured on the first page of *Shenbao*, Shanghai's most prominent Chinese-language newspaper ("Gongjie huaren sishi," *Shenbao*, May 11, 1908, 1).

79 Huang, "Songnan mengying lu," 111.

80 For a history of the rise of professionalism in Republican China, see Xu, *Chinese Professionals and the Republican State*.

81 Shanghai jianzhu shigong zhiweihui, *Dongfang "Bali,"* 4.

82 For example, the British architectural firm Atkinson and Dallas worked regularly with the contractor Zhang Jiguang, a Zhejiang native, and his firm, Flourishing Construction (Xiesheng Yingzao Chang), on projects such as the Fuli Company's headquarters (1905), the Daqing Bank (1907), and the Eastern Cooperative Bank (1911) (He, *Zhang Xiaoliang zhuan*, 31).

83 An 1847 issue of the *Builder* described the travails of Mr. Morson, who "sent to China for accurate drawings and descriptions of the principal druggist's shop in Canton. It was found difficult to obtain drawings which would clearly convey all that was desired, but not so to have a model made; and accordingly native artificers were

employed to construct, in small, an exact counterpart of a shop and house complete; and this is now in Mr. Morson's possession, and supplies information as to the construction of Chinese dwellings, which was not to be obtained at 'The Chinese Exhibition'" (*Builder*, March 6, 1847; see also Crossman, *The Decorative Arts of the China Trade*, 111).

84 "Technical Education in Shanghai," *NCH*, July 15, 1904, 122; "The Chinese Public School," *NCH*, November 18, 1904, 1136.

85 "Report of the Committee Appointed to Deal with the Subject of Technical Education in Shanghai," *Proceedings of the Society and Report of the Council, 1904–5*, 173. See also Mayne to Bland, December 30, 1904, "Shanghai Municipal Council Correspondence, December 1904-February 1905," U1-2-1184, Shanghai Municipal Archives. See Clear and Griffith, "Education and Training of Chinese Students in Engineering," 116.

86 Sopher, *The Profitable Path of Shanghai Realty*, 319.

87 *The Palace Hotel Guide to Shanghai*, 9. The first building in Shanghai to feature an elevator was the Russo-Chinese Bank, completed in 1902 (Chang, ed., *Daduhui cong zheli kaishi*, 203; see also Shanghai jianzhu shigong zhiweihui, *Dongfang "Bali,"* 78). Evidence suggests that the five-story Clarke Boarding House, constructed by Gratton, Scott and Carter in 1903, also featured an elevator ("Shanghai Construit," *L'Echo de Chine*, July 23, 1903, 763).

88 For example, the Palace Hotel was the site of the first International Narcotics Conference, held in Shanghai on February 26, 1909 ("The Opium Campaign," *NCH*, August 28, 1909, 486).

89 See Gore-Booth to the Shanghai Municipal Council, March 11, 1909, "Shanghai Municipal Council Correspondence, Palace Hotel, 1909–1936," U1-14-5970, Shanghai Municipal Archives.

90 Yan, "Shanghai zui gao zhi jianzhu," *Zhonghua shiye jie*, June 10, 1914, 1–4.

91 "Shanghai Municipal Council Correspondence, Palace Hotel, 1909–1936," U1-14-5970, Shanghai Municipal Archives.

92 "Shanghai Municipal Council Correspondence, Palace Hotel, 1909–1936," U1-14-5970, Shanghai Municipal Archives.

93 This involved putting a bamboo fence around the entire premises to prevent inspectors from entering the property until a solution was found to a particular problem. For example, listing in building caused by Shanghai's soft soil was a recurring issue. Shanghai jianzhu shigong zhiweihui, *Dongfang "Bali,"* 78.

94 *The Palace Hotel Guide to Shanghai*. See also "Shanghan huizhong lüguan wuxian dianji," *Waijiaobao*, July 31, 1909, 397.

95 Engineer and Surveyor to Secretary of the Shanghai Municipal Council, December 8, 1916, "Shanghai Municipal Council Correspondence, Palace Hotel, 1909–1936," U1-14-5970, Shanghai Municipal Archives.

96 Report, Godfrey, Municipal Engineer and Surveyor, January 10, 1910, in "Proposed Pagoda," *Municipal Gazette* 3, no. 111 (February 3, 1910): 25.

97 N. E. Cornish, "The President's Address," 22.

98 "Shanghai Municipal Council Report for the Year Ending December 31, 1910, and Budget for the Year Ending December 31, 1911," 272.

99   See, for example, Engineering Society of China, *Report of the Special Committee on Reinforced Concrete*.

100 "Shanghai Municipal Council Report for the Year Ending December 31, 1910, and Budget for the Year Ending December 31, 1911," 272.

101 Report compiled by the Municipal Engineer, March 7, 1910, "Shanghai Municipal Council Report for the Year Ending December 31, 1910, and Budget for the Year Ending December 31, 1911," 276.

102 Report compiled by the Municipal Engineer, March 7, 1910, "Shanghai Municipal Council Report for the Year Ending December 31, 1910, and Budget for the Year Ending December 31, 1911," 276.

103 As the chief engineer and surveyor Godfrey noted, "the fact that a permit is requested for the erection of a 'pagoda' does not alter the fact that it is a 'building,' and the question arises as to whether the Building Rules should be revised, and the height limit imposed by Article XLVIII either increased or deleted" (Report compiled by the Municipal Engineer, March 7, 1910, "Shanghai Municipal Council Report for the Year Ending December 31, 1910, and Budget for the Year Ending December 31, 1911," 276).

104 Landlords to the Shanghai Municipal Council, February 22, 1910, "Shanghai Municipal Council Report for the Year Ending December 31, 1910, and Budget for the Year Ending December 31, 1911," 276. The landlords included A. R. Burkill & Sons, E. D. Sassoon & Co., Simon A. Levy, Hanson, McNeill & Jones, Thos. R. Wheelock, Scott, Christie & Johnson, Ward, Probst & Co., Atkinson & Dallas, and Chen Chun-Hsieh.

105 "Shanghai Municipal Council Report for the Year Ending December 31, 1910, and Budget for the Year Ending December 31, 1911," 276.

106 For example, J. A. Denham, a British transplant and RIBA-registered architect, didn't feel the project was big enough ("Proposed Reinforced Concrete Pagoda in Shanghai," 89).

107 "Proposed Reinforced Concrete Pagoda in Shanghai," 89.

108 "The Pagoda," *NCH*, March 25, 1910, 690.

109 "The Ratepayers' Meeting," *NCH*, March 25, 1910, 680–82; "Ji najuan xiren huiyi jianzao gao ta shi," *Shenbao*, March 23, 1910, 2–6.

110 See Li, *Renwen Shanghai*, 102–11.

111 "The Revolution in China," *NCH*, January 6, 1912, 25.

112 Kang described a utopian future composed of dazzling, tastefully designed garden compounds filled with flowers, insects, and fish set atop soaring structures, where one could breathe fresh air and "swallow the clouds," surrounded by other fantastical jade towers. During Liang's 1903 trip to North America, for example, he remarked that whereas Beijing's stone dwellings often required a descent of several stone steps, creating the sensation that inhabitants lived underground, buildings in New York regularly reached ten to twenty stories high, with its tallest structure soaring thirty-three stories. In fact, the tallest building in New York at the time was the thirty-story Park Row building (Kang and Li, *Datong shu*, 359–60; Liang and Yang, *Xin dalu youji*, 274–75).

113 See Elliott, *The Manchu Way*, 2–8.

1   "Western Models or Chinese: Which Government Should China Choose?" *NCH*, March 7, 1914, 689.

2   Zhang, ed., *Jindai Shanghai chengshi yanjiu*, 62.

3   At the time, one yuan was equivalent to one Mexican silver dollar (Wang Jingyu, ed., *Zhongguo jindai gongye shi zilio*, 2:7–11).

4   Fewsmith, *Party, State, and Local Elites in Republican China*, 46.

5   Tong, "Has Extraterritoriality Outlived Its Usefulness?," 56.

6   "An Act Creating a United States Court for China and Prescribing the Jurisdiction Thereof," 234–38; Scully, *Bargaining with the State from Afar*, 143.

7   Heidenstam, "Shanghai—the Industrial and Commercial Metropolis?," 32.

8   "Engineering Society of China: Paper by Mr. Von Heidenstam," *NCH*, December 13, 1919, 706.

9   Stephens, *Order and Discipline in China*, 48.

10 Kotenev, *Shanghai*, 107; Cassel, *Grounds of Judgment*, 177.

11 In 1915, for example, Chinese officials proposed that the municipal council include several Chinese members to deal jointly with matters affecting Chinese in the whole settlement. Foreign officials countered that the settlement's existing land regulations precluded such inclusion, and a Chinese advisory board was created as a substitute ("Settlement Extension," *Shanghai Municipal Gazette*, March 4, 1915, 55–56).

12 "Chinese on the Council," *NCH*, September 23, 1911, 738.

13 Goodman, *Native Place, City, and Nation*, 16.

14 Andrews, "China's Relations with the United States," *New York Times*, November 25, 1906, SM5.

15 Korigan, "Metiers chinois: Maçons et maçonnerie," *L'Echo de Chine*, December 23, 1909, 1.

16 Crinson, *Rebuilding Babel*, 9–11.

17 See, for example, Kipnis, "Face," 119–48; and Zito and Barlow, *Body, Subject & Power in China*, 103–30.

18 Smith, *Chinese Characteristics*, 16–18; Hu and Lin, *China's Own Critics*, 127–31; Hevia, *English Lessons*, 177–78.

19 Kipnis, "Face," 130; Zito and Barlow, *Body, Subject & Power in China*, 103.

20 Goodman, *Native Place, City, and Nation*, 190.

21 McCormick, *Audacious Angles on China*, 82.

22 Hu and Lin, *China's Own Critics*, 127–31.

23 See Lu, *Qie jie ting zawen*, 98–100; Lu, Yang, and Yang, *Selected Works of Lu Hsun*, 4:129.

24 Lawrence and Schafer, "On the Surface," 4. See also Bohde, "Notes from the Field: Mimesis," 195–97.

25 Semper and Mallgrave, "The Development of the Wall and Wall Construction in Antiquity," 33–42.

26 Chatterjee, "Tectonic into Textile: John Ruskin and His Obsession with the Architectural Surface," 68–97.

27 Simmel, "The Aesthetic Significance of the Face"; Bohde, "Notes from the Field: Mimesis," 197.

28 One shop owner, afraid of losing his business's prominence along an avenue after the municipal council set its storefront farther back from the road, constructed a huge double arch of ornamental ironwork in an attempt to draw customers ("'Young China in the Maloo': Foreign Building in Fashion," *NCH*, October 26, 1912, 228).

29 "United States Should Buy Consular Property in China," *China Weekly Review*, May 3, 1924, 337.

30 Cohen, "American Perceptions of China," 66–67.

31 Schram, ed., *Mao's Road to Power*, 104.

32 *The Threatened Decline and Fall of Great Britain in China*, 17.

33 Chollot to Vissière, November 6, 1893, "Hôtel Consulaire: Construction du premier hôtel consulaire, 1863–1867; Reconstruction de l'hôtel consulaire, 1894–1896," Série B, Carton 28, Conseil d'administration municipale de la Concession Française à Shanghai, Les Archives diplomatiques du Ministère des Affaires étrangères, Nantes. Chollot was born in 1861 in France. He began his studies at l'École des Ponts et Chaussées before leaving school to travel to French-controlled Indochine and participate in the Sino-French War as a captain in the Second Regiment under General Joseph Joffre, the famed French engineer from Montpelier, as part of the Gallieni Mission. Chollot began his professional service as a municipal engineer in Port Arthur, or Lushankou, a Russian-administered treaty port, in 1886. There, he directed the construction of its shipping piers and dry slipways, a project for which he was ultimately decorated with the Order of St. Anne by Russia, a Cross of the Légion d'Honneur by France, and conference of the title of "Mandarin" by the Chinese government. In 1893, Chollot moved to Shanghai to replace the concession's retiring chief engineer Charles Blondin ("L'Arrivée du Comte de Martel à Shanghai," *Le Journal de Shanghai*, May 15, 1930, 4).

34 "Consulat General du Japon à Changhai," *L'Echo de Chine*, October 7, 1911, 549.

35 Scully, *Bargaining with the State from Afar*, 85–89.

36 Ge, *Huyou zaji*, 53.

37 "A New American Crusade: Exhibiting to Europe What Our Skill and Enterprise Accomplish," *New York Times*, January 26, 1902, WF4.

38 "Buildings," 56.

39 "American-Chinese Exposition," *New York Times*, January 7, 1899, 7. Americans were quick to realize the value in exporting model products abroad for promotion purposes. For example, two Oldsmobile automobiles were imported into Shanghai in 1902 (Burke, *My Father in China*, 224).

40 For a discussion on the role of "character" in the colonial context, see Stoler, "Rethinking Colonial Categories: European Communities and the Boundaries of Rule," 141.

41 Hunt, *The Making of a Special Relationship*, 217.

42 Scully, *Bargaining with the State from Afar*, 26.

43 "Land and Buildings for Consular Establishments in China, Japan, and Korea," House of Representatives Report 1109, RG 59, Entry 411, Foreign Service Buildings,

1914–43, Box 19, Buildings in the Orient, National Archives and Records Administration, College Park, MD.

44 Thornton Wilder wrote a semiautobiographical manuscript titled "Chefoo, China" based in part on his family's experience in China (Niven, *Thornton Wilder, A Life*, 20).

45 Wilder to Department of State, telegram, May 26, 1914, "Central Files, Ud 820, 125.8571," National Archives and Records Administration, College Park, MD.

46 Reinsch to Bryan, October 31, 1914, "Central Files, Ud 820, 125.8571," National Archives and Records Administration, College Park, MD.

47 Sammons to Department of State, July 22, 1914, "Central Files, Ud 820, 125.8571," National Archives and Records Administration, College Park, MD.

48 Sammons to Lansing, June 30, 1916; Sammons, to Lansing, August 11, 1916, "Central Files, Ud 820, 125.8571," National Archives and Records Administration, College Park, MD.

49 Atkinson and Dallas Report to the American Consul, Shanghai, November 13, 1914, cited in Report, "Proposed Purchase of Permanent quarters for United States Government Officers at Shanghai—Joint Report and Recommendations by the Judge of the United States Court for China and the American Consul-General at Shanghai," November 13, 1914, 4, "Central Files, Ud 820, 125.8571," National Archives and Records Administration, College Park, MD.

50 Memorandum, Department of State, Office of the Director of the Consular Service, July 1, 1916, "Records of the Foreign Service Buildings Office: Miscellaneous Papers Relating to Buildings in Japan and China," RG 59, Entry 411, Foreign Service Buildings, 1914–43, Box 19, Buildings in the Orient, National Archives and Records Administration, College Park, MD.

51 Memorandum, Department of State, Office of the Director of the Consular Service, July 1, 1916, "Records of the Foreign Service Buildings Office: Miscellaneous Papers Relating to Buildings in Japan and China," RG 59, Entry 411, Foreign Service Buildings, 1914–43, Box 19, Buildings in the Orient, National Archives and Records Administration, College Park, MD.

52 Scully, *Bargaining with the State from Afar*, 144.

53 Sammons to Department of State, June 6, 1914, "Central Files, Ud 820, 125.8571," National Archives and Records Administration, College Park, MD.

54 "Shanghai Americans to Have Million Dollar Club Home," *China Weekly Review*, November 10, 1923, 425. For a history of the American community in Shanghai, see Huskey, "Americans in Shanghai."

55 *NCH*, November 26, 1864, 190.

56 Jackson, *Shaping Modern Shanghai*, 65.

57 "Public Meeting: Annual Meeting of Ratepayers," *NCH*, May 17, 1873, 419.

58 "Meeting: Municipal Council," *NCH*, February 20, 1884, 204.

59 "Shanghai Municipal Council Report for the Year Ending March 31, 1890, and Budget for the Year Ending March 31, 1891," 15.

60 "Shanghai Municipal Council Report for the Year Ending December 31, 1893, and Budget for the Year Ending December 31, 1894," 20.

61   Inaugural Meeting of the Municipal Buildings Committee, April 11, 1912, "Shanghai Municipal Council Correspondence, Municipal Council Buildings, 1912," U1-14-1027, Shanghai Municipal Archives.

62   Turner arrived in Shanghai in 1900, spending four years as a chief assistant under G. B. Atkinson before becoming an architectural assistant within the municipality's Public Works Office. He became a member of RIBA in 1927 ("Biography File, Robert Charles Turner," Royal Institute of British Library and Collections, London).

63   In 1927, British journalist Arthur Ransome coined the term "The Shanghai Mind" to define the peculiar psychological disaffection displayed by many Shanghailanders with respect to the broader economic, political and social context of China (Ransome, *The Chinese Puzzle*, 29–30).

64   Bickers, "Shanghailanders," 161–211.

65   O'Connor, "Architecture, Power and Ritual in Scottish Town Halls," 14–23.

66   "Municipal Buildings," *NCH*, March 8, 1913, 680–82.

67   "Shanghai Municipal Council Report for the Year Ending December 31, 1922, and Budget for the Year Ending December 31, 1923," 234A. In response, Sir Reginald Blomfield, president of RIBA, noted that "justice could only be done to the design by executing it in granite instead of artificial stone as originally intended."

68   "Shanghai Municipal Council Report for Year Ending December 31, 1910, and Budget for Year Ending December 31, 1911," 163; "A Garden City for Shanghai," *NCH*, January 24, 1914, 233.

69   Peirce to Godfrey, May 8, 1912, "Shanghai Municipal Council Correspondence, Municipal Council Buildings, 1912," U1-14-1027, Shanghai Municipal Archives.

70   Peirce to Godfrey, May 8, 1912, "Shanghai Municipal Council Correspondence, Municipal Council Buildings, 1912," U1-14-1027, Shanghai Municipal Archives.

71   Peirce to Godfrey, May 8, 1912, "Shanghai Municipal Council Correspondence, Municipal Council Buildings, 1912," U1-14-1027, Shanghai Municipal Archives.

72   Peirce to Godfrey, May 8, 1912, "Shanghai Municipal Council Correspondence Municipal Council Buildings, 1912," U1-14-1027, Shanghai Municipal Archives.

73   "Shanghai Municipal Council Correspondence, Municipal Council Buildings, 1912," U1-14-1027, Shanghai Municipal Archives.

74   Another story was subsequently added to the building in 1938.

75   "Gongbu ju bugao," *Shenbao*, November 16, 1922, 13; "Ji gongbu ju xin wu zhi luo chengli," *Shenbao*, November 17, 1922, 13.

76   "The Council Building," *NCH*, November 25, 1922, 495–96.

77   "The Council Building," *NCH*, November 25, 1922, 495–96.

78   Kotenev, *Shanghai*, 42.

79   "The Municipal Building," *NCH*, November 18, 1922, 447.

80   McCullough, *The Path between the Seas*, 58; see also Headrick, *The Tentacles of Progress*.

81   Huber, *Channelling Mobilities*, 24–30.

82   Peters, *Building the Nineteenth Century*, 124.

83   McCullough, *The Path between the Seas*, 128.

84   Hobson, *Imperialism: A Study*.

85 Brunschwig, *French Colonialism, 1871–1914*, 142.

86 See "Land and Buildings for Consular Establishments in China, Japan, and Korea," RG 59, Entry 411, Foreign Service Buildings, 1914–43, Box 19, Buildings in the Orient, National Archives and Records Administration, College Park, MD.

87 Otter, "Locating Matter," 55.

88 Fearn, *My Days of Strength*, 130.

89 Lord Salisbury to French Ambassador to England, July 17, 1899, "Concession de Changhai, Janvier-Mars 1899," Correspondance Politique et Commerciale, 1897–1918, Nouvelle Série 266, Ministère des Affaires étrangères, Missions étrangères, Paris; "Anglo-American Alliance in China," *New York Times*, January 6, 1899, 6.

90 Zhang, *Dianshizhai huabao*, 1:15.

91 "Anglo-American Alliance in China," *New York Times*, January 6, 1899, 6.

92 Lord Salisbury to French Ambassador to England, July 17, 1899, "Concession de Changhai, Janvier-Mars 1899," Correspondance Politique et Commerciale, 1897–1918, Nouvelle Série 266, Ministère des Affaires étrangères, Missions étrangères, Paris.

93 Tapernoux, "Le Dossier des Eaux," *Le Courrier de Chine*, October 10, 1908, Série B, Carton 67, Les Archives diplomatiques du Ministère des Affaires étrangères, Nantes.

94 Bexaure to Ministère des Affaires étrangères, July 22, 1899, "Pompiers, Travaux Publiques," Série B, Carton 64, Les Archives diplomatiques du Ministère des Affaires étrangères, Nantes; Eckhardt to Ratard, October 11, 1908, "Tramways and Water," Série B, Carton 66, Les Archives diplomatiques du Ministère des Affaires étrangères, Nantes.

95 Tapernoux, "Le Dossier des Eaux," *Le Courrier de Chine*, October 10, 1908, Série B, Carton 67, Les Archives diplomatiques du Ministère des Affaires étrangères, Nantes.

96 One resident living next to the French post office wrote in to *Le Courrier de Chine* under the pseudonym O. Cainadan to complain about its shoddy construction. The writer feared that "if a blast of wind or something stronger causes the building to collapse, Cainadan will be no more of this world. . . . My ghost will be at your house . . . haunting your nights until your last sigh, Mr. Chollot" (Tapernoux, "Le Dossier des Eaux," *Le Courrier de Chine*, October 10, 1908, Série B, Carton 67, Les Archives diplomatiques du Ministère des Affaires étrangères, Nantes).

97 There remains some question as to whether Chollot was fired or quit on his own accord ("Demission De M. J. J. Chollot," *L'Echo de Chine*, January 17, 1907, 92). Chollot ran again for the French Municipal Council in January 1908, though he was subjected to "vehement attacks" from those opposed to his election and did not win ("The French Municipal Council," *NCH*, January 24, 1908, 189).

98 "Le Bassin des eaux claires," *L'Echo de Chine*, October 17, 1908; Tapernoux "Le Dossier des eaux." *Le Courrier de Chine*, October 10, 1908, Série B, Carton 67, Les Archives Diplomatiques du Ministère des Affaires étrangères, Nantes. The extent of the fiasco even compelled Consul General Ratard to lament the waterworks' unsanitary condition in his annual Bastille Day speech in 1907 ("Choses municipales," *L'Echo de Chine*, August 8, 1907, 1).

99 Tapernoux, "Le Dossier des eaux." *Le Courrier de Chine*, October 10, 1908, Série B, Carton 67, Les Archives diplomatiques du Ministère des Affaires étrangères, Nantes. The process of water filtration involved the rapid introduction of water into several

clay-lined basins at the moment of the Huangpu River's high tide, the point at which the water's entrance level was the same as that of the basin's apron. Sediment was agitated by the introduced water's movement. The water was propelled through the filters via gravity. It collected underneath the filters and was subsequently carried to a purified water reservoir by a tube.

100   "The French Waterworks: The Opening Ceremony," *NCH*, January 15, 1902, 86.

101   "Tramways and Water," Série B, Carton 66, Les Archives diplomatiques du Ministère des Affaires étrangères, Nantes; Bezaure to the Ministère des Affaires étrangères, July 22, 1899, "Pompiers, Travaux Publiques," Série B, Carton 64, Les Archives diplomatiques du Ministère des Affaires étrangères, Nantes.

102   Margerie to Ministère des Affaires étrangères, June 12, 1912; "Pompiers, Travaux Publiques," Série B, Carton 64, Les Archives diplomatiques du Ministère des Affaires étrangères, Nantes.

103   Goodman, *Native Place, City, and Nation*, 190; Lam, "Policing the Imperial Nation," 883.

104   Elvin, "The Gentry Democracy in Shanghai, 1905–1914;" Fewsmith, *Party, State, and Local Elites in Republican China*, 18–36; Zhou, *Shanghai difang zizhi yanjiu (1905–1927)*, 28–80.

105   "Huangpu Conservancy Convention," *NCH*, October 13, 1905, 70.

106   Elvin, "The Gentry Democracy in Shanghai, 1905–1914," 46.

107   Henriot, *Shanghai*, 13.

108   Li, *Wanzhu xiaoxue*, 1–4; "Zalu," *Quanye huixun*, Febraury 9, 1910, 6.

109   Rankin, "State and Society in Early Republican Politics, 1912–18," 260–82.

110   Xue, *Shanghai waitan diming zhanggu*, 84.

111   Following the Small Swords Uprising, the imperial government had deemed the construction of homes between the city wall and the moat illegal for fear such construction could be used the scale the wall in an invasion. Nevertheless, by the late nineteenth century, numerous houses had been constructed on the land, with rents being collected and unreported to imperial authorities by both the city government as well as the Army of the Green Standard. In 1905, debate emerged between the government and the army over whether the land should be considered *gongdi*, public land, or *yingdi*, or army land ("The City Wall: Progress of the Scheme," *NCH*, October 26, 1912, 228; see also Elvin, "The Gentry Democracy in Shanghai, 1905–1914," 158).

112   "Shanghai chai cheng yi zhengwen," *Shenbao*, June 19, 1906, 17; Elvin, "The Gentry Democracy in Chinese Shanghai, 1905–14," 56.

113   "Les murs de la ville Chinoise de Changhai," *L'Echo de Chine*, February 28, 1907, 291.

114   "Communications avec la ville Chinoise de Shanghai," *L'Echo de Chine*, March 28, 1907, 437.

115   Elvin, "The Gentry Democracy in Chinese Shanghai, 1905–14," 56.

116   "Fortes de la cité chinoise," *L'Echo de Chine*, October 24, 1907, 1724.

117   "Shanghai chai cheng wenti," *Shenbao*, July 9, 1908, 4.

118   Zhang, "Jindai Shanghai chengshi tezheng fenxi," 92.

119   "Chai cheng wenti zhi da zuli," *Shenbao*, July 23, 1908, 2; Yao, Zhang, and Yuan, eds., *Shencheng jianshe chunqiu*, 92; Xue, *Shanghai waitan diming zhanggu*, 84–85; Elvin, "The Gentry Democracy in Chinese Shanghai, 1905–14," 56.

120 "Minzheng zhang zancheng chai cheng," *Shenbao*, January 16, 1912, 7; Wu, *Shanghai chai cheng an baogao*, 2.

121 "Chai cheng wenti hui zhi," *Shenbao*, July 16, 1912, 7.

122 "Les murailles et les tramways de la cité," *L'Echo de Chine*, January 27, 1912, 118; "La Revolution en Chine: Les murailles de la cité," *L'Echo de Chine*, February 10, 1912, 144.

123 "Demolition of Chinese City Wall," *NCH*, July 27, 1912, 268; "City-Wall Demolition Scheme," *NCH*, August 17, 1912, 478; "The City Wall: Progress of the Scheme," *NCH*, October 26, 1912, 228.

124 Wu, *Shanghai chai cheng an baogao*, 2.

125 Sabard, "Les murailles de la cité," *L'Echo de Chine*, August 24, 1912, 286.

126 MacGowan, "Lights and Shadows of Chinese Life: A Ramble through a Chinese City," *NCH*, December 13, 1907, 658.

127 "Demolition of City Walls," *NCH*, Jan. 27, 1912, 232; "Demolition of Chienmen," *Peking Daily News*, July 17, 1915, 4.

128 Yeh, *Shanghai Splendor*, 76.

129 "The Municipal Building," *NCH*, November 18, 1922, 447.

130 "Shanghai—the Wonder City of All Asia," *NCH*, May 17, 1924, 275.

131 "Shanghai Municipal Council Report for the Year Ending December 31, 1910, and Budget for the Year Ending December 31, 1911," 163. See also Heidenstam, "Shanghai—the Industrial and Commercial Metropolis?," 24.

CHAPTER 6: NATIONAL ARCHITECTS, NATIONAL ARCHITECTURE

1 See Dikötter, *Exotic Commodities*, 12–22; Wagner, "The Role of the Foreign Community in the Chinese Public Sphere," 423–43; and Ye, *The Dianshizhai Pictorial*.

2 Musgrove, *China's Contested Capital*, 92–93; Tsin, *Nation, Governance, and Modernity in China*, 51–82, 98–103.

3 Gropius, *Internationale Architektur*, 3.

4 Gropius, *Internationale Architektur*, 3.

5 See, for example, Bozdogan, *Modernism and Nation Building*, 3–15; and Oshima, *International Architecture in Interwar Japan*, 15–23.

6 See, for example, Bao, *Fiery Cinema*, 197–262; Lee, *Shanghai Modern*; and Liang, *Mapping Modernity in Shanghai*.

7 Kallee-Dijon, "Architecture and Building Practice in China," 59.

8 Musgrove, *China's Contested Capital*, 92.

9 Lai, *Zhongguo jindai jianzhu shi yanjiu*, 115–80. Xu Shi'er and Xu Hongyu have been identified as China's first foreign-trained architectural students; both studied engineering in China before leaving to study in Japan and England in 1905, respectively. A survey of foreign students at France's École des Ponts et Chaussées between 1880 and 1899 lists four students from Fujian within its ranks. They include Ouang-King-Touan, born April 23, 1860, in Fuzhou, admitted on October 24, 1882, on behalf of the Chinese government; Ling Tsi-Ching, born in 1866 in Fuzhou; Tcheng King-Ping, born in 1866 in Fujian and admitted on May 24, 1887; and Li Tai-Chao, born in 1866 in Fujian and admitted on May 24, 1887 "(École des Ponts et Chaussées: Élèves

externes No. 2, 1880–1899," Les Archives, l'École des ponts ParisTech, Marne-la-Vallée).

10 See Cody, Steinhart, and Atkin, eds., "Introduction," xii–xiii; Van Zanten, "Just What Was Beaux-Arts Architectural Composition?," 23–37; and Ruan, "Accidental Affinities," 30–47.

11 Kuan, "Between Beaux-Arts and Modernism," 184.

12 Grossman, *The Civic Architecture of Paul Cret*, xv.

13 Cret, "The École des Beaux Arts: What Its Architectural Teaching Means," 367–71; Grossman, *The Civic Architecture of Paul Cret*, 210.

14 Chaund, "Architectural Effort and Chinese Nationalism," 534.

15 Kirby, "Engineering China," 137–60.

16 See, for example, Tong, *Tong Jun wenji*, 1:2; Liang and Zhang, "Tianjin tebie shi wuzhi jianshe fang'an," in *Liang Sicheng quanji*, 1:32.

17 In conjunction with their professional practice the partners also established a training course, including classes in engineering technology, design, structure, foreign and Chinese building regulations, surveying, material strength, and Chinese and foreign architectural history (Tong and Yan, "Zhongguo jianzhu jiaoyu," 405–7).

18 In 1933, the firm added another partner and Penn graduate, Tong Jun (1900–1983), and changed its name to Allied Architects (Huagai jianzhu shiwusuo).

19 Cody, *Building in China*, 211–16.

20 "La Librairie Francaise de Shanghai," *Le Journal de Shanghai*, July 14, 1930, 23.

21 Wood, "Presidential Address," *Engineering Society of China* (1920): xxxi.

22 Roger Labonne, "Shanghai sous tous ses aspects," *Le Journal de Shanghai (numéro spécial)*, July 14, 1936, 4.

23 Zhong Qin, "Guomao jianzhu yuanliao wenti," *Shenbao*, November 7, 1933, 9.

24 Cody, *Building in China*, 107–8, 134, 149–50.

25 Chan, "The Institutionalization and Legitimization of Guohua," 545–47.

26 Shanghai jianzhu shigong zhiweihui, *Dongfang "Bali,"* 146, 174. See also Perry, *Shanghai on Strike: The Politics of Chinese Labor*.

27 Musgrove, *China's Contested Capital*, 92.

28 Zhongguo jianzhushi xuehui, *Zhongguo jianzhushi xuehui*. See also *Zhongguo jianzhushi xuehui ding jianzhushi yewu guice*.

29 The group was founded in March 1930 after several of the Shanghai/Shaoxing Carpentry Guild's original members decided to establish a formal society that would unite the city's two largest construction guilds, the Shanghai-Shaoxing or Southern, Construction Guild, organized in October 1907, and the Ningbo-Zhejiang, or Northern, Construction Guild, founded in 1908. Southern (Shanghai/Shaoxing) leaders included Jiang Yusheng, Zhang Xiaoliang, Zhang Xiaoqing, Xie Bingheng, Tao Guilin, among others. Northern (Zhejiang) leaders included Cai Tongrong, Zhu Dexin, Wang Gaosun, Zhu Quantong, Jiang Baozhen, Chen Wushi, and Gui Lansun (He, "Shanghai jindai yingzao ye de xingcheng ji tezheng," 118–24; "Zhongguo jianzhushi xuehui nianhui zhi sheng," *Shenbao*, January 17, 1933, 4).

30 As part of a job bidding process, for example, construction companies were often charged participation fees ranging from ¥10 to ¥100, which was roughly equivalent

to US$3 to US$30. Once the project had been awarded to a particular firm, however, the other unsuccessful firms' fees were rarely returned, prompting widespread complaints and claims of fraud ("Zhenxing jianzhu shiye zhi shouyao," *Jianzhu yuekan* 2, no. 7 [1934]: 41–43).

31 Shanghai jianzhu shigong weiyuanhui, *Dongfang "Bali,"* 116.

32 He, "Du Yangeng yu 'Jianzhu yuekan,'" 188–93. The organization's steering committee consisted of representatives of Shanghai's engineers, contractors, construction magnates, and architects. Members included Tao Guilin, founder of one of Shanghai's most prominent engineering firms, Fuji, which was responsible for the construction of the Sun Yat-sen Mausoleum in Nanjing; Wang Gaosun, director of the Ningbo-Zhejiang construction guild and responsible for the construction for the French Concession's first ten-story building, the Cathay Apartments (now the Jinjiang Hotel); and Xie Bingheng, one of the city's oldest surviving builders, an original director of the Shanghai and Shaoxing construction guild responsible for the construction of the International Settlement's municipal offices. Other notable members included Jiang Zhanggeng, son of Jiang Yuheng and founder of the Jiangyu Construction Company, which was the firm responsible for the construction of Shanghai's Chinese YMCA and the Hua'an Insurance Company; Zhang Xiaoliang, founder of the Jiu Construction Company and leader of the Shanghai construction industry since Yang Sisheng's death in 1908; and Tang Jingxian, a steel manufacturer who traveled to Japan to study steel smelting in 1931 before returning to Shanghai to establish the city's first Chinese-owned competitive steel operations in 1932. Tang moved to Singapore in 1950 and built its first skyscraper, the eighteen-story, 73.8-meter-tall Asia Insurance Building ("Zhang Xiaoliang xiansheng," 1; "Zhang Xiaoliang jun zuochen sishi," *Shenbao*, June 2, 1936, 13; Sun, *Shanghai chengshi guihua zhi*; *Fu ji yingzao chang chengjian dao huai weiyuanhui*).

33 Du lost US$15,000 on the building and, as noted by He, is quoted as declaring that the experience was "seventeen months of bitterness. . . . I'll swear I'll never do any more construction. I can't work in this kind of filthy environment!" (He, "Du Yangeng yu 'Jianzhu yuekan,'" 188).

34 Du, "Shanghai shi jianzhu xiehui lueshi."

35 "Fanguan Oumei hou jin zhu guo, qi jianzhu shu zhi jinzhan, ri ci yue zhuo . . . tongren gannian yi xian jin ziju zhi wu guo, zhang ci cuotuo, shijian luowu, menxin ziwen, qingheyikan . . . cihou yuan geng dongfang jianzhu zhi yuyin . . . yi xiyang wuzhi wenming fa yang wo guo guyou wenyi zhi zhen jingshen" (cited in Shanghai jianzhu shigong zhiweihui, *Dongfang "Bali,"* 149).

36 Du, "Duiyu gaijin Zhongguoshi jianzhu de shangque."

37 Du, "Shanghai shi jianzhu xiehui lueshi," 1.

38 Rujivacharakul, "Architects as Cultural Heroes," 149.

39 Guangzhou's Bureau of Municipality, established in 1918, was the country's first, and under the influence of Sun Ke, son of Sun Yat-sen and appointed city mayor in 1921, the city became an acknowledged model of urban administration in Republican China (Tsin, *Nation, Governance, and Modernity in China*, 51–82, 98–103; Shen, *Shen Yi zishu*, 101).

40 W. E. Fisher, "Experiments Produce Improved Type of Cheap Workers' Home," *China Press*, August 6, 1935, 9.

41 For a brief history of the journal and its role in the history of China's modern architectural development, see Zhu, "Cong 'Zhongguo jianzhu' kan 1932–1937 nian Zhongguo jianzhu sichao yu zhuyao qishi," 17–31.

42 See, for example, "Architects Form Integral Part of Contribution to Civilization," *China Press*, August 23, 1934, 12.

43 Du, "Duiyu gaijin Zhongguoshi jianzhu de shangque," *Shenbao*, April 12, 1936, 20.

44 For a history of the National Products Movement, see Gerth, *China Made*.

45 One book informed its readers that the most surprising difference between living in the country and living in the city was the size of one's house. In the countryside, simple homes tended to consist of one to two stories, while in the city, buildings typically imitated "Western styles" and were taller, with differences in style and construction (Zong Liangchen, *Zenyang jianzhu fangwu*, 40–41).

46 Kirby, *Germany and Republican China*, 145–89.

47 Bian zhu, "Juan tou bian yu," *Zhongguo jianzhu* 3, no. 5 (1935): preface.

48 *Zenyang jianzhu fangwu*, 54.

49 See Young, *Japan's Total Empire*, 3–54.

50 Coble, *Facing Japan*, 26.

51 Shanghai City Government, "Japanese Invasion of Shanghai (January 28–March 7, 1932)," 43–56. See also "Foreign Affairs Association of Japan. The Sino-Japanese Conflict: A Short Survey, Tokyo, 1937," 467–84.

52 Du, "Shanghai shi jianzhu xiehui lueshi," 2.

53 See Zhong Qin, "Guomao jianzhu yuanliao wenti," *Shenbao*, November 7, 1933, 9.

54 Tan, "Hu zhan hou jianzhu zhi jinzhan," *Jianzhu yuekan* 1, no. 6 (1933): 31–32; Tang, *Reconstruction in China*, 329–32.

55 "Jianzhushimen! Nimen tai qi tou lai, kan kan zhe wuqian nian lishi de guo guo, zai dixia toulai, kan kan zhei kexue pengpai de shijie; nimen shenger fangchen, ji ci dongfang yishu, zhengzai fuxing, er xifang kexue, zhengzai jinlai de shihou, nimen gai zenyang fuqi zhei chenzhong de danzi, er qu ta shangle zhei xin jianzhu de lucheng?" (Wen Mingzhang, "Ruhe ta shang xin jianzhu de lucheng," *Shenbao*, September 12, 1933, 9).

56 Kuan, "Between Beaux-Arts and Modernism," 187.

57 He, *Zhang Xiaoliang zhuan*, 38. In 1934, the Nationalist municipal government sent several representatives, including the city's party representative Mao Xiaxuan and Education Bureau representative Nie Haifan, to monitor the election of the Shanghai Architectural Society's board members amid fears of the group's possible communist inclinations ("Shanghai shi jianzhu xiehui di er jie wei qiu huiyuan dahui teji," *Jianzhu yuekan* 2 no. 4 [1934]: 25–41). Society-sponsored films and lectures by intellectuals and officials such as Jiang Kanghu, the well-known Beijing University professor and founder of the Chinese Socialist Party, helped to fan such fears (Kui An, "Benhui di san jie hui yuan da hui ji xiang," *Jianzhu yuekan* 2, no. 10 [1934]: 41–46; "Faqi zujie jianzhu xue shu yanjiang hui jianyue," *Jianzhu yuekan* 3, no. 7 [1935]: 3).

58 "Municipality Passes Ruling on Architects," *China Press*, January 19, 1933, 11; Yang, *Jianzhuxue abc*.

59 *Proceedings: World Engineering Congress, Tokyo, 1929*, 153.

60 Liang and Zhang, "Tianjin tebie shi wuzhi jianshe fang'an," 32.

61 Yang, "Yinhang jianzhu zhi neiwaiguan," 1–3.

62 Kuan, "Between Beaux-Arts and Modernism," 169–92.

63 Lu, "Memorials to Dr. Sun Yat-Sen in Nanking and Canton," 97–101.

64 Thomas F. Millard, "Five Cities in One Comprise Shanghai," *New York Times*, July 29, 1925, 12. Shanghai's five independent municipalities included Nantai, the formerly walled city center; the French Concession; the International Settlement; Zhabei, the district located north of the International Settlement; and Pudong, which was separated from the rest of Shanghai's city center by the Huangpu River.

65 Dong, "Architecture Chronicle," 359.

CHAPTER 7: A CONTESTED MUNICIPALITY

1 Hosie, *Brave New China*, 4.

2 See Carroll, "The Beaux-Arts in Another Register," 315–32; Esherick, ed., *Remaking the Chinese City*; and Musgrove, *China's Contested Capital*, 89–124.

3 For a history of the Greater Shanghai Plan, see Henriot, *Shanghai*, 168–84; Kuan, "Image of the Metropolis," 84–95; Kuan, "Between Beaux-Arts and Modernism" 169–92; and Macpherson, "Designing China's Urban Future," 39–62.

4 Macpherson, "Designing China's Urban Future," 41; Kuan, "Between Beaux-Arts and Modernism," 186.

5 Henriot, *Shanghai*, 26–27.

6 Du, "Kaipi dongfang dagang de zhongyao ji qishi shi buzhou (1)," *Shenbao*, January 17, 1933, 4.

7 Henriot, *Shanghai*, 168–84.

8 Sun, *Jianguo fanglüe*, 126–42.

9 Lai, "Searching for a Modern Chinese Monument," 22–55. Jury members included Shen Yi, director of public works; Ye Yuhu, a railroad expert and president of Jiaotong University; Henry Murphy; Hans Behrents, president of the Engineering Society of China; and Dong Dayou, the city's architectural consultant and an architectural graduate of both the University of Minnesota and Columbia University ("Yewu baogao").

10 Vincent, *The Extraterritorial System in China: Final Phase*, 62–63.

11 Dyce, *Personal Reminiscences of Thirty Years' Residence*, 56.

12 Other names included Capital Road (Guo Jing Lu), Policy Road (Zhengzhi Lu), and National Peace Road (Guo He Lu) (Yao, Zhang, and Yuan, *Shen cheng jianshe chunqiu*, 96).

13 "Yewu baogao," 34.

14 "Shanghai shi zhengfu xinwu jianzhu jingguo," *Zhongguo jianzhu* 1, no. 12 (1933): 8.

15 "Shi gongwuju kaishi qianyi," *Shenbao*, December 23, 1933, 11.

16 "Zhang quanti xuanshou zuo canguan tiyuchang tongxianghui ge tuanti xiangji huanying," *Shenbao*, October 7, 1935, 12.

17 Liang, *Zhongguo jianzhu shi*, 355.

18 A 1934 government report, for example, quoted Public Works Department head Shen Yi's lamentations regarding the public's likely reaction to news that its roof was already growing grass and that birds had already built numerous nests within its lower-hanging eaves. Shen also complained of an article in a German newspaper he had seen during a diplomatic trip to Europe detailing a German traveler's search around the open fields around the new city center for the Mayor's Building ("Zhongguo zhi jianshe," *Jianzhu yuekan* 3, no. 5 [1935]: 45).

19 Jacqueline Tyrwhitt Papers, TyJ/2/1, Victoria and Albert Museum, London.

20 Jacqueline Tyrwhitt Papers, TyJ/2/1, Victoria and Albert Museum, London.

21 Jacqueline Tyrwhitt Papers, TyJ/2/1, Victoria and Albert Museum, London.

22 "Monument Unveiled at Grave of General Frederick Ward," *China Weekly Review,* May 31, 1924, 493.

23 "The Future of the Foreigner in China," *NCH*, October 11, 1924, 16.

24 "Provision of New Town Hall," *Shanghai Municipal Gazette* 23, no. 1249 (May 30, 1930): 216. Harris, a longtime Shanghai resident, was eventually elected to the Shanghai Municipal Council in 1933 before retiring in 1935.

25 "Provision of New Town Hall," 216. The Joint Committee of Shanghai Women's Organizations, one of the earliest and most vocal proponents of the new scheme, also advocated for a formal reception hall to be included so that international visitors and emissaries could be properly greeted and welcomed. Representatives from the committee also pointed out that "the city halls of most Western cities featured rooms whereby the Mayoress or wife of a Chief Commissioner could host public parties and functions. The women of Shanghai, too, desired such accommodation for 'public courtesy'" ("New Town Hall," *Shanghai Municipal Gazette* 23, no. 1258 [July 25, 1930]: 303).

26 "The Majestic Hotel," *NCH*, November 8, 1924, 233.

27 Smith, *I Didn't Make a Million*, 24–25.

28 On May 30, 1925, a group of Chinese protestors marched on the Louza Police Station on Nanjing Road in the International Settlement to demand the release of several other marchers arrested earlier that day in connection with demonstrations against what were seen as unfair foreign-administered labor practices. The police opened fire on the crowd, killing twelve and wounding seventeen, and sparking intense, summer-long Chinese protests that helped to crystallize Chinese opposition to the city's foreign presence (Clifford, *Shanghai 1925*, 66).

29 "Getting Together on the Shanghai Problems," *China Weekly Review,* March 27, 1926, 81.

30 Shanghai Municipal Council, "Shanghai Municipal Council Report for the Year Ending December 31, 1931, and Budget for the Year Ending December 31, 1932," 15.

31 "The Majestic Hotel Site," *Shanghai Municipal Gazette* 24, no. 1301 (April 14, 1931): 174; Shanghai Municipal Council, "Shanghai Municipal Council Report for the Year Ending December 31, 1931, and Budget for the Year Ending December 31, 1932," 15.

32 Shanghai Municipal Council, "Shanghai Municipal Council Report for the Year Ending December 31, 1931, and Budget for the Year Ending December 31, 1932," 16.

33 "New Town Hall," *Shanghai Municipal Gazette* 24, no. 1295 (March 20, 1931): 105.

34 Council member Tsuyee Pei, vice president of the Bank of China and father of the architect I. M. Pei, suggested that "in view of the uncertain future status of the

Settlement and the possibility of a Town Hall being required which would accommodate a greatly increased number of ratepayers, the decision on the type of building to be erected should be deferred" (Shanghai shi dang'anguan bian, *Gongbu ju dangshi hui huiyi lu*, 24:386).

35   Wilden to Poincare, March 26, 1923, "Dossiers concernant Les immeubles consulaires, Shanghai," Série A, Carton 3, A-6, Les Archives diplomatiques du Ministère des Affaires étrangères, Nantes.

36   Société Central des Architectes to Verdier, February 7, 1935, "Dossiers concernant les immeubles consulaires, Shanghai," Série A, Carton 3, A-6, Les Archives diplomatiques du Ministère des Affaires étrangères, Nantes.

37   Jennings, *Imperial Heights*, 123, 129.

38   "Frenchtown Population Jumps 22,540 in Past Twelve Months," *China Press*, October 21, 1932, 5. See also "French Neighbors," *North China Daily News*, October 25, 1933, 8.

39   "Garbage Piles Up in Concession as Walkout Continues: Exhortations Fail to Bring 2,500 Chinese Employees of French Municipal Council Back to Work; Disinfectants to Be Sprayed in Streets," *China Press*, July 6, 1931, 1.

40   L'Administration Municipale, "Projet de Reglement de Construction," ed. la Concession Française Service des Travaux Publics (Shanghai, 1934), 3, Les Archives diplomatiques du Ministère des Affaires étrangères, Nantes.

41   The first floor and location of the tax office included 1,400 square meters of space, and the fourth to sixth floors included 1,670 square meters total ("Rules for Construction of Municipal Offices, 1936," U38-1-1114, Shanghai Municipal Archives).

42   See Morizet, "Maire De Boulogne-Billancourt," *L'Architecture d'aujourd'hui* 5, no. 9 (1934): 5–18.

43   Wright, "Service in the Tradition of Modernity," 305–7.

44   Zhong Qin, "Ouzhou ji Meizhou jianzhu xue qishi," *Shenbao*, May 9, 1933, 11.

45   That such projects could succeed in Shanghai, it was believed, spoke to the firm's "success as an organization, so completely and entirely French, in foreign territory despite bitter, foreign competition, and thus the best proof against the falseness of such opinion" ("Une Equipe des realisateurs français," *Le Journal de Shanghai*, July 14, 1934, 1a).

46   Mallet-Stevens, "Architecture 'd'aujourd'hui,'" *L'Architecture d'aujourd'hui* 6, no. 9 (1935): 73.

47   "Special City Government Anniversary," *NCH*, October 25, 1939, 1. See also Borg, "Japanese Announce Plans for a New Shanghai," 191–92.

48   "Bricks for Civic Centre from Hongkew Ruins," *NCH*, June 8, 1938, 407.

49   "Le Plus Grand Shanghai maintenant et dans l'avenir par Le General Wou Teh-Tcheng, Maire de la Municipalité Chinoise," *Le Journal de Shanghai*, January 14, 1933, 4.

50   See Dong, "Greater Shanghai—Greater Vision," 103. See also Dong, "New Shanghai," 87–98; and Dong, "Architecture Chronicle," 358–62.

51   Du, "Kaipi dongfang gang de zhongyao ji qishi shi buzhao (3)," *Shenbao*, February 14, 1933, 9.

52 "Shanghai Municipal Council Report for the Year Ending December 31, 1931, and Budget for the Year Ending December 31, 1932," 12–13, 15.

53 Dong, "New Shanghai," 87–98.

54 Green, "L'Avenir de Shanghai," *Le Journal de Shanghai*, 6 July 1934, 7; "Shanghai Civic Center Planned," *New York Times*, January 22, 1935, 44.

55 Bryna Goodman has noted "the awkwardness of symbolizing the semi-colonial" (Goodman, "Improvisations on a Semicolonial Theme, or, How to Read a Celebration of a Transnational Urban Community," 6).

56 *Shanghai de jianglai*, 38; Spakowski, "Semi/colonial Futures," 236. Architecture is a recurring index of change in many of the contributions. One participant, Pan Yang'an, wrote of a day when the Shanghai Municipal Council offices were crowned with "Republican flags." Mayor Wu imagined a future that included both foreign advisers and Chinese residents walking through the Civic Center and appreciating its achievements (*Shanghai de jianglai*, 59–60, 65).

CHAPTER 8: EXHIBITING A MODERN CHINESE ARCHITECTURE

1 Mitchell, *Colonising Egypt*, 7–16.

2 Greenhalgh, *Ephemeral Vistas*, 79.

3 Hart, *The I.G. in Peking*, 1:17.

4 Hart, *The I.G. in Peking*, 2:517.

5 Fernsebner, "Material Modernities," 145–88. China's architectural representation at San Francisco prompted Yue Jiazao (1868–1944), a late Qing scholar and member of China's official fair committee, to pen what would become, upon its publication in 1933, China's first Chinese-written architectural history, in an effort to rectify China's perceived architectural slights (Yue, *Zhongguo jianzhu shi*, 1).

6 Lai, *Zhongguo jindai jianzhu shi yanjiu*, 225–29.

7 Peterson, "The 1933 World's Fair," 124.

8 Sewell to Yi, February 6, 1931, Box 52, Folder 2–930, "Series II—Government Correspondence." See also "Summary of China's Involvement," Box 11, Folder 11–125, "Series XI—Exhibits," A Century of Progress Records, Special Collections, University of Illinois at Chicago.

9 Roskam, "Situating Chinese Architecture within 'A Century of Progress,'" 347–71.

10 Liang and Zhang, "Tianjin tebie shi wuzhi jianshe fang'an," 32.

11 "Chunjie jiaqi nei zhi jianzhu zhanlan," *Shenbao*, February 20, 1934, 9. See also Du, "Duiyu gaijing Zhongguoshi jianzhu de shangque," *Shenbao*, April 12, 1936, 12.

12 Hai, "Wanguoshi jianzhu zhi shangque," *Shenbao*, May 23, 1933, 9. In 1931, Saarinen, Bertram Goodhue, and Cret were identified as the three most influential architects in the United States (Grossman, "Paul Philippe Cret," 258n37).

13 Steinhardt, "The Tang Architectural Icon and the Politics of Chinese Architectural History," *Art Bulletin* 86, no. 2 (2004): 228–54.

14 Carroll, *Between Heaven and Modernity*, 163; Xi, "Zhongguo gudai jianzhu shang 'li' de fenxi," *Shenbao*, February 19, 1935, 5.

15 Guo, "Canonization in Early Twentieth-Century Chinese Art History," 1–16.

16   Chan, *The Making of a Modern Art World*; Ho, *Curating Revolution*, 7–8.

17   Wang, "Modernism and Its Discontent in Shanghai," 167–79.

18   "Jianzhu cailiao zhanlanhui," *Shenbao*, October 10, 1935, 9.

19   "Jianzhujie yingyou zhi zeren," 3.

20   Du, "Zuotan zhuishu," 3–4.

21   Chu, "Constructing a New Domestic Discourse," 1081.

22   Esherick, "Modernity and Nation in the Chinese City," 12.

23   Chan, *The Making of a Modern Art World*, 50.

24   The board consisted of more than thirty people, including Ye Gongchuo, Huang Boqiao, Liu Donglei, Gu Lanzhou, Zhang Jiguang, Li Jinpei, Zhao Shen, Shen Yi, Liang Sicheng, Dong Dayou, Wu Qiufan, Li Dazhao, Yao Huasun, Zhu Guixin, Zhuang Daqing, Dao Guilin, and Tang Jingxian.

25   The Greater Shanghai Municipality donated ¥1,000 for the event, while ¥1,200 was collectively pledged by the four major architectural and engineering organizations involved, including the Shanghai Architectural Society, the Chinese Architects' Society, the Chinese Engineering Society, and the Shanghai Builders' Union. The remainder was raised through private contributions ("Zhongguo jianzhu zhanlanhui," *Jianzhu yuekan* 4, no. 3 [1936]: 3–4).

26   "Zhongguo jianzhu zhanlanhui kaimu," 32–35; "Opening of Chinese Structural Show," *NCH*, April 15, 1936, 106; Ye, "Zhongguo jianzhu zhanlanhui shikan: Fakanci," *Shenbao*, April 12, 1936, 20; Du, "Zuotan zhuishu," 3–4.

27   "Faqi Zhongguo jianzhu zhanlanhui," 53.

28   Shen and Lou, "Zhongguo jianzhu zhanlanhui canguan ji," 15. See also Tan, "Zhongguo jianzhu zhanlanhui canguan ji," 11–12.

29   Shanghai jianzhu shigong zhiweihui, *Dongfang "Bali,"* 116.

30   "Zhongguo jianzhu zhanlanhui kaimu," 34. Throughout the exhibition's organization, the exhibition's overall layout and remained an ancillary matter. Prior to the first steering committee meeting, bulletins went out encouraging architects and engineers from around the country to send in examples of their own work for inclusion within the exhibition. Display design was not mentioned until the second meeting, when a committee was created and subsequently headed by Dong Dayou (Du, "Zhongguo jianzhu zhanlanhui de shiming," 4–5).

31   Wang, "Modernism and Its Discontent in Shanghai," 173.

32   In his preface to the exhibition catalogue, for example, Ye Gongchuo reminded readers that housing represented one of the Nationalist Party's four key policy directives, along with clothing, food, and work (Ye, "Fakanci," 1).

33   Du, "Duiyu gaijing Zhongguoshi jianzhu de shangque," 1.

34   Guoli Zhongyang daxue gongxueyuan, jianzhu gongcheng xi, *Canjia Zhongguo jianzhu zhanlanhui zhi yizhi*, 2.

35   Guo, "Bolanhui chenlie ge guan yingzao sheji zhi kaolu," 12–14.

36   Tong, "Jianzhu yishu jishi," 81–88.

37   See Guo, "Fuxing xin Zhongguo jianzhu jihua shu"; Tong, "Jianzhu yishu jishi," 81–88.

38   Lu and Wu, "Women de zhuzhang," *Zhongguo jianzhu* 4, no. 6 (1936): 55–56.

39   Tsu, *Failure, Nationalism, and Literature*, 222–26.

1 Tong, "Foreign Influence in Chinese Architecture," 417.

2 Liang, "Weishenme yanjiu Zhongguo jianzhu," 251–54; Tong, "Wo guo gongongjian-zhu waiguan de jiantao."

3 Rand, "Letter from Shanghai," *New Yorker*, November 6, 1948, 99.

4 Wei, "Da Shanghai jihua," 256.

5 Shaplen, "Reporter at Large: The China Watchers," *New Yorker*, February 12, 1966, 89.

6 *International Meeting of Architects*, 4–5.

7 Le Corbusier, *The City of To-morrow and Its Planning*, 88.

8 In 1968, Jacqueline Tyrwhitt wrote that the physical layout of the imperial Chinese city of Chang'an—which like Beijing was organized as a gridiron pattern—was "astonishingly similar in many respects to Le Corbusier's overall plan for Chandigarh in the location of the capital area, the scale of the walled units and their separation by major thoroughfares" (Tyrwhitt, "The City of Ch'ang-an," 24).

9 Krokker, "The Building Industry," 315–17; "Hospital for Shanghai," 11; "Chinese Art Museum in Shanghai," 76–77; "Satellite Towns of Shanghai," *Kokusai-Kentiku*, 52–55.

10 Lasker, "Shanghai Tomorrow," 314.

11 Easterling, *Extrastatecraft*; Hyde, "Architecture, Modernity, Crisis," 2–3.

12 Wang, "Economic and Social Impact of Export Processing Zones in the Republic of China," 7–28.

13 Easterling, *Extrastatecraft*, 25.

14 Brautigam and Tang, "African Shenzhen," 27–54.

15 Agamben, *State of Exception*, 23.

BIBLIOGRAPHY

ARCHIVES

Archives, L'École des Ponts ParisTech, Marne-la-Vallée

Archives du Ministère des Affaires étrangères, Centre des Archives diplomatiques, Nantes

Archives du Ministère de l'Europe et des Affaires étrangères, La Courneuve

Archives du Séminaire des Missions étrangères, Paris

Baker Business Historical Collections, Harvard University, Boston

British Library, London

Compagnie de Jésus, Archives Jésuites, Vanves

Government Services Office, Hong Kong

Jardine Matheson Archive, Cambridge University Library

Library and Museum of Freemasonry, London

National Archives, Kew, London

National Archives and Records Administration (NARA), College Park, MD

Phillips Library, Peabody Essex Museum, Salem, MA

Royal Institute of British Architects (RIBA) Library and Collections, London

Shanghai Municipal Archives

Special Collections, Shanghai Public Library

Special Collections, University of Hong Kong Libraries

Special Collections, University of Illinois at Chicago

Jacqueline Tyrwhitt Papers, Victoria and Albert Museum, London

OTHER SOURCES

Abramson, Daniel M. *Building the Bank of England: Money, Architecture, Society, 1694–1942.* New Haven: Yale University Press, 2005.

"An Act Creating a United States Court for China and Prescribing the Jurisdiction Thereof." *American Journal of International Law* 1, no. 2 (1907): 234–38.

Adas, Michael. *Machines as the Measure of Men: Science, Technology, and Ideologies of Western Dominance.* Ithaca, NY: Cornell University Press, 1989.

Agamben, Giorgio. *State of Exception.* Chicago: University of Chicago Press, 2005.

———. *"What Is an Apparatus?" and Other Essays*. Stanford: Stanford University Press, 2009.

Alcock, Rutherford. *The Capital of the Tycoon: A Narrative of a Three Years' Residence in Japan*. New York: Harper and Brothers, 1863.

Alder, Ken. *The Measure of All Things: The Seven-Year Odyssey and Hidden Error That Transformed the World*. New York: Free Press, 2002.

All about Shanghai and Environs: A Standard Guide Book: Historical and Contemporary Facts and Statistics. 1935. Reprint, Taipei: Ch'eng Wen, 1973.

Anderson, M. S. *The Rise of Modern Diplomacy, 1450–1919*. London: Longman, 1993.

"Annual General Meeting." In *The Engineering Society of Shanghai: Proceedings and Report of the Council, 1911–12*, 242–43. Shanghai: Kelly and Walsh, 1912.

Appleton, William Worthen. *A Cycle of Cathay*. New York: Columbia University Press, 1951.

Archer, John. "Character in English Architectural Design." *Eighteenth-Century Studies* 12, no. 3 (Spring 1979): 339–71.

Ashworth, Edward. "How Chinese Workmen Built an English House." *Builder*, November 9, 1851, 686–88.

Attiret, Jean Denis. *A Particular Account of the Emperor of China's Gardens near Pekin: In a Letter from F. Attiret, a French Missionary, Now Employ'd by That Emperor to Paint the Apartments in Those Gardens, to His Friend at Paris. Translated from the French by Sir Harry Beaumont*. London: Printed for R. Dodsley; and sold by M. Cooper, 1752.

Ayscough, Florence. "Cult of the Ch'eng Huang Lao Yeh." *Journal of the North-China Branch of the Royal Asiatic Society* 55 (1924): 131–55.

Bailey, Peter. *Leisure and Class in Victorian England: Rational Recreation and the Contest for Control, 1830–1885*. London: Methuen, 1987.

Balfour, George. *Memorandum of the Services of Captain Now Major George Balfour, Madras Artillery, Late Consul at Shanghai*. London: B. W. Gardiner, 1848.

Banno, Masataka. *China and the West, 1858–1861: The Origins of the Tsungli Yamen*. Cambridge: Harvard University Press, 1964.

Barrow, John. *Travels in China: Containing Descriptions, Observations and Comparisons, Made and Collected in the Course of a Short Residence at the Imperial Palace of Yuen-Min-Yuen, and on a Subsequent Journey through the Country from Pekin to Canton*. London: Printed for T. Cadell and W. Davis, 1804.

Beeching, Jack. *The Chinese Opium Wars*. London: Hutchinson, 1975.

Belsky, Richard. *Localities at the Center: Native Place, Space, and Power in Late Imperial Beijing*. Cambridge: Harvard University Asia Center, 2005.

Bergère, Marie-Claire. "'The Other China': Shanghai from 1919 to 1949." In *Shanghai, Revolution and Development in an Asian Metropolis*, edited by Christopher Howe, 1–34. Cambridge: Cambridge University Press, 1981.

———. *Shanghai: China's Gateway to Modernity*. Stanford: Stanford University Press, 2009.

Bhabha, Homi. "Of Mimicry and Man." In *Tensions of Empire: Colonial Cultures in a Bourgeois World*, edited by Frederick Cooper and Ann Laura Stoler, 152–62. Berkeley: University of California Press, 1997.

Bian zhu. "Juan tou bian yu." *Zhongguo jianzhu* 3, no. 5 (1935): preface.

Bickers, Robert A. *Britain in China: Community, Culture and Colonialism, 1900–1949*. New York: St. Martin's, 1999.

———. "Moving Stories: Memorialisation and Its Legacies in Treaty Port China." *Journal of Imperial and Commonwealth History* 42, no. 5 (2014): 826–56.

———. "Shanghailanders: The Formation and Identity of the British Settler Community in Shanghai, 1842–1937." *Past and Present* 159 (1998): 161–211.

Biggerstaff, Knight. "Shanghai Polytechnic Institution and Reading Room: An Attempt to Introduce Western Science and Technology to the Chinese." *Pacific Historical Review* 25, no. 2 (May 1956): 127–49.

Blake, Robert. *Jardine Matheson: Traders of the Far East*. London: Weidenfeld and Nicolson, 1999.

Blomfield, Reginald Theodore. *Memoirs of an Architect*. London: Macmillan, 1932.

Blue, Gregory. "Opium for China: The British Connection." In *Opium Regimes: China, Britain, and Japan, 1839–1952*, edited by Timothy Brook and Bob Tadashi Wakabayashi, 30–47. Berkeley: University of California Press, 2000.

Bohde, Daniela. "Notes from the Field: Mimesis." *Art Bulletin* 95, no. 1 (June 2013): 195–97.

Bond, George E. "Registration: The Case Restated." *Builder*, November 18, 1908, 2.

Borg, Dorothy. "Japanese Announce Plans for a New Shanghai." *Far Eastern Survey* 8, no. 16 (August 1939): 191–92.

Bozdogan, Sibel. *Modernism and Nation Building: Turkish Architectural Culture in the Early Republic*. Seattle: University of Washington Press, 2001.

Brautigam, Deborah, and Tang Xiaoyang. "African Shenzhen: China's Special Economic Zones in Africa." *Journal of Modern African Studies* 49, no. 1 (2011): 27–54.

Bremner, G. A. *Imperial Gothic: Religious Architecture and High Anglican Culture in the British Empire, 1840–1870*. New Haven: Yale University Press, 2013.

———. "Nation and Empire in the Government Architecture of Mid-Victorian London: The Foreign and India Office Reconsidered." *Historical Journal* 48, no. 3 (September 2005): 703–42.

Bremner, G. A., and D. P. Y. Lung. "Spaces of Exclusion: The Significance of Cultural Identity in the Formation of European Residential Districts in British Hong Kong, 1877–1904." *Environment and Planning D: Society and Space* 21 (2003): 223–52.

Brewer, John, and Eckhart Hellmuth, eds. *Rethinking Leviathan: The Eighteenth-Century State in Britain and Germany*. Oxford: Oxford University Press, 1999.

Brunschwig, Henri. *French Colonialism, 1871–1914: Myths and Realities*. New York: Praeger, 1964.

"Buildings." In "Secretary Taft's Visit to Shanghai." Special issue, *Journal of the American Association of China* 2, no. 5 (November 1907): 56.

Burke, James Cobb. *My Father in China*. New York: Farrar and Rinehart, 1942.

Cao Sheng, "Yihuan beichang ji" 1876. Reprinted in *Shanghai zhanggu congshu*, vol. 2, edited by Hu Poan, 946–1033. Shanghai: Shanghai Tongsheshi, 1936.

Carr, Caleb. *The Devil Soldier: The Story of Frederick Townsend Ward*. New York: Random House, 1992.

Carroll, John M. "Slow Burn in China: Factories, Fear, and Fire in Canton." In *Empires of Panic: Epidemics and Colonial Anxieties*, edited by Robert Peckham, 35–55. Hong Kong: Hong Kong University Press, 2015.

Carroll, Peter J. "The Beaux-Arts in Another Register: Government Administrative and Civic Centers in City Plans of the Republican Era." In *Chinese Architecture and the*

Beaux-Arts, edited by Jeffrey W. Cody, Nancy Shatzman Steinhardt, and Tony Atkins, 315–32. Honolulu: University of Hawaiʻi Press, 2011.

———. *Between Heaven and Modernity: Reconstructing Suzhou, 1895–1937*. Stanford: Stanford University Press, 2006.

Carter, John. *The Builder's Magazine: or, a universal dictionary for architects, carpenters, masons, bricklayers, &c. . . . consisting of designs in architecture in every stile and taste . . . together with the plans and sections, . . . the whole forming a complete system of architecture*. London: Printed for E. Newbery, the Corner of St. Paul's Church Yard, in Ludgate Street, 1788.

Cassel, Pär Kristoffer. *Grounds of Judgment: Extraterritoriality and Imperial Power in Nineteenth-Century China and Japan*. Oxford: Oxford University Press, 2012.

Chambers, Sir William. *Designs of Chinese Buildings, Furniture, Dresses, Machines and Utensils*. London: Published for the author and fold by him [*sic*] next Door to Tom's Coffee-house, Russel-Street, Covent-Garden, 1757.

———. *A Treatise on Civil Architecture, in which the Principles of that Art are Laid Down*. London: Printed for the author by J. Haberkorn, 1759.

Chan, Pedith. "The Institutionalization and Legitimatization of Guohua: Art Societies in Republican China." *Modern China* 39, no. 5 (September 2013): 541–70.

———. *The Making of a Modern Art World: Institutionalisation and Legitimatisation of Guohua in Republican Shanghai*. Leiden: Brill, 2017.

Chang Qing, ed. *Daduhui cong zheli kaishi: Shanghai Nanjing lu waitan duan yanjiu*. Shanghai: Tongji Daxue Chubanshe, 2005.

Chatterjee, Anuradha. "Tectonic into Textile: John Ruskin and his Obsession with the Architectural Surface." *Textile: Journal of Cloth and Culture* 7, no. 1 (2009): 68–97.

Chattopadhyay, Swati. "Blurring Boundaries: The Limits of 'White Town' in Colonial Calcutta." *Journal of the Society of Architectural Historians* 59, no. 2 (June 2000): 154–79.

Chaund, William. "Architectural Effort and Chinese Nationalism: Being a Radical Interpretation of Modern Architecture as a Potent Factor in Civilization." *Far Eastern Review* 15, no. 8 (August 1919): 533–36.

Cheng, Ying-wan, and Harvard University East Asian Research Center. *Postal Communication in China and Its Modernization, 1860–1896*. Cambridge: Harvard University Press, 1970.

"Chinese Art Museum in Shanghai." *Architecture d'aujourd'hui* 20, no. 2 (February 1950): 76–77.

Chouban yiwu shimo. Xu xiu siku quanshu. Vol. 419. Shanghai: Shanghai Guji Chubanshe, 1995.

Christ, Carol Ann. "'The Sole Guardians of the Art Inheritance of Asia': Japan and China at the 1904 St. Louis World's Fair." *positions* 8, no. 3 (2000): 675–709.

Chu, Cecilia L. "Constructing a New Domestic Discourse: The Modern Home in Architectural Journals and Mass-Market Texts in Early Twentieth-Century China." *Journal of Architecture* 22, no. 6 (2017): 1066–91.

Chung, Anita. *Drawing Boundaries: Architectural Images in Qing China*. Honolulu: University of Hawaiʻi Press, 2004.

Clancey, Gregory K. *Earthquake Nation: The Cultural Politics of Japanese Seismicity, 1868–1930*. Berkeley: University of California Press, 2006.

Clear, A. C., and D. P. Griffith. "Education and Training of Chinese Students in Engineering." In *Engineering Society of China: Proceedings of the Society and Report of the Council, 1916–1917*, 97–128. Shanghai: Engineering Society of China, 1917.

Clear, Alfred Charles. "Presidential Address." In *Engineering Society of China: Proceedings of the Society and Report of the Council, 1914–1915*, 1–13. Shanghai: Kelly and Walsh, 1915.

Clifford, Nicholas. *Shanghai 1925: Urban Nationalism and the Defense of Foreign Privilege*. Michigan Papers in Chinese Studies, No. 37. Ann Arbor: Center for Chinese Studies, 1979.

Coates, P. D. *The China Consuls: British Consular Officers, 1843–1943*. Oxford: Oxford University Press, 1988.

Coble, Parks M. *Facing Japan: Chinese Politics and Japanese Imperialism, 1931–1937*. Cambridge: Harvard University Press, 1991.

Cody, Jeffrey W. "American Planning in Republican China." *Planning Perspectives* 11 (1996): 339–77.

———. *Building in China: Henry K. Murphy's "Adaptive Architecture," 1914–1935*. Seattle: University of Washington Press, 2001.

———. Introduction to *Chinese Architecture and the Beaux-Arts*, edited by Cody, Nancy Shatzman Steinhardt, and Tony Atkins, xi–xxi. Honolulu: University of Hawai'i Press, 2011.

———. "Minguo shiqi Shanghai de zhuzai fangdi chanye." In *Chengshi jinbu, qiye fazhan he Zhongguo xiandaihua, 1840–1949*, edited by Zhang Zhongli, 263–74. Shanghai: Shanghai Shehui Kexueyuan Chubanshe, 1994.

———. "The Woman with the Binoculars: British Architects, Chinese Builders, and Shanghai's Skyline, 1900–1937." In *Twentieth-Century Architecture and Its Histories*, edited by Louise Campbell, 251–74. London: Society of Architectural Historians of Great Britain, 2000.

Cohen, Warren I. "American Perceptions of China." In *Dragon and Eagle: United States-China Relations: Past and Future*, edited by Michel Oksenberg and Robert B. Oxnam, 54–86. New York: Basic, 1978.

Cohn, Bernard. "Representing Authority in Victorian India." In *Postcolonial Passages: Contemporary History-Writing on India*, edited by Saurabh Dube, 47–69. Oxford: Oxford University Press, 2004.

Conner, Patrick. *Oriental Architecture in the West*. London: Thames and Hudson, 1979.

Cooke, George Wingrove. *China: Being "The Times" Special Correspondence from China in the Years 1857–58*. Wilmington: Scholarly Resources, 1972.

Coomans, Thomas. "Indigenizing Catholic Architecture in China: From Western-Gothic to Sino-Christian Design, 1900–1940." In *Catholicism in China, 1900–Present*, edited by C. Y. Chu, 125–44. New York: Palgrave Macmillan, 2014.

———. "A Pragmatic Approach to Church Construction in Northern China at the Time of Christian Inculturation: The Handbook 'Le missionnaire constructeur,' 1926." *Frontiers of Architectural Research* 3, no. 2 (June 2014): 89–107.

Cornish, N. E. "President's Address." In *The Shanghai Society of Engineers and Architects: Proceedings of the Society and Report of the Council, 1909–1910*, 1–23. Shanghai: North-China Daily News and Herald, 1911.

Cranston, Earl. "Shanghai in the Taiping Period." *Pacific Historical Review* 5, no. 2 (June 1936): 147–60.

Cret, Paul Philippe. "The École des Beaux-Arts: What Its Architectural Teaching Means." *Architectural Record* 23, no. 5 (May 1908): 367–71.

———. "Ten Years of Modernism." *Architectural Forum* 59 (1933): 91–94.

Crinson, Mark. *Empire Building: Orientalism and Victorian Architecture*. London: Routledge, 1996.

———. *Rebuilding Babel: Modern Architecture and Internationalism*. London: I. B. Tauris, 2017.

Crossman, Carl L. *The Decorative Arts of the China Trade: Paintings, Furnishings and Exotic Curiosities*. Suffolk: Antique Collectors' Club, 1991.

Cummins, J. S. *A Question of Rites: Friar Domingo Navarrete and the Jesuits in China*. Aldershot, Hants: Scolar Press, 1993.

Cunningham, Colin. *Victorian and Edwardian Town Halls*. London: Routledge, 1981.

Cunynghame, Arthur. *The Opium War: Being Recollections of Service in China*. Philadelphia: G. B. Zieber and Co., 1845.

Davis, John Francis. *The Chinese: General Description of the Empire of China and Its Inhabitants*. Vol. 2. London: Charles Knight and Co., 1836.

Defoe, Daniel. *The Farther Adventures of Robinson Crusoe*. London: W. Taylor, 1719.

Deng Ming. *Shanghai bainian lueying*. Shanghai: Shanghai Renmin Meishu Chubanshe, 1992.

Denison, Edward, and Guang Yuren. *Building Shanghai: The Story of China's Gateway*. West Sussex, England: John Wiley and Sons, 2006.

———. *Modernism in China: Architectural Visions and Revolutions*. Chichester: John Wiley, 2008.

Des Courtils, Louis. *La Concession Française de Changhaï*. Paris: Librairie du Recueil Sirey, 1934.

Dikötter, Frank. *Exotic Commodities: Modern Objects and Everyday Life in China*. New York: Columbia University Press, 2006.

Dillon, Michael. *China's Muslim Hui Community: Migration, Settlement and Sects*. London: Curzon, 1999.

Dillon, Nara, and Jean Chun Oi. *At the Crossroads of Empires: Middlemen, Social Networks, and State-Building in Republican Shanghai*. Stanford: Stanford University Press, 2008.

Ding Richang and Zhao Chunchen. *Ding Richang ji*. 2 vols. Shanghai: Shanghai Guji Chubanshe, 2010.

Do You Know Shanghai? Canadian Pacific Steamships, 1923.

Dong Dayou. "Architecture Chronicle." *T'ien Hsia Monthly* 3, no. 4 (1936): 358–62.

———. "Greater Shanghai—Greater Vision." *China Critic* 10, no. 6 (August 1935): 103–6.

———. "New Shanghai." *China Quarterly* 1, no. 2 (December 1935): 87–98.

Downing, Charles Toogood. *The Fan-qui in China*. 3 vols. London: Henry Colburn, 1838.

Du Halde, J. B. *Description géographique, historique, chronologique, politique, et physique de l'empire de la Chine et de la Tartarie Chinoise, enrichie des cartes générales et particulieres de ces pays, de la carte générale et des cartes particulieres du Thibet, & de la*

Corée; & ornée d'un grand nombre de figures & de vignettes gravées en tailledouce. La Haye: H. Scheurleer, 1736.

Du Yangeng. "Duiyu gaijin Zhongguoshi jianzhu de shangque." In *Zhongguo jianzhu zhanlanhui huikan*, 1–3. Shanghai: Zhongguo Jianzhu Zhanlanhui Huikan, 1936.

———. "Shanghai shi jianzhu xiehui lueshi." In *Zhongguo jianzhu zhanlanhui huikan*, 1–4. Shanghai: Zhongguo Jianzhu Zhanlanhui Huikan, 1936.

———. "Zhongguo jianzhu zhanlanhui de shiming." In *Zhongguo jianzhu zhanlanhui huikan*, 4. Shanghai: Zhongguo Jianzhu Zhanlanhui Huikan, 1936.

———. "Zuotan zhuishu." *Jianzhu yuekan* 4, no. 3 (1936): 3–4.

Dutta, Arindam. *The Bureaucracy of Beauty: Design in the Age of Its Global Reproducibility.* New York: Routledge, 2007.

Dyce, Charles. *Personal Reminiscences of Thirty Years' Residence in the Model Settlement Shanghai, 1870–1900.* London: Chapman and Hall, 1906.

Easterling, Keller. *Extrastatecraft: The Power of Infrastructure Space.* London: Verso, 2014.

Eaton, Natasha. *Mimesis across Empires: Artwork and Networks in India.* Durham, NC: Duke University Press, 2013.

Edkins, Joseph. "Chinese Architecture [reprinted from the *Journal of the China Branch of the Royal Asiatic Society*]." Shanghai: Kelly and Walsh, 1890.

Elliott, Mark C. *The Manchu Way: The Eight Banners and Ethnic Identity in Late Imperial China.* Stanford: Stanford University Press, 2001.

Elman, Benjamin. "Naval Warfare and the Refraction of China's Self-Strengthening Reforms into Scientific and Technological Failure, 1865–1895." *Modern Asian Studies* 38, no. 2 (2004): 283–326.

Elvin, Mark. "The Gentry Democracy in Chinese Shanghai, 1905–14." In *Modern China's Search for a Political Form*, edited by Jack Gray, 41–65. London: Oxford University Press, 1969.

———. "The Gentry Democracy in Shanghai, 1905–1914." PhD diss., Cambridge University, 1968.

Engineering Society of China. *Report of the Special Committee on Reinforced Concrete.* Shanghai: Kelly and Walsh, 1914.

Esherick, Joseph, and Mary Backus Rankin, eds. *Chinese Local Elites and Patterns of Dominance.* Berkeley: University of California Press, 1990.

———. "Modernity and Nation in the Chinese City." In *Remaking the Chinese City*, edited by Esherick, 1–19. Honolulu: University of Hawai'i Press, 2000.

———. *The Origins of the Boxer Uprising.* Berkeley: University of California Press, 1987.

Fairbank, John King. *Trade and Diplomacy on the China Coast: The Opening of Treaty Ports, 1842–1854.* Cambridge: Harvard University Press, 1964.

Fairbank, Wilma. *Liang and Lin: Partners in Exploring China's Architectural Past.* Philadelphia: University of Pennsylvania Press, 1994.

"Faqi Zhongguo jianzhu zhanlanhui." *Zhongguo bowuguan xiehui huikan* (April 1936): 53.

Farris, Johnathan. *Enclave to Urbanity: Canton, Foreigners, and Architecture from the Late Eighteenth to the Early Twentieth Centuries.* Hong Kong: Hong Kong University Press, 2017.

Fearn, Anne Walter. *My Days of Strength: An American Woman Doctor's Forty Years in China*. New York: Harper and Brothers, 1939.

Fergusson, James. *A History of Architecture in All Countries: From the Earliest Times to the Present Day*. London: John Murray, 1862.

Fernández Navarrete, Domingo. *The Travels and Controversies of Friar Domingo Navarrete, 1618–1686*. Edited by James Sylvester Cummins. Cambridge: Published for the Hakluyt Society at the University Press, 1962.

Fernsebner, Susan. "Material Modernities: China's Participation in World's Fairs and Expositions, 1876–1955." PhD diss., University of California, San Diego, 2002.

Fewsmith, Joseph. *Party, State, and Local Elites in Republican China: Merchant Organizations and Politics in Shanghai, 1890–1930*. Honolulu: University of Hawaiʻi Press, 1985.

Fichter, James R. *So Great a Proffit: How the East Indies Trade Transformed Anglo-American Capitalism*. Cambridge: Harvard University Press, 2010.

Fishel, Wesley R. *The End of Extraterritoriality in China*. Berkeley: University of California Press, 1952.

Flynt, Wayne. *Taking Christianity to China: Alabama Missionaries in the Middle Kingdom, 1850–1950*. Tuscaloosa: University of Alabama Press, 1997.

Foreign Affairs Association of Japan. "The Sino-Japanese Conflict: A Short Survey, Tokyo, 1937." In *Japan's Justification, the Sino-Japanese Conflict, 1931–1941*, vol. 2, *Prelude to Pearl Harbor: Seeds of Conflict*, 467–84. Nedeln, Liechtenstein: Kraus Reprint, 1980.

Fortune, Robert. *Three Years' Wanderings in the Northern Provinces of China: Including a Visit to the Tea, Silk, and Cotton Countries: With an Account of the Agriculture and Horticulture of the Chinese, New Plants, Etc.* London: J. Murray, 1847.

Foucault, Michel. *The Foucault Effect: Studies in Governmentality: With Two Lectures by and an Interview with Michel Foucault*. Edited by Graham Burchell, Colin Gordon, and Peter Miller. London: Harvester Wheatsheaf, 1991.

Freedman, Maurice. "Geomancy." *Proceedings of the Royal Anthropological Institute of Great Britain and Ireland*, no. 1968 (1968): 5–15.

Freeman, Edward Augustus. *A History of Architecture*. London: J. Masters, 1849.

Fu Xinian, Guo Daiheng, Liu Xujie, Pan Guxi, Qiao Yun, and Sun Dazhang. *Chinese Architecture*. English text edited and expanded by Nancy Steinhardt. New Haven: Yale University Press, 2002.

Fuji yingzaochang chengjian daohuai weiyuanhui. Shanghai: Gongchengji Niance, 1936.

Garrett, Valery M. *Heaven Is High, The Emperor Far Away: Merchants and Mandarins in Old Canton*. Oxford: Oxford University Press, 2002.

Ge, Yuanxu. *Huyou zaji*. 4 vols. 1876. Reprint, Shanghai: Shanghai Guji Chubanshe, 1989.

———. *Shanghai fanchang ji*. 3 vols. 1878. Reprint, Taipei: Wenhai Chubanshe Youxian Gongsi, 1988.

Geertz, Clifford. "Centers, Kings, and Charisma: Reflections on the Symbolics of Power." In *Culture and Its Creators: Essays in Honor of Edward Shils*, edited by Joseph Ben-David, Terry N. Clark, Raymond Aron, and Edward Shils, 150–71. Chicago: University of Chicago Press, 1977.

Gerth, Karl. *China Made: Consumer Culture and the Creation of the Nation*. Cambridge: Harvard University Press, 2003.

Giquel, Prosper. *The Foochow Arsenal, and Its results, from the Commencement in 1867, to the End of the Foreign Directorate, on the 16th February, 1874.* Translated by H. Lang. Shanghai: Shanghai Evening Courier, 1874.

Glover, William J. *Making Lahore Modern: Constructing and Imagining a Colonial City.* Minneapolis: University of Minnesota Press, 2008.

Godfrey, C. H. "The President's Address." In *The Shanghai Society of Engineers and Architects: Proceedings and Report of the Council, 1910–1911*, 3–17. Shanghai: Kelly and Walsh, 1911.

———. "Some Notes on Tenure of Land in Shanghai." In *The Engineering Society of China: Proceedings of the Society and Report of the Council, 1912–13*, 43–65. Shanghai: Kelly and Walsh, 1913.

Goodman, Bryna. "Improvisations on a Semicolonial Theme, or, How to Read a Celebration of a Transnational Urban Community." *Journal of Asian Studies* 59, no. 4 (November 2000): 889–926.

———. *Native Place, City, and Nation: Regional Networks and Identity in Shanghai, 1853–1937.* Berkeley: University of California Press, 1995.

Goodman, Bryna, and David Goodman. "Introduction: Colonialism and China." In *Twentieth-Century Colonialism and China: Localities, the Everyday, and the World*, edited by Goodman and Goodman, 1–22. London: Routledge, 2012.

Gordon, Charles George, and Samuel Mossman. *General Gordon's Private Diary of His Exploits in China.* London: Low, Marston, Searle and Rivington, 1885.

Gratton, Frederick M. *Freemasonry in Shanghai and Northern China.* Shanghai: North China Herald Office, 1900.

Gratton, Frederick M., and Robert S. Ivy. *The History of Freemasonry in Shanghai and Northern China Containing a Complete List of All the Regular Lodges and Royal Arch Chapters, & C.* Tientsin, China: North China Print and Pub. Co., 1913.

Greenberg, Michael. *British Trade and the Opening of China, 1800–42.* Cambridge: Cambridge University Press, 1951.

Greenhalgh, Paul. *Ephemeral Vistas: The Expositions Universelles, Great Exhibitions and World's Fairs, 1851–1939.* Manchester: Manchester University Press, 1988.

Gropius, Walter. *Internationale Architektur.* 1925. Reprint, Munich: Open University, 1975.

Grossman, Elizabeth. *The Civic Architecture of Paul Cret.* London: Cambridge University Press, 1996.

———. "Paul Philippe Cret: Rationalism and Imagery in American Architecture." PhD diss., Brown University, 1980.

Guo Hui. "Canonization in Early Twentieth-Century Chinese Art History." *Journal of Art Historiography* 6, no. 10 (June 2014): 1–16.

Guo Yuanxi. "Bolanhui chenjie ge guan yingzao sheji zhi kaolu." *Zhongguo jianzhu* 2, no. 2 (1934): 12–14.

———. "Fuxing xin Zhongguo jianzhu jihua shu." Manuscript, n.d. Special Collections, University of Hong Kong.

Guofan, Zeng. *Zeng Guofan quanji.* Vol. 3. Changsha: Yuelu Shushe, 2011.

Guoli Zhongyang daxue gongxueyuan, jianzhu gongcheng xi. *Canjia Zhongguo jianzhu zhanlanhui zhi yizhi.* Nanjing: Guoli Zhongyang daxue gongxueyuan, 1936.

Guterl, Matthew Pratt. "The New Race Consciousness: Race, Nation, and Empire in American Culture, 1910–1925." *Journal of World History* 10, no. 2 (February 1992): 307–52.

Guth, Christine. "Charles Longfellow and Okakura Kakuzo: Cultural Cross-Dressing in the Colonial Context." *positions: east asian culture critique* 8, no. 3 (Winter 2000): 606–36.

Gützlaff, Karl Friedrich August, and Andrew Reed. *China Opened, or, a Display of the Topography, History, Customs, Manners, Arts, Manufactures, Commerce, Literature, Religion, Jurisprudence, Etc. Of the Chinese Empire.* London: Smith, Elder and Co., 1838.

Haiguan zong shui wu si shu and Stanley Fowler Wright. *Documents Illustrative of the Origin, Development and Activities of the Chinese Customs Service.* Shanghai: Statistical Dept. of the Inspectorate General of Customs, 1937.

Hancock, David. *Citizens of the World: London Merchants and the Integration of the British Atlantic Community, 1735–1785.* Cambridge: Cambridge University Press, 1995.

Hart, Robert. *Entering China's Service: Robert Hart's Journals, 1854–1863.* Edited by Katherine Frost Bruner. Cambridge: Council on East Asian Studies, Harvard University, 1986.

———. *The I.G. in Peking: Letters of Robert Hart, Chinese Maritime Customs, 1868–1907.* Edited by John King Fairbank, Katherine Frost Bruner, and Elizabeth MacLeod Matheson. 2 vols. Cambridge: Belknap Press of Harvard University Press, 1975.

———. *These from the Land of Sinim: Essays on the Chinese Question.* London: Chapman and Hall, 1901.

Hay, Jonathan. "Painting and the Built Environment in Late-Nineteenth-Century Shanghai." In *Chinese Art: Modern Expressions*, edited by Maxwell Hearn and Judith G. Smith, 61–101. New York: Museum of Modern Art, 2001.

He Zhongjian. "Du Yangeng yu 'Jianzhu yuekan.'" In *Di si ci Zhongguo jindai jianzhu shi yanjiu taolunhui lunwenji*, edited by Zhang Fuhe, 188–93. Shanghai: Zhongguo Jianzhu Gongye Chubanshe, 1993.

———. "Shanghai jindai yingzaoye de xingcheng ji tezheng." In *Di san ci Zhongguo jindai jianzhu shi yanjiu taolun huilun wenji*, edited by Wang Tan, 118–24. Beijing: Zhongguo Jianzhu Gongye Chubanshe, 1991.

———. *Zhang Xiaoliang zhuan: Shanghai jindai jianzhuye de lingjun ren.* Shanghai: Shanghai Shehui Kexue Chubanshe, 1997.

Headrick, Daniel R. *The Tentacles of Progress: Technology Transfer in the Age of Imperialism, 1850–1940.* New York: Oxford University Press, 1988.

———. *The Tools of Empire: Technology and European Imperialism in the Nineteenth Century.* New York: Oxford University Press, 1981.

Heidenstam, H. von. "Shanghai—the Industrial and Commercial Metropolis?" In *Engineering Society of China: Proceedings of the Society and Report of the Council, 1919–20*, 5–32. Shanghai: Engineering Society of China, 1921.

Henriot, Christian. *Shanghai, 1927–1937: Municipal Power, Locality, and Modernization.* Berkeley: University of California Press, 1993.

———. "The Shanghai Bund in Myth and History: An Essay through Textual and Visual Sources." *Journal of Modern Chinese History* 4, no. 1 (June 2010): 1–27.

Herbert, Gilbert. *Pioneers of Prefabrication: The British Contribution in the Nineteenth Century.* Baltimore: Johns Hopkins University Press, 1978.

Hevia, James L. *Cherishing Men from Afar: Qing Guest Ritual and the Macartney Embassy of 1793.* Durham, NC: Duke University Press, 1995.

———. *English Lessons: The Pedagogy of Imperialism in Nineteenth-Century China.* Durham: Duke University Press, 2003.

———. *The Imperial Security State: British Colonial Knowledge and Empire-Building in Asia.* Cambridge: Cambridge University Press, 2012.

Hietkamp, Lenore. "The Park Hotel and Its Architect Laszlo Hudec: 'Tallest Building in the Far East' as Metaphor for Pre-Communist China." Master's thesis, University of Victoria, 1998.

"History of the Northern Lodge of China, No. 570, E. C." Undated manuscript. Library and Museum of Freemasonry, London.

Hitchcock, Henry Russell. *Early Victorian Architecture in Britain.* New Haven: Yale University Press, 1954.

———. *Modern Architecture: Romanticism and Reintegration.* New York: Hacker Art Books, 1970.

Ho, Denise Y. *Curating Revolution: Politics on Display in Mao's China.* Cambridge: Cambridge University Press, 2017.

Hoang, Pierre P. *Notions Techniques sur la propriété en Chine, avec un chois d'actes et de documents officiels.* 1897. Reprint, Nendeln: Kraus-Thomson, 1975.

Hobsbawm, E. J. *Nations and Nationalism since 1780: Programme, Myth, Reality.* The Wiles Lectures Given at the Queen's University of Belfast. Cambridge: Cambridge University Press, 1992.

Hobson, J. A. *Imperialism: A Study.* London: J. Nisbet, 1902.

Home, Robert. *Of Planting and Planning: The Making of British Colonial Cities.* London: Routledge, 2013.

"Homicides in China." *Chinese Repository* 3 (May 1834): 38–39.

Hosie, Lady Dorothea. *Brave New China.* London: Hodder and Stoughton, 1938.

"Hospital for Shanghai." *Architectural Forum* 85, no. 8 (August 1946): 11.

Hu Shih and Lin Yutang. *China's Own Critics: A Selection of Essays.* Beijing: China United Press, 1931.

Huang Jinghang, ed. *Yang Sisheng, Ye Chengzhong, Xiansheng Hezhuan.* Shanghai: Tao Xingzhi Jingti, 1936.

Huang Shiquan. "Songnan mengying lu." 1883. Reprinted in *Huyou zaji, Songnan mengying lu, Huyou mengying: Shanghai tan yu Shanghairen congshu,* edited by Zheng Zu'an, 89–149. Shanghai: Shanghai Guji Chubanshe, 1989.

Huber, Valeksa. *Channelling Mobilities: Migration and Globalisation in the Suez Canal Region, 1869–1914.* Cambridge: Cambridge University Press, 2013.

Hübner, Joseph Alexander von. *Promenade autour du monde.* Vol. 1. Paris: Librairie Hachette et Compagnie, 1881.

Hunt, Michael H. *The Making of a Special Relationship: The United States and China to 1914.* New York: Columbia University Press, 1983.

Hunter, William C. *The "Fan Kwae" at Canton before Treaty Days, 1825–1844.* London: K. Paul, Trench and Co., 1882.

Huskey, James Layton. "Americans in Shanghai: Community Formation and Response to Revolution, 1919–1928." PhD diss., University of North Carolina at Chapel Hill, 1985.

Hyde, Timothy. "Architecture, Modernity, Crisis." *Journal of Architectural Education* 69, no. 1 (March 2015): 2–3.

————. *Constitutional Modernism: Architecture and Civil Society in Cuba, 1933–1959*. Minneapolis: University of Minnesota Press, 2012.

International Meeting of Architects. Warsaw, Poland: Warsaw Illustrated Weekly Stolica on behalf of the Association of Polish Architects, 1954.

Irving, Robert Grant. *Indian Summer—Lutyens, Baker, and Imperial Delhi*. New Haven: Yale University Press, 1981.

Issar, Sukriti. "Codes of Contention: Building Regulations in Colonial Bombay, 1870–1912." *Journal of Historical Sociology* 30, no. 2 (June 2017): 164–88.

Jackson, Isabella. *Shaping Modern Shanghai: Colonialism in China's Global City*. Cambridge: Cambridge University Press, 2018.

Jarman, Robert L. *Shanghai Political and Economic Reports, 1842–1943: British Government Records from the International City*. 18 vols. Slough: Archive Editions, 2008.

Jenkins, Eugenia Zuroski. *A Taste for China: English Subjectivity and the Prehistory of Orientalism*. Oxford: Oxford University Press, 2013.

Jennings, Eric T. *Imperial Heights: Dalat and the Making and Undoing of French Indochina*. Berkeley: University of California Press, 2011.

Jiaman, Liang. *Xu Guangqi nianpu*. Shanghai: Shanghai Guji Chubanshe, 1981.

"Jianzhujie yingyou zhi zeren." *Jianzhu yuekan* 3, no. 9–10 (1935): 3.

Johnson, Linda Cooke. *Shanghai: From Market Town to Treaty Port, 1074–1858*. Stanford: Stanford University Press, 1995.

Kallee-Dijon. "Architecture and Building Practice in China." *Architect and Engineer* (October 1940): 59–60.

Kang Youwei. *Datong shu*. 1936. Reprinted in *Chuantong waiyi xia di jinshi lixiangguo; xing Shi congshu*, edited by Li Shizhen. Zhengzhou: Zhongzhou Guji Chubanshe, 1998.

Karl, Rebecca. *Staging the World: Chinese Nationalism at the Turn of the Twentieth Century*. Durham, NC: Duke University Press, 2002.

Kawata, T. *Glimpses of China, 1921*. Tokyo: The Hakubunkwan Printing Co., 1921.

Keay, John. *The Honourable Company: A History of the English East India Company*. New York: Macmillan, 1994.

Keeton, George Williams. *The Development of Extraterritoriality in China*. New York: Fertig, 1969.

Keller, Lisa. *Triumph of Order: Democracy and Public Space in New York and London*. New York: Columbia University Press, 2009.

Kennedy, Thomas L. "Li Hung-Chang and the Kiangnan Arsenal, 1860–1895." In *Li Hung-Chang and China's Early Modernization*, edited by Samuel C. Chu and Kwang-Ching Liu, 197–215. Armonk, NY: M. E. Sharpe, 1993.

Kidambi, Prashant. *The Making of an Indian Metropolis: Colonial Governance and Public Culture in Bombay, 1890–1920*. Burlington, VT: Ashgate, 2007.

King, Anthony D. *The Bungalow: The Production of a Global Culture*. Oxford: Oxford University Press, 1995.

————. *Colonial Urban Development: Culture, Social Power, and Environment*. London: Routledge, 1976.

Kipnis, Andrew. "'Face': An Adaptable Discourse of Social Surfaces." *positions* 3, no. 1 (1995): 119–48.

Kirby, William C. "Engineering China: Birth of the Developmental State, 1928–1937." In *Becoming Chinese: Passages to Modernity and Beyond*, edited by Wen-Hsin Yeh, 137–60. Berkeley: University of California Press, 2000.

———. *Germany and Republican China*. Stanford: Stanford University Press, 1984.

Klekar, Cynthia. "'Sweetness and Courtesie': Benevolence, Civility, and China in the Making of European Modernity." *Eighteenth-Century Studies* 43, no. 3 (2010): 357–69.

Kostof, Spiro. *The City Shaped: Urban Patterns and Meanings through History*. Boston: Little, Brown, 1991.

Kotenev, Anatol M. *Shanghai, Its Mixed Court and Council: Material Relating to the History of the Shanghai Municipal Council and the History, Practice and Statistics of the International Mixed Court, Chinese Modern Law and Shanghai Municipal Land Regulations and Bye-Laws Governing the Life in the Settlement*. Shanghai: North-China Daily News and Herald, 1925.

Kowsky, Francis R. "The Architecture of Frederick C. Withers (1828–1901)." *Journal of the Society of Architectural Historians* 35, no. 2 (May 1976): 83–107.

Krokker, Bruno. "The Building Industry: Modern Buildings in Shanghai." *China Journal of Science and Arts* 30, no. 5 (May 1939): 315–17.

———. "The Deplorable Destruction of the Civic Centre." *China Journal of Science and Arts* 28, no. 2 (February 1938): 64–67.

Kuan, Seng. "Between Beaux-Arts and Modernism." In *Chinese Architecture and the Beaux-Arts*, edited by Jeffrey W. Cody, Nancy S. Steinhardt, and Tony Atkin, 169–92. Honolulu: University of Hawai'i Press, 2011.

———. "Image of the Metropolis: Three Historical Views of Shanghai." In *Shanghai: Architecture and Urbanism for Modern China*, edited by Peter G. Rowe and Seng Kuan, 84–103. New York: Prestel, 2004.

Lai Delin. "Searching for a Modern Chinese Monument: The Design of the Sun Yat-Sen Mausoleum in Nanjing." *Journal of the Society of Architectural Historians* 64, no. 1 (March 2005): 22–55.

———. *Zhongguo jindai jianzhu shi yanjiu*. Beijing: Tsinghua Daxue Chubanshe, 2007.

Lam, Tong. "Policing the Imperial Nation: Sovereignty, International Law, and the Civilizing Mission in Late Qing China." *Comparative Studies in Society and History* 52, no. 4 (2010): 881–908.

Land Regulations and Bye-Laws for the Foreign Settlements of Shanghai, North of the Yang-King-Pang. Shanghai: North-China Herald Office, 1898.

Lane-Poole, Stanley, and F. Victor Dickins. *The Life of Sir Harry Parkes: K.C.B., G.C.M.G., Sometime Her Majesty's Minister to China and Japan*. London: Macmillan and Co., 1894.

Lang, H. *Shanghai Considered Socially*. Shanghai: American Presbyterian Mission Press, 1875.

Lanning, George. "Names and Nicknames of the Shanghai Settlements." *Journal of the North-China Branch of the Royal Asiatic Society* 51 (1920): 81–98.

Lanning, George, and Samuel Couling. *The History of Shanghai*. 1921. Reprint, Taipei: Ch'eng Wen, 1973.

Lasker, Bruno. "Shanghai Tomorrow." *Social Forces* 19, no. 3 (March 1941): 314–26.

Lawrence, Amanda Reeser, and Ashley Schafer. "On the Surface." *Praxis* 9 (2007): 4.

Le Comte, Louis. *Memoirs and remarks: geographical, historical, topographical, physical, natural, astronomical, mechanical, military, mercantile, political, and ecclesiastical, made in above ten years travels through the Empire of China*. London: J. Hughs, 1737.

Le Corbusier. *The City of To-morrow and Its Planning*. New York: Dover, 1929.

Lee, Leo Ou-fan. *Shanghai Modern: The Flowering of a New Urban Culture in Shanghai, 1930–45*. Cambridge: Harvard University Press, 1999.

Legh, Peter. *The Music of the Eye; or Essays on the Vitruvian Analysis of Architecture*. London: Printed for William Walker; James Carpenter and Son; and Priestley and Weale, 1831.

Leibo, Steven A. *Transferring Technology to China: Prosper Giquel and the Self-Strengthening Movement*. Berkeley: Institute of East Asian Studies, University of California, 1985.

Levy, Richard Michael. "The Professionalization of American Architects and Civil Engineers, 1865–1917." PhD diss., University of California at Berkeley, 1980.

Li Hongzhang. *Memoirs of Li Hung Chang*. Translated by William Francis Mannix and John W. Foster. Boston: Houghton Mifflin, 1913.

Li Hongzhang, Gu Tinglong, and Dai Yi. *Li Hongzhang quanji*. 2 vols. Hefei: Anhui Jiaoyu Chubanshe, 2008.

Li Tiangang. *Ren wen Shanghai: Shimin de kongjian*. Shanghai: Shanghai Jiaoyu Chubanshe, 2004.

Li Tinghan. *Wanzhu xiaoxue* 1 (1913): 1–4.

Liang, Samuel Y. *Mapping Modernity in Shanghai: Space, Gender, and Visual Culture in the Sojourners' City, 1853–98*. New York: Routledge, 2010.

Liang, Yuansheng. *The Shanghai Taotai: Linkage Man in a Changing Society, 1843–90*. Honolulu: University of Hawai'i Press, 1990.

Liang Qichao. *Xin da lu youji*. 1904. Reprinted in *Jindai Zhongguo shiliao congkan*, vols. 96–97. Edited by Yang Fei. Taibei: Wenhai Chubanshe, 1967.

Liang Sicheng. "Weishenme yanjiu Zhongguo jianzhu." 1944. Reprinted in *Jianzhu wencui*, 251–54. Beijing: Shenghua Dushu Xinzhi Sanxian Shudian, 2006.

———, ed. *Yingzao suanli*. Beijing: Zhongguo Yingzaoshe Yinxing, 1932.

———. *Zhongguo jianzhu shi*. 1954. Reprint, Tianjin: Baihua Wenyi Chubanshe, 1998.

Liang Sicheng and Zhang Rui. "Tianjin tebie shi wuzhi jianshe fang'an." 1930. Reprinted in *Liang Sicheng quanji*, vol. 1, edited by Yu Zhigong, 32–34. Beijing: Zhongguo Jianzhu Gongye Chubanshe, 2001.

Lindsay, H. H., and Charles Gutzlaff. "Review." *Chinese Repository* 2, no. 12 (April 1834): 549.

Liu, Shih Shun. *Extraterritoriality: Its Rise and Its Decline*. Studies in History, Economics, and Public Law. New York: Columbia University Press, 1925.

Liu Xiang, Gu Yanpei, Lin Sun, and Gui Guoqiang. *Shanghai chenghuang miao daguan*. Shanghai: Fudan Daxue Chubanshe, 2002.

Lu Qianshou and Wu Jingqi. "Women de zhuzhang." *Zhongguo jianzhu* 4, no. 6 (1936): 55–56.

Lu Xun. *Qie jie ting zamen: Lu Xun quanji*. Vol. 6. Beijing: Renmin Wenxue Chubanshe, 1956.

———. *Selected Works of Lu Hsun*. Vol. 4. Translated by Xianyi Yang and Gladys Yang. Peking: Foreign Languages Press, 1956.

Lu Y. C. (Lu Yanzhi). "Memorials to Dr. Sun Yat-Sen in Nanking and Canton." *Far Eastern Review* 25, no. 4 (March 1929): 97–101.

Ma Guangren, ed. *Shanghai xinwenshi (1850–1949)*. Shanghai: Fudan Daxue Chubanshe, 1996.

Macaulay, Thomas. *Speeches by the Rt. Hon. Thomas Babington Macaulay*. New York: Redfield, 1866.

MacFarlane, W. *Sketches in the Foreign Settlements and Native City of Shanghai*. Shanghai, 1881.

Macgowan, D. J. "Modes of Keeping Time Known among the Chinese." *Chinese Repository* (July 1851): 607–12.

Macpherson, Kerrie L. "Designing China's Urban Future: The Greater Shanghai Plan, 1927–1937." *Planning Perspectives* 5, no. 1 (1990): 39–62.

———. *A Wilderness of Marshes: The Origins of Public Health in Shanghai, 1843–1893.* Hong Kong: Oxford University Press, 1987.

Mallet-Stevens, Rob. "Architecture 'd'aujourd'hui.'" *L'Architecture d'aujourd'hui* 6, no. 9 (1935): 73.

Markley, Robert. *The Far East and the English Imagination, 1600–1730*. Cambridge: Cambridge University Press, 2006.

Matheson, James, and James Warren. *The Present Position and Prospects of the British Trade with China: Together with an Outline of Some Leading Occurrences in Its Past History*. London: Smith Elder, 1836.

Mathur, Saloni. *India by Design: Colonial History and Cultural Display*. Berkeley: University of California Press, 2007.

Maybon, Charles, and Jean Fredet. *Histoire de la Concession Française de Changhai*. Paris: Librairie Plon, 1929.

Maynard, W. Barksdale. *Architecture in the United States, 1800–1850*. New Haven: Yale University Press, 2002.

McCormick, Elsie. *Audacious Angles on China*. Shanghai: Chinese American Publications, 1922.

McCullough, David G. *The Path between the Seas: The Creation of the Panama Canal, 1870–1914*. New York: Simon and Schuster, 1977.

Medhurst, Walter Henry. "General Description of Shanghae and Its Environs, Extracted from Native Authorities." *Chinese Miscellany: Designed to Illustrate the Government, Philosophy, Religion, Arts, Manufactures, Trade, Manners, Customs, History and Statistics of China* No. 4. Shanghae: Printed at the Mission Press, 1850.

———. "Reminiscences of the Opening of Shanghai to Foreign Trade." *Chinese and Japanese Repository* 3, no. 15 (October 12, 1864): 79–88.

Mehta, Uday Singh. *Liberalism and Empire: A Study in Nineteenth-Century British Liberal Thought*. Chicago: University of Chicago Press, 1999.

Meihua'anzhu. *Shenjiang shengjing tushuo*. 1894. Reprint. Zhongguo Minsu Xuehui Minsu Congshu, edited by Guoli Beijing Daxue. Vol. 78. Taibei: Dongfang Wenhua Shuju, 1972.

Metcalf, Thomas. *An Imperial Vision: Indian Architecture and Britain's Raj*. Berkeley: University of California Press, 1989.

Meyer, Jeffrey F. "Feng-Shui of the Chinese City." *History of Religions* 18, no. 2 (November 1978): 138–55.

Meyer-Fong, Tobie S. *What Remains: Coming to Terms with Civil War in 19th Century China*. Stanford: Stanford University Press, 2013.

Michie, Alexander. *The Englishman in China during the Victorian Era as Illustrated in the Career of Sir Rutherford Alcock, K.C.B., D.C.L.* 2 vols. London: William Blackwood and Sons, 1900.

Mitchell, Timothy. *Colonising Egypt*. Berkeley: University of California Press, 1988.

———. *Rule of Experts: Egypt, Techno-Politics, Modernity*. Berkeley: University of California Press, 2002.

Montalto de Jesus, C. A. *Historic Shanghai*. Shanghai: Shanghai Mercury, 1909.

Moore, Alasdair. *La Mortola: In the Footsteps of Thomas Hanbury*. London: Cadogan Guides, 2004.

Morizet, Andre. "Maire de Boulogne-Billancourt." *L'architecture d'aujourd'hui* 5, no. 9 (1934): 5–18.

Morley, Ian. *British Provincial Civic Design and the Building of Late-Victorian and Edwardian Cities, 1880–1914*. Lewiston, ME: Edwin Mellen, 2008.

Morrison, Gabriel James. "Inaugural Address by President." In *Shanghai Society of Engineers and Architects: Proceedings of the Society and Report of the Council, 1900–1*, 3–26. Shanghai: "North China Herald" Office, 1901.

Morse, Hosea Ballou. *In the Days of the Taipings, Being the Recollections of Ting Kienchang, Otherwise Meisun, Sometime Scoutmaster and Captain in the Ever-Victorious Army and Interpreter-in-Chief to General Ward and General Gordon; an Historical Retrospect*. Salem, MA: Essex Institute, 1927.

———. *International Relations of the Chinese Empire*. Vol. 1. London: Longmans, Green, 1910–18.

Mou, Zhenyu. "Land, Law and Power: The Cadastre of the French Concession in Shanghai (1849–1943)." *European Journal of East Asian Studies* 14 (2015): 287–312.

Murphey, Rhoads. *Shanghai: Key to Modern China*. Cambridge: Harvard University Press, 1953.

Musgrove, Charles. *China's Contested Capital: Architecture, Ritual, and Response in Nanjing*. Honolulu: University of Hawai'i Press, 2013.

Naquin, Susan. *Peking: Temples and City Life, 1400–1900*. Berkeley: University of California Press, 2000.

Nelson, Louis P. *Architecture and Empire in Jamaica*. New Haven: Yale University Press, 2016.

Nevius, John L. *China and the Chinese*. New York: Harper and Brothers, 1869.

Nield, Robert. *China's Foreign Places: The Foreign Presence in China in the Treaty Port Era, 1840–1943*. Hong Kong: University of Hong Kong Press, 2015.

Nieuhof, Johannes, Johann Adam Schall von Bell, Pieter de Goyer, Jacob de Keizer, and Athanasius Kircher. *An Embassy from the East-India Company of the United Provinces, to the Grand Tartar Cham Emperor of China, Deliver'd by Their Excellencies Peter De Goyer and Jacob De Keyzer, at His Imperial City of Peking*. Translated by John Ogilby. London: Printed by the author (translator) John Ogilby, 1673.

Nilsson, Sten. *European Architecture in India, 1750–1850*. London: Faber and Faber, 1968.

"Notices of Shanghai: Its Position and Extent; Its Houses, Public Buildings, Gardens, Population, Commerce, Etc." *Chinese Repository* 15, no. 9 (1846): 469–72.

Nyíri, Pál. "Extraterritoriality. Foreign Concessions: The Past and Future of a Form of Shared Sovereignty." EspacesTemps.net. www.espacestemps.net/articles/extra territoriality-pal-nyiri.

O'Connor, Susan. "Architecture, Power and Ritual in Scottish Town Halls, 1833–1973." PhD diss., University of Bath, 2016.

Ong, Aihwa, "The Chinese Axis: Zoning Technologies and Variegated Sovereignty." *Journal of East Asian Studies* 4 (2004): 69–96.

Oshima, Ken Tadashi. *International Architecture in Interwar Japan: Constructing Kokusai Kenchiku.* Seattle: University of Washington Press, 2009.

Osterhammel, Jurgen. "Semi-colonialism and Informal Empire in Twentieth-Century China: Towards a Framework of Analysis." In *Imperialism and After: Continuities and Discontinuities*, edited by Wolfgang J. Mommsen and Jurgen Osterhammel, 290–314. London: Allen and Unwin, 1986.

Ottenheym, Konrad A. "Amsterdam 1700: Urban Space and Public Buildings." In *Circa 1700: Architecture in Europe and the Americas*, edited by Henry A. Millon, 119–38. New Haven: Yale University Press, 2005.

Otter, Chris. "Locating Matter: The Place of Materiality in Urban History." In *Material Powers: Cultural Studies, History and the Material Turn*, edited by Tony Bennett and Patrick Joyce, 38–59. London: Routledge, 2010.

Ouchterlony, John. *The Chinese War: An Account of the Operations of the British Forces from the Commencement of the Treaty of Nanjing.* London: Saunders and Otley, 1844.

The Palace Hotel Guide to Shanghai. Shanghai: Palace Hotel, 1909.

Pan Mingquan. *Shanghai fosi daoguan.* Shanghai: Shanghai Cishu Chubanshe, 2003.

Pearson, C. D. "Presidential Address." In *Engineering Society of China: Proceedings of the Society and Report of the Council, 1926–1928*, xxvii–xxxvi. Shanghai: North-China Daily News and Herald, 1928.

Perera, Nihal. *Decolonizing Ceylon: Colonialism, Nationalism and the Politics of Space in Sri Lanka.* New Delhi, India: Oxford University Press, 1999.

Perry, Elizabeth. *Shanghai on Strike: The Politics of Chinese Labor.* Stanford: Stanford University Press, 1993.

Peters, Tom F. *Building the Nineteenth Century.* Cambridge: MIT Press, 1996.

Peterson, Charles S. "The 1933 World's Fair." *Pencil Points* 10 (April 1929): 124.

Peterson, Willard J. "Why Did They Become Christians? Yang T'ing-Yun, Li Chih-Tsao, and Hsu Kuang-Ch'i." In *East Meets West: The Jesuits in China, 1582–1773*, edited by Charles E. Ronan and Bonnie B. C. Oh, 129–52. Chicago: Loyola University Press, 1988.

Phipps, John. *A Practical Treatise on the China and Eastern Trade.* London: Allen, 1836.

Picon, Antoine. *French Architects and Engineers in the Age of Enlightenment.* Cambridge Studies in the History of Architecture. Cambridge: Cambridge University Press, 1992.

Pitcher, Philip Wilson. *In and About Amoy: Some Historical and Other Facts Connected with One of the First Open Ports in China.* Shanghai: Methodist, 1909.

Platt, Stephen. *Autumn in the Heavenly Kingdom: China, the West, and the Epic Story of the Taiping Civil War.* New York: Random House, 2012.

Politzer, Eric. "The Changing Face of the Shanghai Bund, Circa 1849–1879." *Arts of Asia* 35, no. 2 (March/April 2005): 64–81.

Pong, David. "Confucian Patriotism and the Destruction of the Woosung Railway, 1877." *Modern Asian Studies* 7, no. 4 (1973): 647–76.

Port, M. H. *Imperial London: Civil Government Building in London 1850–1915.* New Haven: Published for the Paul Mellon Centre for Studies in British Art by Yale University Press, 1995.

Port, M. H., and Paul Mellon Centre for Studies in British Art. *The Houses of Parliament.* New Haven: Published for the Paul Mellon Centre for Studies in British Art by Yale University Press, 1976.

Porter, David. *Ideographia: The Chinese Cipher in Early Modern Europe.* Stanford: Stanford University Press, 2001.

———. "A Peculiar but Uninteresting Nation: China and the Discourse of Commerce in Eighteenth-Century England." *Eighteenth-Century Studies* 33, no. 2 (1999): 181–99.

Pott, F. L. Hawks. *A Short History of Shanghai, Being an Account of the Growth and Development of the International Settlement.* Shanghai: Kelly and Walsh, 1928.

Powell, Lawrence N. *The Accidental City: Improvising New Orleans.* Cambridge: Harvard University Press, 2012.

Proceedings: World Engineering Congress, Tokyo, 1929. Tokyo: Kogakkai, 1929.

"Proposed Reinforced Concrete Pagoda in Shanghai." In *Shanghai Society of Engineers and Architects: Proceedings of the Society and Report of the Council, 1909–1910,* 89–90. Shanghai: North-China Daily News and Herald, 1911.

Qian Zonghao. *Bainian huiwang: Shanghai waitan jianzhu yu jingguan de lishi bianqian.* Shanghai: Shanghai Kexue Jishu Chubanshe, 2004.

Ransome, Arthur. *The Chinese Puzzle.* London: G. Allen and Unwin, 1927.

Reilly, Thomas H. *The Taiping Heavenly Kingdom: Rebellion and the Blasphemy of Empire.* Seattle: University of Washington Press, 2004.

"Report of the Committee Appointed to Deal with the Subject of Technical Education in Shanghai." In *Shanghai Society of Engineers and Architects: Proceedings of the Society and Report of the Council, 1904–5,* 173–84. Shanghai: Kelly and Walsh, 1906.

Robinson, John Beverley. *Architectural Composition: An Attempt to Order and Phrase Ideas Which Hitherto Have Been Only Felt by the Instinctive Taste of Designers.* New York: Van Nostrand, 1914.

Rogaski, Ruth. *Hygienic Modernity: Meanings of Health and Disease in Treaty-Port China.* Berkeley: University of California Press, 2004.

Roskam, Cole. "Situating Chinese Architecture within 'A Century of Progress': The Chinese Pavilion, the Bendix Golden Temple, and the 1933 Chicago World's Fair." *Journal of the Society of Architectural Historians* 73, no. 3 (September 2014): 347–71.

Rowe, Peter G., and Seng Kuan. *Architectural Encounters with Essence and Form in Modern China.* Cambridge: MIT Press, 2002.

Ruan Xing. "Accidental Affinities: American Beaux-Arts in Twentieth-Century Chinese Architectural Education and Practice." *Journal of the Society of Architectural Historians* 61, no. 1 (March 2002): 30–47.

Ruitenbeek, Klaas. *Carpentry and Building in Late Imperial China: A Study of the Fifteenth-Century Carpenter's Manual "Lu Ban Jing."* New York: E. J. Brill, 1993.

Rujivacharakul, Vimalin. "Architects as Cultural Heroes." In *Cities in Motion: Interior, Coast, and Diaspora in Transnational China*, edited by Sherman Cochran and David Strand, 133–53. Berkeley: Institute of East Asian Studies, 2007.

Ruskin, John. *The Stones of Venice*. New York: Wiley, 1860.

"Satellite Towns of Shanghai." *Kokusai-Kentiku* 28, no. 4 (April 1961): 52–55.

Savage, Kirk. *Standing Soldiers, Kneeling Slaves: Race, War, and Monument in Nineteenth-Century America*. Princeton: Princeton University Press, 1997.

Scarth, John. *Twelve Years in China: The People, the Rebels, and the Mandarins*. London: T. Constable; Hamilton Adams, 1860.

Schram, Stuart, ed. *Mao's Road to Power: Revolutionary Writings 1912–1949*. Vol. 1, *The Pre-Marxist Period*. New York: M. E. Sharpe, 1992.

Schumpeter, Joseph Alois. *Capitalism, Socialism, and Democracy*. London: Allen and Unwin, 1947.

Scriver, Peter. "Empire-Building and Thinking in the Public Works Department of British India." In *Colonial Modernities: Building, Dwelling and Architecture in British India and Ceylon*, edited by Scriver and Vikramaditya Prakash, 69–92. London: Routledge, 2007.

Scully, Eileen P. *Bargaining with the State from Afar: American Citizenship in Treaty Port China, 1844–1942*. New York: Columbia University Press, 2001.

———. "Prostitution as Privilege: The 'American Girl' of Treaty-Port Shanghai, 1860–1937." *International History Review* 20, no. 4 (December 1998): 855–83.

Semper, Gottfried, and Harry Francis Mallgrave. "The Development of the Wall and Wall Construction in Antiquity [London Lecture of 18 November 1853]." *RES: Anthropology and Aesthetics*, no. 11 (Spring 1986): 33–42.

Seward, George F., and United States Consulate. *The United States Consulates in China: A Letter with Enclosures of the Consul-General in China to the Secretary of State*. Washington: Printed for private circulation, 1867.

Shanghai City Government. "Japanese Invasion of Shanghai (January 28–March 7, 1932). A Record of Facts. Secretariat, City Government of Greater Shanghai." In *Prelude to Pearl Harbor; Seeds of Conflict*, 43–56, vol. 1, *China's Plea for Help, the Sino-Japanese Conflict, 1931–1941*. Nendeln: Kraus Reprint, 1980.

Shanghai de jianglai. Shanghai: Zhonghua Shuju, 1934.

Shanghai jianzhu shigong weiyuanhui. *Dongfang "Bali": Jindai Shanghai jianzhu shihua*. Shanghai: Shanghai Wenhua Chubanshe, 1991.

"Shanghai Nanjing lu shangdian zhuangkuang." *Zhonghua shiye jie*, April 1914, 1–18.

"Shanghai shi jianzhu xiehui lue shi." In *Zhongguo jianzhu zhanlanhui huikan*, 1–4. Shanghai: Zhongguo Jianzhu Zhanlanhui Huikan, 1936.

Shanghai shi shizhongxin qu chengjianshe weiyuanhui. *Jianshe Shanghai shi zhongxinqu cheng sheji shu*. Shanghai: Shanghai Shi Zhengfu Mishu Chu, 1930.

———. *Yewu baogao*. Shanghai: Shanghai Shi Zhengfu, 1930.

"Shanghai shi zhengfu xinwu jianzhu jingguo." *Zhongguo jianzhu* 1, no. 12 (1933): 1–9.

Shanghai shidang'anguan, ed. *Gongbuju dongshihui huiyi lu*. 28 vols. Shanghai: Shanghai Guji Chubanshe, 2001.

Shanghai tan yu Shanghairen. Shanghai: Shanghai Guji Chubanshe, 1989.

Shanghai zujie zhi bian zuan weiyuanhui, Shi Meiding, Ma Changlin, and Feng Shaoting. *Shanghai zujie zhi*. Shanghai: Shanghai Shehui Kexueyuan Chubanshe, 2001.

Shen Airen and Lou Huanzhao. "Zhongguo jianzhu zhanlanhui canguan ji." *Minli xunkan*, April 1936, 15–16.

Shen Yi. *Shen Yi zishu*. Taibei: Zhuanji Wenxue Chubanshe, 1985.

Sheng Yuehan daxue wushi nian xhilüe, 1879–1929. Taibei: Taiwan Sheng Yuehan Daxue Tongxuehui, 1972.

Shih, Shumei. *The Lure of the Modern: Writing Modernism in Semicolonial China, 1917–1937*. Berkeley Series in Interdisciplinary Studies of China. Berkeley: University of California Press, 2001.

Shoemaker, Robert B. "The London 'Mob' in the Early Eighteenth Century." *Journal of British Studies* 26, no. 3 (July 1987): 273–304.

Sigel, Louis. "Revolutionary Diplomacy: A Reexamination of the Shanghai Peace Conference of 1911." *Papers on Far Eastern History* 19 (March 1979): 111–43.

Simmel, Georg. "The Aesthetic Significance of the Face." 1901. Reprinted in *Essays on Sociology, Philosophy and Aesthetics*, edited by Kurt H. Wolff, 276–81; translated by Lore Ferguson. New York: Harper Torchbooks, 1959.

Skinner, G. William. *The City in Late Imperial China*. Stanford: Stanford University Press, 1977.

Slade, John. *Narrative of the Late Proceedings and Events in China*. Canton: Canton Register Press, 1839.

Smedley, J. D. "Chinese Buildings." *Engineering Society of Shanghai: Proceedings of the Society and Report of the Council, 1904–5*, 155–69. Shanghai: Kelly and Walsh, 1905.

Smith, Adam. *An Inquiry into the Nature and Causes of the Wealth of Nations*. Edited by James E. Thorold Rogers. Oxford: Clarendon, 1869.

Smith, Arthur Henderson. *Chinese Characteristics*. New York: Revell, 1894.

Smith, George. *A Narrative of an Exploratory Visit to Each of the Consular Cities of China, and to the Islands of Hong Kong and Chusan: In Behalf of the Church Missionary Society, in the Years 1844, 1845, 1846*. London: Seeley, Burnside, and Seeley, 1847.

Smith, Richard J. "Ritual in Ch'ing Culture." In *Orthodoxy in Late Imperial China*, edited by Kwang-Ching Liu, 281–310. Berkeley: University of California Press, 1990.

Smith, Whitey. *I Didn't Make a Million*. Manila: Philippine Education Company, 1956.

Soane, John, and David Watkin. *Sir John Soane: The Royal Academy Lectures*. Cambridge: Cambridge University Press, 2000.

Sopher, Arthur, and Theodore Sopher. *The Profitable Path of Shanghai Realty*. Shanghai: Shanghai Times, 1939.

Spakowski, Nicola. "Semi/colonial Futures: Visions of Shanghai's Future in Prewar China." *Twentieth-Century China* 42, no. 3 (October 2017): 234–54.

Stafford, Francis E., and Hanchao Lu. *The Birth of a Republic: Francis Stafford's Photographs of China's 1911 Revolution and Beyond*. Seattle: University of Washington Press, 2009.

Staunton, Sir George. *Remarks on the British Relations with China, and the Proposed Plans for Improving Them*. London: Edmund Lloyd, 1836.

Steinhardt, Nancy Shatzman. *Chinese Imperial City Planning*. Honolulu: University of
Hawaiʻi Press, 1990.

———. "The Tang Architectural Icon and the Politics of Chinese Architectural History."
Art Bulletin 86, no. 2 (June 2004): 228–54.

Stephens, Thomas B. *Order and Discipline in China: The Shanghai Mixed Court, 1911–27.*
Seattle: University of Washington Press, 1992.

Stoler, Ann Laura. "Rethinking Colonial Categories: European Communities and the
Boundaries of Rule." *Comparative Studies in Society and History* 31, no. 1 (January
1989): 134–61.

———. "Sexual Affronts and Racial Frontiers: European Identities and the Cultural Politics of Exclusion in Colonial Southeast Asia." *Comparative Studies in Society and History* 34, no. 3 (July 1992): 514–51.

Sun Changfu and Chen Yunqian. "Cong minzu taidu kan Wusong tielu de xingfa." *Kaifang
shidai*, no. 1 (2005): 60–71.

Sun Ping. *Shanghai chengshi guihua zhi*. Shanghai: Shanghai Shehui Kexueyuan Chubanshe, 1999.

Sun Zhongshan. *Jianguo fanglüe*. 1925. Reprint, Shenyang: Liaoning Renmin Chubanshe, 1994.

Tan Zidian. "Zhongguo jianzhu zhanlanhui canguan ji." *Jianzhuyue kan* 4, no. 3 (1936): 11–12.

Tang Liangli. *Reconstruction in China: A Record of Progress and Achievement in Facts and
Figures*. Shanghai: China United Press, 1935.

Tang Zhenchang, Shen Hengchun, and Qiao Shuming. *Shanghai shi*. Shanghai: Shanghai
Renmin Chubanshe, 1989.

Taylor, Charles. *The Story of Yates the Missionary, as Told in His Letters and Reminiscences*. Nashville: Sunday School Board, Southern Baptist Convention, 1898.

Taylor, Jeremy E. "The Bund: Littoral Space of Empire in the Treaty Ports of East Asia."
Social History 27, no. 2 (May 2002): 125–42.

*The Threatened Decline and Fall of Great Britain in China: A Review of the Present Political
Situation in China*. Shanghai: Gazette, 1903.

Tiffany, Osmand. *The Canton Chinese: or, the American's Sojourn in the Celestial Empire.*
Boston: James Munroe, 1849.

Tong, Hollington K. "Has Extraterritoriality Outlived Its Usefulness?" *Millard's Review of
the Far East*, December 13, 1919, 56.

Tong Jun. "Foreign Influence in Chinese Architecture." *T'ien Hsia Monthly* 6, no. 5 (May
1938): 410–17.

———. "Jianzhu yishu jishi." 1937. Reprinted in *Tong Jun wenji*, 1:81–88. Beijing: Zhonguo
Jianzhu Gongye Chubanshe, 2001.

———. "Woguo gonggong jianzhu waiguan de jiantao." 1946. Reprinted in *Tong Jun
wenji*, 1:118–21. Beijing: Zhonguo Jianzhu Gongye Chubanshe, 2001.

Tsin, Michael. *Nation, Governance, and Modernity in China: Canton, 1900–1927.* Stanford:
Stanford University Press, 1999.

Tsu, Jing. *Failure, Nationalism, and Literature: The Making of Modern Chinese Identity,
1895–1937.* Stanford: Stanford University Press, 2005.

Tyrwhitt, Jacqueline. "The City of Ch'ang-an: Capital of the T'ang Dynasty of China."
Town Planning Review 39, no. 1 (April 1968): 21–37.

Upton, Dell. *Another City: Urban Life and Urban Spaces in the New American Republic.* New Haven: Yale University Press, 2008.

Vacher, Helene. *Projection coloniale et ville rationaliseé: Le rôle de l'espace colonial dans la constitution de l'urbanisme en France, 1900–1931.* Aalborg, Denmark: Aarhus University Press, 1997.

Van Zanten, David. "Just What Was Beaux-Arts Architectural Composition?" In *Chinese Architecture and the Beaux-Arts,* edited by Jeffrey W. Cody, Nancy Shatzman Steinhardt, and Tony Atkins, 23–40. Honolulu: University of Hawai'i Press, 2011.

———. "Second Empire Architecture in Philadelphia." *Philadelphia Museum of Art Bulletin* 74 (1974): 9–24.

Victoir, Laura. "Hygienic Colonial Residences in Hanoi." In *Harbin to Hanoi: The Colonial Built Environment in Asia, 1840–1940,* edited by Victoir and Victor Zatsepine, 231–50. Hong Kong: University of Hong Kong Press, 2013.

Vidler, Anthony. *The Scenes of the Street and Other Essays.* New York: Monacelli, 2011.

Vincent, John Carter. *The Extraterritorial System in China: Final Phase.* Cambridge: East Asian Research Center and Harvard University Press, 1970.

Viollet-le-Duc, Eugène-Emmanuel. *Discourses on Architecture.* Translated by Henry Van Brunt. Boston: J. R. Osgood and Company, 1875.

Wagner, Rudolf. "The Role of the Foreign Community in the Chinese Public Sphere." *China Quarterly,* no. 142 (June 1995): 423–43.

Wakeman, Frederic, Jr., and Wen-hsin Yeh, eds. *Shanghai Sojourners.* Berkeley: University of California Press, 1992.

Walzer, Michael. "On the Role of Symbolism in Political Thought." *Political Science Quarterly* 82, no. 2 (June 1967): 191–204.

Wang, Bogong, Sheng Cao, and Shanghai tong she. *Taiping jun, xiaodaohui luan hu shiliao.* 1873. Reprint, Taibei: Wenhai Chubanshe, 1968.

Wang, Kwei-Jeou. "Economic and Social Impact of Export Processing Zones in the Republic of China." *Industry of Free China* 54, no. 6 (December 1980): 7–28.

Wang Tao. *Yingruan zazhi.* China, 1875.

Wang Yiyan. "Modernism and Its Discontent in Shanghai: The Dubious Agency of the Semi-colonized in 1929." In *Twentieth-Century Colonialism and China: Localities, the Everyday, and the World,* edited by Bryna Goodman and David Goodman, 167–79. London: Routledge, 2012.

Wasserstrom, Jeffrey. "Cosmopolitan Connections and Transnational Network." In *At the Crossroads of Empires: Middlemen, Social Networks, and State-Building in Republican Shanghai,* edited by Nara Dillon and Jean Chun, 206–24. Stanford: Stanford University Press, 2008.

———. *Global Shanghai, 1850–2010: History in Fragments.* London: Routledge, 2009.

Wei Shu. "'Da Shanghai jihua' qishilu jindai Shanghai bijie dushi zhongxin kongjian xingtai de liubian." PhD diss., Tongji Daxue, 2007.

Wheatley, Paul. *The Pivot of the Four Quarters: A Preliminary Enquiry into the Origins and Character of the Ancient Chinese City.* Chicago: Aldine, 1971.

White, R. B. *Prefabrication: A History of Its Development in Great Britain.* London: Her Majesty's Stationery Office, 1965.

Wilson, Andrew. *The "Ever-Victorious Army": A History of the Chinese Campaign under Lieutenant Colonel C. G. Gordon and the Suppression of the Tai-Ping Rebellion*. Edinburgh: William Blackwood and Sons, 1868.

Wilson, Jon E. *The Domination of Strangers: Modern Governance in Eastern India, 1780–1835*. London: Palgrave Macmillan, 2008.

Wilton-Ely, John. "The Rise of the Professional Architect in England." In *The Architect: Chapters in the History of the Profession*, edited by Spiro Kostof, 180–208. Berkeley: University of California Press, 2000.

Wisse, Geert. "Manifold Beginnings: Single-Sheet Papers." In *The Papered Wall: The History, Patterns and Techniques of Wallpaper*, edited by Lesley Hoskins, 8–21. London: Thames and Hudson, 2005.

Wong, J. Y. *Deadly Dreams: Opium, Imperialism and the Arrow War (1856–1860) in China*. Cambridge: Cambridge University Press, 1998.

Wong, John D. *Global Trade in the Nineteenth Century: The House of Houqua and the Canton System*. Cambridge: Cambridge University Press, 2016.

Wong, V. L. *The Low Library: A History*. Shanghai: St. John's University, 1924.

Wood, Arthur Prescott. "Presidential Address." In *The Engineering Society of China: Proceedings of the Society and Report of the Council, 1919–1920*, x–xxxv. Shanghai: Kelly and Walsh, 1920.

Wood, Frances. *No Dogs and Not Many Chinese: Treaty Port Life in China 1843–1943*. London: John Murray, 1998.

Wood, William Wightman. *Sketches of China*. Philadelphia: Carey and Lea, 1830.

Wright, Arnold, and H. A. Cartwright. *Twentieth Century Impressions of Hongkong, Shanghai, and Other Treaty Ports of China: Their History, People, Commerce, Industries, and Resources*. London [etc.]: Lloyds Greater Britain Publishing, 1908.

Wright, David. "John Fryer and the Shanghai Polytechnic: Making Space for Science in Nineteenth-Century China." *British Journal for the History of Science* 29, no. 1 (March 1996): 1–16.

Wright, Gwendolyn. "Tradition in the Service of Modernity: Architecture and Urbanism in French Colonial Policy, 1900–1930." *Journal of Modern History* 59, no. 2 (June 1987): 291–316.

Wright, Mary. *The Last Stand of Chinese Conservatism: The T'ung-Chih Restoration, 1862–1874*. New York: Atheneum, 1966.

Wu Jiang. "Baohaosi zai Shanghai de yingxiang" In *Megacities 2000 Conference Proceedings*, edited by Department of Architecture, University of Hong Kong, 2–9. Hong Kong, 2000.

———. *Shanghai bainian jianzhu shi, 1840–1949*. Shanghai: Tongji Daxue Chubanshe, 1997.

Wu Xin. *Shanghai chai cheng an baogao*. Shanghai, 1914.

Xu, Xiaoqun. *Chinese Professionals and the Republican State: The Rise of Professional Associations in Shanghai, 1912–1937*. Cambridge: Cambridge University Press, 2001.

Xu Jingzhi, *Chinese Architecture: Past and Contemporary*. Hong Kong: The Sin Poh Amalgamated (H.K.), 1964.

Xu Yinong, *The Chinese City in Space and Time: The Development of Urban Form in Suzhou*. Honolulu: University of Hawai'i Press, 2000.

Xu Zhichao and "Shanghai youdian zhi" bian zuan weiyuanhui. *Shanghai youdian zhi.* Shanghai: Shanghai Shehui Kexueyuan Chubanshe, 1999.

Xue Liyong. *Shanghai waitan diming zhanggu.* Shanghai: Tongji Daxue Chubanshe, 1994.

———. *Waitan de lishi he jianzhu.* Shanghai: Shanghai Shehui Kexueyuan Chubanshe, 2002.

Yang Junshi. *Jianzhuxue abc. Abc congshu.* Shanghai: ABC Congshushe Yinshua, Shijie Shuju, 1928.

Yang Kuan. *Zhongguo lidai chidu kao.* Shanghai: Shangwu Yinshuguan; Xinhua Shudian Zong Kingshou, 1955.

Yang Zhaohui. "Yinhang jianzhu zhi neiwaiguan." *Zhongguo jianzhu* 1, no. 4 (October 1933): 1–3.

Yao Jinxiang, Zhang Shengyuan, and Yuan Gang. *Shencheng jianshe chunqiu.* Shanghai: Tongji Daxue Chubanshe, 1993.

Yates, Matthew Tyson. *Ancestral Worship and Fung-Shuy. [Read at the Missionary Quarterly Meeting, Shanghai, September 16th, 1867.].* Shanghai: Shanghai Recorder, 1867.

Ye Gongchuo. "Fakanci." In *Zhongguo jianzhu zhanlanhui huikan,* 1–2. Shanghai: Zhongguo Jianzhu Zhanlanhui Huikan, 1936.

Ye Xiaoqing. *The Dianshizhai Pictorial: Shanghai Urban Life, 1884–1898.* Ann Arbor: Center for Chinese Studies, University of Michigan, 2003.

Yeh, Catherine Vance. *Shanghai Love: Courtesans, Intellectuals, and Entertainment Culture, 1850–1910.* Seattle: University of Washington Press, 2006.

———. "Where Is Shanghai? Maps and the Struggle to Define the Image of the City between 1860 and 1930." In *Peking, Shanghai, Shenzhen,* edited by Kai Vockler and Dirk Luckow, 506–11. Frankfurt: Campus Verlag, 2000.

Yeh, Wen-Hsin. *Shanghai Splendor: Economic Sentiments and the Making of Modern China, 1843–1949.* Berkeley: University of California Press, 2007.

Yorke, G. J. "The Princely House: The Story of the Early Years of Jardine Matheson and Company in China, 1782–1844." Undated manuscript. Special Collections, University of Hong Kong.

Young, Louise. *Japan's Total Empire: Manchuria and the Culture of Wartime Imperialism.* Berkeley: University of California Press, 1999.

Yu Yue. *Chongxiu Shanghai xianzhi.* China: Wumen Xian Shu, 1871.

Yuan Jicheng. *Jindai Zhongguo zujie shigao.* Beijing: Zhongguo Caizeng Jingji Chubanshe, 1988.

Yue, Meng. "Hybrid Science versus Modernity: The Practice of the Jiangnan Arsenal, 1864–1897." *East Asian Science, Technology, and Medicine,* no. 16 (1999): 13–52.

———. *Shanghai and the Edges of Empires.* Minneapolis: University of Minnesota Press, 2006.

Yue Jiazao. *Zhongguo jianzhu shi.* 1933. Reprint, Shanghai: Shanghai Shudian, 1996.

Yule, Henry. *Hobson-Jobson: A Glossary of Colloquial Anglo-Indian Words and Phrases, and of Kindred Terms, Etymological, Historical, Geographical, and Discursive.* 1886. Reprint, London: Routledge and Keegan Paul, 1985.

Zeng, Pu. *Nie hai hua.* 1931. Reprint, Beijing: Tuanjie Chubanshe, 2007.

Zhang, Yingjin. *The City in Modern Chinese Literature and Film: Configurations of Space, Time, and Gender.* Stanford: Stanford University Press, 1996.

Zhang Qiming. *Dianshizhai huabao: Dake tang ban.* 15 vols. Shanghai: Shanghai Huabao Chubanshe, 2001.

Zhang Song. "Jindai Shanghai Chengshi Tezheng Fenxi." In *Di sici Zhongguo jindai jianzhushi yanjiu taolunhui lunhui ji,* edited by Zhang Fuhe and Jiang Tan, 87–101. Shanghai: Zhongguo Jianzhu Gongye Chubanshe, 1993.

"Zhang Xiaoliang xiansheng." *Muye jie* (1940): 1–2.

Zhang Zhongli, ed. *Jindai Shanghai chengshi yanjiu.* Shanghai: Shanghai Renmin Chubanshe, 1990.

Zheng Zu'an. "Shanghai 'huayuan yangfang' qu de xingcheng he lishi tese," *Shanghai chengjian dang'an* (February 2004): 33–37.

"Zhongguo jianzhu zhanlanhui kaimu." *Zhongguo bowuguan xiehui huibao,* May 1936, 32–35.

Zhongguo jianzhushi xuehui. *Zhongguo jianzhushi xuehui: Zhangcheng, yewu guize, gongshou jie yue, fuhui yuan lu.* Shanghai: Zhongguo Jianzhushi Xuehui, 1926.

Zhongguo jianzhushi xuehui ding jianzhushi yewu guize. *Zhongguo jianzhushi xuehui ding jianzhushi yewu guize.* Shanghai, 1947.

Zhou Songqing. *Shanghai difang zizhi yanjiu (1905–1927).* Shanghai: Shanghai Shehui Kexueyuan Chubanshe, 2005.

Zhu Yongchun. "Cong 'Zhongguo Jianzhu' Kan 1932–1937 Nian Zhongguo Jianzhu Sichao Yu Zhuyao Qishi." In *Zhongguo jindai jianzhu yanjiu yu baohu,* edited by Zhang Fuhe, 17–31. Beijing: Tsinghua Daxue Chubanshe, 2001.

Ziskin, Rochelle. *The Place Vendôme: Architecture and Social Mobility in Eighteenth-Century Paris.* Cambridge: Cambridge University Press, 1999.

Zito, Angela. "City Gods, Filiality, and Hegemony in Late Imperial China." *Modern China* 13, no. 3 (July 1987): 333–71.

———. *Of Body and Brush: Grand Sacrifice as Text/Performance in Eighteenth-Century China.* Chicago: University of Chicago Press, 1997.

Zito, Angela, and Tani E. Barlow. *Body, Subject and Power in China.* Chicago: University of Chicago Press, 1994.

Zong Liangchen. *Zenyang jianzhu fangwu.* Shanghai: Shangwu Yinshuguan Faxing, 1933.

INDEX

Dongbei University, 206
Dongdajiu, 151, 156
dougong (bracket sets), 13, 166, 181
drainage and sewage, 49, 60, 93
Du Halde, Jean Baptiste, 15
Du Yangeng, 167–68, 169, 179, 194, 201, 207, 244n33
Dule Monastery, 204
Dupré (municipal engineer), 90
Dupré, A., 91, 92

E

ecclesiastic architecture, 94. *See also* Holy Trinity Cathedral; Trinity Church
École des Beaux-Arts, 190. *See also* Beaux-Arts style
economic zoning models, 212–13
Edan, Benoît, 60, 61, 71
Ede, F. G., 204
educational architecture, 111, 112 *fig.*, 231n40
electricity, 93, 123, 127, 148, 183
elevators, 121, 123, 183, 234n87
Engineering Society of China, 131, 246n9
Engineering Society of Shanghai (Shanghai Society of Engineers and Architects), 114, 116, 126, 232n60
engineering standards, 117–18, 233n69. *See also* standardization and professionalization
engineers, 120–21, 149–50, 202, 203; educational curriculum, 161–62, 243n17; engineering firms, 204, 206; professional societies, 114, 116, 131, 201, 232n60, 246n9, 250n25; registration, 116–18, 232n63, 232–33n67. *See also* infrastructure projects
Estournelles de Constant, Paul Henri d', 150
Ever Victorious Army, 66; monument to, 73, 74–76, 76 *fig.*
export processing zones (EPZ), 212–13
extraterritoriality: abolition of, 179, 210; architecture and, 7–12, 81, 104, 161, 209; Britain and, 7, 31–33, 49; and the Chinese republic, 128–29, 130–31; and courts, 131; France and, 34, 218n51;

and international expositions, 196; justification for, 32, 130; legacy of, 211, 212–14; legal apparatus, 7, 8–9, 32, 37–38; modernity and, 175, 195; physical plan for, 33–38; roots of, 32; in Shanghai compared with other zones, 9–10; Taiping Rebellion and, 65; taxation and, 107; United States and, 32–33, 140, 142, 218n51
Ezra, Edward, 141

F

façades, 133–35, 140, 148, 150
face, 133–35, 150, 153, 156, 158
factories, 130–31
Factory system, 19, 20 *fig.*, 21–24, 22, 38
Falls, T. J., 83
Fan Wenzhao, 165 *fig.*, 200, 208
fengshui, 28–29, 125–26
figural sculpture: Protet statue, 89–90, 90 *fig.*; in storefront displays, 111
fire insurance, 43–44, 46, 220n96
fireplaces, 112, 115
fires, 52, 61, 230nn15,17; building regulations and, 108, 112
flour mills, 131
Flourishing Construction (Xiesheng Yingzao Chang), 233n82
Folger Shakespeare Library, 162
Forbidden City, 166, 198, 204
foreign settlements: Chinese residents of, 49, 59–60, 77, 106; creation of, 5–7, 36–38; governance of, 60, 68–69, 78, 79–81; housing for refugees in, 54, 59, 66–68, 77; links between, 61, 62 *map*, 86–87; maps of, 79, 80 *fig.*; public construction projects, 60–61; taxation in, 61, 107–8; women in, 22, 37. *See also* American Settlement; British Settlement; French Concession; International Settlement
foreign trade, 17–19, 21–22, 36–37, 38. *See also* commerce; Factory system; opium trade; treaty ports
Foucault, Michel, 12

Rand, Christopher, 211

Ratard, French Consul General, 153, 240n98

rats, 108, 114, 229n8

real estate, 68, 77, 113, 116, 127

recession, 77

refugees, 53, 54, 59, 66–68, 67*fig.*, 77, 107. *See also* sojourners

Reid, Dr. Gilbert, 130

reinforced concrete pagoda, 123–28, 124*fig.*, 235n103

Republic of China, 128–29, 197, 198, 249n56; in Taiwan, 212–13. *See also* Greater Shanghai Plan; nation building; Nationalist party and government

residential architecture, 11, 28, 31, 200. *See also* housing

Respondentia, 22, 23

RIBA. *See* Royal Institute of British Architects

roads, 87, 90, 102, 125, 150, 154, 156–58; building distance from, 108, 146; footways, 60; in Greater Shanghai Plan, 180, 186; names of, 69, 180, 224n52, 246n12; maintenance, 93, 172; street lights, 60, 61; street signs, 60; widening of, 70

Robertson, Daniel Brooke, 35, 51, 221n119, 223n38

roofs, 13, 42, 43, 92, 111, 137, 208; defects, 152, 220n88, 247n18; tiled, 172, 181, 204

Roussel de Courcy, Marie-René, 47

Royal Institute of British Architects (RIBA): approval of plans, 147; members and associates, 112, 228n56, 235n106, 239nn62,67

Ruskin, John, 134

Russell & Company, 38, 40, 46, 53; compound of, 43, 44*fig. See also* Cunningham, Edward

Russian consulate, 49, 137–38, 139*fig.*

S

Saarinen, Eliel, 200, 249n12

Sammons, Thomas, 141

Sapajou, "A Vision of a Future Ambition," 185*fig.*

Sassoon & Company, 68, 235n104

Scarth, John, 53–54

schools, 82, 119, 120, 167. *See also* architecture: study abroad; educational architecture

Scott, George Gilbert, 94–97, 228nn56,64. *See also* Holy Trinity Cathedral

Scott, Harding & Company, 121. *See also* Scott, Walter

Scott, Walter, 121, 123, 232n60. *See also* Palace Hotel

Second Empire architecture, 87

Second Opium War, 65–66

self-government bureaus, 154–55

Self-Strengthening Movement (Ziqiang Yundong), 81–82, 161

semi-colonialism, 8–9, 249n55

Semper, Gottfried, 134

settling (of buildings), 90, 122, 125

Seward, George F., 100, 229n77

Shanghai: as chaotic, 210–12; contrast with Guangzhou, 34, 35, 38–39, 50; as cosmopolitan community, 5, 34, 52, 81, 92, 106, 114, 117, 149; maps of, 5*map*, 6*map*, 27*map*, 37*fig.*, 79, 80*fig.*, 176*fig.*; population of, 8, 30, 46, 49, 54, 179; as trading port, 19, 27, 31, 38, 50, 63, 175, 179; urban landscape, 31–32. *See also* Bund, the; Chinese city; extraterritoriality; foreign settlements; French Concession; International Settlement; treaty ports

Shanghai Architectural Society, 167–68, 201, 206, 244n32, 245n57, 250n25; fourth general assembly, 168*fig.*

Shanghai Builders' Union (Shanghai Shi Yingzaochang Tongye Gonghui), 166, 243n29, 250n25

Shanghai Club, 99

Shanghai county magistrate, 27–28, 218n35; yamen of, 28, 31, 58, 61

Shanghai Land Investment Company, 189

Shanghai massacre (1927), 163

Shanghai Municipal Council: adoption of modernist architecture, 187; and building regulations, 108, 122–23, 228n56, 234n93; Electricity Committee, 127; establishment of, 7, 93; members of, 93, 247n24; offices of, 135, 143–47, 249n56; proposal to add Chinese members, 236n11; and registration of architects and engineers, 117, 232n63, 232–33n67; resignation of, 210. *See also* French Concession Municipal Council; International Municipal Council

Shanghai Municipal Council Offices, 143–49, 148 *fig.*, 158, 239n74; preliminary scheme, 147 *fig.*

Shanghai Municipal Gazette, 124 *fig.*, 127

Shanghai municipal government (Nationalist), 163, 174, 178–79, 245n57. *See also* Greater Shanghai Municipality; Greater Shanghai Plan

Shanghai Museum, 201, 202 *fig.*, 203, 204

Shanghai Mutual Telephone Company Ltd., 123, 147

Shanghai of To-day, 158

Shanghai Polytechnic Institution and Reading Rooms (Gezhi Shuyuan), 84–85, 85 *fig.*, 86, 226n18

Shanghai Society of Engineers and Architects (Engineering Society of Shanghai), 114, 116, 126, 232n60

Shanghai Volunteer Corps, 102, 144, 146, 148, 171, 222n11

Shanghai Waterworks Company, 151, 153

Shanghai Workers Guild, 201

Shanghailanders, 145, 148, 239n63

Shanghai's future (Shanghai de jianglai), 195, 249n56

Shen Baozhen, 85

Shen Wenhong, 167

Shen Yi, 167, 201, 203, 246n9, 247n18, 250n24

Shenbao: architectural articles and columns, 170, 171–72, 200; image of concrete pagoda, 127; obituary of Yang Sisheng, 233n78

shipbuilding, 82–84, 109

Simms, Hardy, 148

Simpson, Cecil, 116

Sincere department store, 111

Singapore, civic buildings, 146

Sino-French War, 136

skyscrapers, 123–27, 150, 164, 192, 200, 244n32; New York, 235n112

Small Swords Uprising, 53–54, 55–58, 61, 70–71, 72 *fig.*, 76; aftermath of, 105, 197, 241n111; Battle of Muddy Flat, 58, 222n11; memorials, 70–73, 72 *fig.*, 89, 156. *See also* refugees

Smith, Adam, 16

Smith, Arthur, 223n33; *Chinese Characteristics*, 133

Snyder, Reo., *Map of Shanghae*, 37 *fig.*

Society for the Research of Chinese Architecture (Zhongguo Yingzao Xueshe), 200, 203, 204, 206

Society of Chinese Architects (Zhongguo Jianzhushi Xuehui), 166, 167, 169, 206, 250n25

soil issues, 125, 147, 234n93

sojourners, 30, 49, 61, 109–10, 119, 145, 213

South City Roadworks Board, 154

South Lake, 204

Spain, consular jurisdiction, 218–19n51

special economic zones, 213

St. John's University, 111; Anniversary Hall, 111, 112 *fig.*; Schereschewsky Hall, 111, 231n40

standardization and professionalization, 106, 115–18, 120–21, 168–69, 172. *See also* architects: registration of

Staunton, George Thomas, 34

storefronts, 110–11, 135, 237n28

Strachan, George, 50, 98, 226n25

street names, 69, 180, 224n52, 246n12

"Streets of Shanghai" exhibit (1934), 199

Suez Canal, 9, 150

Summer Palace, 66, 73, 204

Sun Yat-sen, 128, 154, 179, 181; Mausoleum, 164, 179, 244n32; Memorial Hall, 164

Supplemental Treaty of the Bogue (1843), 32